THE
END
OF
EMPIRE?
THE
TRANSFORMATION
OF THE
USSR
IN
COMPARATIVE
PERSPECTIVE

THE INTERNATIONAL POLITICS OF EURASIA

Editors:
Karen Dawisha and Bruce Parrott

THE INTERNATIONAL POLITICS OF EURASIA

Volume 9

THE
END
OF
EMPIRE?
THE
TRANSFORMATION
OF THE
USSR
IN
COMPARATIVE
PERSPECTIVE

Editors:
Karen Dawisha and
Bruce Parrott

M.E. Sharpe

Armonk, New York
London, England

Library of Congress Cataloging-in-Publication Data

The end of empire? The Transformation of the USSR in Comparative Perspective/
edited by Karen Dawisha and Bruce Parrott.
p. cm. — (International politics of Eurasia ; v. 9)
"This book is the ninth in a series of ten volumes produced by the Russian Littoral
Project, sponsored jointly by the University of Maryland at College Park and the
Paul H. Nitze School of Advanced International Studies of
the Johns Hopkins University"—CIP pref.
Includes bibliographical references and index.
ISBN 1-56324-368-7 (cloth : alk. paper).
— ISBN 1-56324-369-5 (pbk. : alk. paper)
1. Imperialism—Case studies—Congresses. 2. Post-communism—Congresses.
3. Soviet Union—Politics and government—Congresses.
4. Former Soviet republics—Politics and government—Congresses.
I. Dawisha, Karen, 1949– .
II. Parrott, Bruce, 1945– . III. Series.
JC359.E53 1996
321. 9'2'0947—dc20
96-21985
CIP

Printed in the United States of America

Dedicated to the memory of
Dankwart Rustow,
in appreciation of his unrivaled contribution to
teaching, scholarship, and international understanding
on three continents over the last half century.
His erudition, gentle humor, and humanity will be
greatly missed by all who knew him.

Contents

About the Editors and Contributors

Karen Dawisha is professor and director of the Center for the Study of Post-Communist Societies at the University of Maryland, College Park. She graduated with degrees in Russian and politics from the University of Lancaster in England and received her Ph.D. from the London School of Economics. She has served as an advisor to the British House of Commons Foreign Affairs Committee and was a member of the Policy Planning Staff of the U.S. State Department. Her publications include *Russia and the New States of Eurasia: The Politics of Upheaval* (coauthored with Bruce Parrott, 1994), *Eastern Europe, Gorbachev and Reform: The Great Challenge* (1989, 2nd ed. 1990), *The Kremlin and the Prague Spring* (1984), *The Soviet Union in the Middle East: Politics and Perspectives* (1982), *Soviet-East European Dilemmas: Coercion, Competition, and Consent* (1981), and *Soviet Foreign Policy Toward Egypt* (1979).

Bruce Parrott is professor and director of Russian Area and East European Studies at the Johns Hopkins University School of Advanced International Studies, where he has taught for twenty years. He received his B.A. in religious studies from Pomona College in 1966, and his Ph.D. in political science in 1976 from Columbia University, where he was assistant director of the Russian Institute. His publications include *Russia and the New States of Eurasia: The Politics of Upheaval* (coauthored with Karen Dawisha, 1994), *The Dynamics of Soviet Defense Policy* (1990), *The Soviet Union and Ballistic Missile Defense* (1987), *Trade, Technology and Soviet-American Relations* (1985), and *Politics and Technology in the Soviet Union* (1983).

Mark R. Beissinger is professor of political science and director of the Center for Russia, East Europe, and Central Asia of the University of Wisconsin, Madison. In addition to numerous articles and book chapters, he is author of *Scientific Management, Socialist Discipline, and Soviet Power* (1988), and a contributing coeditor of *The Nationalities Factor in Soviet Politics and Society* (1990).

Carole Fink, professor of history at the Ohio State University and author of *The Genoa Conference: European Diplomacy, 1921–1922* (awarded the George Louis Beer Prize of the American Historical Association), *Marc Bloch: A Life in History*, and numerous articles on twentieth-century international history, is currently writing a book on the Polish Minority Treaty of June 1919.

Michael Graham Fry is professor of international relations in the School of International Relations at the University of Southern California. He is a historian of the twentieth-century international system. His research interests include North Atlantic diplomacy, Anglo-European affairs, and great-power involvement in the Middle East. His most recent book, the Festschrift for Donald Cameron Watt, was *Power, Personalities, and Policies* (1993).

Miles Kahler is Rohr Professor of International Relations in the Graduate School of International Relations and Pacific Studies at the University of California, San Diego. He has been senior fellow for international political economy at the Council on Foreign Relations (1994–96) and chair of the editorial board for *International Organization.*

David A. Lake is professor of political science at the University of California, San Diego. At the time his chapter was written he also served as research director for international relations at the Institute on Global Conflict and Cooperation.

Ali A. Mazrui is Albert Schweitzer Professor in the Humanities and Director of the Institute of Global Cultural Studies at State University of New York, Binghamton; Albert Luthului Professor-at-Large in the Humanities and Development Studies at the University of Jos in Nigeria; and Andrew D. White Professor-at-Large Emeritus and Senior Scholar at Cornell University. He has written numerous books, including *Cultural Forces in World Politics* (1990).

Robert I. Rotberg is president of the World Peace Foundation of Cambridge, Massachusetts, and coordinator of the South African Program of the Harvard Institute for International Development. He also teaches at the Kennedy School of Government at Harvard. He was professor of history and political science at MIT for nineteen years, then academic vice president at Tufts University, and finally served as president of Lafayette College before returning to Harvard. He is the author or editor of more than thirty books and many articles on Africa and the Caribbean.

Dankwart A. Rustow, Distinguished Professor Emeritus at City University of New York, earlier served at Princeton, Columbia, and the Brookings Institution. His publications include *Comparative Political Dynamics* (ed., 1991), *Turkey: America's Forgotten Ally* (1987), *Oil and Turmoil: America Faces OPEC and* *the Middle East* (1982), *Philosophers and Kings: Studies in Leadership* (ed., 1970), and *A World of Nations: Problems of Political Modernization* (1967).

Hendrik Spruyt is assistant professor of political science at Columbia University. He has recently published *The Sovereign State and Its Competitors* (1994), "Institutional Selection in International Relations" (*International Organization*, 1994), and "Decline Reconsidered" (*Harvard International Review*, 1995).

S. Frederick Starr, Distinguished Fellow at the Aspen Institute, has authored or edited several major books on Russian history, culture, and political-economic developments, including *The Legacy of History in Russia and the New States of Eurasia* (ed., 1994). In recent years, he has chaired the U.S. government's external advisory committee on research in Russia and the other Newly Independent States. Dr. Starr was previously president of Oberlin College.

Roman Szporluk is M.S. Hrushevsky Professor of Ukrainian History at Harvard University. Most recently, he edited *National Identity and Ethnicity in Russia and the New States of Eurasia* (1994). His earlier publications include *Communism and Nationalism: Karl Marx versus Friedrich List, The Political Thought of T.G. Masaryk,* and *Russia in World History: Selected Essays of M.N. Pokrovsky* (editor and cotranslator).

Solomon Wank is professor emeritus of history at Franklin and Marshall College and former editor of *Austrian History Yearbook* (1989–96). He is the editor of several books and author of numerous articles on diplomacy and politics in the late Habsburg empire. His most recent work is as editor of *Aus dem Nachlass Aehrenthal: Briefe und Dokumente zur österreichisch-ungarischen Innen- und Aussenpolitik 1885–1912* (1994).

Preface

This book is the ninth in a series of ten volumes produced by the Russian Littoral Project, sponsored jointly by the University of Maryland, College Park, and the Paul H. Nitze School of Advanced International Studies of the Johns Hopkins University. As directors of the project, we share the conviction that the transformation of the former Soviet republics into independent states demands systematic analysis of the determinants of the domestic and foreign policies of the new countries. The series of volumes is intended to provide a basis for comprehensive scholarly study of these issues.

This volume was shaped by our view that future scholarship about the post-Soviet world requires both specialized research and broad-gauge studies that carefully juxtapose the breakup of the Soviet empire with the transformation of other multinational empires. Although vitally important, such comparative studies do not currently exist. Analogies between contemporary Russian behavior and the restoration of empire during the Russian Revolution, or between "Weimar Russia" and trends in Germany during the 1920s and 1930s, have shaped Western perceptions but have not been subjected to rigorous analysis. The history of international relations shows that an uncritical acceptance of historical analogies can easily lead statesmen to adopt self-defeating policies.

The principal purpose of this volume is to compare the Soviet/post-Soviet upheaval with the decline and transformation of other twentieth-century multinational polities, including the Habsburg, Ottoman, tsarist, imperial German, French, and British empires. The main questions to be analyzed include the following: (1) How do the circumstances of an empire's collapse affect the disposition of the imperial nationality to reconstitute it, and the capabilities of nonimperial nationalities to resist? (2) How does the development of democracy in a major state affect its foreign policy, and would the consolidation of democracy in Russia constrain Russian imperial impulses? (3) How might the international community affect the chances that a new Russian empire will be created?

and (4) For the non-Russian Soviet successor states, what are the alternatives to direct Russian control or total independence?

A careful analysis of these critical questions can be provided by comparing the Soviet/post-Soviet upheaval with the historical trajectories of other twentieth-century multinational empires. The aim is to identify the causes of imperial decline, the manner in which imperial legacies have shaped the national identities and external relations of the states that have emerged from disintegrating empires, and the factors that have promoted or impeded the reconstitution of collapsed empires. By combining theory with history and analyzing several case studies, the volume seeks to illuminate the dynamics and possible outcomes of the transformation of the USSR.

We would like to thank the contributors to this volume for their help in making this phase of the Russian Littoral Project a success and for revising their papers in a timely fashion. We would also like to express our gratitude to the discussants, who prepared detailed written comments on the papers and greatly assisted in giving the conference coherence and momentum: George Breslauer, University of California, Berkeley; Jon Jacobson, University of California, Irvine; Gail Lapidus, Stanford University; George Liska, School of Advanced International Studies; Kendall Myers, Foreign Service Institute; Alvin Rubinstein, University of Pennsylvania; Avi Shlaim, St. Antony's College, Oxford; Ronald Suny, University of Chicago; and David Wilkinson, University of California, Los Angeles.

We would also like to thank the Institute for Global Conflict and Cooperation at the University of California, San Diego, for hosting the conference, and the Social Science Research Council's Committee for International Peace and Security for cosponsorship. In addition, we are grateful to Janine Draschner for her skillful and calm handling of the complex logistics of the conference (including getting many of the paper presenters out of the January 1996 blizzard and onto planes bound for San Diego), and for her unstinting labor in preparing the final manuscript. For invaluable assistance with preparation of this book, we also thank Stacy VanDeveer, Trevor Wysong, Melissa Rosser, all at the University of Maryland. Kathleen Hancock from the University of California, San Diego, also ably assisted as rapporteur.

Above all we would like to acknowledge the contribution that Dankwart Rustow made to what was to be his last conference. His chapter in this volume is outstanding, displaying his brilliance and his sure-footed but graceful grasp of the ebb and flow of empires. His presence at the San Diego conference was truly memorable. He made seminal contributions to every session, chiding the group at one point that we risked not imperial but "empirical overreach." Lunches and dinners on the veranda overlooking the Pacific were yet a further occasion to continue the lively debates and discussions, along with his wife Margrit, spiced with stories about his early years in Germany and Istanbul. He will be truly missed, yet his many contributions, both professional and personal, will always be remembered.

Russian Littoral Project

The objective of the Russian Littoral Project is to foster an exchange of research and information in fields of study pertaining to the international politics of Eurasia. The interaction between the internal affairs and foreign policies of the new states is studied in a series of workshops that have taken place in the United States, Europe, and Eurasia between 1993 and 1996. Scholars are invited from the new states, North America, and Europe to present papers at the workshops.

Focusing on the interaction between the internal affairs and the foreign relations of the new states, the project workshops examine the impact of the following factors: history, national identity and ethnicity, religion, political culture and civil society, economics, foreign policy priorities and decision making, military issues, and the nuclear question. Each of these topics is examined in a set of three workshops, first with respect to Russia, then with respect to the western belt of new states extending from Estonia to Ukraine, and finally with respect to the southern tier of new states extending from Georgia to Kyrgyzstan.

The Russian Littoral Project could not have been launched without the generous and timely contributions of the project's Coordinating Committee. We wish to thank the committee members for providing invaluable advice and expertise concerning the organization and intellectual substance of the project. The members of the Coordinating Committee are: Dr. Adeed Dawisha (George Mason University); Dr. Bartek Kaminski (University of Maryland); Dr. Catherine Kelleher (NATO Headquarters, Brussels); Ms. Judith Kipper (Center for Strategic and International Studies); Dr. Nancy Lubin (JNA Associates); Dr. Michael Mandelbaum (the School of Advanced International Studies); Dr. James Millar (the George Washington University); Dr. Peter Murrell (University of Maryland); Dr. Martha Brill Olcott (Colgate University); Dr. Ilya Prizel (the School of Advanced International Studies); Dr. George Quester (University of Maryland); Dr. Alvin Z. Rubinstein (University of Pennsylvania); Dr. Blair Ruble (The Kennan Institute); Dr. S. Frederick Starr (Aspen Institute); Dr. Roman Szporluk (Harvard University); and Dr. Vladimir Tismaneanu (University of Maryland).

We are grateful to the Smith Richardson Foundation for funding the workshops from which this book is derived; we are especially grateful to Mark Steinmeyer for his firm support of the project from the beginning. For funding the workshops on which several other volumes are based, we express our thanks to the MacArthur Foundation (particularly Kennette Benedict and Andrew Kuchins), the Pew Charitable Trusts (particularly Kevin Quigley and Peter Benda), the National Endowment for the Humanities, and the Ford Foundation (in particular Geoffrey Wiseman).

We also wish to thank President William Kirwan of the University of Maryland, College Park, and President William C. Richardson of the Johns Hopkins University, who have given indispensable support to the project. Thanks are also due to Dean Irwin Goldstein, Associate Dean Stewart Edelstein, Director of the Office of International Affairs Marcus Franda, and Department of Government and Politics Chair Jonathan Wilkenfeld at the University of Maryland, College Park; to Provost Joseph Cooper and Vice-Provost for Academic Planning and Budget Stephen M. McClain at the Johns Hopkins University; to Professor George Packard, who helped launch the project during his final year as dean of the School of Advanced International Studies (SAIS), to SAIS Dean Paul D. Wolfowitz, and to SAIS Associate Dean Stephen Szabo.

Finally, we are grateful to M.E. Sharpe for producing a first-rate series, in particular to Ana Erlic who has worked unstintingly, and to Patricia Kolb, whose confidence in the success of the project and the volumes is deeply appreciated.

Karen Dawisha
University of Maryland
at College Park

Bruce Parrott
The Johns Hopkins University
School of Advanced International Studies

THE
END
OF
EMPIRE?

THE
TRANSFORMATION
OF THE
USSR
IN
COMPARATIVE
PERSPECTIVE

I

Theoretical Perspectives on the Forms and Development of Empires

1

Analyzing the Transformation of the Soviet Union in Comparative Perspective

Bruce Parrott

The collapse of the Soviet Union has demolished the international political order of the past half-century and has inaugurated a tumultuous process of imperial disintegration, state-building, and potential imperial reconstruction. Scholars seeking to understand this geopolitical upheaval face intellectual impediments rooted not only in the enormity and complexity of the process itself but also in the structure of the disciplines relevant to its study. The customary scholarly division of labor between the study of international relations and the study of comparative politics has generally prevented most social scientists from giving sustained attention to the hybrid character of the growth and decline of empires; the Soviet upheaval demands interpretive frameworks that bridge this academic dividing line.[1] Mainstream research on the Soviet Union was long characterized by a "metrocentric" outlook that focused on the Russian core of the state and neglected its "peripheral" nations and territories; the Soviet collapse has dramatically multiplied the number of societies whose interaction with Russia and the rest of the world requires careful study. In the Communist era, analysts often adopted narrow research specialties in order to sift nuggets of information from mountains of low-grade Soviet ore; today they face an avalanche of new information that taxes their assimilative capacities and makes the identification of general trends unusually difficult. With a few exceptions, historians of Russia and the USSR have shied away from comparative imperial history (as have the historians of most other empires); today the insights of comparative imperial history and decolonization are essential.

To be sure, the nature and consequences of the upheaval in the lands of the former USSR cannot be understood without benefit of the fruits of academic specialization. Deeper Western understanding of the trends in Eurasia will depend on the creation of specialized studies that meld the perspectives of various academic disciplines, utilize research methods drawn from the study of other countries, and mine the rich data contained in newly opened archives and post-Soviet publications.[2] Taken alone, however, specialized studies will be inadequate to clarify the tectonic sociopolitical changes that have been set in motion in Eurasia. Only systematic, large-scale comparisons can help focus scholarly research and test the assumptions that must be made in order to draw general conclusions from detailed empirical studies. Sensing the need for larger interpretive frameworks, some observers have drawn parallels between the Soviet upheaval and the breakup of the Habsburg Empire, between contemporary Russia and the Weimar interlude in German imperial history, and between post-Soviet ethnic conflicts and the violent disintegration of Yugoslavia. But as these three examples show, the choice of particular historical parallels may tacitly incorporate quite divergent expectations about the nature and outcome of the Soviet upheaval. Historical analogies must be selected and interpreted on the basis of careful comparisons rather than on the basis of intuition or the coincidental timing of events. Only such an analytical approach can move public discussion beyond proclamations of the inevitable death of the "last of the great multinational empires" and nearly simultaneous prophecies of its impending rebirth.

Despite the need, few scholars have taken up the challenge of comparing the disintegration of the USSR with the transformation and aftermath of other multinational imperial structures. The tsarist and Soviet empires have not customarily figured in comparative studies of such empires.[3] Moreover, most recent works on the broad theme of empire in international relations typically treat empire as one aspect of a great power's geopolitical strategy while neglecting the distinctive inner workings of multinational polities and the consequences of imperial demise.[4] Put differently, the aftermath of empire has received little attention from recent theorists of international politics. A few specialists on the former Soviet Union have pointed out the need for comparative studies of the USSR's breakup and have published valuable articles containing thoughtful comparative observations, and at least one group of scholars has recently produced a book on the subject.[5] Nonetheless, the general topic requires additional study that draws on the insights of specialists knowledgeable about different empires and that centers on a common set of analytical questions.

Such an undertaking might be structured in a number of ways. This book is designed to compare the Soviet/post-Soviet upheaval with the fates of other twentieth-century empires, particularly the Ottoman, Habsburg, and tsarist empires, imperial Germany, and the French and British empires. It goes without saying that different cases might have been chosen for purposes of comparison, and that different choices would have strongly influenced the aspects of imperial experience highlighted in the chapters that follow. However, a decision has been made to focus on a limited number of modern empires to allow for more rigorous analysis. Focusing on the twentieth century concentrates attention on the broad historical forces, ranging from international military competition to socioeconomic modernization and the growth of nationalism, that have posed special challenges for imperial political structures.

The book has been designed to address a common set of questions about specific aspects of the transformation of these empires. The chapters in the first section set these questions in a broad intellectual and theoretical context. Most of the following chapters analyze more than one empire in terms of a specific aspect of imperial transformation. These specific aspects are (1) the distinctive character and consequences of each empire's disintegration; (2) the structure and behavior of the successor states created on the former imperial periphery; and (3) the internal dynamics and external conduct of the metropolitan successor state, if any, established during the postimperial aftermath. The author of each paper devoted to one of these aspects of the transformation of the USSR has been asked to discuss the same aspect of the transformation of the tsarist empire. The question of whether the process of imperial reconstitution will be repeated in the lands of the former Soviet Union is thus built into the organization of the volume. The final chapters draw some conclusions from the comparisons presented in the preceding chapters and discuss the alternative paths that the post–Soviet upheaval might follow in the future.

The present chapter has two purposes. First, it aims to lay the intellectual groundwork for accurate comparisons by examining the provenance and connotations of the notion of empire and the complex role of the idea in contemporary thinking about international affairs. Despite widespread use of the term in public and scholarly discussion, the meanings ascribed to the word "empire" are various and contradictory. Second, the chapter sets forth a series of hypotheses and speculations. In some instances these propositions rest on a knowledge of non-tsarist and non-Soviet empires that might be called, at best, modest. Nonetheless, the discussion provides a point of departure that I hope will facilitate comparison and synthesis of the ideas of scholars who have a detailed knowledge of the particular empires analyzed in this volume.

Empires and Imperialism

The study of empires has a complex intellectual history fraught with political controversy and contradictory ideological conceptions.[6] Before the nineteenth century, "empire" had multiple meanings. During the preceding three centuries it was sometimes equated with the idea of a universal political order; with the notion of the state; with monarchy; or with a physically large political entity encompassing diverse peoples.[7] Perhaps the most common meaning of the term was the syncretistic notion of a state headed by an emperor or a monarch and including culturally distinct peoples. In this dynastic conception of empire, the key relationship lay between the emperor and his subjects; although the indigenous peoples of the imperial periphery were often judged to be inferior, the most salient political distinctions in the empire were customarily between noble elites and the lower classes, not among ethnic groups. In keeping with this orientation, the imperial apparatus of rule generally made little effort, by modern standards, to change the cultures or institutions of peripheral peoples.[8]

As dominant Western notions of the legitimate locus of political sovereignty changed, so too did the prevailing meaning of empire. The advent of nationality as a key criterion of political differentiation and of nationalism as a potential instrument of political mobilization fundamentally altered the internal dynamics of empires. Partly in consequence, by the middle of the twentieth century the term was commonly used to denote a political structure in which one nation dominated others, often on the basis of an authoritarian metropolitan state. There was, however, no consensus on the meaning of empire. Some writers took authoritarianism—that is, the presence of an emperor, in fact if not in name—to be the most important criterion for the existence of an empire. Other observers regarded national domination of subordinate nations as the key indicator, whether or not the metropolitan state was governed by democratic procedures. Still others, of Marxist persuasion, regarded domination by a capitalist state as the key criterion, thereby excluding the possibility of socialist empires.

Changes in the content of the concept of empire were accompanied by changes in its moral coloration. This change of outlook, it should be said, did not proceed in a linear fashion. In the seventeenth and eighteenth centuries traditional conceptions of empire encountered harsh criticisms from some metropolitan political thinkers. These critics decried the cruelties inflicted on the native inhabitants of peripheral territories, and warned that efforts to sustain large transoceanic empires against the wishes of assertive settler colonies could destroy the metropolitan state itself.[9] However, such criticisms were not widely applied to overland empires consisting primarily of contiguous territories, and during the nineteenth century a wave of political and economic changes revived the impulse of major states to construct transoceanic empires, now conceived of primarily as territories to be controlled rather than as lands to be settled by inhabitants of the metropolitan state. Thus the nineteenth and early twentieth centuries came to represent the apogee of Western empire building and imperial thinking.

Between the mid-nineteenth and mid-twentieth centuries the concept of empire collided with more powerful oppositional currents generated by two central tenets of modern political ideology: democracy and national self-determination. Although these constituent elements of modern political thought contain numerous ambiguities and internal contradictions, they swamped the favorable associations previously attached to the word empire and removed it as a term of positive political discourse. In the nineteenth century, the majority of Western statesmen and commentators regarded empire as a positive phenomenon. By the mid-twentieth century, as Mark Beissinger has pointed out, the concept had become a term of opprobrium whose applicability to existing political structures was generally one facet of an ideological struggle over whether those structures should be perpetuated or dismantled.[10] Later we shall ask whether empires can exist in an intellectual and cultural environment that denies their legitimacy as political entities, and if so, how.

In this chapter, empire denotes a dominant society's control of the effective sovereignty of two or more subordinate societies that are substantially concentrated in particular regions or homelands within the empire.[11] Empires are more than conventional foreign alliances between the metropolitan state and other states—even foreign alliances that endure over long periods of time—although in some historical cases the two categories overlap. According to the definition used in this discussion, empires differ from nation-states by virtue of the nonintegration of their constituent societies into a single political community; they differ from alliances and from great-power hegemony over small states by virtue of the metropolitan center's domination of the peripheral societies' internal affairs as well as their external relations.[12]

Thinking of empire in more restrictive terms, we can distinguish a type called *modern empire*. A modern empire relies on control by a particular kind of metropolitan society, namely a dominant nation, over the sovereignty of subordinate nations.[13] It is distinguished from premodern empires by the presence of nationalism and by a number of other features that make nationalism possible: a relatively clear demarcation of territory, the beginnings of a sense of citizenship, and a level of socioeconomic development that expands the share of the population available for mobilization into the political arena.[14] In a moment we shall explore the problematic nature of the relationships between empire and nationhood. For the moment, suffice it to say that this narrower definition focuses attention on latter-day empires, rather than on empires in the prenationalist era.[15]

Like the notion of empire, the notion of imperial control is not easy to pin down. Metropolitan control of peripheral societies may be exercised in the political-military, the economic, and the cultural spheres. In any given empire, metropolitan control may exist in all three of these spheres, but in other cases it may not. As Roman Szporluk points out in chapter 3, it is much easier for a metropolitan nation to control peripheral nations over which it has a plausible claim of cultural superiority, and to do so at relatively low military cost. By contrast, metropolitan control over nations that regard the metropolitan nation as culturally inferior is more costly in political-military terms and more difficult to sustain over time. There is no inherent reason that a metropolitan nation cannot maintain its control under these conditions, but it can do so only if it has preponderant military means and is prepared to pay high political-military and economic costs.

In this connection we should note that the exercise of metropolitan control is not necessarily equivalent to material exploitation of peripheral societies, and that within a given empire the relationship between control and the distribution of material benefits may change over time. An empire based initially on political and economic exploitation of peripheral societies may gradually evolve into an imperial structure in which political dominance is combined with economic subsidies to the peripheral societies. A gradual shift of this sort occurred in the Soviet Union's forty-five-year relationship with the East European members of the Soviet bloc; apparently a similar shift transpired in Russia's economic relations with several non-Russian Soviet republics while Moscow still dominated Soviet political life.[16] Similarly, Miles Kahler shows in chapter 12 that in sub-Saharan Africa after the mid-1950s, continued French control rested on political-military pressures from the metropole but also entailed the provision of significant material subsidies.

Michael Doyle has usefully differentiated among the metrocentric, pericentric, and systemic traditions of analyzing empires. The metrocentric approach enjoyed its widest currency in the nineteenth and early twentieth centuries, when the wave of European conquests in Africa and Asia suggested that the key to understanding empires lay in the imperial motives and behavior of the European metropolitan powers. This metrocentric view of empire was subsequently challenged by a pericentric conception that came into vogue partly as a consequence of the rise of anticolonial movements and the dismantling of the major West European colonial empires. The role of peripheral societies in the demise of these empires encouraged scholars to pay attention to the part played by conditions on the periphery in the original construction and evolution of empires. The pericentric approach required students of the development of empires to take account of "two calendars"—the rate and direction of change in the metropolitan core and the rate and direction of change in the peripheral territories.[17] A third, systemic tradition of analysis locates the roots of empires not in the characteristics of individual metropolitan states or peripheral societies, but in the international political competition among major states for various forms of power and wealth, including control over peripheral regions and populations.

The notions of empire and imperialism are thus related but distinct. An empire is a political structure that possesses or possessed some historical durability, whereas imperialism is an aspect of great-power behavior. Imperialism may lead to the creation of empires and help sustain them, but imperialism does not always lead to empire. For instance, intense competition among metropolitan powers may make peripheral societies an object of external pressure and intrusion yet also prevent some of them from being incorporated into a single, consolidated empire. China after the mid-nineteenth century comes to mind as an example of a society that was an object of contention among rival imperialist powers. Moreover, as suggested by the pericentric model, direct resistance from peripheral societies may fend off or defeat imperialist efforts to create or maintain an empire.

Conceptualizing empire in terms of the relationships among societies and nations rather than simply in terms of the relationships among states suits the complexity of the subject. Studies of international relations that focus on states tend to regard the goals and interests of states as self-evident. Even studies that seek to examine the play of organized groups behind the facade of the state tend to think of the interests of these groups themselves as being self-evident—for example, the pursuit of power and wealth. Although such motives certainly play a central role in determining the behavior of states, cultural and emotional identifications also shape the prevailing understanding of the state's "national interests." For example, under a rational calculus of state interest, the Nazi regime of the 1930s should have pursued a cautious external policy. Instead it pursued a belligerent imperial strategy, partly because much of the nation whose interests were thought to be at stake lived in eastern Europe, beyond the borders of the German state.[18]

Although comparing empires in terms of societies and nations rather than states alone has advantages, it also poses special intellectual challenges. The advantage of studying empires as relationships among states is that states are relatively easy to identify. They have government leaders and formal institutions such as treasuries and armies, and they make specific political claims on their subjects or citizens. Societies and nations, on the other hand, are far harder to identify and demarcate. When do social subgroups belong to a single political community, and when not? What if one subgroup in a territory believes that all the inhabitants belong to a single political community, while another subgroup rejects this notion? The human boundaries of nations are often matters of dispute and can change over time. Depending on the prevailing criteria of national self-identification, a single nation can encompass diverse ethnic groups, but ethnic groups that once regarded themselves as members of one nation also can begin to regard themselves as separate nations. Nations are fluid entities that persist only if they are actively perpetuated through political and cultural mechanisms, because ultimately each generation of the nation dies and each new generation's collective and personal experiences can vary radically from those of the preceding generation.

Similarly, the intensity of national identification may vary strongly among the distinct social and regional subgroups of a single nation.[19] As chapter 3, by Roman Szporluk, notes with respect to Russia, such variations are most obvious in the middle stages of nation building, when nationalist intellectuals or state leaders seek to foster national awareness in a larger population, especially one that consists mainly of peasants. But substantial discrepancies in national identification can persist long after a nation is "complete." Variations in the content and distribution of national feelings among the millions of people who make up a single nation frequently prevent observers from agreeing on the strength and character of nationalism within the group as a whole.

Empires, Nation-States, and Patterns of Transformation

In conventional usage, the concept of empire and the concept of nation-state are often treated as a dichotomy. This, however, is an oversimplification produced by the reification of historically changeable entities. Many contemporary nation-states began as empires that consisted of culturally disparate groups that lacked a sense of shared identity and were only gradually transformed into a national community identified with the state.[20] Nineteenth-century thinkers tended to think of nation building as a process through which small ethnic groups were incorporated into larger national entities. However, developments in the twentieth century have shown that the process of sociopolitical mobilization can turn ethnic groups loosely identified with a state into secessionist nations that destroy it. Whether this second process is likely to prevail over the first in any particular case depends on numerous factors. These include the numerical ratios between various ethnic groups, the geographic concentration or dispersion of each group, the intensity of ethnic attachments to a territorial homeland whose boundaries differ substantially from those of the whole state, the degree of cultural affinity or distance among the state's constituent groups, and the economic and career opportunities available to the various ethnic elites within the existing state structure.[21] In short, the dividing line between a sense of ethnic distinctiveness and a sense of national separateness is not permanent, and one can change into the other. In analyzing particular cases, both sides of the picture must be examined. Under what conditions is an ethnic group likely to be transformed into a full-fledged nation, and under what conditions is a nation likely to become a "mere" ethnic component of a more inclusive national society?

One key factor that has sustained modern empires and reduced their susceptibility to breakdown has been an aggressive form of metropolitan nationalism. Sometimes this variety of nationalism has arisen more or less spontaneously from political and cultural groups outside the government; sometimes it has been generated by governmental programs calculated to promote "official nationalism" within the society. Students of Russia have often suggested that the emergence of popular Russian national identity coincided with the state's creation of a multinational empire, thereby fusing the sense of Russian nationhood with the habit of imperial domination. Other European states, according to this view, developed a distinctive sense of national identity before establishing their empires. They therefore experienced less confusion about the human boundaries of the nation and were—by implication at least—better prepared to shift to non-imperial forms of behavior.[22]

Although plausible at first glance, this proposition bears the marks of essentialist thinking about supposedly immutable patterns of national behavior. The latter part of the nineteenth century was, after all, the heyday of West European imperial expansion into Africa and Asia, and also the period when many inhabitants of West European states were first imbued with a sense of a distinctive national identity.[23] In France, for example, the peasantry was taught to identify with the nation only in the decades between 1870 and 1910—precisely the period when France launched a vigorous effort to build a new transoceanic empire and French nationalism shifted from liberalism toward radicalism and xenophobia.[24] Nor is it certain that all West European states developed a clear-cut national identity during this period.[25] In a metropolitan state, any long-term sense that national identity is inextricably linked to an imperial vocation is probably due more to the geographical nature of the empire than to the timing of its creation. In transoceanic empires, geographical barriers and the separation of populations favor the development of a sense of metropolitan identity distinct from the empire as a whole; in overland empires the physical mingling of territories and populations tends to impede the development of a clear-cut metropolitan national identity.

Imperial Forms and Soviet Empire

Many observers have drawn a distinction between formal empires, which encompass metropolitan and peripheral societies within a single state, and informal empires, in which a metropolitan state dominates the external and internal affairs of other nominally independent states. The distinction between formal and informal empires has only limited value as a guide to the actual distribution of power between the dominant and peripheral nations. The distribution of power within either a formal or an informal empire can vary sharply, just as it can in non-imperial states. Strictly speaking, the Warsaw Pact was an informal empire; yet the degree of Soviet control over its East European members was extremely high due to the USSR's military might and willingness to intervene, its police and party penetration of East European societies, and its economic leverage over these dependencies.

Nevertheless, the distinction between formal and informal empires is important because an informal empire may allow the metropolitan state to defuse anti-imperial resistance from peripheral societies or from other great powers and thereby reduce the political and economic costs of maintaining the empire. As Miles Kahler shows in chapter 12, under certain circumstances the relatively low costs of informal empire, especially when augmented by the metropolitan government's ability to obscure these costs from the metropole's ordinary citizens, can make this pattern of control more tenable than that of formal empire. Rather like scholarly discussions of empire, scholarly debates over the notion of informal empire have become intertwined with ideological struggles over the rights of former colonies and the obligations of the European powers that once directly controlled them.[26] However, the concept of informal empire is analytically useful so long as the metropolitan threat or use of military force is an integral element of the concept.

Thus far we have assumed that the Soviet Union was an empire; but was it? The Soviet Union manifestly *had* an empire in Eastern Europe and, for a time, in East Asia; but was the USSR *itself* an empire? Answering this question is complicated by the existence of different definitions of empire and by the difficulty of determining whether one nation or several nations exist within a particular state—especially when the state's ideology exalts the notion of a monolithic society and prohibits objective study of this question. A case could be made that the Soviet Union was a multinational state but not an empire—at least not a Russian empire. Official Soviet ideology did not clearly proclaim the superiority of the Russian nation over the other nations of the USSR, and significant numbers of most ethnic minorities came to regard themselves first and foremost as citizens of the USSR. In some respects, there was a perverse equality among ethnic groups: not only was Soviet citizenship extended to non-Russians as well as Russians, but Russians, too, were exterminated in large numbers under Stalin and repressed under his successors. The case for the Soviet Union as a Russian empire would be more clear-cut had Stalin made non-Russians the sole targets of the mass terror and the purges.

On the other hand, a number of considerations do argue for classifying the USSR as an empire. For much of its life the Soviet regime emphatically maintained that relations between Russians and national minorities were similar in Imperial Russia and the Soviet Union, and its operational policies toward mass education and senior political appointments were based on a pervasive assumption that Russian culture and language were superior to those of all other Soviet nationalities.[27] Moreover, the regime maintained a comprehensive internal structure of ethnically defined territorial-administrative units, particularly the national republics of the USSR, which were based on historical ethnic homelands and helped sustain or deepen distinct national identities among the principal ethnic minorities. Not least, real or alleged proponents of the interests of ethnic and national minorities met especially harsh persecution or physical liquidation, and under Stalin several small ethnic groups suspected of disloyalty were deported to Siberia and Central Asia with great loss of life. Thanks to Stalin's reliance on an authoritarian brand of official Russian nationalism to lend cohesion to the Soviet state, ethnic Russians were not tried or executed on such charges. On balance, then, the USSR can reasonably be called an empire—but an empire with special features that may make the dynamics of its transformation and aftermath unusual, as we shall see later in this chapter.[28]

The Dissolution and Aftermath of Empires

Because history is not unilinear, to speak of particular empires in terms of clear-cut life cycles of creation, disintegration, and postimperial aftermath is an oversimplification. Historically, some empires have waxed and waned more than once, and many have expanded in some regions while contracting in others. Nevertheless, a rough division of the evolution of empires into these three stages is heuristically useful for the delimitation of the subject of this book. The central task of the book is not to provide a comprehensive discussion of the causes that have contributed to the disintegration of the empires selected for analysis. The main goal is to analyze and explain what has happened in the wake of imperial disintegration. The book outlines those features and aspects of the process of disintegration that have substantially shaped the course of later events.[29] It explores the enduring effects of the imperial experience on the constituent societies that emerged from the breakdown of each empire. And it examines the impact of these factors on the political prospects and behavior of the metropolitan and peripheral successor states following the demise of the old imperial order.

The principal cases selected for comparison with the Soviet Union suggest the wide range of possible outcomes that may follow imperial disintegration and that might in theory ensue from the breakup of the USSR. Notwithstanding their substantial differences from one another, the Ottoman and Habsburg empires exemplify semitraditional authoritarian polities that succumbed to diverse internal and external pressures and were never reconstituted. By contrast, the fractured tsarist monarchy, a semitraditional authoritarian polity that was destroyed by many of the same pressures, was ultimately reconstituted as a totalitarian empire within a single state. Imperial Germany exemplifies an empire, based on an uneasy mixture of authoritarian and democratic principles, which was deprived of its colonial territories by victorious military rivals and reorganized on liberal-democratic lines, but which soon developed into a totalitarian state aggressively committed to building a new empire. The British and French empires represent cases in which external and internal pressures prompted a democratic metropolitan state gradually to relinquish its formal empire. These two cases also demonstrate that under certain conditions a democratic metropolitan state may relinquish control of colonial territories in a relatively peaceful fashion, but that under other conditions a democratic state may wage protracted wars against decolonization and may establish an informal empire in some of the territories previously under its formal control.

Reasoning a priori rather than solely in historical terms, we can delineate more fully the possible outcomes of the disintegration of a formal empire. Regarded from a territorial standpoint, the most radical outcome involves the disintegration of the entire empire, including the metropolitan core itself. In such cases, the pieces of the old empire may be assembled into a new empire by another metropolitan state. Less drastic outcomes include a metropolitan society's loss of control over all its peripheral territories, the loss of some of these territories, renewed control over the entire periphery, or expansion into additional territory beyond the periphery.[30] In some instances the metropolitan society may relinquish formal control but retain informal control over former peripheral possessions.

When an imperial upheaval deprives the metropolitan society of the capacity to restore either formal or informal control over peripheral territories, several other long-term outcomes are conceivable. These include the creation of a federation or confederation encompassing both the metropolitan society and the peripheral societies; hegemony by the metropolitan successor state over the foreign relations of peripheral successor states; an interstate alliance between the metropolitan state and fully independent peripheral successor states; and an alliance or alliances between peripheral successor states and other major powers, generally directed against the metropolitan successor state.

The prospects for a federal, and to a lesser extent a confederal, outcome are undermined by the dynamics of disintegration, at least in the short term. In cases of imperial disintegration, newly independent nations and states generally continue to rely on imperial or anti-imperial rhetoric as a means of shoring up their shaky national identities. Even in instances where there is no significant residual imperial impulse in the metropolitan state, this dynamic impedes the creation of close formal linkages on nonimperial terms.[31] In the long run, however, even the federal option is conceivable under certain conditions, such as overlapping national identities and strong mutual interest in economic integration.[32]

Influences on the Outcomes of Imperial Transformations

Understanding the outcomes of past imperial transformations and the possible outcomes of the Soviet Union's transformation requires us to analyze the net effects of a wide range of factors. In schematic terms, some of the most important factors are (1) the nature of the international environment, (2) the character of nationalism among the dominant and subordinate nationalities, (3) the role of political violence in the creation and maintenance of the empire, (4) the liberalization of the empire's political structures, (5) the armed forces' behavior and level of cohesion, (6) national economic resources and international economic relations, and (7) the political and economic strategies of peripheral societies during and after the breakup of the empire. The challenge of studying imperial transformations is that the number of causal variables is large, and in numerous cases similar final outcomes may result from very different combinations of causes. There is, in short, no substitute for comparative analysis combined with close empirical study of particular imperial episodes.

The Nature of the International Environment

The international environment of imperial disintegration may be thought of as consisting of geopolitical, institutional-normative, and cultural elements. The geopolitical trigger for the decline or demise of an empire may be a general war, intermittent and less intense military conflicts spanning many years, or nonviolent economic and political pressures generated by other states. Although all three forms of geopolitical pressure may figure in the fate of specific empires, this need not be so, and the relative salience of the three factors varies substantially from one case to another.

Intuitively it seems that each form of geopolitical pressure is likely to propel a disintegrating empire in a different direction, although historical contingencies make it impossible to draw any hard and fast inferences on this score. An empire's defeat in general war may strip away peripheral territories but simultaneously give rise to attitudes and myths that strengthen the impulse to reconstitute the broken empire. Chapter 11, by Carole Fink, explains how a "stab-in-the-back" theory conducive to neo-imperial thinking developed in Germany after Germany's defeat in World War I.[33] By contrast, a cumulating series of limited but costly military defeats in struggles over the control of peripheral societies may create a sense of inevitable decline and gradually undermine the determination of the imperial elite to cling to the remaining peripheral territories. Something of this sort may have occurred in the Ottoman Empire, although not all the members of the elite shared such an outlook.[34] Finally, imperial collapse in the absence of either general war or a string of smaller-scale defeats, as in the case of the USSR, may profoundly discredit the old imperial political structure and thereby weaken any imperial pretensions inherited by the metropolitan successor state. Although myths of external enemies acting in league with internal conspirators are certain to arise, they may be more difficult to instill in a significant part of the metropolitan citizenry without the concrete evidence of foreign hostility furnished by large-scale military conflict.

The outcome of imperial transformations is also affected by prevailing international political and legal norms. In the wake of World War II and the powerful anticolonial movements that it unleashed, the doctrine of national self-determination has been accepted on a worldwide basis, and the nation-state, however loosely defined, has been accepted as a form of political organization morally preferable to empire. Although elastic in application, these norms have raised new obstacles to the maintenance or reconstitution of formal empires.

The effect of such norms, of course, depends in large measure on the behavior of the major states that shape the course of international affairs. In the nineteenth century, as Solomon Wank suggests in chapter 4, the Ottoman and Habsburg empires each depended in different measure on other major powers to shore up their faltering control of their peripheral territories, and for several decades these powers provided such support, primarily for reasons of self-interest. By the time of World War I, however, the doctrine of self-determination and national independence had become a political weapon used selectively by the warring powers to promote the disintegration of their military adversaries.

After World War II the doctrines of self-determination and national independence became tools of struggle in the Cold War, as the United States and the Soviet Union vied for influence over the emerging anticolonial movements of the Third World. As Michael Fry shows in chapter 5, the United States did not launch a frontal attack on the West European colonial empires because it required the support of the West European states in the continental struggle against the Soviet bloc and wished to prevent Soviet inroads in the Third World. But neither did the United States endorse the continued existence of Western Europe's formal colonial empires. Instead, it followed a complex policy intended to court pro-Western independence movements, prevent the rise of anti-Western movements for national liberation, and to facilitate, in some regions, the transformation of West European formal empires into informal empires.

More subtle forms of international influence on the process of imperial disintegration can be exercised by nonstate actors. These groups may include active peripheral-society diasporas situated outside the empire. This is particularly true in instances where military defeat or collapse has left an empire's future in the hands of foreign powers amenable to the influence of these diasporas. For example, the influence of the Czech and Slovak diasporas on U.S. policy toward the disposition of the Habsburg lands following World War I facilitated the creation of an independent Czechoslovak state in the postwar peace settlement.[35] By contrast, the settlement also contributed to the incorporation of the Bohemian Germans—who for obvious reasons lacked such international leverage—into the same multiethnic state on terms that many of them found unacceptable.

The Character of Nationalism Among the Dominant and Subordinate Nationalities

In various guises, nationalism has both sustained and destroyed modern empires. Recognizing the destabilizing potential of nationalist movements to generate demands for popular sovereignty, traditional empires built on dynastic principles have generally feared metropolitan as well as peripheral nationalism; by contrast, empires that have completed the transition to active forms of mass political participation (whether or not this participation is democratic) have generally welcomed nationalism among the members of the dominant nationality. Empires torn between the wish to limit participation and the desire to promote industrial development have had an ambivalent policy toward official nationalism of this variety. On balance, however, metropolitan nationalism has more often buttressed empires, whereas peripheral nationalism has almost invariably undermined them.

This suggests that the weak or comparatively late development of national consciousness within the metropolitan society, coupled with a high level of national consciousness in some or all of the peripheral societies, has historically reduced the chances that an empire will survive or be reconstituted. Ottoman Turkey and, in a peculiar sense, the Habsburg Empire, appear to fit this proposition. As shown by Dankwart Rustow in chapter 7, national consciousness developed quite late in Anatolian Turkey, and international circumstances made the survival of the Turkish nation contingent on abandoning many of the Ottomans' old imperial claims. In the Austro-Hungarian empire, the situation was more complicated, but functionally much the same. At the end of World War I most Austrian Germans favored unification with Germany instead of the restoration of the Habsburg Empire; and the revanchist forces in Hungary, which had been severely truncated by the postwar peace settlement, were too weak to reestablish their control over other nations except in league with a more powerful ally such as Germany.

Conversely, more resilient empires may be characterized by relatively powerful metropolitan nationalism and weak nationalism in a number of the peripheral societies, as in the tsarist case and in Nazi Germany. Here, weak nationalism should be construed not only to mean a low level of national consciousness in the peripheral societies but also to include sharp interethnic divisions within those societies, even when the ethnic consciousness of each component element is comparatively well developed. One feature of Nazi Germany's expansion into eastern Europe before World War II was the way in which it played on the radical variant of the concept of self-determination—that is, self-determination not for the "national" populations of established east European states, but for ethnic minorities within them. In this fashion, metrocentric and pericentric conditions interacted to increase the potential for imperial reconstitution and expansion. It might be argued that a roughly similar "objective" situation exists with respect to Russia and some other Soviet successor states, such as Georgia, where Russia has played on Georgia's internal ethnic divisions and internal separatist tendencies to try to establish its dominance over the country. Although arguably an exaggeration, the analogy is nonetheless suggestive.

The impact of "diasporas" of the majority nationality on the process of imperial transformation must also be taken into account. As a rule, the presence in the peripheral societies of a large group of settlers from the empire's dominant nationality is likely to heighten the metropolitan core's resistance to the dissolution of the empire, whereas the presence of only a small population of this kind tends to weaken the impulse to preserve or restore the empire in adjacent territories.[36] Similarly, the existence of a majority-nationality diaspora outside the historic boundaries of the empire may foster an impulse for imperial expansion. Thus an apparent parallel exists between the ethnic German diaspora as a contributing cause of Nazi expansion into East-Central Europe and the potential international consequences of the ethnic Russian diaspora in the non-Russian successor states of the USSR. In each case, the struggle over an inclusive or restricted definition of citizenship in the metropolitan successor state stands out as an important arena of political struggle.[37] In each case, too, the breakup of established states made the issue of citizenship much more salient. In 1918 the breakup of the Habsburg Empire invigorated the *Grossdeutsch* conception of an inclusive German nation; in 1991 the breakup of the USSR similarly forced Russians to consider whether the Russian nation consisted solely of the inhabitants of Russia or included ethnic Russians in other successor states.

On the other hand, whether "demand pull" from a dominant-nationality diaspora actually constitutes a major cause of imperial restorationism is an open question. In each case under study, we must ask whether the dominant-nationality diaspora actually favored the reconstitution of the empire or whether politicians in the metropolitan successor state merely imputed to the diaspora their own imperial goals. Here it is important to avoid primordialist thinking about ethnic groups' national identities and loyalties. Whether a dominant-nationality diaspora will seek incorporation into a renewed empire depends partly on the tenor of its historical relations with the ethnic groups in the peripheral successor state. The orientation of such a diaspora will also hinge on the treatment it receives from peripheral successor states and on the economic benefits conferred by membership in those states relative to those available in the metropolitan successor state. It is a familiar observation that individuals embrace national identities not only on the basis of intrinsic cultural legacies, but also on the basis of concrete political and economic calculations. Due to such contingencies, as S. Frederick Starr suggests in chapter 10, the ethnic Russian diaspora may play a less salient role in Russia's future relations with other post-Soviet states than many observers initially expected.

The Role of Political Violence in the
Creation and Maintenance of the Empire

The long-term effects of internal violence under an empire are likely to affect both the dynamics and aftermath of its dissolution. Depending on the particular circumstances, the nature of the agents of political violence and the character of its targets can contribute to divergent patterns of change. Although equally destructive in human terms, state-sponsored violence directed against peripheral societies may be considerably less harmful to the empire than violence directed against the metropolitan nationality itself. State violence against the dominant nationality may erode official nationalism as a basis of the imperial elite's legitimacy, thereby undermining the empire and possibly blocking its reconstitution. As noted earlier, this is a distinctive and perhaps unique feature of the Soviet/post-Soviet case. Over the long term, Stalin's murderous policies toward all groups of Soviet citizens gave rise to anti-Soviet nationalism both among the USSR's national minorities and among the Russians themselves. The rise of antistate nationalism among ethnic Russians was an unusual aspect of the Soviet upheaval and was arguably the most powerful catalyst of imperial dissolution. Stalin manipulated official Russian nationalism to maintain the political cohesion of the empire, but the emergence of a new strain of Russian nationalism which regarded Russians as the chief victims of the Soviet regime deprived it of that crucial source of cohesion.[38]

Conversely, a history of communal violence, especially communal violence directed by national minorities against members or groups of the metropolitan society, may harden the dominant nationality's unwillingness to accept the personal risks entailed by dissolution of the imperial state. Large-scale violence of this sort does not appear to have occurred in the non-Soviet cases examined in this book, but its implications can be grasped from the history of the Yugoslav crisis. By heightening the fears of the Serbian metropolitan population and the Serbian diaspora in other former Yugoslav republics, memories of Croatian atrocities against Serbs during World War II impeded the peaceful secession of Croatia and other republics from the Yugoslav federation. In the lands of the former USSR, by contrast, the low incidence of communal violence directed against the dominant Russian population by non-Russians (as distinguished from anti-Russian violence carried out by the Soviet state) may increase the probability of a broadly peaceful dissolution of the empire. Such historical legacies, of course, are brought to bear on contemporary events partly through the political strategies and machinations of current political leaders (which will be discussed below in more detail). But it is also true that the legacies create a predisposition toward peaceful acceptance of imperial dissolution or violent resistance against it.

Liberalization of the Empire's Political Structures

Internal liberalization appears to be a necessary—but not a sufficient—condition for the peaceful dissolution of an empire. Much depends on the geographic distribution of liberalizing impulses inside the empire and on the timing of these impulses relative to one another. It may be that nonviolent imperial disintegration requires the coincidence of liberalizing trends in the metropolitan and the peripheral societies, and that liberalization in the imperial center or the periphery alone is inadequate. This appears to be an important difference between the Soviet and Yugoslav cases. In the USSR the rise of an anti-imperial democratic movement in Russia and of anti-imperial movements in several non-Russian Soviet republics was nearly simultaneous. In Yugoslavia secessionist reform movements in the peripheral societies became predominant when liberal reformers in the Serbian core had already been defeated by authoritarian forces under the leadership of Slobodan Milosevic. Milosevic opportunistically manipulated an authoritarian variant of Serbian nationalism to prevent the peaceful dissolution of Yugoslavia. Boris Yeltsin, motivated by a mixture of principle and opportunism, harnessed a liberal strand of Russian nationalism to promote the peaceful dismantling of the Soviet state.

As a broad proposition, twentieth-century democracies seem far less able (than do authoritarian regimes)—to create and sustain empires especially overland as opposed to transoceanic empires. In her chapter analyzing Weimar Germany's failed attempt at democratization, Carole Fink asks whether contemporary Russia may be replicating that experience and thereby moving toward a revival of past imperial policies. Although there are several significant parallels, fundamental differences exist between the two countries' prior experiences with the domestic exercise of imperial power and their resultant attitudes toward liberal democracy. Some recent students of democratization have argued that the desire to escape arbitrary rule has a larger impact on popular attitudes than does the anticipation of material benefits from democratic government.[39] In Weimar Germany, the previous, relatively benign course of the semi-authoritarian imperial system gave German citizens little warning of the coming horrors of Nazism. Contemporary Russia, on the other hand, has already endured one of the worst totalitarian regimes in history; its struggles toward democracy are occurring amid recollections of the mass deaths inflicted during Stalin's imperial reign. A critical question is how deeply these horrors will remain embedded in the society's memory after the generation that experienced them passes from the scene. But the contrast in historical sequences suggests that most Russians will balk at returning to full-fledged authoritarianism and that their present reluctance to make personal sacrifices to build a new empire may persist despite the wide-spread national mood of imperial nostalgia.

In weighing the likely impact of internal political arrangements on the external behavior of any metropolitan successor state, it is important to bear in mind the distinction between states with established democratic systems and states undergoing democratization. The argument that established democracies do not wage war on one another has led many contemporary observers to assume that a democratic Russia will be nonimperial. However, the applicability of this proposition to Russia's relations with the other Soviet successor states, even those that are democratically oriented, is not self-evident. The post-Soviet states are not stable democracies, nor in many cases have they established clear-cut national identities that are fully distinct from one another. Under these conditions, democratic debate and elections might weaken imperialist forces among the dominant nationality, but democratic practices might also give advocates of empire an arena in which to win converts among rank-and-file citizens disillusioned by the hardships of the past five years.[40] One might speculate that in a case like Russia's, where the international and domestic economic costs of a neo-imperial policy would be extremely painful for the general population, democratization decreases the likelihood of imperial reconstitution through large-scale military action, but does not preclude efforts to re-establish control of portions of the empire through political and economic pressures coupled with low-level military coercion.

The Role of the Armed Forces

In many modern empires, the military establishment has been strongly commit-ted to the empire and has played a central role in maintaining it against internal as well as external perturbations. This is due partly to the frequent tendency to equate the empire's survival with the security of the metropolitan core, and also to the close association between the empire's survival and the political status of the military as an institution. The military may exist to protect the empire, but the empire may also exist to protect the military.

Consequently, in cases of imperial disintegration, the military establishment may harbor a strong desire to reclaim lost peripheral territories. In transoceanic empires, threats to the metropole and the appearance of new military missions may induce the armed forces to accept a more circumscribed geographic role that downgrades the significance of peripheral territories with marginal strategic importance.[41] But in overland empires the military establishment is likely to be much more reluctant to give up its bases in peripheral territories thought to be essential to the defense of the metropolitan core. Self-interest apart, the growth of perceived threats to the metropole is likely to strengthen military commanders' desire for the reconstitution of a fractured empire. In some cases, the military establishment may favor an informal pattern of empire that restores many of its strategic assets and enhances its mission without provoking strong peripheral opposition that could embroil it in major counterinsurgency operations.

When neo-imperial goals cannot be attained by political or economic means, an empire can be rebuilt only through the use of military force or a credible threat of its use. This underscores the importance of the metropolitan successor state's real military capabilities. Depending on the circumstances surrounding the empire's disintegration, the armed forces may suffer greatly or not at all. A long period of political and economic turmoil inside the metropolitan successor state may spill over into the military establishment and undermine its ability to revive the empire by force. In extreme cases, a high level of domestic economic and cultural turmoil may destroy the cohesion of the military establishment and even cause military commanders to become preoccupied with securing their personal welfare at the expense of any broader objectives. In these cases, elements within the military may endorse and lobby for a renewal of empire, but they may not be able to provide the means to achieve it.

Aside from its role as lobbyist and potential instrument of imperial restoration, the military establishment may affect the policies of the metropolitan state in one other fashion. Earlier I suggested that restorationist impulses are likely to be especially pronounced in the wake of a large-scale war that deprives the metropolitan core of its peripheral territories but does not destroy the core itself. Here the spillover from military experience into civilian life can be crucial. The huge numbers of soldiers required for modern interstate warfare may provide fertile soil for revanchist ideologies, and a rapid demobilization of forces may inject these neo-imperial ideas into civilian political life. This process, for example, appears to have had a substantial effect on the political atmosphere in Weimar Germany. In such circumstances, massive military demobilization in the wake of a general war may paradoxically create a greater long-term danger of imperial restoration than would efforts to pare back even a large imperial military establishment in peacetime. In this respect, the relatively peaceful dismantling of the Soviet empire has so far generated fewer pressures for imperial reconstitution than a general war would probably have created.

National Economic Resources and International Economic Relations

In cases of imperial disintegration, the prospects for reconstituting the empire in any form are shaped by the metropolitan successor state's level of economic development vis-à-vis the peripheral successor states and other major powers. If the metropolitan center possesses a preponderance of resources compared with the peripheral states, it stands a greater chance of reasserting political control over them, especially if they are economically unattractive to the other international actors that might supplant the former metropole as their main economic partner.

The post-disintegration prospects for a metropolitan reassertion of economic control are usually greater in overland than in transoceanic empires, since the level of economic integration between the metropolitan and peripheral societies is ordinarily higher at the time of the empire's breakup. As Hendrik Spruyt notes in his chapter, the regions of the Soviet Union had an unusually high level of economic integration, compared with other states or economic unions. Under such circumstances, the sheer magnitude of the task is likely to make an economic reorientation toward the outside world more difficult for peripheral successor states. Moreover, if their economies have been organized on the highly inefficient principles of socialist central planning, escaping the economic orbit of the former metropole will be especially difficult unless they enact the fundamental domestic economic reforms necessary for them to participate successfully in the international economy. The established imperial economic infrastructure of communications, transportation, and energy supply may also make peripheral successor states susceptible to pressures and manipulation from the metropolitan successor state.

On the other hand, not all peripheral successor states are equally vulnerable to metropolitan economic manipulation. Some may possess large stocks of valuable natural resources that can be developed jointly with outside powers and used to bolster economic growth and state revenues. Nor is smallness an inherent obstacle to the establishment of economic independence in peripheral successor states. In the increasingly open global economy, small successor states can be economically viable if they undertake necessary economic reforms and pursue effective economic policies.[42] In the last three decades a number of small states in Asia have capitalized on international trade and investment flows to prosper and grow at rates that are the envy of the Western powers.

Whatever the vulnerabilities of the peripheral successor states, the likelihood of a neo-imperial assertion of control also depends on the economic calculations of the metropolitan successor state itself. Earlier I noted that imperial political control over peripheral societies sometimes coincides with metropolitan subsidies to these same societies. However, as Spruyt points out, a policy based solely on economic objectives may lead a metropolitan successor state to eschew this kind of costly imperial relationship in favor of more profitable ties with commercial partners outside the former empire. The worse the economic condition of the metropolitan society, the greater the internal pressures to avoid subsidizing an imperial relationship with peripheral successor states, particularly large states, since the domestic opportunity costs to the metropole are painfully high. In the post-Soviet case, it is still unclear whether Russia will attempt to reestablish imperial control on such terms.

Political and Economic Strategies of Peripheral Societies

It must be emphasized that the probability of the reconstitution of empire hinges in significant measure on trends inside the peripheral successor states themselves. A great deal depends on the level of professional skills inherited from the imperial era and on the political talents of the leaders who come to power after the empire disintegrates. In addition, much depends on the depth of ethnic and socioeconomic cleavages within the peripheral societies. Skilled peripheral elites committed to building strong states and effective economies constitute a major barrier to the reassertion of metropolitan control; scarcely less important is their ability to bridge domestic economic and ethnic cleavages that might be exploited from outside. Skilled elites increase a peripheral society's chances of parrying metropolitan political pressures and deflecting arguments designed to convince ordinary citizens that superior economic benefits are available from a reconstructed empire. In cases where a sizable peripheral-society diaspora exists in advanced foreign countries, members of the diaspora may supply the resources needed to bridge both economic-administrative and political gaps in the abilities of the new state's indigenous elites.

The adroitness with which a new elite manages foreign and security relations is another vital consideration. Skilled leadership is essential for establishing "geopolitical name recognition"—that is, a clear-cut national identity and political acceptance by major powers that can assist the successor state and possibly fend off intrusions from the old metropolitan core. The level of cooperation among the peripheral successor states also affects the prospects for imperial reconstitution. Such cooperation may be more effective in the aftermath of transoceanic empires, in which metropolitan-peripheral linkages are weaker and the metropolitan successor state is more apt to encounter logistical obstacles if it seeks to project its power into the former peripheral territories. If peripheral states attain significant military capabilities, either by virtue of internal resources or by acquiring fragments of the imperial armed forces, the probability of a reconstitution of formal empire also declines, so long as the metropolitan successor state is unwilling to pay a high domestic and diplomatic price to attain this objective.

In any case of imperial disintegration, a central issue in assessing the long-term outcome is the degree of diversity or uniformity among the peripheral successor states. Will most of the empire's peripheral successor states possess a similar capacity or incapacity for survival, or will there be major variations among them? The answer to this complex question appears to hinge on both the legacy left behind by the metropole and on the relative staying power of the imperial legacy vis-à-vis the peripheral society's pre-imperial legacy of political and cultural traditions. In chapter 8, Robert Rotberg notes the broad similarities among most of the African states that emerged following the disintegration of the European colonial empires, but he also points out the rather distinct political and institutional characteristics of some Asian successor states that emerged from the same empires. Similarly, the Ottoman successor states of southern Europe were apparently more capable of sustaining an independent existence than were the Arab societies that were taken under European tutelage after World War I.

The case of the Soviet empire is unusual in this respect. In the quest to transform both peripheral and metropolitan societies, the Soviet state went to extremes that most other imperial states neither imagined nor were capable of. The various peripheral successor states may therefore have been imbued with a powerful common legacy. On the other hand, these societies entered the Soviet era with distinct national cultures and histories, and elements of these pre-Soviet heritages have resurfaced since the late 1980s. It may therefore be the case that these societies will evolve in quite different ways, and that their ability to survive as independent states will vary accordingly. Whichever of these propositions is closer to the truth, it will have a major bearing on the aftermath and the overall outcome of the disintegration of the Soviet empire.

Conclusion

Analyzing the transformation of the Soviet Union in comparative perspective offers a valuable path toward fuller understanding of this momentous process of imperial disintegration and upheaval. But it does not exempt scholars from the task of wrestling with the particular circumstances and substance of post-Soviet developments. As the following chapters show, some of the writers believe that international and domestic circumstances have made the restoration of a formal empire in the territories of the former USSR nearly impossible. But other scholars, who lay more stress on the enduring social and psychological legacies of the Soviet system, believe that such an outcome is quite conceivable. In part, these differences of opinion stem from divergent appraisals of the political durability of the peripheral successor states and the depth of long-term national support in those countries for independence. In addition, the authors' distinct views stem from varying judgments, implicit or explicit, about Russia's prospects for successful democratization. Not least, the differences stem from divergent assessments of the depth of Russian imperial nostalgia, on the one hand, and Russia's present political-military and economic capacity to realize new imperial dreams, on the other.

By itself the comparative approach cannot resolve such intellectual issues. But it can perform the essential function of helping us to see the Soviet transformation against a broad intellectual backdrop. Widening our field of vision sensitizes us to the multitude of factors at work in this vast upheaval and helps us pose the right analytical questions. Comparative analysis can alert us to the mixed outcomes that may occur in Russia's relations with various peripheral successor states. It also can help us identify those cases in which the relationship between Russia and a given peripheral successor state will depend not only on developments in each country but on the sequence—the two calendars—according to which those national developments occur. Finally, comparative analysis can help us sift and interpret the voluminous new evidence that will surface as the powerful currents buffeting the Soviet successor states—or should we say the post-Soviet states?—sweep them onward.

Notes

I am greatly indebted to David Wilkinson and the other participants in the Conference on the Disintegration and Reconstitution of Empires for their helpful comments on an earlier version of this chapter.
1. One pioneering book that takes the hybrid quality of empires into account is Michael Doyle, *Empires* (Ithaca: Cornell University Press, 1986).
2. For an initial effort to chart this new intellectual terrain, see Karen Dawisha and Bruce Parrott, *Russia and the New States of Eurasia: The Politics of Upheaval* (New York: Cambridge University Press, 1994); and Dawisha and Parrott, series eds., *The International Politics of Eurasia*, vols. 1–9 (Armonk, NY: M.E. Sharpe, 1994–96).
3. See, for instance, Doyle, *Empires*. See also "Colonialism" and "Empires" in *International Encyclopedia of the Social Sciences*, vol. 3, pp. 1–12, and vol. 5, pp. 41–49. A pioneering early study that does compare Russia's imperial practices with those of other empires is S. Frederick Starr, "Tsarist Government: The Imperial Dimension," in Jeremy Azrael, ed., *Soviet Nationality Policies and Practices* (New York: Praeger, 1978), pp. 3–38.
4. Paul Kennedy, *The Rise and Fall of the Great Powers* (New York: Random House, 1987); Jack Snyder, *Myths of Empire: Domestic Politics and International Ambition* (Ithaca: Cornell University Press, 1991); and Charles Kupchan, *The Vulnerability of Empire* (Ithaca: Cornell University Press, 1994).
5. See, for example, Alexander Motyl, "From Imperial Decay to Imperial Collapse: The Fall of the Soviet Empire in Comparative Perspective," in Richard R. Rudolph and David E. Good, eds., *Nationalism and Empire: The Habsburg Empire and the Soviet Union* (New York: St. Martin's, 1992), pp. 15–44; John-Paul Himka, "Nationality Problems in the Habsburg Monarchy and the Soviet Union: The Perspective of History," in ibid., pp. 79–94; Mark Beissinger, "The Persisting Ambiguity of Empire," *Post-Soviet Affairs* 11, no. 2 (1995): 149–85; and Karen Barkey and Mark von Hagen, eds., *Imperial Collapse: Causes and Consequences* (Boulder, CO: Westview Press, forthcoming). Two early book-length comparative treatments of the USSR's disintegration are Rudolph and Good, eds., *Nationalism and Empire*, and Uri Ra'anan et al., eds., *The Break-Up of Multinational States*. These two works contain valuable insights, but each was completed before the final collapse of the USSR and the establishment of the post-Soviet successor states. See also W. Raymond Duncan and G. Paul Holman Jr., eds., *Ethnic Nationalism and Regional Conflict: The Former Soviet Union and Yugoslavia* (Boulder, CO: Westview Press, 1994).
6. See Wolfgang J. Mommsen, *Theories of Imperialism*, trans. P.S. Falla (Chicago: University of Chicago Press, 1980); Doyle, *Empires*, chs. 1, 6.
7. Anthony Pagden, *Lords of All the World: Ideologies of Empire in Spain, Britain and France, c.1500–c.1800* (New Haven: Yale University Press, 1995).
8. This broad generalization groups together early empires that varied substantially in their attitudes toward the cultural assimilation, institutional restructuring, and religious conversion of peripheral societies. David Wilkinson has informed me that the ancient Egyptian, Chinese, Roman, and Arab empires all devoted considerable efforts to one or

another of these goals. In my opinion, however, even when such efforts occurred, they could not produce the kind of comprehensive change of language, popular culture, and social structure that modern governments are capable of effecting through mass education, mass communication, and regular bureaucratic contacts with individual members of society.

9. Pagden, *Lords of All the World,* pp. 6, 178–95. These criticisms were reinforced by the virtually complete loss of the empires of Britain, France, and Spain in the Western Hemisphere during the late eighteenth and early nineteenth centuries.

10. In addition to chapter 6 of this volume, see Beissinger, "The Persisting Ambiguity of Empire," pp. 152, 156–57.

11. This concept of empire is a slightly modified version of the ideas developed by Michael Doyle in *Empires.* In stipulating that there must be at least two subordinate societies, I follow Alexander Motyl, who distinguishes empires from bifurcated states such as Czechoslovakia. Alexander Motyl, "Thinking about Empire: A Conceptual Inquiry with Some Implications for Theory," in Barkey and von Hagen, eds., *Imperial Collapse.*

12. The distinction between empire and foreign-policy hegemony is drawn from Doyle, *Empires,* p. 40.

13. One significant feature of Doyle's pioneering book is how little attention it gives to the topic of nationalism.

14. Benedict Anderson, *Imagined Communities* (London: Verso, 1983), pp. 19, 90. For the effects of higher levels of socioeconomic development and potential mass participation on absolute monarchies and other traditional polities, see Samuel Huntington, *Political Order in Changing Societies* (New Haven: Yale University Press, 1967), chs. 1, 3.

15. The appellation "modern" is not meant to signify that such empires have necessarily been equipped to prosper or survive in the twentieth-century world—only that major components of these empires have achieved a significant level of modern socioeconomic development.

16. See the economic statistics cited in Tables 3.2 and 3.3 of Marek Dąbrowski and Rafał Antczak, "Economic Transition in Russia, Ukraine, and Belarus in Comparative Perspective," in Bartlomiej Kaminski, ed., *Economic Transition in Russia and the New States of Eurasia* (Armonk, NY: M.E. Sharpe, 1996), pp. 46–47. It is necessary to say "apparently," because data on Russian price and monetary subsidies to the non-Russian republics are available only for the end of the Soviet era.

17. Tony Smith, *The Pattern of Imperialism: The United States, Great Britain, and the Late-Industrializing World Since 1815* (New York: Cambridge University Press, 1981), pp. 85–86.

18. On this point see Richard Rosecrance's review of Charles Kupchan, *The Vulnerability of Empire,* in "Overextension, Vulnerability, and Conflict: The 'Goldilocks Problem' in International Strategy (A Review Essay)," *International Security* vol. 19, no. 4 (1995): 156–58.

19. E.J. Hobsbawm, *Nations and Nationalism Since 1780: Programme, Myth, Reality* (New York: Cambridge University Press, 1990); Robert J. Kaiser, *The Geography of Nationalism in Russia and the USSR* (Princeton: Princeton University Press, 1994), chs. 1–2. Contrast this sociological approach with the emphasis on ideas and elites in Liah Greenfeld, *Nationalism: Five Roads to Modernity* (Cambridge: Harvard University Press, 1992).

20. See Hugh Seton-Watson, *Nations and States: An Enquiry into the Origins of Nations and the Politics of Nationalism* (Boulder, CO: Westview Press, 1977), ch. 2.

21. One factor contributing to the successful consolidation of nation-states has been

the willingness of dominant ethnic or territorial groups to grant members of other groups access to countrywide markets and mobility into top-level careers, thereby coopting potential separatist elites and fostering their identification with the state as a whole. This sort of access helped contain the centrifugal force of Scottish nationalism within the United Kingdom, for example (Anderson, *Imagined Communities,* p. 90). Ethnically or territorially distinct elites are more likely to begin to regard themselves and their kinsmen as separate nations when they are denied broad economic and career opportunities that link them with the state; the rise of nineteenth-century Latin American nationalism and movements for separation from the Spanish Empire provides a case in point (ibid., pp. 56–58).

22. This is one explanation of Russian nationalism—but not the sole explanation—offered by Richard Pipes in his introduction to *Handbook of Major Soviet Nationalities,* Zev Katz, Rosemarie Rogers, and Frederic Harned, eds. (New York: Free Press, 1975), pp. 1–2; see also Dawisha and Parrott, *Russia and the New States of Eurasia,* p. 26.

23. In thinking about this issue, another factor must also be borne in mind. At least three of these metropolitan states (England, France, and Spain) had built (and subsequently lost) empires in the Western Hemisphere before they underwent the development of modern-day nationalism.

24. Eugen Weber, *Peasants Into Frenchmen: The Modernization of Rural France, 1870–1914* (Stanford, CA: Stanford University Press, 1976); Hobsbawm, *Nations and Nationalism Since 1780,* pp. 12, 44, 60–61, 79; cf. Kaiser, *The Geography of Nationalism,* chs. 1–2. Indeed, Hobsbawm maintains that one of the three basic criteria of European nationhood during this period was "a proven capacity for conquest" (p. 38). One difference between the Russian and French patterns of development may be that France's elites acquired a sense of belonging to a single nation earlier than did Russia's elites and had a greater administrative capacity to use mass education and other socializing processes to create a French nation that ultimately incorporated the peasantry.

25. In the case of the British Empire, it is an interesting question whether a single British nation ever fully crystallized, since the metropolitan core continued to consist of English, Scottish, and Welsh populations that regarded themselves as members of distinct ethnonational groups, as well as many Irish inhabitants who favored separation from the United Kingdom. See Michael Hechter, *Internal Colonialism: The Celtic Fringe in British National Development, 1536–1966,* paperback ed. (Berkeley and Los Angeles: University of California Press, 1977).

26. In this connection, see Richard Rosecrance, *The Rise of the Trading State: Commerce and Conquest in the Modern World,* paperback ed. (New York: Basic Books, 1986), pp. 53–55, and Smith, *Patterns of Imperialism,* pp. 69–84.

27. In stressing these continuities, the Stalinist regime abandoned the anti-imperial stance of early Marxist historiography and distorted the historical record of tsarism to depict these relations as essentially benign. Lowell Tillett, *The Great Friendship: Soviet Historians on the Non-Russian Nationalities* (Chapel Hill: University of North Carolina Press, 1969); Dawisha and Parrott, *Russia and the New States of Eurasia,* pp. 32–33.

28. It has sometimes been suggested that the Russian Federation is also an empire, partly because about twenty percent of its population consists of non-Russians and some of its constituent governmental units are ethnically defined. However, three features make this characterization seem inappropriate: (1) the state has adopted a broad definition of the nation that encompasses all inhabitants of Russia, not just ethnic Russians; (2) ethnically defined units make up only about one-third of the eighty-nine components of the federation; and (3) there is now generally far more opportunity for the politically unfettered development of the cultural identities of non-Russian ethnic groups than there was in the Soviet era. The latter point holds true despite Moscow's extremely brutal war in Chechnia

against Chechen forces claiming independence for their territory, which is located inside Russia's internationally recognized borders.

29. In Russian history, for example, explaining the collapse of the tsarist regime is not equivalent to explaining the establishment of the Soviet empire under Bolshevik aegis— although some common factors obviously figure in both kinds of explanation.

30. It is sometimes forgotten, for instance, that the USSR of the 1920s represented only a partial reconstitution of the tsarist empire—lacking as it did Finland, eastern Poland, the Baltic States, and Moldavia.

31. Beissinger, "The Persisting Ambiguity of Empire," p. 153.

32. In this scenario, one or more of the peripheral societies has a weak or exiguous sense of national identity. If the old metropolitan core relies on negotiation and economic and cultural incentives rather than on military and economic coercion, an erstwhile empire might be territorially reconstituted as a democratic state lacking imperial domination of the peripheral societies in question. In this case the territorial identity of the empire would be preserved (at least in part), but the voluntary integration of two or more of its component societies into a single political community would cause the state's imperial features to disappear within those territories.

33. Of course, such an outcome also depends on whether or not the metropolitan state is politically and culturally reconstructed under the control of the victors. The different policies adopted toward Germany after World War I and after World War II illustrate the difference.

34. In chapter 4 of this volume Solomon Wank shows that the Ottoman elite failed to make the internal reforms necessary to preserve the empire, but that after at least a century of imperial decline, the Young Turks who came to power in the early twentieth century were committed to reviving the empire.

35. For background, see Carol Skalnik Leff, *National Conflict in Czechoslovakia: The Making and Remaking of a State, 1918–1987* (Princeton: Princeton University Press, 1988), pp. 150–52.

36. In this respect modern empires appear to differ from earlier transoceanic empires. In these early empires, the settler colonies generally possessed sufficient military and technological advantages to subdue the indigenous population, as well as approximate military-technological parity with the metropolitan society. This made movements among the settlers for independence from the metropolitan core more feasible and more likely. In modern empires the dominant nationality's advantage as settlers is more difficult to sustain over time, as the requirements of economic development generate technical skills and more assertive attitudes among the indigenous population. This increases the settlers' incentive to remain part of the empire.

37. On the establishment of an ethnocultural rather than a more restrictive territorial definition of citizenship in Germany before World War I, see Rogers Brubaker, *Citizenship and Nationhood in France and Germany* (Cambridge: Harvard University Press, 1992), pp. 114, 126–30, and 165–68. Brubaker emphasizes the differences between pre-Nazi and Nazi citizenship laws; but a substantial element of continuity existed as well. See also Peter Alter, "Nationalism and Liberalism in Modern German History," in Roger Michener, ed., *Nationality, Patriotism and Nationalism* (St. Paul, MN: Paragon House, 1993), pp. 90–91, 96.

38. John Dunlop, *The Rise of Russia and the Fall of the Soviet Empire* (Princeton: Princeton University Press, 1993).

39. Giuseppe Di Palma, *To Craft Democracies: An Essay on Democratic Transitions* (Berkeley and Los Angeles: University of California Press, 1990).

40. For a historical analysis that argues that democratizing countries are more likely to wage war than are either stable democracies or stable authoritarian systems, see Edward

Mansfield and Jack Snyder, "Democratization and War," *Foreign Affairs* vol. 74, no. 3 (1995): 79–97.

41. For instance, the pre–World War I British military establishment initially resisted redeploying forces from distant colonies to meet the German navy's growing threat to Great Britain, but as the threat became more obvious the military supported and quickly carried out a major redeployment to the European theater (Kupchan, *Vulnerability of Empire*, pp. 106–28). However, as Miles Kahler notes in chapter 12 of this volume, even though the French and British armed forces were both responsible for the defense of transoceanic empires, the French military establishment vigorously resisted the actual dismantling of empire, whereas the British military did not.

42. Gertrude Schroeder, "On the Economic Viability of New Nation-States," *Journal of International Affairs* vol. 45, no. 2 (1992): 549–74.

2

The Rise, Fall, and Future of the Russian Empire

A Theoretical Interpretation

David A. Lake

The Russian Empire has been at the center of global politics throughout the twentieth century. The expansion of the Russian Empire into eastern Europe served as the primary catalyst for the Cold War. The collapse of the empire, beginning in 1989, rightly signaled the end of the forty-five-year frost. Today, important segments of Russian society yearn for the return of the empire—a development that, were it to occur, would surely impose a deep freeze on now warm East–West relations. Understanding the rise, fall, and future of the Russian Empire is central to the successful management of foreign affairs in the closing days of the "American century."

The study of imperialism was once at the heart of the discipline of international relations. It is now typically treated as a footnote, of interest primarily to more historically inclined scholars. This is increasingly unfortunate. The collapse of the Soviet Union rendered transparent the imperial nature of the Russian-dominated political system. Yet, we lack today the necessary theoretical tools to understand and explain the empire, its demise, or its future.

In this chapter, I build upon the rich if now forgotten literature on imperialism and pose a general theory of empire, in two parts. First, I summarize a theory of relational contracting in which empire is but one of several possible relationships between polities. Drawing upon economic theories of the firm, empire is understood metaphorically as roughly equivalent to integration within a single firm. Empires are most likely to emerge when scale economies are large, the expected costs of opportunism in an anarchic relationship are high but decline with hierarchy, and governance costs are low or do not escalate significantly with hierarchy. Like many other theories in international relations, the theory of relational contracting focuses on relations between states—not on their domestic attributes. The features of the theory most relevant to the Russian Empire are summarized here; fuller versions of the theory are presented elsewhere.[1] In the second part of this chapter, focusing on the internal characteristics of polities, I review a theory of the monopoly power of the state. Relaxing the stark assumption of internal unity central to the first approach, the second model suggests that autocracies will tend to possess an imperial bias in their foreign policies. Again, only the relevant features are discussed here; the theory is presented and tested more systematically in an earlier essay.[2] The two theories are intimately related, operate together, and jointly form a general theory of empire. I do not attempt to assess which part is analytically more important in the Russian case; rather, features of both models are at work simultaneously in this and, I suspect, other instances as well.

One of the great anomalies of the Russian Empire was its peaceful demise. Many analysts, even those sensitive to the internal decay of the Communist regime, predicted that the empire would fall with a bang, not a whimper. Nonetheless, the end of the Russian Empire was spearheaded and accepted—even if not fully anticipated or supported—by the Soviet elite. The theories presented here identify processes of endogenous change that ultimately produce the collapse of empire. Under conditions obtaining in the Soviet Union by the 1980s, they imply that shrinking the empire would improve welfare and would, therefore, be acceptable to the political leadership. This is, perhaps, one of the biggest differences between traditional theories of imperialism and the general theory examined here.

This chapter is a theoretical reflection on the nature, causes, and duration of empires. It is decidedly not an empirical study of empires in general, or of the Russian Empire in particular. The theory is applied to the Russian case, but only at the level of broad interpretation. Specialists will no doubt find the approach unsatisfying, but I believe there is value in seeing the rise, decline, and possible future of the Russian Empire through a new and, I hope, more powerful set of lenses. The chapter is divided into five principal parts. I first briefly review existing theories of empire. The second section defines *empire* and places it along a continuum of other possible relationships between polities. I present, in the third section, a theory of relational contracting and, in the fourth section, a theory of the monopoly state. The final section examines implications of the combined theory for the future and policy.

Theories of Empire

Three main theories divide the study of empire.[3] Metrocentric theories focus on dispositional features of imperial states and identify a range of internal characteristics associated with expansion. Vladimir I. Lenin's theory of imperialism is a classic example: faced with a falling rate of profit at home, capitalist states are driven to build empires as they search for new outlets for their accumulating surpluses.[4] Explanations of Russian imperialism that emphasize either cultural traits or the expansionist nature of communist ideology are metrocentric theories.

Pericentric theories emphasize conditions in the colonial states and territories. In this view, states are drawn into empires by events and conditions in the outlying areas. John Gallagher and Ronald Robinson articulate this approach most clearly in their thesis, "The Imperialism of Free Trade."[5] Great Britain, they argue, pursued the same goals around the world; what differed was the ability or willingness of peripheral elites and governments to serve British interests. Although it preferred an informal empire based on policies of free trade, Britain opted for more formal control in areas where local rulers were too weak to ensure an open economy or other imperial competitors threatened to close the area to trade. Pericentric theories of Russian imperialism include those that highlight the varying conditions in the Eastern European states after World War II or focus on the nature and strength of the new governments in the several successor states.

Finally, systemic theories of empire highlight the struggle between great powers for influence around the globe. Realist theories, for instance, predict that security or power-maximizing states will build empires to counterbalance the capabilities of potentially hostile competitors.[6] In the Russian case, systemic theories focus on the state's continuing fear of Germany after World War II and its need to build a Soviet buffer in Eastern Europe, or on Russia's current need to reestablish control over the successor states to remain a great power in world affairs.

There is sufficient evidence in the historical record to sustain each of these theories as a viable explanation of imperialism. Any instance of empire is likely to combine elements drawn from all three approaches. Several recent studies have succeeded in integrating these frameworks into a consistent and powerful whole.[7] Nonetheless, these synthetic theories, while sensitive to variations in informal and formal empires, continue to abridge the full range of variation in relations between polities; this both limits the explanatory utility of the theories and creates a selection bias in their research designs. Perhaps more important for our purposes here, these theories are static and cannot explain imperial change. The theory discussed below seeks to rectify both of these limitations: the first part is explicitly relational, and thus combines elements from metrocentric, pericentric, and systemic theories; the second part is strictly metrocentric.

Empire as a Political Relationship

Originally used as an invective against Napoleon's expansionist policies in Europe, imperialism has been defined in a variety of ways.[8] Classical realists follow the original usage; for Hans Morgenthau, any state that does not accept the territorial status quo is ipso facto imperialist.[9] For others, empire is associated

Figure 2.1. **A Continum of Political Relations**

Locus of Rights of Residual Control

Anarchy   Hierarchy

Alliance   Protectorate   Informal Empire   Empire/Confederation

Relationship

with the direct or indirect economic domination of peripheral areas; in an extreme and somewhat perverted sense, it has also been used to refer to any economic exchange between states of unequal wealth.[10] Analysts have also identified various types of empires, with the most common distinction being between informal and formal systems of rule. Despite their differences, all of these various usages share a common view of empire as the control of one polity by a second.[11] In a less than helpful way, the debate over what is and is not an empire has typically fractured over the instruments of control, not the condition or degree of control itself.

Defined as a relationship in which one polity is controlled by another, empire can be more fully understood as an endpoint along a continuum defined by the degree of hierarchy between two polities.[12] This continuum is illustrated in Figure 2.1. A *polity* is an organized political community that has experienced or could potentially experience self-rule. Despite rather severe problems of operationalization, as discussed by Bruce Parrott, any attempt to analyze existing empires must at least envision a past or an alternative future in which the constituent parts were or could become independent entities.[13] Polities, as defined here, differ from acephalous political communities, which lack any central organization, and from other political communities that are below the minimum efficient scale to survive as independent entities. It follows from this definition that the basic unit of analysis may change with variations in internal political organization or minimum efficient size. Throughout this chapter, Russia is taken to be the basic polity both within the formal empire, embodied in the Soviet Union, and in the informal empire, which linked the Soviet Union with the nominally sovereign states of Eastern Europe. It is for this reason that I use the term "Russian" Empire rather than the more common "Soviet" empire.[14]

The degree of relational hierarchy, in turn, is defined by the locus of rights of residual control. All relationships between two parties, whether entered into voluntarily or as a result of coercion, can be considered to be based upon some *contract* that specifies explicitly or implicitly the terms under which they will pool their efforts and resources—broadly referred to here as cooperation—and the residual rights of control retained by each.[15] Cooperation by itself does not establish control. When two states agree to some joint activity, they do not necessarily establish control over one another. Rather, control occurs when one side imposes constraints on the other's residual decision-making rights.

Contracts are, simply, agreements that define the terms of the relationship between two actors. Contracts can be completely or incompletely specified. The former type details numerous contingencies and sets forth appropriate responses by the parties; the latter contains blanks that are filled in by the parties as necessary. With costly information, bounded rationality, or any other constraint on perfect foresight, no contract can address all contingencies in all possible states of the world. In practice, then, all contracts are imperfectly specified and thus leave a varying residual of unspecified rights, obligations, and actions. The *rights of control* fall to the party with the ability to make decisions in this residual. It is important to note that the term *right* does not necessarily imply a formal, de jure recognition by both parties of one's authority to exercise control over the residual; the term can simply reflect an informal, de facto ability of one party to control actions of the other in some areas. Rights of control differ from mere influence, however, in that they constitute an enduring pattern of control within an ongoing relationship.

In anarchy, which defines one end of the continuum of political relationships, each party possesses full residual rights of control; while constrained by its environment, each state is master of its own fate in that area of rights not previously ceded in the contract. Anarchic relations, of course, characterize the majority of international relations; some scholars even understand anarchy to be the defining characteristic of international politics.[16] An alliance, such as the North Atlantic Treaty Organization, or a free trade agreement, like the General Agreement on Tariffs and Trade, are well-known examples of contracts between states in anarchy.

In hierarchy, at the other end of the continuum, one party—the dominant member—possesses the right to make residual decisions, while the other party—the subordinate member—lacks this right. Thus, the dominant state possesses control over all resources and assets not specifically reserved to the subordinate actor in the contract. It is irrelevant to the definition of hierarchy whether the relationship is entered into voluntarily or through the pain of battle and whether control rests on military force or economic dependence. How control is exercised is separate from the condition of control, and it is the latter that defines relational hierarchy. At least two forms of hierarchy exist. In empire, one partner cedes substantial rights of residual control directly to the other; in this way, the two polities are melded together in a political relationship in which one partner controls the other. The European empires of the nineteenth century remain classic examples. In a second form of hierarchy, confederation, the constituent members themselves remain equal but cede substantial residual rights to a third party or federal state.

This definition of empire as a hierarchical transfer of the rights of residual control does not differ in its fundamentals from others posed in this volume. Miles Kahler, in chapter 12, also distinguishes between confederations, which operate with joint decision making, and empires, in which one society assumes sole decision-making authority over the internal and external policies of another—or, to use my terms, where one party possesses all rights of residual control.[17] Bruce Parrott defines empire as a dominant society's control of the effective sovereignty of two or more subordinate societies—with effective sovereignty analytically congruent with complete rights of residual control.[18] While similar in form and content to both Kahler's and Parrott's definitions, a focus on the degree of hierarchy and on the locus of the rights of residual control reveals more clearly, I believe, the continuous nature of relationships between polities.

At least two types of intermediate relationships between alliance and empire have been salient historically.[19] In a protectorate, one state cedes control to another over important areas of national policy, most notably foreign affairs. Although the terms vary, such grants of control are typically broad, are made for extended periods of time, and are irrevocable. Such delegations of authority transfer residual rights of control in the designated areas from the protected state to the protector and severely constrain the former's ability to influence the policy choices the latter makes for it. Britain extended a de jure protectorate over the so-called native states of India and a de facto protectorate over what is now the United Arab Emirates during the nineteenth and early twentieth centuries. Through the organization of Commonwealth of Independent States (CIS), Russia is attempting to impose a protectorate, at least, over the other successor states.[20]

Informal empire is the second salient intermediate form. Informal empire differs from its more formal counterpart only in the breadth of the residual rights of control transferred from the subordinate to the dominant state. In formal empire, the imperial state's control of residual rights in the subordinate partner is nearly total, whereas in informal empire, the control is substantial but less than complete. This definition differs from tradition, in which the distinction between formal and informal empire rests on the mechanism rather than on the degree of control, with informal empire defined as indirect rule by local proxy.[21] Although the process of control is important and easily conflated with outcome, the key distinguishing factor is the extent of the residual rights that remain in the domain of the subordinate member. The most striking modern example of an informal empire was the Soviet bloc that was established in Eastern Europe following World War II.[22]

"Pure" conditions of anarchy or hierarchy seldom exist. Even in primarily consultative relations between allies, some degree of control may be exercised over residual choices. Similarly, in empire, local officials are often given some independence in responding to local conditions. Thus, conceived in this way, we can begin identifying degrees of hierarchy along the continuum of relations. As examples, we can note that Russia's post–World War II relations with the states of Eastern Europe were less hierarchic than its current relations with the constituent republics of the former Soviet Union. Among the successor states today, some (the Baltics) have opted for noncooperation; some are emerging as protectorates, a relationship in which Russia continues to control their foreign policies; and others—the CIS notwithstanding—are being reintegrated into an informal Russian empire.[23]

Relational Contracting

Theories of relational contracting, first developed in economics, were originally designed to explain the institution of the firm. However, they also provide a general approach to understanding social organization.[24] The key insights of the relational contracting approach are, first, that the transaction is the unit of analysis, and, second, that transactions can be carried out in a variety of governance structures—or what I have called relations in the previous section. Stated another way, the approach views the structures in which particular transactions occur as variable and endogenous. The central hypothesis is that parties choose relations in order to economize on resources, or in other words, to maximize benefits from exchange and minimize transactions costs. In short, actors choose the relationship that is most efficient for conducting the transaction so as to maximize the resources that can be used for other valued purposes.

In international politics, three variables are critical to the decision of whether to cooperate with another party, and, if so, what kind of relationship to form. The three variables to consider are scale economies, expected costs of opportunism, and governance costs. Scale economies determine the gains from cooperation. The expected costs of opportunism reflect the risk of cooperating with the partner. These costs decrease as hierarchy increases, thus creating the principal impetus toward empire. Governance costs are incurred in safeguarding the relationship and, if necessary, coercing the other party; governance costs increase with hierarchy and deter states from empire. Together these three variables determine the choice of relationship. Small scale economies, which might otherwise thwart cooperation, may still produce a relationship between the parties if the expected costs of opportunism and governance costs are even smaller. High expected costs of opportunism, which again might undermine cooperation, may still permit a relationship if governance costs are sufficiently low—although in this case the relationship will be relatively hierarchic. The logic behind these inferences is developed in the following sections.

Scale Economies

The gains from cooperation are the great forgotten variable in current theories of international relations. In many theories, the gains from cooperation are either assumed to exist or are treated as fixed, as when it is assumed that prisoner's dilemma is the characteristic game of international politics or that games are typically repeated.[25] But total gains from cooperation cannot be fixed or assumed; rather, they vary as a function of scale economies. The larger the scale economies, the greater the gains from cooperation, whether the focus of cooperation is a material good for trade, security, or another joint activity that requires input of scarce resources from one or both parties.[26]

Scale economies are defined by the relationship between changes in production inputs and outputs. Returns to scale remain constant when increases in the quantity of factors employed in production lead to an equal and proportionate increase in the quantity of output. Under decreasing returns to scale, increased inputs produce less than proportionate increases in output, and under increasing returns, increased inputs lead to more than proportionate increases in output. Scale economies arise in three ways: through a division of labor, through use of or changes in technology, or when positive externalities are internalized in a relationship.

Through specialization and exchange, parties can reap the gains from a division of labor. The law of comparative advantage is based precisely on this insight. Yet, other activities that are not commonly understood to involve tradable goods can produce the same sorts of benefits. In the realm of security, for instance, states may specialize in certain activities and exchange their output: If one state builds a deepwater navy and protects sea lanes, while another builds a land army and concentrates on territorial defense, both countries may increase security while expending fewer total resources. A division of labor may also be utilized in different types of political relationships; specialization and exchange can occur between two states in an anarchic relationship or between an imperial state and its colony. The difference between the two situations lies not in the transaction itself but in the political arrangement that governs the transaction.

Security is also a "natural" monopoly that, due to the technology of production, often possesses increasing scale economies over some substantial geographic area.[27] Technological changes that apply more energy to the productive process, facilitate standardization, or break complex tasks into simpler and repetitive parts are also likely to produce greater scale economies, as will any production method that requires a large, fixed, initial investment. Increasing technical proficiency with output—or learning by doing—is equally important. In the economic arena, such technological innovations are the driving force behind the growth of ever-larger firms and, in the views of some, regional trade arrangements and economic unions.[28] In the security realm, technological innovations that lower the cost of projecting force, create advantages for the offense, or favor forward-based defenses will increase scale economies and enlarge the optimal area over which to produce defense.[29] The advent of steam-power technology provides one example: in addition to reducing the costs of maintaining a global navy, the use of steam power also required an extensive network of overseas coaling stations, some of which were integrated into the European empires while others remained independent.

Positive externalities are benefits from an activity that extend beyond the party producing the good. They are pervasive in the environmental and security arenas, but are less common in traditional economic exchange.[30] For example, the security produced by a state may benefit others within the international system as well. If a state blocks another's drive for hegemony, it benefits other states within the system. Likewise, if a front-line state deters expansion by another, it protects those states that lie to its rear. By internalizing their separate defense efforts within a single cooperative relationship, both parties can potentially improve their individual welfare by reducing redundant production.

A division of labor, technological change, and positive externalities can all increase scale economies and heighten incentives for parties to cooperate. Stated more strongly, a division of labor, improved technologies, or positive externalities are necessary conditions for cooperation. For a cooperative venture to succeed, there must be some advantage to at least one party from pooling resources and efforts with the other that cannot be obtained unilaterally; otherwise, states are better off relying upon their own resources. As scale economies increase, so does the probability of cooperation—when all other factors are held constant. Yet, because scale economies are potentially the same across alternative political relationships, these efficiency gains cannot explain the choice between, say, an alliance and an empire. This remains a function of the expected costs of opportunism and of governance costs, discussed in the next two sections.

Lacking "natural" geographic borders, Russia has long been favored by the substantial scale economies of its natural monopoly in security. By expanding eastward and westward, it greatly increased the area from which it could extract resources without enlarging substantially the borders it was required to defend. The technological advances inspired by World War II also placed a premium on offensive military operations from forward bases—creating a new impetus for expansion, especially into Eastern Europe. In what was often described as a buffer strategy, the object of expansion was to project force and fight future wars as far as possible from Russia's national territory; an identical military strategy, reflecting the same increased scale economies, informed American defense planning after World War II.[31] These same technological scale economies continue to exist today.

In the economic arena, the internal division of labor made possible by the empire was an important impetus for expansion. Unable to compete effectively on world markets due to the inefficiencies of the command economy, and fearful of political manipulations of trade by the West, the Soviet Union relied upon a division of labor within the empire, with different regions specializing in different goods (on the more limited division of labor between Russia and the informal empire, see next section). With the end of Communist rule, the stifling effects of the command economy have been reduced and Russia is going through a severe crisis of economic adaptation. If economic reform is eventually successful, and Russia specializes in its areas of international comparative advantage, this drive for an imperial division of labor will be diminished (see below).

Expected Costs of Opportunism

When involved in a cooperative relationship, states risk three kinds of opportunistic behavior by their partners. As Glenn Snyder has posited, they may be *abandoned;* more generally, partners may shirk responsibility by formally or informally abrogating agreements. States may be *entrapped* by their partners into undesired conflicts, wars, or other activities.[32] As such, entrapment is often a problem of moral hazard in which commitments, once issued, cause the partner to act in a more risky, negligent, or aggressive fashion than before. Finally, states may be *exploited*—a closely related form of opportunism that Snyder does not address. Having settled upon an initial division of the benefits and costs of the relationship, partners can subsequently seek to alter the terms of agreements and obtain more favorable distributions of the joint gains.

When it occurs, in whatever form, opportunism is costly for the state. Its partner either contributes less to the joint enterprise than promised, forces the state to divert its own resources toward undesired ends, or seizes a greater share of the joint gain than anticipated. Abandonment, for instance, reduces not only the partner's contribution but also, in some cases, the efficacy of the state's own efforts; if the state has specialized in a land-based army and its partner has agreed to provide the complementary naval defense, the latter's abandonment may leave the former more vulnerable than if it had produced both an army and navy of its own.

The cost to the state of such behavior is determined by its own opportunity cost. When it possesses alternatives that it values almost as much as the one in question, a state's opportunity cost is relatively low; it can shift from relationship to relationship easily and without a significant loss in welfare. When there are no attractive alternatives, the state's opportunity cost is high and changing relations is a more consequential decision with more deleterious welfare implications. The greater the state's opportunity cost, the greater is the harm—or actual cost—the partner can inflict upon it.

Opportunity costs are determined by the degree to which assets are relationally specific; that is, whether they possess more value in one use and relationship than in others.[33] Assets can be highly flexible and easily transferred from one application to another or highly specialized and difficult to redirect. The more relationally specific the asset, the greater are the opportunity costs incurred by the state.

The probability that the partner will act opportunistically, in turn, is a function of the governance structure the actors choose to construct. The ability of any polity to act opportunistically is determined by its rights of residual control; the greater the residual rights, the greater the discretion of the actor to behave in ways that may—intentionally or unintentionally—undermine cooperation.

Thus, by implication, the probability that the partner will engage in opportunistic behavior decreases with relational hierarchy. In an alliance, for instance, each partner retains complete residual rights and, thus, wide discretion. Even though it may agree to declare war if a third state attacks the first, the partner nonetheless retains the right to decide who attacked whom and how many resources it will actually commit to the conflict. Therefore, in anarchic relations, ceteris paribus, the probability of a partner behaving opportunistically is comparatively high. In an empire, at the other extreme, states merge their formerly autonomous decision-making processes and transfer rights of residual control to the dominant member. The dominant state now decides—to continue with the same example—who is the victim of any attack (presumably itself), who is the aggressor, and how many resources its partner must mobilize.

The expected cost of opportunism is a function of its actual cost, which is constant across the range of alternative relations, and its probability, which declines with relational hierarchy. Thus, the expected costs of opportunism decrease as relations between the parties become more hierarchic. All other things considered, states should prefer to bind their partners through greater hierarchy. The fewer the residual rights of control retained by the partner, the lower the potential for opportunism and, in turn, the expected costs. More than any other relational factor, it is the desire to reduce the potential for opportunism by their partners that drives states toward empire.

The underlying potential for opportunism by Russia's partners has always been relatively high.[34] As a great power, Russia has long been a regional threat and it has a demonstrated record of aggrandizement against its neighbors—many of whom were drawn into the empire during and after World War II. Indeed, before the war many in eastern Europe perceived Germany as the lesser of two evils, and sought to use the Reich as a counterweight to an even more distasteful Russian imperialism.[35] Russia's regional dominance only increased with the defeat of Germany. Rather than emerging as a good neighbor, the Soviet Union exited the war as a revisionist regional power against whom neighboring states would normally balance rather than bandwagon. Similarly, eastern Europe, and particularly the northern tier states of Czechoslovakia, eastern Germany, Hungary, and Poland, had been integrated into the prewar European market economy. Economically, as well as politically and socially, these states were part of Europe, and the economic turn toward Russia was, to put it simply, unnatural. The attraction of the West, moreover, was reinforced by America's postwar economic vitality. Czechoslovakia's and Poland's initial interest in participating in the Marshall Plan provided continuing evidence to the Soviet Union of the pull of the Western economic and political systems. On both security and economic grounds, Russia was justifiably concerned that its regional partners would abandon it at the first opportunity—as indeed they did between 1989 and 1991.

This high potential for opportunism by Russia's partners had two effects. First, it meant that cooperation could take place only within a relatively hierarchical relationship, in order to reduce the potential for opportunistic action by the peripheral areas against Russian interests. This was a critical determinant of

Russia's imperial strategy.[36] Second, in the informal empire, where the probability of opportunism remained higher than within the boundaries of Soviet Union, Russia chose not to develop an extensive division of labor—and, in turn, not to accumulate substantial relationally specific assets—in order to reduce the actual costs of opportunism should it occur. While Russia periodically pushed for a greater division of labor in its relations with the eastern Europeans, this was never a sufficiently high priority to break the political logjam either within the Soviet Union itself or in its relations with its partners.[37] In short, Russia forsook some of the gains from cooperation in order to limit the possible costs of opportunism by its subordinate partners. The high risk of opportunism, therefore, reduced the potential gains from empire and ultimately contributed to its demise. This reflects one of the most striking contradictions of empires: Hierarchy emerges in response to a partner's potential opportunism, but the high likelihood that a state's partners are unreliable restricts the division of labor and, thereby, the benefits from empire.

Governance Costs

States incur governance costs in creating and maintaining relations. These costs take two analytically distinct forms: compensation for distorted incentives and coercion.[38] Whereas opportunism declines with the degree of relational hierarchy, governance costs increase with relational hierarchy. As a result, governance costs deter states from pursuing more hierarchic relations.

The loss of residual control distorts incentives to use resources efficiently in the subordinate party. When parties to an agreement retain full rights of residual control—as in anarchy—they are motivated to cooperate in the most efficient manner possible so as to save resources for other valued purposes. Just as individuals are best motivated when they are claimants on the profits of a firm, so are states best motivated by the freedom to use their resources in any way they choose. As the subordinate party's residual control shrinks, its incentives change; the resources saved by efficient cooperation are themselves subject to increasing control by the dominant state and, thus, less valuable to the subordinate. As the subordinate party's residual control recedes, incentives in other areas of economic and political life are distorted as well. By definition, as residual rights decline, the dominant state is exercising control over a greater range of behavior and, by implication, directing resources to uses the subordinate party would not choose on its own. As the residual rights of control shift from one party to the other, distortions to the subordinate member's incentives multiply.[39] In the case of the Russian Empire, at least under the Soviet Union, many of these distortions were integral to and followed from the command economy imposed by Moscow on the formal and informal satellites.

In a purely voluntary relationship, distortions in its partner create for the dominant state both additional costs of monitoring and control and, somewhat paradoxically, the need for greater side payments to the subordinate member. The effect of these distorted incentives can be partially corrected by additional contractual provisions that mandate certain actions by the subordinate party. When this contractual solution is adopted, however, the dominant state must employ additional resources to monitor and safeguard the new provisions. As the distortions increase with a higher degree of relational hierarchy, the resources employed by—and, therefore, the costs to—the dominant state must increase as well. Yet, contracting cannot remove distortions entirely. Monitoring and safeguarding additional areas of behavior are subject to diminishing marginal returns. It is also efficient to shift the locus of residual control from one party to the other precisely when it is difficult to specify future contingencies; as a result, it is very costly to safeguard against all possible distortions.

Because of its inherent distortions, increasing hierarchy—ceteris paribus—reduces the welfare of the subordinate party. To gain the subordinate party's willing consent to a hierarchic relationship, the welfare losses created by these distortions must be compensated by some transfer or side payment from the dominant state—increasing the costs to the latter. As the subordinate partner's residual control declines, and the distortions increase, so must the compensation package offered by the dominant state. The system of subsidies granted by Russia to the peripheral areas of its formal and informal empire is a prime example of compensation to ensure compliance. As this example confirms, increasing hierarchy raises the costs to the dominant state of governing the subordinate partner.

Distortions in the subordinate member will also accumulate over time, ultimately undermining the basis for the hierarchic relationship. Indeed, in part because of these accumulating distortions, empire becomes an "obsolescing bargain" eventually doomed to failure.[40] Each distortion requires actors within the subordinate party to adjust their own behavior in individually rational but nonetheless socially inefficient ways, thereby producing further distortions in the economy. Over time, the accumulated distortions will become manifest in declining growth rates and economic stagnation (if not absolute decline).[41] At any moment in time, the dominant state will offer a compensation package just sufficient to keep the subordinate party from rebelling or otherwise breaking the relationship. As the distortions increase with time, the compensation package must also increase, raising the net cost of the relationship for the dominant member. In this way, empires and other hierarchic relationships eventually become obsolete; from the dominant state's point of view, a structure of costs and benefits that was attractive early in the relationship becomes ever less appealing as the relationship matures and the distortions and compensating side payments grow—as eventually occurred even in the Russian Empire. All else held constant, any hierarchic relationship will eventually become costly on net to the dominant state. The more hierarchic the relationship, the sooner the break-even point will be reached.[42]

Although it fits awkwardly within the neoclassical economic approach that informs relational contracting theories, coercion is a fact of life in international relations.[43] The governance costs incurred in correcting and compensating distortions in the subordinate party are rooted in problems of contracting under costly information. Coercion is a substitute for contracting. It can be used by the dominant state to correct distortions by eliciting appropriate behaviors from the subordinate party. Likewise, it can be used to secure compliance with a hierarchical relationship without granting compensation for the resulting distortions. Like contracting, coercion requires the use of scarce resources and, therefore, is costly to countries that use or threaten to use it. This is clearly true for direct military action, but it holds equally for other sanctions such as trade embargoes (which, if effective, reduce the sanctioning country's terms of trade).

As with the other governance costs, the costs of creating and maintaining a relationship through coercion increase with hierarchy. The more hierarchic the imposed relationship, the smaller the subordinate actor's rights of residual control and the greater its resistance both at the outset and throughout the course of the relationship. The greater the resistance, the greater the coercion necessary to support a given relationship.

Greater coercion will also be required over time as distortions increase in the subordinate party. The obsolescing bargain is not alleviated when the relationship rests on coercion rather than on a voluntary contract—indeed, the problem may be magnified, as coercion may prevent the subordinate party from negotiating an end to some of the more pernicious distortions created by the imperial state. Thus, the governance costs of acquiring control over others and maintaining a relationship either by contract or coercion increase as relations move from anarchy to hierarchy. They also increase over time, especially in more hierarchic relations, because of the accumulation of distortions in the subordinate party.

The importance and effects of governance costs are observed in Russia's creation of an informal empire in Eastern Europe after World War II. The costs were relatively low, thereby permitting a hierarchical relationship to emerge. Most importantly, the costs of establishing control over the region were absorbed in the defeat of Germany and, from the perspective of postwar relations, were "sunk." In other words, Russia's new postwar position of dominance in Eastern Europe meant that the past costs of coercion need not figure in the future equation. All Russia needed to consider were the future costs of governing territories it already effectively controlled.[44] The governance costs of maintaining the informal empire were also relatively low, mostly taking the form of low-paid occupation troops. Moreover, these direct governance costs were offset by substantial resource extractions from Eastern Europe. In the period 1946–56, reparations paid to the Soviet Union totaled $14–$20 billion. Large implicit trade subsidies added to this amount. By one estimate, the Soviet Union extracted on net $1 billion per year from Eastern Europe until 1956.[45] Even if it did not produce a profit in the early postwar years, the informal empire clearly did not constitute a significant drain on Soviet coffers.

These governance costs, however, grew incrementally but inexorably over time. Because of the revolts in East Germany in 1953 and Hungary in 1956, which together signaled widespread dissatisfaction with conditions in the region and with Russia's domination, the resource flow from Eastern Europe to the Soviet Union began to dwindle and, eventually, reverse itself. Direct extractions were terminated, and implicit trade subsidies began to flow into rather than out of the region.[46] After the oil shocks of the 1970s, which raised the price of oil everywhere outside the Soviet bloc, the informal empire in Eastern Europe became an ever greater liability to Russia. According to one estimate, Soviet aid to Eastern Europe in all forms amounted to approximately $134 billion between 1971 and 1980 alone.[47] As late as 1988, the Soviet subsidy to Eastern Europe was estimated—by the Russians themselves—to be $17 billion per year.[48] As suggested by the obsolescing bargain, the empire eventually turned on itself— prompting a reevaluation of Soviet-East European ties, a loosening of Russian control in the repeal of the Brezhnev Doctrine, and finally the decision not to prevent the disintegration of the informal empire.

The Monopoly State

Like many theories of international relations, the theory of relational contracting presented here assumes that states are unitary actors. In other words, the theory treats the state, defined now as a domestic political actor, as a perfect agent for a society that seeks to maximize aggregate welfare, however substantively determined. The theory then draws inferences about likely national behaviors from the attributes of the actors, the external environment, and changes in that environment. This is a powerful form of theorizing in international relations, but it has obvious limitations. In particular, the state as an international actor is not unitary, and the state as a domestic actor is not a perfect agent for its society. At the very least, the state exploits its relative autonomy or "agency slack" to pursue its own welfare or the welfare of particularistic groups that capture it. Following now common usage, the benefits so obtained by the state can be grouped under the broad heading of *rents* and the behavior employed by the state to acquire these benefits can be referred to as *rent-seeking*. The current section of this chapter discards the assumption that the state is a perfect agent in favor of the assumption that it seeks to maximize its rents. Working within the same microeconomic framework that informs the theory of relational contracting, I examine the implications of agency slack and its relationship to empire.

Theories of rent-seeking are widespread in political science.[49] By lobbying the government, groups can encourage adoption of restrictionist policies that reduce competition for goods and services, increase price, and transfer wealth or rents from consumers to themselves. Tariffs, because of the limitations they place on imports, are a classic restrictionist instrument; state licensing and certification for various professions produce the same result. Lenin's theory of imperialism can be recast in these terms, with capitalists earning rents from the monopolization of external markets. Jack Snyder's more recent study points to the same central tendency: seeking to improve their own welfare, groups enter into rent-seeking coalitions that produce tendencies toward expansion and—from the perspective of the larger society—overexpansion.[50]

Often neglected in this literature is the fact that the state itself possesses significant monopoly power and can earn rents for its officials or critical groups upon whom it depends for political support.[51] This shift in focus from social rent-seeking to state rent-seeking, even though the rents may ultimately end up in the hands of politically important social actors, has two analytical advantages. First, societal models are based implicitly on a pluralist view of politics that is most appropriate for the study of democratic polities; a focus on the state facilitates the analysis of a broader range of political regimes. Second, a focus on the state allows for the use of simple models from public finance theory and insights from the literature on the optimal size and shape of nations to deduce specific hypotheses on the links between rent-seeking and empire.

The State as Monopolist

All states specialize in producing public goods. Since consumers would normally free ride, the state's monopoly on the legitimate use of force gives it a comparative advantage in this area; indeed, its comparative advantage is so strong that the state is often the only producer of such goods and enjoys a natural monopoly. The state's monopoly of force, however, also allows it to expand beyond the provision of public goods and to displace private producers from other economic activities. At an extreme, the state can own and regulate the entire economy. By exercising its power as a monopoly producer of goods and services, the state earns rents for itself or for redistribution among politically influential groups upon whom it is dependent for support. By doing so, the state exploits the broad mass of citizens for the gain of its own officials.

Like any other monopolist, the state creates rents by restricting the supply of the good(s) under its control and raising prices above the competitive market level. The difference between the monopoly price and the cost of production is the rent earned by the state.

Like a private monopolist, the state can also use advertisements—called propaganda in politics—to stimulate demand; it may also use its authority to inflate demand indirectly, as when it threatens other states in order to increase society's demand for security. When demand is stimulated, the rents earned by the state increase. States can also obfuscate the true costs of production, thereby rendering public control over their activities more difficult and increasing the rents earned. Obfuscation of this sort is, in part, a function of the good being produced. Public goods, the production of which depends upon the authoritative ability of the state to tax consumers, typically lack privately produced counterparts against which to measure government performance. States also tend to specialize in goods (like education) with only long-run and difficult-to-measure links between inputs (teachers' salaries, instructional methods) and outputs (knowledge).[52]

Because of their monopoly powers and patterns of specialization, all states earn some rents, regardless of how easily the states are controlled by their mass publics. As the costs to society of controlling rent-seeking increase, however, a state will extract higher rents and will expand its control over ever greater areas of economic activity—further increasing its rents by monopolizing production in those areas.

The command economy of the Soviet Union was, perhaps, the most extreme case of a centralized state monopoly controlling most forms of economic activity and earning substantial rents. While no direct measures of state rent-seeking are available for any polity (indeed, if the earlier arguments are correct, states will intentionally obfuscate their budgets, making such estimates virtually impossible) the level of rent-seeking by the Soviet state appears to have been quite high. The number of state officials and party members who benefited from these rents was sufficiently large that no single individual amassed the personal fortune of, say, Ferdinand Marcos of the Philippines, the political elites of the Soviet Union did enjoy substantial benefits relative to the average consumer due to their privileged access to a wide range of goods and services in an economy of acute scarcity.[53]

Public Control of State Power

The state's ability to earn rents is dependent upon the public's ability to control the monopoly power of the state. Just as states can regulate private monopolies "in the public interest," and thereby limit the rents these firms earn, so can publics regulate the monopoly powers of states. Whether and how well publics perform this role is a function of the costs of monitoring the state and enforcing the public will.

In order to control the state, individuals must first monitor its performance and acquire information on the real costs of production. Information problems loom large. Costs can often be assessed only by comparing production in two or more countries. Effective monitoring is itself a public good, subject to the problem of free riding; because no citizen has any incentive to invest in acquiring information, collective investment in monitoring occurs only at suboptimal levels. A state can also raise the costs of monitoring by intentionally obfuscating its budget, limiting access to information about other countries, and so on. The higher the costs to the public of acquiring information on state performance, the greater latitude state officials have to engage in rent-seeking activities.

Once public assessment of state performance and level of rents has occurred, citizens have two instruments through which to control state behavior: *exit* and *voice*.[54] Through exit, individuals move and reduce the state's market for the goods it is producing. Discipline is imposed upon the state, in other words, by shrinking its consumer base, reducing its rents, and thereby punishing it for undesirable behavior. This is, however, a blunt instrument of public control. Voice—or, more generally, political participation—disciplines the state by separating or threatening to separate state officials from their offices. The citizens stay, but the composition of the state changes, the mere threat of which may induce state officials to limit their rapacious behavior. Voice can take many forms, from voting, to campaign contributions, to mass unrest, to active rebellion. At the aggregate level, the costs of political participation vary by regime type. For instance, in most democracies, where elections are the primary focus of political participation for the majority of citizens, it is relatively costless to exercise voice via the vote. At the other extreme, autocratic states typically suppress political dissent and participation. Voting, if it occurs at all, is ineffective in removing officials from power. In autocracies, to replace or effectively threaten a ruler requires either mass unrest or some form of armed rebellion—activities that carry considerably higher individual costs, including the possibility of death. In these polities, voice is very costly for the average citizen and, as a result, seldom exercised.

On average, the higher the costs of political participation, the greater the state's ability to earn rents will be. Thus democracy, as a more open political system, is a comparatively effective mechanism for controlling the state. More closed, autocratic systems are far less powerful tools to this end. There are always some costs to monitoring and controlling the state. Therefore, all states earn some rents. Nonetheless, the level of rents earned by the state will be lower in democratic and higher in more autocratic polities.

The Soviet Union was, to use the terms developed here, a rent-seeking autocracy. It limited information about its own activities and those of other states abroad—thereby raising the costs of monitoring its monopoly power. It restrained the freedom of its citizens to exit the political system and stifled political participation—further raising the costs of controlling its monopoly power. As a result, the Soviet state—like its tsarist predecessor—enjoyed broad monopoly powers which it appears to have used to produce substantial rents.

Rent-Seeking and Empire

The ability to earn rents creates an imperialist bias in a state's foreign policy. Intuitively, rents make each unit of territory more profitable to the state, giving it an incentive to acquire and rule more area; successful rent-seeking thus creates a larger optimal size for the political unit.[55] It follows from the arguments in the previous section that autocratic states possess a larger optimal size and, in turn, a tendency toward expansion.

For all states, an optimal size exists defined by the costs of collecting revenue and providing goods and services to their citizens, on the one hand, and the

Figure 2.2. **The Optimal Size of Political Units**

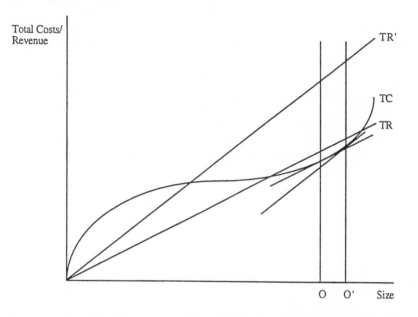

revenues earned by taxes collected as payment for these goods and services, on the other. This relationship is depicted in Figure 2.2. The costs of producing goods and services and collecting taxes is reflected in the total cost curve (TC); the curve here is drawn in its traditional shape, with an initial portion of increasing returns and a later segment of decreasing returns to scale. As the size of the political unit increases, total costs begin to rise more rapidly. Each additional unit of territory also produces additional revenue: the state becomes the new local monopoly supplier of goods and services, and it taxes its new consumers accordingly. Total revenue increases with size, and is represented by the total revenue curve (TR). As shown in Figure 2.2, there is a single optimal size of the political unit where the marginal revenue from an additional unit of territory equals the marginal costs of production and collection in that unit; geometrically, this occurs at point O, where the slopes of the TR and TC curves are equal (demonstrated by the line segment parallel to TR and tangent to TC).

In the real world, there is no reason to expect either total revenue to rise monotonically (i.e., TR forms a straight line) or total costs to increase in an orderly manner over distance (i.e., the TC curve is smooth). Rather, the state is more likely to act as a discriminating monopolist, effectively taxing different regions at different rates depending upon the costs to the publics in those areas of controlling the state. This type of discriminatory policy would produce a kinked TR curve, with multiple segments of varying slope. Likewise, the goods and services provided and the costs of production and revenue collection are likely to vary in different areas, meaning that the TC curve will also be kinked. If either the TC or TR curve is kinked, there may be multiple equilibria and more than one optimal size for the political unit. This is especially like to occur when the constituent parts of an empire differ culturally, geographically, and administratively in their relations with the imperial center. Which equilibrium obtains at a particular moment can, for our purposes, be attributed to historical circumstances, although this could obviously be specified further if necessary. In any case, the possible presence of multiple equilibria suggests that slight variations in revenues and costs may produce radical changes in the optimal size of the political unit. Thus, we might observe extreme changes in the size of the political unit arising from somewhat smaller changes in the underlying conditions.

Rents earned by the state, whether retained by state officials or redistributed to key support groups, increase the optimal size of the political unit. Each unit of territory now produces greater revenue for the state. The greater the revenue, the greater the costs that can be borne to capture that revenue in equilibrium. In short, each additional unit of territory is now worth more to the state, and the state is willing to bear a higher marginal cost to control it. Thus, a state with an increased rent-seeking capacity has an incentive to expand until marginal revenue and marginal cost are once again equalized at a new, larger size; or, equivalently, the optimal size for an autocratic state will be greater than that for a more democratic state. Geometrically, as illustrated in Figure 2.2, rents cause the total revenue line to rotate counterclockwise from the origin (TR' > TR) and the equilibrium size to expand (O' > O).[56] This relationship also holds true in reverse. As the rent-seeking capacity of a state declines, total revenue falls (e.g., from TR' to TR) and the optimal size of the unit contracts (from O' to O). If the revenue and cost curves are kinked, small changes in rents may again produce large changes in optimal size.

In sum, the greater the rent-seeking ability of the state, the larger its optimal size. This relationship will manifest as an imperialist bias in a state's foreign policy. The lesser the rent-seeking ability of the state, the smaller its optimal size and imperialist bias. When the constituent units of the empire differ in ways that affect the costs of producing state goods and services or the revenue generated by them, there may be multiple equilibria and more than one optimal size. If so, dramatic and discontinuous change in the optimal size of the state is possible.

The relationship between rents and optimal size appears to have held true in the former Soviet Union. For centuries, Russia has been autocratic. It has also been expansionist, spreading eastward and westward until it filled the Eurasian continent. For most of the last four hundred years, Russia has been the world's largest empire.[57] This is not, of course, to attribute the enormous size of the Russian Empire solely to state rent-seeking. There are many other autocratic states that do not grow to dominate continents, just as there are countries of nearly continental size with very limited monopoly powers. The factors and trade-offs identified in the theory of relational contracting—scale economies, expected costs of opportunism, and governance costs—operate simultaneously and can either reinforce or counteract the effects of state rent-seeking. Yet, an analysis based solely on the theory of relational contracting would not distinguish between, say, the Baltic states, formally incorporated into the Russian Empire, and Poland, integrated only into the informal empire. Relational contracting theory cannot explain fully why the former were wholly subsumed within the Soviet Union, while the latter retained its nominal sovereignty and greater residual rights of control. Conversely, the theory of the monopoly state presented in this section suggests that the Baltic states and others were incorporated into the formal empire at least in part due to the imperialist bias of autocratic Russia. The reconstitution of the dismantled tsarist empire by the Communists once they had consolidated political power also supports this inference.

The Rent–Growth Trade-Off and the Dynamics of Empire

Like all rent-seeking, state rent-seeking distorts the economy and reduces rates of economic growth.[58] Over time, as the distortions accumulate, the state can improve its returns by reducing rents, freeing the economy from monopoly restrictions, and stimulating growth. By the logic of the model presented in the previous section, as the state turns from seeking rents to encouraging growth, the optimal size of the political unit will contract. At this new equilibrium, with higher growth rates, reduced rents, and a smaller optimal size, the state is at least marginally better off than if it had retained its old economic strategy and remained at its former size. While there may be distributional consequences within the state—with factions more dependent upon rents opposing the contraction and those likely to gain from growth pushing for reform—the increase in their aggregate welfare suggests that state leaders will nonetheless support the reduction in the size of territorial unit that follows from the shift from rents to growth.

State rent-seeking benefits the state but harms society. The transfer of rents from citizens to state officials or their political supporters creates social deadweight losses due to both the less-efficient use of resources and directly unproductive activities. The latter category includes the state's efforts to obfuscate its rents and citizens' efforts to monitor and restrain state rent-seeking; the social costs of directly unproductive activities may be substantial.[59]

As the state exercises its monopoly powers, citizens respond by adjusting their own economic activity: they choose not to invest in areas that compete with the state, they fail to invest in potential growth areas that might be expropriated by the state, or they reduce their work effort because returns are depressed by state extractions. To offset these distortions, the state typically creates selective incentives that, in turn, produce secondary distortions in the economy. For example, the Soviet Union kept the price of bread artificially low to help maintain minimal levels of public support. This low price, however, prompted consumers to substitute bread for other food and nonfood goods, reducing the rate of return in other sectors—which, in turn, required a second round of state intervention to sustain investment levels. The end result of selective interventions is a vicious cycle of increasing inefficiency that ultimately impedes economic growth and, at an extreme, may even produce absolute economic decline. Again, the command economy of the Soviet Union demonstrates clearly the inefficiencies produced by politically motivated economic distortions.

As the economy grows, the demand for all goods and services grows as well. Holding the level of monopoly extraction constant, this growth benefits the state by increasing the market and, hence, the total rents earned. While growth benefits society as a whole, it also improves the total returns for the state and its constituent groups. As the economy declines or contracts, the demand for goods and services falls, harming the monopoly state. As distortions accumulate in the economy, the state thus faces a trade-off: increase the level of rent-seeking, which slows the rate of growth; or stimulate growth, which requires reducing its rents. At any moment in time, the state chooses the combination of rents and growth that maximizes its total return. As the distortions increase and the rate of growth declines over time, the state will shift away from rent-seeking and toward growth. To use a common metaphor, the state—if successful—enjoys a larger piece of pie on net; even though its share is proportionately smaller with reduced rents, the pie is larger with higher growth than it would be otherwise. As a result, the state, or the groups that receive rents created by the state, are better off and can be expected to support the change in economic strategy.

As deduced previously, as the state reduces its rent-seeking, the optimal size of the political unit will contract. In Figure 2.2, the total revenue curve falls (TR < TR') and the equilibrium moves toward the origin (O < O'). The change in optimal size is a natural consequence of the change in economic strategy, and will therefore be accepted by the beneficiaries of state rents. Given the possibility of multiple equilibria, as noted in the previous section, and some uncertainty about the exact location of these equilibria, leaders may be surprised by the extent of the change in the optimal size of the state; but, having arrived at this new equilibrium, they will have no incentive to change it. This suggests that even substantial alterations in the territorial unit can occur with political support from the beneficiaries of the "old" system.

Finally, factions within the state or groups that receive a share of state rents may be affected by the shift in strategy in different ways. Like the military and related industries, which prospered under the former Soviet Union, groups whose interests are tied to state rents and who are unable to compete effectively in a freer economy will oppose the new emphasis on growth. They also would benefit from a reconstitution of the empire, and will form a core constituency in favor of rebuilding an imperial system. Groups that are less dependent upon state rents and more competitive will be the primary supporters of reform; they will also form the core of the anti-imperialist coalition. Focusing on the distributional implications of state rent-seeking clarifies who should and should not support the empire—but distributional issues do not negate the larger point. As rent-seeking creates a vicious cycle of distortions and as growth rates fall, the state as a whole benefits from and can be expected to shift to a growth-oriented economic strategy. This shift necessarily implies a reduction in the optimal size of the territorial unit. This reduction, finally, will be accepted by central political leaders and their associated constituencies.

Thus, just as distortions in the subordinate state create an obsolescing bargain when viewed through the lens of relational contracting theory, state rent-seeking produces an inevitable dynamic toward the dissolution of empire—this time catalyzed by distortions within the dominant state itself. In both theories then, empires must eventually decline—a process that will unfold with the support of state leaders. Furthermore, the obsolescing bargain and the rent–growth trade-off can interact, hastening the day of imperial reckoning. Since the costs of empire tend to rise as distortions in the subordinate polity accumulate, rents earned by the imperial state will decline—reinforcing tendencies toward a contraction in the optimal size of the empire.[60]

As a stylization at least, the collapse of the Soviet Union closely fits this analysis. Growth rates in the Soviet Union declined throughout the 1970s, essentially stagnating by the early 1980s. To combat stagnation and revitalize the Soviet system, Mikhail Gorbachev sought to reduce the heavy hand of the state-managed command economy and stimulate new economic growth. He also undertook a series of political reforms designed to increase public control over the state and thereby institutionalize the new constraints on state power, which would in turn help reinforce and preserve the economic reforms.[61] As the Gorbachev reforms took hold, and as the leadership simultaneously sought to reduce the drain posed by the informal empire in Eastern Europe, the Soviet Union began to fracture. More specifically, key political entrepreneurs in the republics began to recognize both that the centralized system was no longer viable or appropriate and that the Soviet leadership would not resist efforts by peripheral areas to seek greater independence. Seizing this opening, these same political entrepreneurs pushed for greater autonomy and, as the theory predicts, the Soviet leadership capitulated more or less willingly. Both Soviet and republic leaders were surprised by the extent of the dissolution, but not by the general tendency.[62] Indicating the importance of political jurisdictions, and the variations in costs and revenue they both represent and create, the Soviet Union fractured along the lines of its federal republics—but no further, at least as of this writing.[63] Today, the same segments of the Russian political economy that oppose the reforms led by Boris Yeltsin (and others) support the rebuilding of the empire, while liberalizing segments generally oppose renewed imperialism.

Although there are, no doubt, many details that do not fit this stylization, the expectations of the theory and the general empirical record are remarkably congruent. Under an autocratic system of rule, the Soviet Union became one of the largest empires in history. As the economy stagnated under the weight of the state monopoly, growth-oriented reforms were eventually enacted. In turn, the territorial unit contracted—in this case quite sharply. Interestingly, the importance of state rent-seeking is clearer in the decline of the Russian Empire than in its rise, which is more overdetermined. The analysis here is offered only as a theoretical interpretation, not as a test of the theory nor as empirical fact. Nonetheless, the interpretation is suggestive, I believe, and offers an explanation for the relatively peaceful nature of the collapse of the Soviet Union.

Implications for the Future and Policy

Russia's informal empire in Eastern Europe was made possible by an unusual circumstance; as noted, the costs of establishing hierarchy in the region were sunk in the course of defeating Germany in World War II. While some limited hierarchy might have been expected in the region in any event, the coercive control of Eastern Europe obtained as a by-product of the war lowered effective governance costs and allowed a greater degree of hierarchy than would otherwise have been possible. Contiguous empires in the core of the international system are rare; the other empires examined in this volume are the other principal exceptions. Over the last five hundred years, most empires have been formed in the periphery of the global system, where state structures were either very weak or, in some cases, nonexistent. Today, as Iraq discovered, the costs of coercing established states into imperial relationships are simply too high. The creation of new empires are likely to be rare events.[64] Virtually the only exception to this generalization is the area of the former Soviet Union, where the successor states are now dealing with the afterglow of a centralized, hierarchical, and imperial political system. For this reason, I confine the discussion in this section to relations between Russia and the other successor states.

The economies of scale that produced the Soviet Union and, indeed, the informal empire in Eastern Europe largely remain in place today, but in a somewhat attenuated form. In the security realm, the technological gains from forward bases still exist. Nonetheless, the more general threats from Germany and the West that sustained the military economy of the Soviet Union have diminished with the end of the Cold War. In the economic arena, the distributional effects of the imperial collapse are critical. If the economic reformers and the competitive sectors of the economy that support them prevail, then Russia and the other successor states will turn toward international markets, and the need for an internal, imperial division of labor will decline. On the other hand, if the conservatives and the uncompetitive sectors dominate, then a shift toward a more autarkic economic strategy will necessitate a return to an internal division of labor. Not all of the successor states are likely to fall one way or the other in terms of preferred economic strategy, and there will be considerable variation in attitudes toward reintegrating the imperial economy. By opening their own markets and financially and politically supporting economic liberalization within the successor states, the United States and other powers can help tip the political balance within these states in favor of the economic reformers and away from the imperialists.

The internal hierarchy of the Soviet Union allowed for substantial investments in relationally specific assets. While these investments were a natural by-product of the internal division of labor, they were made possible by Soviet leaders' confidence that they could control the potential for opportunism by the subordinate members of the empire. As a result, there emerged over time in the Soviet Union highly specialized military bases outside Russia (e.g., missile testing and launching ranges); pipelines that traversed republics; integrated raw materials, processing plants, or manufacturing enterprises that spanned regions; and so on. Because the expected costs of opportunism within the empire were relatively low, facility locations were chosen not based on minimizing asset specificity between the republics but according to other economic and political criteria.

Today, even though the imperial hierarchy has collapsed, the specific assets remain. The potential for opportunism by one or both sides in any transaction is now considerably higher. Recognizing the higher expected costs of opportunism, one or both parties will be reluctant to utilize or rely upon such assets. In the prevailing anarchy, the successor states must either run the risk of exploitation by their partners or undertake costly investments that duplicate the partner's assets as a hedge against opportunism. The higher expected costs of opportunism create a mutual interest in re-creating some form of hierarchy. The high level of relationally specific assets between the successor states, which remain as a residue of the old empire, will create important and voluntary pressures to rebuild some degree of economic and political hierarchy in the region.[65] Since any empire not built entirely on coercion necessarily involves some exchange of benefits between center and periphery, a situation that Karen Dawisha calls autocolonization—or voluntary subordination within a political hierarchy—is necessarily present.[66] In the aftermath of the old Russian Empire, these pressures are likely to be especially strong.

The fact that hierarchy can be welfare enhancing for both Russia and the other successor states creates an important policy dilemma for the West. While analysts generally concur that preventing the reintegration of the Russian Empire is an essential policy goal, they also agree that stimulating growth and investment in the economies of the successor states is equally if not more important. To the extent that the efficient use of specific assets underlies both policy goals, as it does at present, an inherent contradiction exists. If relationally specific assets matter, then the West cannot have it both ways. It may need to encourage greater hierarchy to stimulate growth. Or, to inhibit greater hierarchy, it must provide greater direct assistance targeted at building specific assets tied to states outside the former Soviet Union.

The governance costs to Russia of rebuilding the hierarchy, however, are likely to vary across the successor states. In some, most notably the Baltics, Russian suzerainty has been broken—in part with the aid and encouragement of the West. To re-create hierarchy in this area would require high levels of coercion and possibly result in conflict with Europe and the United States. The Baltic states are likely to remain outside Russia's control, even if they are not free from Russian influence on an episodic basis. Other states pushing for inclusion in the Western security sphere, such as Moldova, are hoping to achieve a similar level of independence. Lowering the hurdle for inclusion in Western political and security institutions will facilitate this end. At the other end of the spectrum, Russian troops remain in nearly all of the CIS states—placing them in much the same position as, say, Poland in 1945. Some successor states, plagued by internal weakness, have appealed to Russia for political and military support—and, like Georgia, have been brought back under Russia's hierarchical umbrella. Short of discouraging the use of coercion and encouraging the removal of Russian troops, which often remain by mutual consent, the leverage of the Western states over these governance costs is quite limited. Where hierarchy is necessary, the West should encourage mutual, voluntarily negotiated restrictions on potential opportunism. This is likely to produce movement toward confederation—a more benign form of hierarchy—rather than empire.

Over the next decade, we will observe a wide range of new political relations among the successor states, perhaps varying by issue area, that are all designed to reap the benefits of continuing scale economies while controlling problems of opportunism created by the imperial residue of specific assets. The greater the scale economies, the more likely it is that some form of cooperation will emerge between Russia and the other successor states; the smaller the scale economies, the more likely it is that the successor states will search for ties to Western states and the international economy more generally. The larger the specific assets, the greater the expected costs of opportunism and the more likely it is that relations between Russia and the successor states will once again become hierarchical. The smaller the governance costs of re-establishing and maintaining hierarchy, the more likely a new Russian empire will emerge. On balance, although the calculations here remain highly informal, some degree of hierarchy appears likely to reemerge from the wreckage of the Soviet Union. We are unlikely to see, a decade from now, anarchic relations between Russia and the other successor states. Relations in the region will not look like those between autonomous, sovereign, "Westphalian" states that characterize much of international politics. Rather, we are likely to find a range of relations, varying from protectorates to informal empires to empires and confederations. To understand relations between the successor states, the nineteenth-century colonial empires and Soviet–East European relations before 1989 are likely to provide analogies that are more instructive than European diplomacy and more helpful than mainstream international relations theory.

Western states do have some ability to influence the direction of change in the former Soviet Union. Opening Western economies to the goods and services of the East and integrating former communist states into Western political and security institutions creates new and attractive options for the successor states and reduces the imperial pull of Russia. At the same time, the West should support noncoercive, voluntary confederations created to cope with problems of opportunism; given the tension between stimulating growth and impeding the reconstruction of the empire, inhibiting the emergence of new hierarchies between Russia and the other successor states cannot be an absolute objective for the West. The challenge will be to reassure Russia that its security and economic needs can be met outside of its former empire.

Equally important to the unfolding of the empire, however, is the future of the monopoly state in Russia. As with all states, this is not a matter of rent-seeking and imperialism or no rent-seeking and no imperialism. All states earn some rents; the question is simply of more or less bias. The critical determinant is the outcome of Russia's current internal political struggle. Who will emerge victorious: the groups privileged under the old autocratic system and dependent upon rent-seeking within the empire, or the democratic forces aligned with economic liberalizers and anti-imperialist groups? The future of democracy in Russia is, thus, intimately linked with both economic reform and the empire.

In this case, all good things go together—at least from the point of view of the United States and other concerned states. Support for democratic forces or economic reformers in Russia strengthens the anti-imperialists. Likewise, strong signals that the West will resist coercive attempts to reconstitute the empire weaken the autocratic and conservative economic forces. Integrating Russia and the other successor states into the open international economy and into Western political and security institutions—moves recommended largely for reasons of relational contracting—can help reinforce the domestic position of groups committed to democracy, economic reform, and life within current borders.

Conclusion

This chapter, as the title asserts, is an interpretation of the rise, fall, and future of the Russian Empire informed by theories of relational contracting and the monopoly state. It is written from the perspective of an international relationist, not a scholar of Russian history, economics, or politics. While the case provides interesting variation on many of the independent variables in the general theory, and might otherwise constitute an appropriate series of observations for assessing its validity, the data necessary for rigorous tests have not been systematically assembled. In the limited purposes of this essay, the overall theory has provided two lenses through which to view a complicated history and has highlighted some patterns in the record that were previously ignored. Perhaps the most important contribution of the theory, in my view, lies in suggesting how—contrary to the expectations of many—the informal empire in Eastern Europe and the formal empire embodied in the Soviet Union could disintegrate peacefully. The theory also provides a sketchy road map for the future. Most pointedly, it suggests that at least some of the successor states are likely to be reintegrated into an informal, if not formal, Russian empire either voluntarily, in order to realize scale economies while minimizing the expected costs of opportunism, or by force, especially if the antireform forces prove politically triumphant in Russia. One thing is clear. As they mature, relations between the successor states are unlikely to resemble those between the autonomous, sovereign states often thought to characterize international politics. To understand the future, we must return to the study of imperialism.

Notes

I would like to thank Scott Bruckner and Adam Stulberg for research assistance, conducted long ago, that nonetheless contributed to this paper. I would also like to thank Jeff Frieden, James Goldgeier, Wendy Lake, Jack Snyder, Celeste Wallander, David Wilkinson, and the series editors for helpful comments. Selected portions of this chapter are reprinted from David A. Lake, "Anarchy, Hierarchy, and the Variety of International Relations," *International Organization* 50, no. 1 (1996): 1–33. Copyright 1996 by the IO Foundation and the Massachusetts Institute of Technology.

1. David A. Lake, "Anarchy, Hierarchy, and the Variety of International Relations," *International Organization* 50, no. 1 (1996): 1–33; and *Entangling Relations: American Foreign Policy in Its Century* (forthcoming).

2. David A. Lake, "Powerful Pacifists: Democratic States and War," *American Political Science Review* 86, no. 1 (1992): 24–37.

3. This taxonomy and the labels are from Michael W. Doyle, *Empires* (Ithaca: Cornell University Press, 1986).

4. Vladimir Lenin, *Imperialism: The Highest Stage of Capitalism* (New York: International Publishers, 1939).

5. John Gallagher and Ronald Robinson, "The Imperialism of Free Trade," *The Economic History Review*, 2nd ser., 6, no. 1 (1953): 1–15.

6. See, for example, Kenneth N. Waltz, *Theory of International Politics* (Reading, MA: Addison-Wesley, 1979). The best extended discussion of imperialism from a realist perspective remains Benjamin J. Cohen, *The Question of Imperialism: The Political Economy of Dominance and Dependence* (New York: Basic Books, 1973).

7. Tony Smith, *The Pattern of Imperialism: The United States, Great Britain, and the Late-Industrializing World Since 1815* (New York: Cambridge University Press, 1981); Doyle, *Empires;* and P.J. Cain and A.G. Hopkins, *British Imperialism*, 2 vols. (New York: Longman, 1993).

8. Pablo Gonzáles Casnova, "Imperialism," in Joel Krieger, ed., *The Oxford Companion to Politics of the World* (New York: Oxford University Press, 1993), p. 410.

9. Hans Morgenthau, *Politics Among Nations: The Struggle for Power and Peace*, 5th rev. ed. (New York: Alfred A. Knopf, 1978), p. 57.

10. Harry Magdoff, *The Age of Imperialism: The Economics of U.S. Foreign Policy* (New York: Monthly Review, 1969); Johan Galtung, "A Structural Theory of Imperialism," *Journal of Peace Research* 8 (1971): 81–109.

11. See Cohen, *The Question of Imperialism,* p. 16.

12. On the concept of relational hierarchy, see Oliver E. Williamson, *The Economic Institutions of Capitalism: Firms, Markets, and Relational Contracting* (New York: Free

Press, 1985); and Thráinn Eggertsson, *Economic Behavior and Institutions* (New York: Cambridge University Press, 1990).

13. See Bruce Parrott, chapter 1 of this volume.

14. Moreover, in the theory of relational contracting developed in this chapter, there is no analytic reason to distinguish between the empires that predated the Soviet Union, existed under seven decades of communism, and are likely to follow the demise of the Soviet Union.

15. This is a slightly stronger definition of cooperation than the existing standard in the literature, which emphasizes only mutual adjustment of policies. See Robert O. Keohane, *After Hegemony: Cooperation and Discord in the World Political Economy* (Princeton: Princeton University Press, 1984), p. 12.

16. Waltz, *Theory of International Politics*. On the concept of sovereignty as constitutional independence, see Alan James, *Sovereign Statehood: The Basis of International Society* (Boston: Unwin and Hyman, 1986).

17. In chapter 12, Kahler also defines empire as a monopoly of external ties. This characteristic of empire naturally and logically follows from hierarchy and can be thought of as a derived feature of empire.

18. Parrott, in chapter 1 of this volume, and Dawisha, in chapter 14 of this volume, follow Alexander J. Moytl and restrict empire to relations between one core state and two or more peripheral societies. Moytl, "Thinking about Empire: A Conceptual Inquiry with Some Implications for Theory," in Karen Barkey and Mark von Hagen, eds., *Imperial Collapse: Causes and Consequences* (Boulder, CO: Westview Press, forthcoming). There is little analytic reason for this restriction. The Strategic Trust Territory of the Pacific, formed as an American empire after World War II, is hierarchical even though there is only one subordinate polity. Of the other definitions in this volume, Hendrik Spruyt conflates the process of creation, through coercion, with the outcome of empire. Dawisha adds a requirement of intentionality, while I prefer to allow for the possibility of unwitting empire.

19. A third intermediate relationship may also exist between alliances and protectorates. In what is commonly called a sphere of influence, the dominant state (e.g., Russia) precludes the subordinate state (e.g., Finland) from entering into relationships with third parties—a weak infringement on the latter's residual rights of control, but an infringement nonetheless. The possible relationships discussed in the text and illustrated in Figure 2.1 are not exhaustive. For a discussion of the variety of intermediate relations that is related to but does not directly use the definition of hierarchy developed here, see W.W. Willoughby and C.G. Fenwick, *Types of Restricted Sovereignty and of Colonial Autonomy* (Washington, DC: Government Printing Office, 1919; reprint, *The Inquiry Handbooks,* vol. 16, Wilmington, DE: Scholarly Resources, 1974). Despite its breadth, this work did not anticipate many modern relationships, including free trade areas, economic unions, or political unions.

20. For a related discussion, see Philip G. Roeder, "From Hierarchy to Hegemony: Patterns of Security Among the Soviet Successor States," in David A. Lake and Patrick Morgan, eds., *Regional Orders: Building Security in a New World* (University Park: Pennsylvania State Press, 1997).

21. Doyle, *Empires,* pp. 38, 42.

22. The problem with recognizing any informal relationship is that the exercise of residual rights of control is evident only in out-of-equilibrium behavior. In the case of an informal empire, for instance, when the limited rights of the client are understood by both parties, no resistance occurs, no overt coercion is necessary, and the local government complies with the wishes of the dominant state *as if* in an alliance. Only if the client tests its constraints or the patron's patience will the informal imperial controls become mani-

fest. As a result, informal relationships can be discerned only by observing interactions over extended periods in order to increase the chances of encountering anomalous behaviors. The imperial nature of Soviet–East European relations was made clear even though the relationship was informal: the subordinate peoples consistently tested the limits of informal Soviet rule, sparking suppressions of local dissent in East Germany in 1953, Hungary in 1956, Czechoslovakia in 1968, and (indirectly) Poland in 1981.

23. See Karen Dawisha and Bruce Parrott, *Russia and the New States of Eurasia: The Politics of Upheaval* (New York: Cambridge University Press, 1994); Len Aron and Kenneth M. Jones, eds., *The Emergence of Russian Foreign Policy* (Washington, DC: United States Institute of Peace, 1994); and Michael Mandelbaum, ed., *Central Asia and the World* (New York: Council on Foreign Relations, 1994).

24. Williamson, *Economic Institutions;* and Eggertsson, *Economic Behavior.* For applications to international relations, see Keohane, *After Hegemony;* and Beth V. Yarbrough and Robert M. Yarbrough, *Cooperation and Governance in International Trade: The Strategic Organizational Approach* (Princeton: Princeton University Press, 1992). A frequent criticism of this approach is that states, unlike firms, are not fully rational, cannot accurately calculate transactions costs, do not value resources for alternative uses, and do not optimize across alternatives. It is unlikely that firms possess these characteristics or perform these activities well either. Much of modern microeconomic theory is devoted to studying the causes and consequences of such departures from unbounded rationality and complete and perfect information. For a strong defense of the comparative efficiency of political as opposed to economic markets, see Donald Wittman, *The Myth of Democratic Failure: Why Political Institutions are Efficient* (Chicago: University of Chicago Press, 1995). Although Wittman focuses on democratic political regimes, it is precisely the departures from this democratic ideal that motivates the theory of the monopoly state below.

25. For example, see Keohane, *After Hegemony*, pp. 67–78.

26. For cooperation to occur, only one party needs to enjoy larger scale economies; one-sided gains can be redistributed to the partner to induce the necessary adjustments in its policies. By themselves, scale economies tell us little about the distribution of the joint gain between the parties. This is determined by a separate but related bargaining game, the outcome of which will be determined by differences in the opportunity costs of the actors (see the next section).

27. Richard Bean, "War and the Birth of the Nation-State," *Journal of Economic History* 33 (1973): 203–21; Frederic C. Lane, *Profits from Power: Readings in Protection Rent and Violence-Controlling Enterprises* (Albany: State University of New York Press, 1979).

28. Helen V. Milner, "Firms, States, and the Creation of Regional Trade Blocs," in Edward Mansfield and Helen V. Milner, eds., *The Political Economy of Regionalism: The Second Wave* (New York: Columbia University Press, forthcoming).

29. George Quester, *Offense and Defense in the International System* (New York: John Wiley and Sons, 1977).

30. Security externalities among allies point to an important exception. See Joanne Gowa, *Allies, Adversaries, and International Trade* (Princeton: Princeton University Press, 1994).

31. See David M. Glantz, *The Military Strategy of the Soviet Union: A History* (London: Frank Cass, 1992), esp. pp. 176–80; and R. Craig Nation, *Black Earth, Red Star: A History of Soviet Security Policy, 1917–1991* (Ithaca: Cornell University Press, 1992). Edward N. Luttwak, *The Grand Strategy of the Soviet Union* (New York: St. Martin's, 1983), p. 19, suggests that a forward-based strategy was not, in fact, central to postwar planning and politics. On the comparison with the United States, see Lake, *Entangling Relations.*

32. On abandonment and entrapment, see Glenn H. Snyder, "The Security Dilemma in Alliance Politics," *World Politics* 36 (1984): 461–95.

33. Benjamin Klein, Robert G. Crawford, and Armen A. Alchian, "Vertical Integration, Appropriable Rents, and the Competitive Contracting Process," *Journal of Law and Economics* 21 (1978): 297–326. Asset specificity can also be understood as the transactions costs of changing relations.

34. For a comparison of the expected costs of opportunism to the United States and Soviet Union after 1945, see Lake, "Anarchy, Hierarchy, and the Variety of International Relations."

35. David J. Dallin, *Soviet Russia's Foreign Policy, 1939–1942* (New Haven: Yale University Press, 1942), p. 242.

36. Czechoslovakia, at first, and Finland, throughout the postwar period, were allowed a substantially longer leash by Moscow than the other states of the region. Nation, *Black Earth*, p. 177, notes that this "rested upon an intact national consensus and positive orientation toward the USSR that did not exist elsewhere."

37. Randall Stone, *Satellites and Commissars: Strategy and Conflict in the Politics of Soviet-Bloc Trade* (Princeton: Princeton University Press, 1995).

38. For reasons of space, this chapter does not discuss a third set of governance costs: safeguards on the dominant state. Briefly, relational hierarchy shifts the locus of opportunism from the subordinate partner to the dominant state. As the partner's rights of residual control decline, the rights of the dominant state over it expand—increasing the potential that the latter will act opportunistically toward the former. In the absence of coercion, the subordinate partner will not submit to this vulnerable position unless the behavior of the dominant state is adequately and credibly safeguarded in the agreement. As a result, dominant states must undertake costly actions to bind themselves to the terms of the contract and, especially, to commit to exercise their expanded residual control in a non-opportunistic manner. These costs appear less relevant to the Russian case. For a more detailed discussion of the costs of safeguards on the dominant state, see Lake, "Anarchy, Hierarchy and the Variety of International Relations."

39. This argument has a direct analog in the case of private firms; see Sanford J. Grossman and Oliver D. Hart, "The Costs and Benefits of Ownership: A Theory of Vertical and Lateral Integration," *Journal of Political Economy* 94 (1986): 691–719.

40. The term *obsolescing bargain* was originally used to describe shifts in bargaining leverage between states and firms. See Raymond Vernon, *Sovereignty at Bay: The Multinational Spread of U.S. Enterprises* (New York: Basic Books, 1971). Its usage is equally appropriate here.

41. Mancur Olson, *The Rise and Decline of Nations: Economic Growth, Stagflation, and Social Rigidities* (New Haven: Yale University Press, 1982), argues that accumulating interest groups would have the same effect. Olson's argument runs parallel to but is nonetheless distinct from the one advanced here.

42. Solomon Wank, in chapter 4 of this volume, suggests that under these circumstances, imperial states inevitably try to appease the subordinate polity and correct the distortions that follow from hierarchy by devolving a greater degree of autonomy onto the peripheral unit. This may be a common response to the obsolescing bargain. However, it is important to recognize that it is not the devolution of authority per se that causes imperial disintegration but the obsolescing bargain that drives both the initial response (devolution) and the eventual outcome (collapse).

43. The most sophisticated study of conflict within a neoclassical approach is Jack Hirshleifer, *Economic Behaviour in Adversity* (Chicago: University of Chicago Press, 1987).

44. This contrasts with the situation facing the United States in Western Europe. See Lake, "Anarchy, Hierarchy, and the Variety of International Relations."

45. Zbigniew K. Brzezinski, *The Soviet Bloc: Unity and Conflict*, rev. and enl. (Cambridge: Harvard University Press, 1967), pp. 285–86.

46. The record of the debate over implicit prices subsidies is vast. See Michael Marrese and Jan Vanous, *Soviet Subsidization of Trade with Eastern Europe: A Soviet Perspective*, Research Series, no. 52 (Berkeley: University of California Institute of International Relations, 1983); Paul Marer, "The Political Economy of Soviet Relations with Eastern Europe," in Sarah Meiklejohn Terry, ed., *Soviet Policy in Eastern Europe* (New Haven: Yale University Press, 1984); Jozef M. van Brabant, "The USSR and Socialist Economic Integration: A Comment," *Soviet Studies* 36 (1984): 127–38; Keith Crane, *The Soviet Economic Dilemma of Eastern Europe* (Santa Monica: RAND, 1986); and Kazimiera Z. Poznanski, "Opportunity Cost in Soviet Trade with Eastern Europe: Discussion of Methodology and New Evidence," *Soviet Studies* 40 (1988): 290–307. On the politics of implicit trade subsidies, see Stone, *Satellites and Commissars*.

47. Valerie Bunce, "The Empire Strikes Back: The Transformation of the Eastern Bloc from a Soviet Asset to a Soviet Liability," *International Organization* 39 (1985): 1–46.

48. Stone, *Satellites and Commissars*, p. 45.

49. See Mancur Olson, *The Logic of Collective Action* (Cambridge: Harvard University Press, 1965); and Olson, *Rise and Decline of Nations*. For a sense of this concept's impact on the discipline, see Jeffrey S. Banks and Eric A. Hanushek, eds., *Modern Political Economy: Old Topics, New Directions* (New York: Cambridge University Press, 1995).

50. Jack Snyder, *Myths of Empire: Domestic Politics and International Ambition* (Ithaca: Cornell University Press, 1991).

51. But see Lane, *Profits from Power*; Douglass C. North, *Structure and Change in Economic History* (New York: W.W. Norton, 1981); and Lake, "Powerful Pacifists."

52. From a social welfare point of view, these goods may be most efficiently produced by the state. For example, since parents are uninformed about the best educational methods and since their children will suffer the consequences of poor choices, it may be appropriate to vest this production activity in centralized hands—even recognizing that the state will act as a monopolist in this area as well.

53. Nonetheless, it would appear that the Soviet state was not as rapacious as it might have been, given its domestic political system (see the next section). I do not address here whether this stemmed from a commitment to communist ideology, some other internal factor, or—more likely, I believe—from the always threatening international environment in which the Soviet Union was embedded. On this last point, see North, *Structure and Change*. The important conclusion, however, is that the Soviet state most likely did earn higher rents than relevant democratic states, like the United States, that shared a similar position in the international environment.

54. Albert O. Hirschman, *Exit, Voice, and Loyalty: Responses to Decline in Firms, Organizations, and States* (Cambridge: Harvard University Press, 1970).

55. On the optimal size of nations, see Bean, "War and the Birth of the Nation-State"; David Friedman, "A Theory of the Size and Shape of Nations," *Journal of Political Economy* 85 (1977): 59–77; Leonard Dudley, "Punishment, Reward, and the Fortunes of States," *Public Choice* 74 (1992): 293–315; Donald Wittman, "Nations and States: Mergers and Acquisitions; Dissolutions and Divorce," *American Economic Review (Papers and Proceedings)* 81 (May 1991): 126–29; Beth V. Yarbrough and Robert M. Yarbrough, "International Contracting and Territorial Control: The Boundary Question," *Journal of Institutional and Theoretical Economics* 150 (1994): 239–64; and Ronald Findlay, "Towards a Model of Territorial Expansion and the Limits of Empire" (manuscript, 1994). For a more philosophical treatment, see Robert A. Dahl and Edward R. Tufte, *Size and Democracy* (Stanford, CA: Stanford University Press, 1973).

56. For expositional clarity, I assume the total cost curve does not change when the state earns rents. This is obviously a simplification. Even if costs increase modestly with state rent-seeking, the imperialist bias will still arise. For a discussion of why changes in costs will tend to be smaller than changes in revenue, see Lake, "Powerful Pacifists," p. 27.

57. Russia is also the third largest empire in human history. Rein Taagepera, "Size and Duration of Empires: Systematics of Size," *Social Science Research* 7 (1978): 108–27, esp. 117, 126.

58. Olson, *Rise and Decline of Nations*; also Mancur Olson, "Dictatorship, Democracy, and Development," *American Political Science Review* 87 (1993): 567–76.

59. Focusing on social rent-seeking, but with a logic parallel to that developed here, Stephen P. Magee, William A. Brock, and Leslie Young, *Black Hole Tariffs and Endogenous Policy Theory: Political Economy in General Equilibrium* (New York: Cambridge University Press, 1989), demonstrate that rent-seeking, under certain conditions, can escalate to consume virtually the entire national product. See also Jagdish N. Bhagwati, "Directly Unproductive, Profit-Seeking DUP Activities," *Journal of Political Economy* 90 (1982): 69–90.

60. Note, however, that autocratic states may be able to hold onto empire longer than more democratic states. Rents earned by the state provide a cushion against the rising costs of distortions in the subordinate polity. These accumulating distortions, however, lead empires to end earlier than if rents were the only factor at issue.

61. On the functioning of the command economy and the various reforms, see Zbigniew Brzezinski, *The Grand Failure: The Birth and Death of Communism in the Twentieth Century* (New York: Macmillan, 1990); Anders Åslund, *Gorbachev's Struggle for Economic Reform,* updated and rev. ed. (Ithaca: Cornell University Press, 1991); János Kornai, *The Socialist System: The Political Economy of Communism* (Princeton: Princeton University Press, 1992).

62. On the push for independence, see Walter C. Clemens, Jr., *Baltic Independence and Russian Empire* (New York: St. Martin's, 1991); Ronald Misiunas and Rein Taagepera, *The Baltic States: Years of Dependence, 1940–1990,* enl. and updated ed. (Berkeley and Los Angeles: University of California Press, 1993).

63. In Chechnia and in the Caucasus more generally, the dominant non-Russian culture and history of opposition to central rule may yet produce a further unraveling of the Russian empire.

64. Within the core, what were once empires were consolidated into centralized states (e.g., France and Germany)—suggesting that the line between empire and nation-state may be ambiguous. As recent trends in Spain, Britain, Canada, and elsewhere suggest, the progression from empire to nation-state may not be unidirectional. Once-centralized states may now be unraveling, and if they are to remain unified the heavy hand of imperial repression may be required. At the same time, we may in the future observe the creation of some voluntary hierarchies in the form of confederations. The European Union is well on its way toward this end.

65. In chapter 6 of this volume, Mark Beissinger cites the example of Kazakhstan, where the absence of expertise and spare parts has led the government to transfer operational authority of several dozen petrochemical, ore refining, and machine building enterprises to a Russian holding company.

66. Dawisha, chapter 14 of this volume.

II
Imperial Disintegration

3

The Fall of the Tsarist Empire and the USSR

The Russian Question and Imperial Overextension

Roman Szporluk

Introduction

The Russian state collapsed twice in the twentieth century. In 1917, the Russian Empire disintegrated while it was fighting and losing a foreign war. The Soviet Union broke apart in 1991, in peacetime, several decades after it had won the greatest war in Russia's long history of wars. The first state collapsed before the Communists took power; the second, when it was under Communist rule.

Many works have been written—and even more will be written—about causes of the breakup of both the Russian Empire and the USSR.[1] Our task here is much more modest—to focus on certain distinct "factors" ("circumstances," "conditions") which substantially contributed to these events, without claiming, however, that these are sufficient or necessary "causes" of what happened.

Unlike empires of modern times that fell while their former metropoles were gradually being transformed into "normal" nations and nation-states, the tsarist—and then the Soviet—empire fell apart before a modern Russian nation and a Russian nation-state had emerged. A major factor in the imperial collapse in 1917, and in the Soviet collapse in 1991, proved to be conflict between the imperial state and an emergent Russian nation or "society." In both cases, "Russia" contributed to the fall of "Empire." This leads us to the conclusion that both empires failed to solve the "Russian Question"—arguably their most important nationality question.

Another major factor in the fall of both the Russian and Soviet empires was their overextension. They established their hegemony over nations and territories that refused to recognize Russia and /or the USSR as a superior civilization, a higher form of economy and government—qualities which an empire must possess if its rule is not to be based on coercion alone. To maintain hegemony over them in the absence of such recognition required a disproportionate reliance on coercion, and this made Russian rule in "Europe" a heavy burden on the Russian people, which in turn further contributed to the alienation of the Russians from "their" state. These were additional obstacles to the formation of a modern Russian nation. Thus, the inclusion of non-Russian peoples under Imperial/Soviet rule negatively affected the conditions under which the Russians lived. Having been called—and coerced—by their rulers, both tsarist and Communist, to serve "the great cause" of the empire, the Russians found it very difficult to establish for themselves a political identity distinct from and independent of empire.

Because of this special focus, the historical account of this essay is highly selective in facts and problems mentioned. We are interested in those elements of the past experience which may be a useful guide for the identification of the future trends, from which one may draw some lessons. Hegel's famous quip that "the only lesson history teaches is that men do not learn any lessons from history" is usually quoted out of context: Hegel did say not that nothing else was to be learned from history—the problem, he said, was that people did not know how to find the deeper meaning behind concrete events.[2]

What do we mean by empire? There are many definitions available and we do not propose to offer a new one here. Instead, we shall help ourselves to some descriptions of empire by others which appear to be helpful in our study. Thus, Ghita Ionescu sees "three basic elements" in an empire: (1) "a strong political center, animated by a historical mission of expansion," (2) "religious or ideological coercion," and (3) "a sense of final purpose" in its elite.[3]

For Dominic Lieven, "an empire has to be a great power," but it must also "play a major role in shaping . . . the values and culture of an historical epoch. To be a great power has implications as regards resources, ideologies, expansionist temptations and cultural styles which, in historical terms, are implicit in the concept of empire."[4]

Finally, Istvan Hont sees an empire as "a kind of territorial state-system within which entire populations or nations (even if they might retain the appearance of being the inhabitants of a distinct and separate territory) are considered as either superiors or inferiors." Hont agrees with Michael W. Doyle that "Empire . . . is a relationship, formal or informal, in which one state controls the effective political sovereignty of another political society. It can be achieved by force, by political collaboration, by economic, social, or cultural dependence."[5]

Thus, following these authors, we conclude that to qualify as an empire a polity needs to be a great power and to be internationally recognized as such; to extend over a large territory and to include different peoples under different legal and administrative systems; to be endowed with a sense of ideological or religious mission that transcends considerations of power politics; and to act as a leader in the sphere of culture.

The Tsarist Empire

Russia began to call itself an empire only in 1721, but it had in fact become an empire long before Peter I renamed his country. Peter's assumption of a Western title (at that time in Europe there was one other polity in the same class, the "Holy Roman Empire" ruled by the Habsburgs)—is rightly associated with his—and Russia's—orientation toward and identification with "Europe."

Empire in the East

But long before these changes in titles, Muscovy had already become an empire. A key event in this process took place in the reign of Ivan the Terrible—the so-called "Conquest of Kazan." Andreas Kappeler rightly devotes a chapter titled "Gathering of the Lands of the Golden Horde from the 16th to the 18th Century" in his account of the rise of the Russian Empire.[6]

Subsequently, Muscovite Russians and Volga Tatars and other eastern, mainly Turkic and Islamic peoples, lived under one jurisdiction. The Muscovite elites worked out a modus vivendi with the elites of the eastern peoples, with whom their ancestors had been acquainted during the so-called Mongol rule over Muscovite Russia. Richard Pipes has noted that the Russians were successful in assimilating those (eastern) nations whose nobility did not enjoy the same privileges their Russian counterparts had, but the Russians were a "complete failure" in the Western provinces, where the local nobles had traditionally been better off than they.[7] Under Moscow, the Russian and Tatar elites established a cooperative relationship and Moscow's further expansion to the east was facilitated by this Muscovite-Tatar cohabitation.[8] The Muscovites and the peoples of the Volga and farther east lived together in a polity to which concepts taken from the West European experience did not apply: Moscow's "Eastern Empire" was formed before the age of modern nations and nationalism, and in areas where Western ideas, if known at all, were accessible only via Moscow.

Empire in the West

Things were quite different in Russia's western domains. The Muscovite state also expanded to the West before Peter's time, in the fifteenth and sixteenth centuries, gaining Novgorod and parts of the Grand Duchy of Lithuania, a vast polity that at one time extended over what we know today as Belarus, Ukraine, and western regions of Russia. Those western acquisitions brought areas previously exposed to Western influences into the Muscovite realm, but they were not strong enough to counterweigh the eastern character of the Russian state. The first "Westernization" of Moscow came in the seventeenth century when the tsar established his overlordship over the formerly Polish-ruled parts of Ukraine to the east of the Dnieper, and also over the city of Kiev. The result was the transformation of Russian culture under the impact of Ukrainian or "West Russian" (including Belorussian) infusions, which prompted some Russian scholars to connect the emergence of a modern Russia to this "Ukrainization" of Muscovy in the seventeenth and eighteenth centuries.[9]

The next major step in the Europeanization of Russia came under Peter the Great. In addition to the many changes in cultural, administrative and military spheres, Peter gained new territories from Sweden, including the site where St. Petersburg itself, Russia's new capital, was built, and also the Baltic provinces, the present-day Estonia and Latvia. In the partitions of Poland in the late eighteenth century, Catherine II added most of Poland's Ukraine (except Galicia) and all of today's Belarus and Lithuania. Finally, in 1815, under Alexander I, Russia acquired even the central Polish lands, with Warsaw, Lublin, Kielce, and Kalisz, which came to be known as the "Congress Kingdom." A little earlier, in 1809, Russia acquired Finland from Sweden, thus adding a Protestant nation to the mainly Protestant Estonians and Latvians and Baltic Germans who had been under Russia since Peter.

Thus, besides the Orthodox and Muslims (and Russia gained many of the latter in the Crimea and other formerly Ottoman possessions), this newly enlarged Russia included millions of Jews, Catholics (including Catholics of the Uniate rite), and Protestants. This kind of imperial expansion into "Europe" had no analogy in the European experience. The West European empires expanded overseas—while Russia, concurrently with eastern conquests, was establishing its rule over regions and peoples who were more "European" than Russia itself. In this respect the Habsburg expansion into the Balkans and parts of Poland (1772, 1795) was different because Vienna was more "Western" than any of its new acquisitions. To be sure, modern Western nations had been built by conquest. But those conquests happened long before the age of nationalism, and this factor in the end made it possible for the Bretons, the Burgundians, and the Provençals to recognize the primacy of Paris and eventually to become "French." As the Russians were soon to learn, it would prove much harder—if at all possible—to convince the new European subjects of St. Petersburg that they should become Russian. However backward the East Europeans may have been in comparison with the British, French, or Germans, they were, or thought themselves to be, more "advanced" than their Russian masters. As new ideas of nationality arose, these new subjects increasingly saw themselves as Poles (in old Poland only nobles were "Polish"), Finns, Ukrainians, Lithuanians, Estonians, and so on. If the Russians were to learn from the experience of the West, they should have sought to forge a new common identity with the Tatars and other peoples ruled by Muscovy, just as England, Wales and Scotland had combined to produce a common British identity.[10]

Empire in the Age of Nationalism

Instead of working to bring together the peoples and religions it had already had, Russia entered the age of nationalism by annexing a nation that would prove to be its relentless and irrepressible enemy.

In his influential book on the rise and fall of "Russia as a Multinational Empire," Andreas Kappeler says:

> The Polish national movement first, and most strongly, undermined the Russian Empire. It challenged not only the government but also a large part of the Russian society, and it influenced the Lithuanians, Belorussians and Ukrainians, who had been dependent on the Polish nobility for centuries and had been influenced by Polish culture. The Poles played this leading role once again in the crisis of the Soviet Empire at the end of the twentieth century.[11]

Throughout the nineteenth century Poland represented the most celebrated case of a nation seeking to recover its freedom. There was a series of Polish uprisings directed against Russia, which played the role of Poland's main oppressor. Poland was a proud nation which had been deprived of its state, and the Russian Empire was forced to deal with the Polish question at a time when the fundamental issues of Russian nation formation had not been solved.

At about the same time East-Central and Eastern Europe became attracted to the ideas, originally formulated in Germany, that nationality was a cultural community based on language, and that nations and languages form families. Scholars and writers among the Czechs, Serbs, Russians, and others discovered that their languages and thus their nations formed a single "Slavic" family. Some drew from this intellectual discovery an additional political conclusion: the Slavs should unite, there should be "Slavic solidarity," if not a single Slavic state. But there were difficulties when it came to implementing the idea, as Frantisek Graus points out: "The only independent Slav country, Russia, was the most backward region in Europe, where serfdom continued until 1861 and where the non-aristocratic population had no privileges whatsoever." The Czechs felt themselves, rightly, much more advanced than the Russians, to whom being Slavic meant becoming Russian, but "the biggest problem . . . was presented by the Poles," who suffered under their fellow Slavs' oppression.[12]

The Russians felt they had to legitimate their presence in Europe in conformity with the new ideas of nationality then arising in Europe. They began to write the history of the Empire and its predecessors as a Russian *national* history. Kappeler argues that in their drive to become—and be accepted as—"European" the Russians constructed their history (and redefined their relationship with the East) by employing concepts derived from the West. Their nineteenth-century historians had taught the Russians to look at the Empire as the national state of the Russians—and the new philology and ethnography defined the Russians as a Slavic and Orthodox Christian people. In the works of the great Russian historians of the nineteenth century, "the history of a multinational empire of Russia became Russian history."[13]

This in turn meant relegating the non-ethnic Russians—some of whom had lived with the Russians in one state for centuries—as "inorodtsy," or aliens, in short—as Russia's "minorities," if not outright its colonial peoples. This approach overlooked a fundamental difference recently noted by Geoffrey Hosking: "Britain *had* an empire, but Russia *was* an empire—and perhaps still is." The British empire, Hosking explains, was distant (Ireland was the exception) and the British people were therefore able to detach themselves from it "without undue distress." On the other hand, the "Russian empire was part of the homeland, and the 'natives' mixed inextricably with the Russians in their own markets, streets and schools—as indeed they still do."[14]

Clearly, Russia's identification with the Slavs, and the redefinition of the country in European categories, had certain long-term implications for Moscow's relations with the Russian East. It was not immediately obvious to all that moving the capital from Moscow to St. Petersburg, which brought Russia closer to "Europe," also made Russia's domestic "Orient"—Kazan and beyond—more foreign, more distant. The "Slavic Idea," which contributed to undermining the dynastic principle in the Habsburg monarchy and helped create a cultural and spiritual barrier between "the Slavs" and the Germanic and Romance peoples, gave the Russians a sense of being the senior and most powerful member of the family of Slavonic nations in Europe; but, on the other hand, if taken seriously, it delegitimized on ethnic grounds Russia's presence in the East, in "Asia."

But these implications would become clear only in the twentieth century. In the later half of the eighteenth and during much of the nineteenth, the building blocs of Russian national history were assembled. The new history made Muscovite and then St. Petersburg Russia a direct heir of the Byzantine Empire, and through it of ancient Greek culture, and the leader of the Orthodox world.

The Byzantium myth, or popular belief that Byzantine or Greek influence had a formative influence on Russian culture and politics, and thus identity, "is one of the great mystifications of all of European cultural history." According to Edward L. Keenan, "it is difficult to identify a single native Muscovite who knew any significant amount of Greek before the second half of the seventeenth century."[15] But this idea gave historical support to the imperial Russian dream of the "reconquest" of Constantinople, the Tsargrad or "Tsar's City," from Islam.

Another myth linked Muscovy to medieval Kiev. In fact, Muscovite Russians did not have an awareness of being a continuation of Kiev until others told them. "These people were not even thinking of Kiev."[16] It was only after Ukraine was attached to Russia in the seventeenth century that Moscow's Kiev connection was established and projected into the medieval past. This tie was reaffirmed during the partitions of Poland when most of Ukraine and all of Belarus found themselves within Russia: the Kiev myth served to counter Polish claims, and was later also invoked to deny Ukrainian demands for recognition as a nation distinct from the Russians.[17]

It should come as no surprise that the Russians reinterpreted their historic experience with the Tatars while they were adding Kiev and Byzantium to their pedigree. Tatars came to be seen in terms of the "Tatar (or Mongol) Yoke" myth. According to this account, medieval Rus had suffered under this yoke, and there were numerous wars fought against the Tatars, resulting in, among other things, the conquest of a *Moslem* Kazan by *Christian* Russians.

These ideological constructions of the eighteenth century set the stage for the nineteenth-century controversies so well known to, and so beloved by, intellectual historians of Russia. Of these the most famous has been the Slavophile-Westernizer debate. However deeply their participants may have disagreed on Russia's relations with "Europe," they all thought of Russia in terms they had adopted from that very "Europe." The Slavophile defenders of Russian uniqueness understood their Russia to be Slavic and Orthodox—they did not admit the Tatars to their community. In other words, their understanding of Russia was shaped by the Western theories. Eurasianism, which would argue that Russians and their Eastern peoples belonged to one community, was not invented until after 1917. In the meantime, theory-dependency was a common Russian disorder.[18]

Russian empire-building proceeded in two directions, then: first, in association with Kazan Moscow undertook a movement eastward; somewhat later, but especially after gaining East Ukraine and Kiev, it undertook a movement to the West. Russia's Eastern drive proved to be more successful—despite religious and cultural barriers, than its drive to the West—despite the religious and cultural affinity between Russians and their immediate neighbors there. Russia's nineteenth-century conquests in the Caucasus and Central Asia, however, were openly colonial, and were of the same kind as European colonial ventures overseas, e.g., the French conquest of North Africa. In the nineteenth century the Russians looked at "the East" with European spectacles if not eyes.[19]

The Empire and the Russians

This vast empire, which extended from the Baltic to the Pacific, and, within Europe, included lands and peoples from Finland to Bessarabia and Crimea, faced profound political and social problems in "Russia proper"—problems which were complicated by the fact that no one knew where "Russia proper" ended and where "Empire" began, for, as we have already noted, Russia did not *have* an empire, it *was* one.

In a crude summary of its political and social history we may say that in the course of the nineteenth century the tsarist state was challenged by those Russians who believed in revolution as a means for solving Russian problems and those who preferred reform. The revolutionary tradition included the Decembrist

Insurrection of 1825 ("the first Russian revolution"), the activities of Alexander Herzen in exile, the rise of revolutionary movements and political terrorism, which led among other things to the assassination of Alexander II (1881), peasant disturbances, industrial strikes, the emergence of Marxist circles and the formation of the Russian Social Democratic party (1898), its split into the Bolshevik and Menshevik wings and then into separate parties, the revolution of 1905. The revolutionary camp viewed the questions Russia faced at the beginning of the twentieth century as being so fundamental—the abolition of monarchy, liquidation of landlord property, struggle against capitalism—that only revolution could solve them.

There was a parallel "bourgeois," liberal and democratic, constitutional alternative to tsarist autocracy which included people active in regional and local self-government, professional associations, an independent press, and educational and cultural societies. The establishment of the Duma in 1906, and the survival of this representative body until 1917, suggested that the state might gradually evolve toward, if not democracy, then at least liberal constitutionalism.

In the meantime, the supporters of the absolute monarchy began to abandon their traditional dynastic legitimism in favor of nationalist or ethnic ideas of identity. In the early twentieth century a Russian nationalist movement emerged which viewed the empire as a nation-state of the Russians. It treated all others as "aliens" and called for denying them the rights the "real Russians" were to enjoy. During the reigns of Alexander III (1881–94) and Nicholas II (1894–1917) this chauvinist current won increasing support in the official court circles.

Needless to say, not only ethnic Russians participated in the revolutionary or reformist (or even pro-tsarist) movements: in all camps persons of virtually all ethnic backgrounds were present, which was understandable considering that in the early twentieth century ethnic Russians, or Great Russians as they were then called, formed less than half of the Empire's population, with Ukrainians, Poles, Belorussians, Jews, Finns, Armenians, Georgians, and Tatars being among the most numerous "minorities." However, while the more traditionalist elements of the minorities accepted the monarchy as legitimate, its growing identification with Russian nationalism made it difficult for even the most conservative or loyal ethnic to believe in the tsar. Needless to say, the nationalities also had their own ethnic parties and organizations and movements.

Poland was the most serious of all of Russia's nationality problems. The official circles of Russia, and most of its public opinion, considered the Polish question solved by the arrangements adopted at the Congress of Vienna in 1815, and regarded the Polish question an internal matter of the three states in which Poles lived. This was not the point of view of the Poles, as demonstrated by the uprisings of 1830–31 and 1863–64 and the major role played by Russian Poland in the revolution of 1905. In Poland, and in Finland and Latvia especially, as well as in the Caucasus region, 1905 was as much a social as a national revolution.[20]

In 1905 the names of two Poles who would win prominence after 1917—Jozef Pilsudski as the founder of an independent Polish state and Feliks Dzierzynski as the founder of the Soviet secret police—first became known to a wider public. At the same time the Ukrainian, Lithuanian and Belorussian national movements, which originally developed within the Russian Empire in a social and cultural confrontation with the Poles, declared themselves in opposition to Russian autocracy. Moreover, the Poles began to see these nationalities as their allies against Russia. The Finns, Estonians, and Latvians also developed an anti-imperial outlook.

From War to Revolution, 1914–17

We shall never know which way Russia would have gone had war not interfered in 1914. But it did. By 1916–early 1917 it was clear that Russia was losing the war. Even more than the war with Japan of 1904–5, the Great War exposed and exacerbated Russia's unsolved issues and problems. A series of crises led to the abdication of the tsar and the fall of the monarchy in March 1917. A new Russia was headed by a Provisional Government drawn from the Duma parties. The Russian people were, or so it seemed, in charge of their state. A general election was to be held to select a Constituent Assembly which would establish Russia as a democratic and progressive country and solve the most pressing issues, such as land reform and the rights of the nationalities and religious groups; in short, it would complete and ratify the formation of a modern Russian nation along Western lines.

Within months, in November 1917, the Provisional Government was out and the Bolsheviks were in with their own, "Soviet" government. Small wonder that quite a few students and even occasional popular accounts write that "in 1917, the Bolsheviks under Lenin's leadership overthrew the tsar." But the Bolsheviks did not overthrow the tsar. They overthrew Russia's first democratic government.

Again, historians list a variety of "causes" and circumstances, such as the continuation of a highly unpopular war, that made it possible for Lenin and his comrades to seize power, first in Petrograd and Moscow, and then, after a bloody civil war, to establish their rule in most of the old Empire.

1917: The Fall of the Empire and the Unmaking of a Nation

Why did a democratic Russia survive only a little over half a year? Why did the Bolsheviks win? All three events in their sequence and connection—the fall of the monarchy, the fall of democracy, and the victory of the Bolsheviks—were a proof that the Russian nation-making process had not been completed by 1917.

The population of Russia—here we have in mind the "core" of ethnic Russian people—remained divided along several fault lines. The educated (or "bour-geois") urban society was alienated from the imperial state; a large part of the industrial working class was alienated not only from the state but also from "society"; and, most fundamentally, the masses of the peasantry, i.e., a majority of the Russians, were living in a world separated both socially and culturally from the bourgeois society and the urban world. It is well known that the Bolshe-viks were able to take advantage of the peasantry in their struggle for power even though their program, as became evident very quickly, had been thoroughly inimical to its interests and aspirations. But in 1917, as Pipes explains, "the peasant was revolutionary in one respect only: he did not acknowledge private ownership of land." Even though most of the arable land was in the peasants' possession, they "craved" the land of the landlords, merchants, and noncommu-nal peasants. Pipes sees in "the prevalence of communal landholding in Euro-pean Russia . . . along with the legacy of serfdom,- a fundamental fact of Russian social history." The collapse of tsarism is explainable by "deep-seated cultural and political flaws that prevented the tsarist regime from adjusting to the eco-nomic and cultural growth of the country," and these flaws became fatal under the conditions of war. "We are dealing here with a national tragedy whose causes recede deep into the country's past."[21]

Pipes further elaborates on this point:

> The problem with Russian peasants was not oppression, but isolation. They were isolated from the country's political, economic, and cultural life, and therefore unaffected by the changes that had occurred since the time that Peter the Great had set Russia on the course of Westernization. . . . The peasantry remained steeped in Muscovite culture: culturally it had no more in common with the ruling elite or the intelligentsia than the native population of Britain's African colonies had with Victorian England.[22]

One may remain not fully convinced by Pipes in his assessment of the peasantry's economic condition and yet recognize the force of his argument about the negative consequences of the peasants' cultural and legal isolation from "society." Perhaps that isolation would have been less tight if the energy and resources the empire spent (and wasted) on Russifying the non-Russians— and most expensively of all, Poland—had been devoted to "Russifying" the peasants in the Great Russian countryside—e.g., by teaching them to read and write. This is just one illustration of how the Polish Question profoundly—and fatally—affected Russia's internal development.

Mark R. Beissinger is right that "the national self-assertion of Russia's minor-ities did not bring down the Tsarist regime," and that "nationalist elites . . . cautiously went about declaring national states in the chaos and confusion that ensued." However, it is hard to agree with him that "the Tsarist system collapsed on its own."[23]

At the time, to those who viewed Russia in light of European history, and they included a majority of educated Russians, the Russian nation or society had emancipated itself from the imperial state in March 1917 and was beginning to establish Russia as a "normal country." Surely they were right to celebrate the fall of the monarchy as the conclusion of a long political struggle, going back to the Decembrists and most immediately to the revolution of 1905, even if the immediate cause of the overthrow was a spontaneous popular demonstration. In this sense the Russian March 1917 was seen by analogy with the revolutions of 1789 and 1848 in "Europe." However, few people then noticed that the bulk of the Russian population, the peasants, had not yet been transformed into nationally conscious Russians—unlike their cousins elsewhere who had by then become French, or German (or, within the Russian Empire, Polish, Finnish, or Lithuanian). The leaders who took power after March did not do enough to "nationalize" the masses—to bring the country people into a larger imagined community of the Russian nation. Indeed, it is arguable that the part of ethnically Ukrainian peasants (whom official Russia termed "Little Russians") that displayed an awareness of themselves as Ukrainians by nationality was relatively larger than the portion of ethnic "Great Russian" peasants who thought in terms of a Russian nation and state. If this was the case, perhaps some reconceptualization of the revolution of 1917 is in order. Scholars generally assume that while there was a social revolution in Russia in 1917, there was no *Russian* "national problem" in Russia itself. In conformity with this view, the subject of the Russian revolution belongs to social history, and this social history acquires an additional national coloring, secondary in importance to the real social issue in ethnic borderlands, such as Ukraine—but not in Russia "proper."[24] However, if Pipes is right about the relation of Russia's peasants to the state and the society of "their" country, if class conflict between the rural masses and the urban society in Russia was so deep that it prevailed over any kind of interclass national solidarity—as confirmed by the events of 1917 and the subsequent civil war—a conclusion about the failure of Russian nation building is warranted.[25]

The argument that November 1917 constituted the "unmaking of a nation" can be further supported by the program and actual policies of the Bolsheviks, since they viewed Russia, in the words of Pipes, "as a springboard for world revolution."[26] It is highly implausible that the peasants and workers who supported the Bolsheviks also considered world revolution their highest priority. Can such a people be a nation and still succumb to a group of obvious dreamers, if not outright madmen, launching a world socialist republic? The Russian historian Yurii Got'e noted in his diary on 22 January 1918: "What kind of nation is this that allows such experiments to be performed on itself?"[27]

The Soviet Union: Ideology, Geopolitics, and Nations

After it was formally constituted in 1922–24, the Soviet Union was a restored Russian empire in important and self-evident respects. This was acknowledged as early as the 1920s by some Russian exiles who had been bitter enemies of Communism but now thought that because the Bolsheviks had saved Russia from breakup they should be supported by "Russian patriots." Such a call for support was a minority view but there was a common recognition that under the Red Flag Russia remained Russia. The Soviet state was also very different, however. Leaving aside the obvious contrast between an essentially conservative tsarism and the revolutionary, "transformationalist" Soviets, the following points are especially relevant in this review.

First, the tsars did not regard their principles suitable for the entire globe and they did not aspire to unify the world under one—their—authority; the Soviet state was not only ideological, but it considered its ideology valid universally and its form of government destined for adoption everywhere. In the words of Ernest Gellner, Soviet communism was "to an extent unusual and perhaps unique in the history of social systems, the implementation of an elaborate, total, all-embracing and deeply messianic *theory*."[28]

Second, compared with imperial Russia the Soviet state was significantly reduced in size and even more significantly transformed in its population mix. Those nationalities that before 1914 had been the most "Western," the farthest advanced on the road to modern nationhood, did not remain with Russia after the revolution: Finland, Poland, Latvia, Estonia, and Lithuania had emerged as sovereign states. Since these were the nations that by general consensus were the most advanced, and more "European" than the Russians, the Soviet Union was more of a Russian state than tsarist Russia had been. Indeed the census of 1926 recorded a Russian majority in the USSR, while before 1914 the Russians had only a plurality.[29]

Third, although it was so much more "Russian" than its predecessor, the country was called Union of Soviet Socialist Republics and was internally organized according to ethnic or linguistic criteria as a federation of socialist nation-states which reserved for themselves the right, acknowledged in all Soviet constitutions, freely to secede from the Union. This provision was not the result of benevolence on the part of the regime. By 1922, the most "European" dependencies of the empire had seceded. Those who tried but failed to become independent states in 1918–20—Ukraine, Belarus, Armenia, Georgia, and Azerbaijan—received an acknowledgment of their efforts and continuing quest for recognition: as formally equal partners of Russia, i.e., the RSFSR, they joined a "new" entity, the USSR. This took place after a dispute between Lenin and Stalin, who had proposed instead to include Ukraine, Belarus, Georgia, Armenia, and Azerbaijan as autonomous republics within the RSFSR.

The establishment of the USSR raised the question of the identity of "Russia proper" and its relation to the USSR. Formally, Russia became a nation state, a constitutional equal of Ukraine or Belarus. But at the same time the RSFSR remained more than that. In 1922, the future Kazakhstan, Uzbekistan, Turkmenia, Krygyzstan, and Tajikistan (under different names) belonged to the

Russian Federation, which was thus a Slavic-Turkic and Christian-Moslem entity. Only after 1924, in a major territorial-national reorganization of Central Asia, did these areas leave the RSFSR and join the USSR directly. But even afterward the RSFSR retained a whole panoply of autonomous republics, districts, regions, each named after an ethnic group, and was thus a smaller replica of the USSR within the USSR.

The Tatar Autonomous SSR was the most important of the republics within the Russian Federation, and as Tatarstan it remains the most important unit within present-day Russia. Stalin refused to grant the Tatars the status of a Union republic on the spurious argument that Tatarstan did not border on a foreign territory and thus would not be able to exercise its constitutional right of secession. But perhaps history rather than geography lay behind Stalin's real motives: Kazan became part of the same state as Moscow long before Tashkent or Baku or even Kiev had found themselves under Moscow or St. Petersburg. The Russians and Tatars were together first under the khans of the Golden Horde, and then again, uninterruptedly from Ivan the Terrible to Nicholas II.

From this historical summary it is possible to identify some of the factors that secured the Bolshevik survival in power. On one hand, the Bolsheviks appealed to Russian patriotism when they defended the integrity of what most Russians considered to be their country. Former tsarist generals and officers volunteered their services to Lenin and Trotsky in 1920 during the Polish-Soviet war, which from the Russian nationalist point of view was about saving Kiev for Russia, and from the Polish point of view was a war first to help the Ukrainians in their struggle for independence and then a war for Poland's survival as a nation (while for Lenin and his comrades it was a means to promote revolution in Europe).[30] On the other hand, because they had started out as resolute opponents of Russian nationalism, the Bolsheviks found support among members of Russia's oppressed nationalities who provided crucial support to the Bolsheviks in the battles of the civil war. These included Poles, Finns, and Latvians, who remained in the USSR after the war because their homelands were "capitalist" countries. The Soviet cause also found some supporters beyond the old Russian empire: for them, like for Lenin, the Polish war was to make the Russian revolution international—and the Polish victory was the world revolution's defeat.

Other, more conventional, geopolitical factors also helped the Soviets. The war against Germany dragged on until November 1918, and the war-exhausted victors were unwilling to intervene in Russia. Also, the Western powers were firmly committed to preserving the territorial integrity of Russia after the expected fall of Communism and thus they refused to help the nationalists in the borderlands. (Let us recall that the United States had great problems with recognizing the independence of Finland and the Baltic states—even while refusing to recognize Soviet Russia.)

The Soviet Utopia

After 1917, the Russian nation-building process was interrupted or sidetracked by the Communist experiment, in which an empire was restored, or, more precisely, a new empire was founded on an expressly anti-national, universalist ideological foundation. The Communist state defined itself in global terms—as an alternative to "capitalism" and its political, social and cultural order. Its aims were much greater than just to be good for Russia and the other Soviet republics—Lenin and his comrades in 1917 had had something different in mind. The USSR was to provide an alternative model of modernity, superior to that represented by the "West."

After 1917, the Bolsheviks persuaded themselves that their system, and therefore their leadership, would extend far beyond such reluctant parts of the old empire as Poland or Finland: they really believed that they represented the prototype of a single global civilization. Even for Stalin, "socialism in one country" was only a beginning.[31] Because the Soviets considered their system superior and suitable for other countries, they imposed it on the states of East Central Europe that they controlled after 1945. But, in the end, there was neither socialism nor one country.[32]

Internationalism or Overextension?

This essay argues that practicing internationalism as Moscow understood it—or overextension—was the undoing of the Soviet Union just as overextension had been a major factor in the collapse of imperial Russia. The seeds of the eventual collapse of the USSR were planted at the time of its greatest military and political triumph—during and after World War II.

First, in 1939–40, the Soviets annexed the Baltic states and eastern Poland, that is, the Western regions of today's Ukraine and Belarus.[33] Then, after 1944, they imposed the Soviet system on those formerly independent states of Central and Eastern Europe which had found themselves under Soviet control at the end of the Second World War.[34] There, too, Sovietism was seen as a form of Russian domination. These nations had a strong sense of being different from Russia and wanted to emulate the West.

Perhaps the decline of the Soviet Union began with the first signs of the breakup of the unity of the Communist world. The Stalin-Tito conflict and the expulsion of Yugoslavia was the first breach, and the next, and much more important, one was the Sino-Soviet split.

While there can be no question that geopolitically nothing could surpass the importance of the Moscow-Beijing break, Poland posed a challenge to the Soviet Communist ideology that it had no way of countering. Starting with the workers' strike in Poznan in June 1956, followed by workers' strikes in Gdansk in 1970, in Radom in 1976, and in Gdansk again in 1980, and culminating in the rise of a multimillion Solidarity, Polish workers hit Soviet Communism at the heart of its foundation, as a "workers' state." None of this is meant to diminish the role of the workers' strikes in East Germany in 1953, or that of the Hungarian revolution of 1956, or the Prague Spring of 1968. But it was precisely because of the fact that the Polish strikes were organized by workers and led by an electrician whose proletarian credentials were impeccable (and certainly more authentic than those of any of the leaders in Poland or in the USSR), that Poland could delegitimate the Soviet model on its own ground. This feat could not have been achieved by peasants or intellectuals or priests or students. And the fact that the workers were both Polish and Catholic added a broader historical perspective to their struggle—making it another act in the centuries-long contest between a Catholic Poland and an Orthodox Russia.

After 1945 the Poles challenged Soviet Communism just as their nineteenth- and early twentieth-century predecessors had historically done from the Kosciuszko Insurrection of 1794 to the workers' and students' strikes in Warsaw and Łodz in 1905. The history of Poland after 1945 confirms Kappeler's assessment of the Polish Question's role in the decline and fall of the Soviet empire.

In an exercise in counterfactual history, let us imagine that after 1944, the Soviet Union had allowed a "Finlandized" Poland, instead of attempting to Sovietize/Russify it. There would have been no "Polish October" of 1956, and thus no Polish impact in the Bloc, no "Solidarity". . . . (And if they had allowed Estonia, Latvia and Lithuania to remain formally outside the USSR, the Soviets would have been spared quite a few more troubles at home, such as the attitude reflected in the Baltic slogan: "Moscow insists on treating us like all the other nationalities—so we shall help all them to become like us.") By suggesting a continuity between Kosciuszko and Walesa, we want to underline the fact that in most of Eastern and Central Europe the Soviet system was perceived as a Russian product and a form of Russian domination.

Over thirty years ago, Rupert Emerson described the post-1945 world: "Colonialism was on the way out far more speedily than had seemed at all possible. Only the old Czarist empire remained intact, undergoing the novel rhythms of Communist development, while the European satellites opened up a new dimension of empire."[35] Confirming this assessment of the origins of Communist East Europe from the other end, three decades later, another scholar, Raymond Pearson, saw a "momentum of decolonization" at work in the dissolution of communist East Europe.[36]

Why Did the Soviet Empire Fall?

Of course, the Soviet empire in Europe did not fall when it did simply because the East Europeans resented the colonial status of their countries, the workers felt exploited, and the intellectuals made fun of Soviet ideology. The collapse followed the popular realization which came with the Cold War that the Communist

Grand Design had failed. As Pearson put it, "the Cold War strained and distorted the Soviet Empire to a hitherto unrecognised degree, proving as debilitating . . . as were the First and Second World Wars. In its excessive and finally intolerable military, economic and political demands, the Cold War fulfilled the function of a surrogate Third World War." Eric Hobsbawm reached an identical conclusion: "Internationally speaking, the USSR was like a country comprehensively defeated, as after a major war—only without a war."[37] And as factors in this outcome, he continued, Eastern Europe was "the Achilles heel of the Soviet system, and Poland (plus, to a lesser extent, Hungary) its most vulnerable spot."[38]

Why should Eastern Europe have been the "Achilles heel"? Wasn't the whole communist project international in its very essence? In answering this question we need to go beyond the issue of the Cold War.

The Soviet system was based on the idea that while the nation-state was a normal political form for the period of capitalism, socialism by its very nature was international or rather supranational. This international force would compete with and ultimately overtake the capitalist system—which consisted of sovereign nation-states. However, as early as the 1930s, under Stalin, the USSR began to identify itself with the tsarist empire's military traditions and foreign policies and the Russian nation was given the status of "elder brother."

The public and official identification of the Soviet Union with tsarist Russia became even stronger during and after the Second World War. But even as the USSR came to resemble tsarist Russia, and to assign a leading position to the Russian language and nation, it did not renounce its claim to represent the prototype of a new socialist civilization that was superior to that of "capitalism," and one that in the end would replace it in the whole world. It was this kind of "internationalism" that the East Europeans had to deal with after 1945.

After Stalin's death, in a changed international situation, Nikita S. Khrushchev renewed the old Communist challenge to capitalist powers. The new party program offered a precise schedule of when the USSR would outpace first Western Europe and then the United States in various economic and social indicators. Soviet leaders were convinced that competing with the West required making the USSR at least equal militarily with the United States, and countering the United States everywhere, especially in the Third World. As they said in Moscow in the 1970s, this had to be done because "The United States is intervening in Soviet internal affairs in every part of the globe."

For a time, the Soviets seemed to be winning. Then it became increasingly clear that the Soviets would be unable to "produce a social order of both Virtue and Plenty"—indeed not even one of those things. "To add insult to injury," Ernest Gellner wrote, "the Japanese and other East Asians showed that Western capitalism can indeed be overtaken, but that it can be done by a Confucian rather than a Marxist adaptation of the ideas of Adam Smith."[39]

This realization caused a loss of faith—or where faith had been lacking, produced a firmer determination to oppose Communism. The East Europeans could see more easily than Soviet citizens that the West was winning. They would have agreed with Kenneth Minogue and Beryl Williams, who character- ized communism as "an abortive form of modernization" and "a mimicry that claim[ed] to be superior to the original performance." [40]

The East Europeans always knew that to see the original performance one had to go west. Besides, they had had their own reasons not to think very highly of anything associated with Russia and to reject Russian claims to superiority. They would agree with Benedict Anderson who wondered in 1983 if the USSR was not more reminiscent of its nineteenth-century imperial predecessor than a pre- cursor of a twenty-first century organization of humankind. (In a new preface dated February 1991, Anderson was more specific, suggesting that "by the open- ing of the new millennium little will remain of the Union of Soviet Socialist republics except . . . republics.")[41]

The Empire Breaks Up

From the breakup of the Soviet external empire in Europe we must turn to the fall of the USSR: from the Achilles heel to Achilles.

One can cite many "causes" of that momentous event—we *feel* that events of such enormity deserve nothing less—and the list of candidates is appropriately impressive. It is certainly impossible to ignore and also impossible to precisely weigh the personal factor—Mikhail Gorbachev. The cause which lay behind the East European collapse also helps explain the fall of the USSR, that is, the Soviet defeat in the Cold War. And the fall of Eastern Europe became a contributing cause of the breakup of the USSR. It was an axiom of Western Sovietology that the USSR would never give up its control over Central and Eastern Europe because the loss of East Europe would delegitimize Communism within the USSR.[42]

What actually happened closely followed the "script" written by Randall Collins, a Weberian sociologist with no special expertise in the field. Arguing on the basis of a broad comparative survey, Collins concluded that "all major geo- political processes appear to be working against the continuation of Soviet world power." "If an overextended imperial state," such as the Russian Empire/USSR, "becomes embroiled in ethnic and political conflicts within a distant client state, there is a strong tendency for these foreign instabilities to become gradually incorporated inside the imperial state's own boundaries." Collins therefore thought it "highly likely that, once a first round of serious crises caused the loss of Eastern Europe or other distant territory, cumulative processes of internal weakening would be set in motion, culminating in the eventual loss of the next tier of ethnically distinct conquest: the Baltic states, the Ukraine, the Caucasus, and the central-Asian Moslem territories . . . ."[43]

What an outsider like Collins had so presciently anticipated came as a surprise to experts. Right up to the Soviet Union's fall, it was widely held that the Soviets had succeeded in building an urban and industrial society, indeed, had found a noncapitalist path to modernity, and had carried out a socialist equivalent of nation building by creating a Soviet people that remained multiethnic and whose members spoke many languages but also had Russian as their common language. This was indeed the intention of the Soviets, except that they did not call the Soviet people a nation, sovetskaia natsiia, but used the term sovetskii narod instead. But, they promoted Soviet patriotism and taught the young the history of "The Great Patriotic War of the Soviet People." There was never any doubt that being a Soviet citizen was an identity overriding ethnicity: "My address is not a house or a street—my address is: USSR." Everything in the official characterization of "Soviet people" corresponded to the conventional Western definition of a political or civic nation. Over sixty years ago the émigré scholar N.V. Ustrialov, in an article titled "On the Soviet Nation," noted (approvingly) that the Soviets were turning all peoples of the USSR into a nation defined politically and ideologically, not ethnically.[44]

Western scholarship tacitly, and often openly, understood "Soviet" in this sense. Books and articles were written and conferences held about Soviet workers, Soviet youth, Soviet music, ballet, and sport; lively debates about the political ambitions of a new Soviet middle class took place until virtually the end; and at least one foreign expert, unsolicited, advised Moscow about "inventing the Soviet national interest." People spoke about institutional pluralism in the USSR and they had in mind Soviet institutions. So when glasnost and perestroika came it was natural of them also to expect the emergence of new Soviet political parties, movements, and associations.

But little of the sort emerged. When the Cold War ended, as Eric Hobsbawm writes, "the international debacle encouraged secessionism in the republics where nationalist sentiment was strong." However, Hobsbawm is convinced that

> the disintegration of the Union was not due to nationalist forces. It was due essentially to the disintegration of central authority, which forced every region or sub-unit of the country to look after itself. . . . The country moved towards a pluralist electoral politics at the very moment that it subsided into economic anarchy. . . . It was an explosive combination, for it undermined the shallow foundations of the USSR's economic and political unity.[45]

If such was the case, then we must say that a Soviet society did not exist. Otherwise an alternative to central authority would have emerged within a Soviet Union framework. Nationalism did not arise because the central state collapsed. The Soviet state collapsed because there was no Soviet society to defend it—and no authentic institutions from which a new Soviet leadership could emerge. As Anatoly Khazanov put it, the Soviet system was totalitarian, and "a virtual absence of civil society in the multiethnic Soviet state implied that the cooperation

was most likely to be achieved by means of ethnic solidarity."[46]
The state did not break up into "regions," but into republics—and of various sizes. The Russian republic extended from the Baltic to the Pacific, with a population of over 150 million. Collins gave us a more persuasive explanation than Hobsbawm, and did so even *before* the event, of why the breakup occurred as it did:

> The formal machinery for the dismemberment of the Soviet Union is already in place. The fifteen largest ethnically distinct areas are officially autonomous states, possessing local machinery of government . . . In current practice, this autonomy has little effect, as the armed forces, monetary system, and economic planning are controlled by organs of the central government and political control is organized by a single national Communist Party. The importance of the autonomous-ethnic-state structure, rather, is that it both maintains ethnic identities and provides organizational framework that would allow genuinely separate states to emerge whenever the central government were seriously weakened.[47]

The discourse that replaced Marxism-Leninism in the Soviet Union's final days was the discourse of nation. Moscow did not create modern nations in the Soviet space: they emerged *despite* the efforts of the Soviet regime to the contrary. This explains why at first national movements were led mainly by writers, poets, artists, and scholars in the fields of humanities: all other spheres of public life had been Soviet. However, when they realized the Soviet ship was sinking, some heretofore Soviet figures decided to become "national" politicians. There were "born again" Uzbeks, Ukrainians, Georgians, and others. With the Moscow center gone, and where the societies and nations were particularly weak, these ex-Communists became masters of their new countries without even pretending to share power with the nationalist intelligentsia. Collins had seen it coming: "The projected disintegration of the Soviet Union would most likely occur under the leadership of dissident communist politicians. Given the current monopoly of communists over political organization in the Soviet Union, it would be difficult for political change to come about in any other way, at least initially."[48]

The Secession of Russia

Even Collins, however, did not predict *Russia*'s secession from the Empire. Who could have imagined that a former party secretary from the Urals, by defying the Kremlin, would attain the post of president (the first ever) of an independent Russia?

This was exactly what Boris N. Yeltsin did. Historians will argue forever about "objective" and "subjective" factors in the fall of the USSR, but John Barber is right when he says about the events of 1990–91: "The Soviet Union did not simply collapse: it was destroyed by the action of its opponents. . . . The alliance of reform Communists and anti-Communist 'democrats' did not obtain state power in Russia by default."[49] In June 1990 the Russian Republic declared its "sovereignty," and this move was followed by a sequence of actions, including the creation of the office of President of Russia, and these moves "all steadily advanced the Russian republic towards full statehood."[50]

However, as George F. Kennan pointed out, while the Russian declaration of sovereignty simply "ranked the Russian nation with the various other peripheral entities in the former Soviet Union," this action posed "a mortal threat to the Soviet Union itself." The Soviet Union was becoming "an empty shell, without people, without territory, and with no more than a theoretical identity."[51]

Russia's Choices

Under the tsars and under Communists, as we saw, Russia failed to make the transition from an empire to a nation-state. Tension and then open conflict between the imperial state and an emergent Russian nation or "society" was a major factor in the imperial collapse in 1917 and in the Soviet collapse in 1991. In both cases, although in different ways, "Russia" contributed to the fall of "Empire." Thus we arrive at a conclusion close, though not identical, to that of Mark R. Beissinger. Beissinger points out that "since the emergence of modern state-building within the Tsarist empire, state and empire have proven extremely difficult to separate, profoundly conditioning the collapse of the Russian empire, the demise of the USSR, and the context in which post-Soviet politics is now being played out."[52] In this essay we go further, and argue that the failure in state-building was a result of the more fundamental failure in Russian nation formation.

In this respect Anatoly Khazanov provides a very illuminating analogy from another case of transition from imperial nationality to nation, one which helps us to understand the present Russian situation. According to Khazanov, the Russians in the Soviet Empire—and we may also suppose their predecessors in imperial Russia—"remained at the Ottoman stage of national identity." This means that they identified their country, Russia, with the Soviet Union much like the Turks used to identify Turkey with the Ottoman Empire. Khazanov argues that the Soviet nationality policy was "detrimental" to the formation of the Russian nation and allowed the rulers "to pass off imperial interests for Russian national interests." He concludes that the formation of a modern Russian nation has not yet been completed. Whether Russia will be a civic or an ethnic nation remains an open question.[53]

Are Russians in the post-Soviet Russian Federation (the country's official name) solving "the Russian Question" more successfully than their imperial predecessors?

Let us first take a look at geography. One often hears, in Russia and abroad, that post-1991 Russia is an "artificial" creation because there is no historical precedent for a Russia in its present boundaries. That is true, but the same may be said about a great number of states existing in today's Europe, not to mention Asia or Africa. Before 1990, there was no Germany in its current boundaries. The Poland established in 1945 had never existed before. Turkey, whose shape on the map looks to all—except the Kurds—so natural and "normal," was seen in the 1920s as an "artificial" creation of the post-Ottoman settlement. And yet that new Turkey was even more "unhistorical" than post-Soviet Russia.

Needless to say, in all these cases deep and painful reappraisals were necessary before the respective nations could agree on what they accepted Germany, Poland, and Turkey to be. (And very dramatic events had to happen before General de Gaulle could make the French accept that Algeria was not a part of France after all.)

These examples help us to appreciate the identity problems of contemporary Russia. But to understand Russian discomfort with geography one must go back to Russian history. History helps us understand why Kiev, which was under Moscow "only" from 1667, became the capital of a newly independent country in 1991, while Kazan, under Moscow for more than a hundred years longer than Kiev, is the capital of a republic *within* Russia.

Russia's relations with Ukraine, and the Russian-"Asian" nexus remain on top of the Russian national agenda today. Many Russians feel that the question of their country's cultural and political "location" (Is Russia in "Europe" or does it form the core of "Eurasia"?) depends on how one solves these questions.

Ukrainian-Russian relations have received relatively close scrutiny and need not be summarized here except by noting that virtually all political circles in Russia continue to question the very existence of a Ukrainian nationality, even though, for tactical reasons, some prefer not to admit this openly. There is reason to think, however, that behind the controversies about the Black Sea fleet or the status of Crimea lies the refusal to accept Ukraine as a state independent of Russia.[54]

The Russian-"Eastern" connection as an issue in defining the identity of Russia receives less attention even though, as this essay shows, it is historically tied to Russia's self-definition as a nation and a state. One of the unexpected consequences of the Chechen conflict may be a greater focus on the question of the nationality problem *within* the Russian Federation. An example of how serious these problems are taken to be by at least some policy makers and scholars may be found in the account of a symposium held in Moscow in 1995, and titled "Russia under the Conditions of Strategic Instability." The following fragment from a statement of N.N. Moiseyev reveals what that symposium was about:

> If we think about it profoundly, we shall see that the two millennia of our life with the Tatars and their ancestors have formed similar mentalities in us. And that is why our synthesis with the Islamic world is realistic, provided there is a sufficiently deep mutual respect and understanding. But if we do not attain it, we shall be in trouble [*nam grozit beda*]. I am sure of this.[55]

To this one might predictably respond by saying that all sorts of things, including quite off-the-mark ones, are heard these days in Moscow. Why should it matter what Academician Moiseyev says?[56] Indeed, these days policy makers and influential analysts in Moscow do devote much more attention to how to "recover" Minsk, Almaty, and Kiev than to worrying about how not to "lose Kazan." They think more about restoring an empire—will it call itself the Third Empire?—and less about building a state (the Second Republic?). Perhaps they are being realistic: the first empire lasted several centuries; the second—seventy years; while the first republic, the only democracy Russia ever knew until the fall of the USSR, survived a mere eight months.

But the restorers of the empire may also be wrong. They may be repeating the fatal mistakes of their tsarist and Soviet predecessors, who, Henry Kissinger says, suffered from "the Russian mania for new conquests." Only a few "were wise enough to realize that, for Russia, 'the extension of territory was the extension of weakness'. . . . In the end, the communist empire collapsed for essentially the same reasons that the tsars' had."[57]

If a "mania for conquests" links the current elites to the tsarist and Soviet past, so does the neglect of the condition of the Russian people. When Alexander Solzhenitsyn asserts that a Russian nation does not exist today, his words bring to mind the points both Pipes and Got'e made about the 1917 era. Solzhenitsyn deplores "the stratification of Russians as if into two separate nations" and illustrates his meaning as follows: "the immense provincial-village heartland, and an entirely disparate minority in the capital, alien to it in thought and westernized in culture." Solzhenitsyn sees a sign of Russia's national "Catastrophe" in "today's amorphous state of Russian national consciousness, in the grey indifference toward once's national affinity and an even greater apathy to compatriots in dire straits." One does not need to share his views or accept his language but he does offer an insight into the condition of Russia that usually escapes the attention of observers—as revealed by their astonishment at how the Russians vote. But the real catastrophe of Russia, says Solzhenitsyn, is summed up in these words: "our dying out."[58]

What Solzhenitsyn calls a national "Catastrophe," professional demographer V.I. Kozlov describes in only slightly less apocalyptic terms: "The Extinction of the Russians: A Historic-Demographic Crisis or a Catastrophe?"[59] Kozlov says that if the current trends continue, by 2000 the number of Russians in the Russian Federation will decrease by 7–9 million compared with 1989, while in "the near abroad" the number of Russians will be down to 20 million (from about 25 million). Kozlov notes with some concern that in 1989 the Russian Federation's net population gain was 289,200 Russians and 287,100 non-Russians. (His concern is understandable, for in 1989 there were 119.9 million Russians in the Russian Federation, where they constituted 81.5 percent of its population.) It is impossible to tell whether the current (as of March 1996) president of Russia and his defense minister have thought of the long-term implications of Chechnya in light of these statistics.[60]

In his account of his mission to Moscow the former U.S. ambassador to the USSR, Jack F. Matlock, concluded that

> Two things do seem as certain as anything in human affairs can be: 1. The Soviet system cannot be rebuilt. . . . 2. The Russian empire cannot be reassembled, even if the Russian people nurse an emotional attachment for an ill-understood past and are periodically victimized by demagogues. Only a healthy Russian economy could bear the cost, but the economy cannot be cured if Russia embarks on an imperialist course.[61]

Matlock reminded his readers that "Russia can no longer afford an empire, however acquired. If the twentieth century taught us anything, it is that empires are costly burdens." He also noted an aspect which is strangely missing in Russian thinking about how to restore the empire: the expected resistance by the former republics. For Russia too, he thought, "internal nation building is the principal challenge. . . . Russia . . . must, in the long run, reform or fall apart."[62]

History teaches that nations, and their leaders, rarely learn their lessons. There is no guarantee that wise and friendly counsel like that offered by the former ambassador will be taken into account by those who form Russian opinion or those who make decisions for their country.

In 1991, it looked as if Russia would lead the entire post-Soviet space in economic reforms and democratization—just as before Russia had been the driving force of Sovietization. Those Russians who had not accepted the disintegration of the empire but who supported democracy and a market economy had reason to hope that Russia's political and cultural leadership in de-Sovietization would make it possible for the Russian empire to be restored—this time in a liberal or "Western" form.

But for this to have a chance to happen, economic and political reforms had to be safe in Russia itself. In 1996, this was less obviously the case than it had been five years earlier. Politically, the Communists have been able to gain most from the condition—and mood—which Solzhenitsyn describes. The Communists are also the most determined and best organized promoters of imperial restoration. But their vision of "re-integration" is not that of the democrats or liberals. Today's Russians, like those of an earlier generation, have to choose between different *Russias*, and not simply between competing parties and leaders. Do they prefer a territorially diminished Russia as it exists now, struggling to build a democracy and a market economy, or a Russia which the Communists promise will bring back to them Kiev and Tashkent and more, but at the cost of democracy and a free economy?

Notes

1. Among the earliest attempts to set the agenda for such future investigations, see Alexander Dallin, "Causes of the Collapse of the USSR," *Post-Soviet Affairs*, vol. 8, no. 4

(October-December 1992), pp. 279–302. For comparative approaches to the study of imperial decline and the rise of nations see essays by Richard L. Rudolph, Alexander J. Motyl, William O. McCagg, Jr., Miroslav Hroch and John-Paul Himka, in Richard L. Rudolph and David F. Good, eds., *Nationalism and Empire. The Habsburg Empire and the Soviet Union* (New York: St. Martin's Press, 1992), pp. 3–93.

2. For a sound and concise outline of the relevant history see "The Legacies of History" in Karen Dawisha and Bruce Parrott, *Russia and the New States of Eurasia: The Politics of Upheaval* (Cambridge and New York: Cambridge University Press, 1994), pp. 23–56.

3. Ghita Ionescu, *The Break-up of the Soviet Empire in Eastern Europe* (Baltimore, MD: Penguin, 1965), p. 7.

4. Dominic Lieven, "The Russian Empire and the Soviet Union as Imperial Polities," *Journal of Contemporary History*, vol. 30 (1995), pp. 607–36. Quotation on p. 608.

5. Istvan Hont, "The Permanent Crisis of a Divided Mankind: 'Contemporary Crisis of the Nation State' in Historical Perspective," in John Dunn, ed., *Contemporary Crisis of the Nation State?* (Oxford, UK, and Cambridge, MA: Blackwell, 1995), p. 172, quoting from Michael W. Doyle, *Empires* (Ithaca: Cornell University Press, 1986), p. 45.

6. Andreas Kappeler, *Russland als Vielvoelkerreich. Entstehung, Geschichte, Zerfall* (Muenchen: C.H. Beck, 1992), pp. 24–56.

7. Richard Pipes, "Introduction: The Nationality Problem," in Zev Katz, Rosemarie Rogers, and Frederic Harned, eds., *Handbook of Major Soviet Nationalities,* (New York: The Free Press; London: Collier Macmillan, 1975), p. 2n.

8. Edward L. Keenan, "Muscovy and Kazan: Some Introductory Remarks on the Patterns of Steppe Diplomacy," *Slavic Review*, vol. 26, no. 3 (1967), pp. 548–58.

9. Nikolai Sergeevich Trubetskoy, *The Legacy of Genghis Khan and Other Essays on Russia's Identity*, ed. by Anatoly Liberman (Ann Arbor, Mich.: Michigan Slavic Publications, 1991); "The Ukrainian Problem," pp. 244–67, originally published as "K ukrainskoi probleme," *Evraziiskii vremennik*, 5, 1927, pp. 165–84.

10. Linda Colley, *Britons: Forging the Nation, 1707–1837* (New Haven: Yale University Press, 1992), p. 6: "Great Britain did not emerge by way of a 'blending' of the different regional or older national cultures contained within its boundaries. . . . Britishness was superimposed over an array of internal differences in response to contact with the Other, and above all in response to conflict with the Other." Thus, what united the English, Scots, and Welsh was their shared hostility to Catholicism— but this also kept the Irish out of the British nation. We should not assume a priori that in Russia the distance between the Orthodox and the Moslems made it impossible for them to fight together against a common "Other": in fact, on many occasions Russia's Moslems fought together with the Orthodox Russians against Catholic and Protestant powers. But this is something the Russians later chose not to remember. (See note 55.)

11. Andreas Kappeler, *Russland als Vielvoelkerreich*, p. 179.

12. Frantisek Graus, "Slavs and Germans," in Geoffrey Barraclough, ed., *Eastern and Western Europe in the Middle Ages* (New York: Harcourt Brace Jovanovich, 1970), p. 26.

13. Kappeler, *Russland als Vielvoelkerreich*, pp. 9–18, especially p. 15.

14. Geoffrey Hosking, "The Freudian frontier," *The Times Literary Supplement*, March 10, 1995, p. 27, rev. of Susan Layton, *Russian Literature and Empire: The Conquest of the Caucasus from Pushkin to Tolstoy* (Cambridge: Cambridge University Press, 1994). See also Mark Bassin, "Russia between Europe and Asia: The Ideological Construction of Geographical Space," *Slavic Review*, vol. 50, no. 1 (Spring 1991), pp. 1–17.

15. Edward L. Keenan, "On Certain Mythical Beliefs and Russian Behaviors," in S.

Frederick Starr, ed., *The Legacy of History in Russia and the New States of Eurasia* (Armonk, N.Y., and London, England: M.E. Sharpe, 1994), p. 27.

16. Keenan, "On Certain Mythical Beliefs," p. 23. Also see Edward L. Keenan, "Muscovite Perceptions of Other East Slavs before 1654—An Agenda for Historians," in Peter J. Potichnyj et al., eds., *Ukraine and Russia in Their Historical Encounter* (Edmonton: Canadian Institute of Ukrainian Studies Press, 1992), pp. 20–38.

17. See, for example, David Saunders, *The Ukrainian Impact on Russian Culture, 1750–1850* (Edmonton: Canadian Institute of Ukrainian Studies Press, 1985); Zenon E. Kohut, *Russian Centralism and Ukrainian Autonomy: Imperial Absorption of the Hetmanate, 1760s–1830s* (Cambridge, Mass.: Ukrainian Research Institute, distr. by Harvard University Press, 1988), and Marc Raeff, "Ukraine and Imperial Russia: Intellectual and Political Encounters from the Seventeenth to the Nineteenth Century," in Peter J. Potichnyj, Marc Raeff, Jaroslaw Pelenski, and Gleb N. Zekulin, eds., *Ukraine and Russia in Their Historical Encounter* (Edmonton: Canadian Institute of Ukrainian Studies Press, 1992), pp. 69–85. For a broader perspective on the nineteenth-century Polish-Ukrainian-Russian triangle, see the two strikingly original monographs by Daniel Beauvois: *Le noble, le serf et le revizor: La noblesse polonaise entre le tsarisme et les masses ukrainiennes (1831–1863)* (Paris: Archives contemporaines, 1984), and *La Bataille de la terre en Ukraine, 1863–1914: Les polonais et les conflits socio-ethniques* (Lille: Presses Universitaires de Lille, 1993).

18. Andrzej Walicki, "Russian Social Thought: An Introduction to the Intellectual History of Nineteenth-Century Russia," *The Russian Review*, vol. 36, no. 1 (January 1977), pp. 1–45.

19. This may be the place to note that, as Alfred J. Rieber has argued, the imperial Russian historical experience included importantly "a struggle on two levels for hegemony over the borderlands"—with the peoples the empire ruled or sought to rule, and with other empires. See Alfred J. Rieber, "Struggle over the Borderlands," in S. Frederick Starr, ed., *The Legacy of History* (Armonk, N.Y., and London, England: M.E. Sharpe, 1994), p. 86. This aspect of imperial history is not directly related to our argument and cannot be addressed here.

20. Alfred J. Rieber has drawn attention to a very close interconnection between the problem of the non-Russian nationalities and the revolutionary movement in Russia proper. The policies of Russification directed against the minorities generated not only nationalism in response but also facilitated the spread of revolutionary agitation, the ideas of populism and Marxism, among the Finnish, Jewish, Baltic, and Transcaucasian populations. It was the more assimilated non-Russians who joined the Russian revolutionary movement. "In 1905 the tsarist autocracy reaped the whirlwind of its errant cultural sowing." Alfred J. Rieber, "Struggle over the Borderlands," p. 81.

21. Richard Pipes, *Russia under the Bolshevik Regime* (New York: Alfred A. Knopf, 1993), pp. 494, 497.

22. Ibid., p. 493.

23. Mark R. Beissinger, "The Persisting Ambiguity of Empire," *Post-Soviet Affairs*, vol. 11, no. 2 (1995), p. 160.

24. John-Paul Himka, "The National and the Social in the Ukrainian Revolution of 1917–20: The Historiographical Agenda," *Archiv fuer Sozialgeschichte*, 34, 1994, 95–110, who writes on p. 110: "As important as the assimilation of the new social history of the Russian revolution is, the history of the Ukrainian revolution had something more to it than the Russian revolution: the national factor."

25. Ronald Grigor Suny, "Ambiguous Categories: States, Empires and Nations," *Post-Soviet Affairs*, 1995, vol. 11, no. 2, p. 192: "Muscovy and Imperial Russia were successful

in integrating the core regions of their empire, often referred to as the *vnutrenniye gubernii*, into a single nationality . . . but . . . maintained and intensified differences between the Russian core and the non-Russian peripheries." Interestingly enough, also in his *The Revenge of the Past. Nationalism, Revolution, and the Collapse of the Soviet Union*, (Stanford: Stanford University Press, 1993), Suny analyzes all the major nationalities problems in the Russian empire in and after 1917—with one exception, the Russians, as if the revolution and civil war had not been *the* Russian *national* problem.

26. Pipes, *Russia under the Bolshevik Regime*, p. 497.

27. Iurii Vladimirovich Got'e, *Time of Troubles*, translated, edited and introduced by Terence Emmons (Princeton: Princeton University Press, 1988), p. 103.

Earlier, on November 16, 1917, Got'e wrote: ". . . Russia is betraying and selling out, and the Russian people wreak havoc and raise hell and are absolutely indifferent to their international fate. It is an unprecedented event in world history when a numerous people, which considers itself a great people, a world power despite all kinds of qualifications, has in eight months dug itself a grave with its own hands. It follows that the very idea of a Russian power, a Russian nation, was a mirage, a bluff, that this only seemed to be so and was never a reality." (*Time of Troubles*, pp. 80–81.)

The view that "1917"—meaning November 1917—stands for a national catastrophe in Russian history has more recently been stated by many Russians, including those who blame the policies of the tsarist empire for the conditions that made that catastrophe possible. Thus, for example, Ilia Gerasimov, "Rossiyskaia mental'nost' i modernizatsiia," *Obshchestvennye nauki i sovremennost'*, no. 4 (1994), p. 72, sees in the year 1917 "the failure of the Russian national idea." (For an identical evaluation of 1917, see also Boris Zemtsov, " 'Otkuda est' poshla . . . rossiiskaia tsivilizatsiia,' " *Obshchestvennye nauki i sovremennost'*, no. 4 [1994], pp. 51–62.)

28. Ernest Gellner, "Nationalism in the Vacuum," in Alexander J. Motyl, ed., *Thinking Theoretically about Soviet Nationalities, History and Comparison in the Study of the USSR* (New York: Columbia University Press, 1992), p. 247.

29. Robert J. Kaiser, *The Geography of Nationalism in Russia and the USSR* (Princeton: Princeton University Press, 1994).

30. Piotr S. Wandycz, *Soviet-Polish Relations, 1917–1921* (Cambridge, MA: Harvard University Press, 1969), Norman Davies, *White Eagle, Red Star: The Polish-Soviet War, 1919–1920* (London: Macdonald, 1972), and Paul Latawski, ed., *The Reconstruction of Poland, 1914–1923* (London: Macmillan 1992).

31. For an argument that Soviet "internationalist" outlook should be taken seriously even when the USSR had allegedly been a nationalist power, see Roman Szporluk, "Conflict in Soviet Domestic and Foreign Policy: Universal Ideology and National Tradition," in William Zimmerman and Harold K. Jacobson, eds., *Behavior, Culture, and Conflict in World Politics* (Ann Arbor, MI: University of Michigan Press, 1993), pp. 275–90, in which some of relevant literature is cited.

32. For my earlier attempt to address this question see "After Empire: What?" *Daedalus*, vol. 123, no. 3 (Summer 1994), pp. 21–39.

33. There are many good studies of the Baltic states under the Soviets and their struggle for independence, e.g., Anatol Lieven, *The Baltic Revolution: Estonia, Latvia, Lithuania, and the Path to Independence* (New Haven: Yale University Press, 1993).

For a brief overview that includes the Balts, as well as West Ukrainians and West Belorussians and Moldavians, see Roman Szporluk, "The Soviet West—or Far Eastern Europe?" *East European Politics and Societies*, vol. 3, no. 3 (Fall 1991), pp. 466–82.

34. *The Soviet Bloc: Unity and Conflict*, by Zbigniew Brzezinski, originally published in 1960, is a classic.

35. Rupert Emerson, *From Empire to Nation. The Rise to Self-Assertion of Asian and African Peoples* (Boston: Beacon Press, 1960), p. 36.

36. Raymond Pearson, "The making of '89: Nationalism and the dissolution of communist Eastern Europe," *Nations and Nationalism*, vol. 1, no. 1 (1995), pp. 69–79, cit. on p. 75.

37. Eric Hobsbawm, *The Age of Extremes: A History of the World, 1914–1991* (New York: Pantheon Books), 1994, p. 492.

38. Ibid., p. 475.

39. Ernest Gellner, "Nationalism in the Vacuum," in Motyl, ed., *Thinking Theoretically*, p. 248.

40. Kenneth Minogue and Beryl Williams, "Ethnic Conflict in the Soviet Union: The Revenge of Particularism," in Motyl, ed., *Thinking Theoretically*, p. 241.

41. Benedict Anderson, *Imagined Communities:Reflections on the Origin and Spread of Nationalism* (London: Verso, 1983), p. 12, and rev. ed. (London and New York: Verso, 1991), p. xi.

42. See, for example, Joseph Rothschild, *Return to Diversity: A Political History of East Central Europe since World War II* (New York and Oxford: Oxford University Press, 1989), pp. 75 and 221, and Ken Jowitt, *New World Disorder:The Leninist Extinction* (Berkeley and Los Angeles: University of California Press, 1992), pp. 217–18.

43. Randall Collins, *Weberian Sociological Theory* (Cambridge and New York: Cambridge University Press, 1986), p. 203.

44. N.V. Ustrialov, "O sovetskoi natsii," in *Nashe vremia* (Shanghai: [no publ.], 1934), pp. 38–39, cited in Roman Szporluk, "Nationalities and the Russian Problem in the USSR," *Journal of International Affairs*, vol. 27, no. 1 (1973), p. 40. For the contrary argument that "the Soviet Union was not conceived or institutionalized as a nation-state," see Rogers Brubaker, "Nationhood and the national question in the Soviet Union and post-Soviet Eurasia: An institutional account," *Theory and Society*, vol. 23, no. 1 (February 1994), pp. 50–52. (See also Suny, "Ambiguous Categories," *Post-Soviet Affairs*, vol. 11, no. 2, p. 190, for this shocking comment: "There was shockingly little effort to create a 'Soviet nation.'") I would also qualify the view that the Soviets institutionalized ethnicity at the republic level. This was the case mainly in the cultural sphere. (Ukrainian schools existed only in Ukraine, Latvian—only in Latvia, etc.) Soviet propaganda took great pride that most republics were "already" multiethnic and were becoming more so; for this reason it singled out Kazakhstan, where Kazakhs were a minority, as a model Soviet republic. An interrepublic "exchange of cadres" was an openly proclaimed policy. For an excellent analysis of the Soviet approach to nationality and ethnicity see Teresa Rakowska-Harmstone, "Chickens Coming Home to Roost: A Perspective on Soviet Ethnic Relations," *Journal of International Affairs*, vol. 42, no. 2 (1992), pp. 519–48, and Anatoly M. Khazanov, *After the USSR: Ethnicity, Nationalism, and Politics in the Commonwealth of Independent States* (Madison and London: University of Wisconsin Press, 1995), pp. 3–51.

45. Eric Hobsbawm, *The Age of Extremes: A History of the World, 1914–1991* (New York: Pantheon Books, 1994), pp. 492–93.

46. Khazanov, *After the USSR*, p. 28. Cf. ibid., p. 231: "Authoritarian capitalism suppresses civil society but still has to tolerate . . . some forms of societal self-organization. . . . In contrast, totalitarian communism resulted in the utter destruction of civil society." Also, John A. Hall, *Coercion and Consent: Studies on the Modern State* (Cambridge: Polity Press, 1994), p. 146, stresses that "one important legacy of communism, namely its destruction of civil society . . . made the liberalization of communist regimes virtually impossible."

47. Collins, *Weberian Sociological Theory*, p. 204.

48. Ibid., p. 207.

49. John Barber, "Russia: a Crisis of Post-imperial Viability," in John Dunn, ed., *Contemporary Crisis of the Nation State*, p. 39. See also John B. Dunlop, *The Rise of Russia and the Fall of the Soviet Empire* (Princeton: Princeton University Press, 1993), and "Russia: Confronting a Loss Of Empire," in Ian Bremmer and Ray Taras, eds., *Nations and Politics in the Soviet Successor States* (Cambridge and New York: Cambridge University Press, 1993), pp. 43–72.

50. Barber, "Russia," ibid., p. 40,

51. George F. Kennan, "Witness to the Fall," *New York Review of Books*, November 16, 1995, p. 10. (Review of Jack F. Matlock, Jr., *Autopsy on an Empire: The American Ambassador's Account of the Collapse of the Soviet Union*. New York: Random House, 1995.)

52. Mark R. Beissinger, "The Persisting Ambiguity of Empire," *Post-Soviet Affairs*, p. 158.

53. Khazanov, *After the USSR*, pp. 239–40.

54. Roman Solchanyk, "Russia, Ukraine, and the Imperial legacy," *Post-Soviet Affairs*, vol. 9, no. 4 (1993), pp. 337–365, and "Ukraine, The (Former) Center, Russia, and 'Russia,'" *Studies in Comparative Communism*, vol. 25, no. 1 (March 1992), pp. 90–107, analyses the current political problem against a historical background.

55. "Rossiia v usloviakh strategicheskoi nestabil'nosti. (Materialy 'kruglogo stola')," *Voprosy filosofii*, no. 9 (1995), p. 7. It is ironic that Moiseyev also felt the need to tell his elite audience that "few people remember that during the seizure of Kazan all regiments of the Russian army were under command of Tatar princes—not those descended from Genghiskhan but the natives of the Volga region." (Ibid., p. 4.) (Moiseyev also had a strongly negative commentary on the West Ukrainians, who he thought had been corrupted by the Catholic West and thus had acquired a "mentality" more alien than that of the Tatars.)

56. According to Galina Starovoitova (lecture at Harvard University, March 12, 1996), the establishment of the "Islamic Party of Russia" and its participation in the elections of December 1995 should be seen as one of the repercussions of the Chechnia crisis in Russia's politics. For ethnopolitical processes among the Tatars and the Chuvash in Russia today, see Victor A. Shnirelman, *Who Gets the Past? Competition for Ancestors among Non-Russian Intellectuals in Russia* (Washington, D.C.: The Woodrow Wilson Center Press; Baltimore and London: The Johns Hopkins University Press, 1996).

57. Henry Kissinger, *Diplomacy* (New York: Simon and Schuster, 1994), p. 176. Kissinger concludes: "The Soviet Union would have been much better off had it stayed within its borders after the Second World War and established relations with what came to be known as the satellite orbit comparable to those it maintained with Finland." (Ibid.) This brings to mind Khazanov's maxim: "Overextension is a common pitfall of empires." (*After the USSR*, p. 10.)

58. See Aleksandr Solzhenitsyn, *"The Russian Question" at the End of the Twentieth Century*, trans. by Yermolai Solzhenitsyn (New York: Farrar, Straus and Giroux, 1995), pp. 104–105.

59. V.I. Kozlov, "Vymiranie russkikh: istoriko-demograficheskii krizis ili katastrofa?" *Vestnik Rossiiskoi Akademii Nauk*, vol. 65, no. 9 (September 1995), pp. 771–77. See also Mark G. Field, "The Health Crisis in the Former Soviet Union: A Report from the 'Post-War' Zone," *Social Science and Medicine*, vol. 41, no. 11 (1995), pp. 1469–78.

60. See Khazanov, *After the USSR*, pp. 247–71, for important data on ethnic trends in various parts of the former Soviet Union, especially in Central Asia and the Russian Federation.

61. Jack F. Matlock, Jr., *Autopsy of an Empire: The American Ambassador's Account of the Collapse of the Soviet Union* (New York: Random House, 1995), p. 737.
62. Ibid., pp. 738–39. For a discussion of Russian national and state identity in the framework of the Russian Federation today, see Marie Mendras, "La Russie dans les tetes," *Commentaire*, vol. 18, no. 71 (Automne 1995), pp. 501–9.

4

The Disintegration of the Habsburg and Ottoman Empires

A Comparative Analysis

Solomon Wank

There has been a great deal of scholarly interest in recent years in the rise and fall of empires. Since 1989, the topic has engendered four major conferences, including the one that produced the essays in this volume.[1] The works of, among others, Michael Doyle, Paul Kennedy, Alexander Motyl, William McCagg, Imanuel Geiss, Geir Lundestad, and S.N. Eisenstadt further attest to this interest.[2] The aforementioned works differ in chronological scope, historical focus, and level of abstraction, but they all point to empire as a form of political structure *sui generis,* with an inherent dynamic that leads, over time, to its decline and disappearance. "It is difficult to escape the conclusion," writes Geir Lundestad, "that empires contain within them the seeds of their own destruction."[3] This theoretical perspective raises several questions with regard to the disintegration of the Habsburg and Ottoman Empires. Was it more than a coincidence that, despite their obvious differences in foundational ideologies and military and administrative organizations, the Habsburg and Ottoman Empires from the sixteenth century onward, followed, in Cemal Kafadar's words, "more or less the same rhythms until both disappeared as ruling houses in the aftermath of the First World War"?[4] Was it the imperial structure of the two empires as such, and not any particular institutional or cultural characteristic, or the presence of diverse nationalities on their territories, that was their most basic feature and the one that inevitably led to their decay? Did the Habsburg and Ottoman Empires rise and fall according to a pattern that is more or less visible in the experiences of other historical empires?

The answers that emerge from the comparative analysis presented here of the disintegration of the Habsburg and Ottoman Empires tend to support the idea of the distinctive structure of empires and some general pattern underlying their rise and fall. The conclusions reached here are, however, offered without finality and in hope of furthering discussion. For practical reasons, this discussion will concentrate on the last one hundred years of the existence of the Habsburg and Ottoman Empires, with brief excursions into their earlier histories to illuminate the extended process leading to their collapse.

Several preliminary remarks are necessary before proceeding further. The first is a caveat. My field of detailed expertise is the Habsburg Empire; I lack an equivalent expertise in Ottoman history. I have gleaned what I know about the Ottoman Empire from secondary sources.[5] Hence, the parallels I draw between developments in the two empires may reflect the unequal fund of knowledge. A second caveat concerns the term *Habsburg Empire*. As used here it refers to the "German" Habsburg Empire that split off from the Spanish Habsburg Empire in 1521, after which the former went its own way. Another geographical note relates to the papers's concentration on the European (Rumelian) part of the Ottoman Empire. In part, this is because I am more familiar with developments in the Balkans than in Asia Minor, but the emphasis is justified also on grounds of relative importance. Bernard Lewis points out that "Rumelia . . . [was] the main centre and stronghold of the Empire and the home of its governing *élites*[6] . . . and the Balkans [were] for long the centre of gravity of the Ottoman Empire."[7]

A third preliminary remark concerns the discussion in this chapter of the "health" of the Habsburg and Ottoman Empires on the eve of war in 1914. In order to avoid misunderstanding, it is important to stress that the analysis here is not a comparison of the wide range of political, social, economic, and cultural activities in the two empires. Health refers to the health of the imperial political structure as manifested in the center–periphery relationship. It is in this regard that the two empires are commensurable. The following section is offered to clarify what I mean.

"The Sick Man of Europe"

There is general agreement among historians that the Ottoman Empire in 1914 was "the sick man of Europe"—internally and externally weak and in the throes of a continuing process of disintegration, with its leaders desperately trying to save what was left of their empire. The Habsburg Empire, on the other hand, was, according to several recent Habsburg historians, holding up well, and was not at all comparable to the decrepit Ottoman Empire. These historians dismiss all talk of the decline and fall of the Habsburg Empire as "misplaced determinism."[8] Rather than a long process of decline leading to the empire's dissolution, they see a quite different historical trajectory. After almost falling apart in the revolutions of 1848, the Habsburg Empire rebounded and grew stronger instead of declining. On the eve of World War I, the empire was, according to these same historians, more stable and prosperous than at any time in its modern history, and the nationalities problem had abated.[9] Elsewhere, I have argued that there is some validity to this rosy picture with regard to economic growth but not very much with regard to political stability or the abatement of the nationalities problem. In fact, a considerable amount of instability existed beneath the surface.[10] The surface stability might be interpreted as resignation on the part of the leaders of the various nationalities in the face of existing political and diplomatic realities in the years before 1914, rather than as acceptance of the empire as such. Thomas Masayrk spoke for many non-German and non-Magyar national leaders when he stated in 1913:

> Just because I cannot indulge in dreams of its [the Habsburg Empire's] collapse and know that whether good or bad, it will continue, I am most deeply concerned that we should make something of this Austria."[11]

If Masayrk and the leaders of the various nationalities resigned themselves to the perceived reality that the Habsburg Empire might continue to exist for some indefinite period, they did so without committing themselves to perpetuate it in its existing form. In the given situation, they concentrated on improving the positions of their ethnic groups within the existing structure, while at the same time they continued to press for some form of autonomy, which generated pressures within the system that produced an underlying instability.[12]

The question of the health of the Habsburg Empire in 1914 may be debatable, but it is also beside the point. Whatever its socioeconomic condition, the imperial Habsburg political elite saw its empire as bordering on dissolution—the next candidate for sick man of Europe. Four days before Austria–Hungary's declaration of war on Serbia, Count Alexander Hoyos, a highly ranked foreign ministry official and one of the architects of the war policy, declared in a tone of anguished bravado: "We are still capable of resolve! We do not want to nor ought to be a sick man. Better to be destroyed quickly."[13] In a more subdued tone, Baron Leopold von Andrian-Werburg, the highly respected and influential Austro-Hungarian consul general in Warsaw (1911–14), summed up the same mindset in his account of the beginning of the war, written in 1916 and only recently published.

> Before the murder of the archduke and also after the murder, there prevailed under the impression of our weak behavior during the Balkan war, deep depression among our military leaders and in the diplomatic milieu surrounding the [foreign] minister. . . . We are heading for collapse and partition and do not defend ourselves. . . . After Turkey comes Austria. That is the catchword in Eastern Europe.[14]

The sense of impending doom strongly influenced the imperial political elite's calculations in favor of war in July 1914. Pessimism about the future was, of course, not exclusive to Habsburg statesmen. To a greater or lesser extent—an important distinction—domestic pressures impinged upon foreign policy in all of the major European countries.[15] However, only in Vienna was the pessimism so deep that it led the emperor and his advisers to initiate the war of 1914.[16]

There is a curious paradox in the juxtaposition of social and economic progress with elite fears of imminent dissolution. Even those historians who positively assess the former acknowledge the existence of the latter without, however, trying to explain it, beyond describing the fear as unjustified or irrational.[17] But there is no contradiction here. What triggered the imperial Habsburg elite's fears of the imminent dissolution of the empire were the effects of relatively rapid and uneven economic growth on the social and nationalist movements since 1848. These movements strengthened the centrifugal forces in the empire, while at the same time they weakened the ties between the imperial center at Vienna and the peripheral regions that were the bases of imperial rule. From the perspective of the Habsburg ruler and his advisers, the deterioration of the relationship between Vienna and its various crown lands indeed gave cause for pessimism.

Of course, the emperor and the Habsburg imperial elite had options. Some form of reorganization along federal lines might have given the Habsburg state a new lease on life. But even if that were possible, Otto Brunner is correct in pointing out that such a reform would have spelled the end of the Habsburg Empire and the imperial concept no less than if they had been destroyed by war and revolution. Neither Emperor Francis Joseph I (1848–1916) nor the heir apparent Archduke Francis Ferdinand, Brunner continues, could have sponsored such a reorganization, even if they had possessed the freedom to do so.[18] Much the same can be said about the last Ottoman sultans and their advisers. Roderic Davison points out that all of the reform efforts by the traditional elite and the Young Turks in the one hundred years before the Ottoman Empire's disintegration were aimed at preserving the empire, that is, maintaining the hegemony of the imperial center; for that reason their efforts failed.[19] The rulers and political elites of both empires clung to eroded ideas of dynastic-imperial power and universalism, a point to which I return later in the section, "Decay and Decline of the Habsburg and Ottoman Empires."

It is worth noting that even a victory by the Central Powers in World War I probably would not have ensured the continuations of the Habsburg and Ottoman states as empires. Alan Sked argues that if the Central Powers had won the war the Habsburg Empire "would have survived intact and probably expanded."[20] This argument, however, is belied by Sked's claim that in the event of victory the empire would have been reduced to a military and economic appendage of Germany, "with little future as an independent state."[21] Survival in that condition would have been tantamount to the end of the Habsburg Empire as an imperial political construct. The same is true for the Ottoman Empire. Germany's *Mitteleuropa* plans called for the reduction of Turkey to a vassal state.[22] "We must ... prepare ourselves for the fact," reported the Austro-Hungarian military attaché in Constantinople, "that the Germans will strive to consider all of Turkey as their exclusive area for expansion."[23]

The Pattern of Empire

The Habsburg and Ottoman Empires, like all historical empires, were collections of formerly independent or potentially independent historical-political entities that came under the sway of the Habsburg and Osmanli dynasties. The two empires—again, like all historical empires—were not really *states* in the sense of a society "characterized by the integration of its components" into a single political community of "social interaction and cultural values."[24] An imperial government, Michael Doyle continues, "is a sovereignty that lacks a community" and "the influence of shared commitments."[25] That was true of the Habsburg and Ottoman Empires. Ottoman leaders, according to Roderic Davison, "served faith and state but they had no sense of solidarity with the people they ruled."[26] William McNeill states that "Ottoman rulers and ruled shared common values across a narrow range of encounter."[27] The lack of a coherent *Staatsidea* binding together the domains of the Habsburg Empire was recognized by a prominent adviser to Emperor Francis Joseph I, foreign minister Count Gustav Kálnoky, who opined in the mid-1880s:

> Since the time when the Habsburg territorial possessions were first united, the monarchy has developed more in the sense of a power [*Macht*] than in the sense of a state [*Staat*]. Power and purpose in external matters were more recognizable than its purpose as a state.[28]

The absence of any coherent internal purpose and the failure to create a common identity eroded the legitimacy of both empires, and created a vacuum that was eventually filled by new nationalisms.

Efforts by the Habsburg and Ottoman governments in the second half of the nineteenth century to counter nationalist movements by fostering a common identity, which is discussed in the section "Decay and Decline of the Habsburg and Ottoman Empires," came much too late. Alexander Motyl maintains that for imperial integration to be successful an empire must be territorially contiguous and the relative power of the core elite must be "overwhelming" compared to that of the peripheral elites. Incorporation must come during an empire's ascendancy, when the core is "still flush with victory ... , peripheral elites are still resource poor ... , and international threats are minimal."[29] Measured by these criteria, the Habsburg and Ottoman attempts at integration were bound to fail. By the second half of the nineteenth century, both empires were declining and neither empire's core elites and ethnic groups (Germans and Turks, respectively) were strong enough relative to peripheral elites and territorial nationalities to incorporate them into an imperial or state nationality.

The Germans were the largest single nationality in the Habsburg Empire, but they were not a majority, and no one nationality constituted a majority. The Germans made up a relatively small segment of the population, considerably smaller than, say, the Russians did during the tsarist empire. In 1910, 12 million Germans (1.9 million in the Hungarian part of the empire) made up 23.9 percent of the Habsburg Empire's total population of 51 million. By comparison, the Magyars comprised 20.2 percent, Slavs 45 percent, Romanians 6.4 percent, and Italians 2 percent. Czechs and Poles, the two strongest Slavic nationalities, comprised 12.6 percent and 10 percent respectively. With the exception of an increase of Magyars and Poles and a small decrease in the number of Germans (chiefly through assimilation in Hungary), the population shares of the empire's nationalities changed little between 1880 and 1910. So, for example, in 1910, Germans made up 35.6 percent of the Austrian part of the empire's 28 million people. This is a slight decrease from 36.8 percent in 1880, but it was enough to arouse fears of demographic stagnation and feelings of vulnerability that contributed to the development of a defensive nationalism, especially in the German areas of Bohemia.[30]

In the Ottoman Empire, the relative size and growth rate of the Turks compared to the various minorities is difficult to determine. Ottoman census methods classified the population by religious (*millet*) affiliation. This was true even of the first truly comprehensive census of 1881–82, and succeeding censuses.[31] The total population of the Ottoman Empire in 1876 is estimated at 35 million—15 million in Europe and 20 million in Asia and Africa. Muslims numbered 21 million against 14 million Christians. The latter were overwhelmingly Greek Orthodox, but not necessarily ethnic Greeks. The Turks, the largest single nationality, numbered 12.8 million—2.1 million in Europe, and most of the rest in Anatolia. Of 9 million non-Turkish Muslims, 4.7 million were Arabs. The Slavs, the largest non-Muslim ethnic group, numbered 6.2 million, Armenians 2.4 million, and Greeks 2 million.[32] The number of Turks seems to have remained about the same until 1914, although after the 1878 Treaty of Berlin, their relative share of the population increased.[33] The treaty stripped the empire of its major Balkan possessions, removing 6.5 million Christians from Ottoman control.[34] That transformed the Ottoman state into a largely Muslim one whose main territory lay in Asia Minor and the Middle East. Census reports reflect the change. Between 1881–82 and 1906, the total Ottoman population increased from 17.1 million to 20.9 million. Muslims numbered 12.5 million and non-Muslims 4.5 million in the 1881–82 census; in 1906 the figures were 15.5 million and 5.5 million.[35] The number of non-Muslims had declined by 1914 to 3.5 million out of a total population of 18.5 million as the empire shrank even more after the Balkan Wars of 1912–13.[36] The Turks became a majority of the population but in an economically backward empire that was in an advanced stage of decay.[37]

The lack of homogeneity in empires is derived from the way they are created and ruled. Empires, Alexander Motyl writes, are formed by transforming "distinct societies with autonomous institutions and regional elites into politically subordinate civil societies."[38] The distinctiveness of the subordinated societies continues to exist, but their political sovereignty has been extinguished or sharply reduced. In effect, the elites of the subordinated societies are reduced to the status of vassals. The relationship between the imperial center (the hereditary lands with their seat in Vienna for the Habsburgs and in Anatolia and Constantinople [later Istanbul] for the Osmanli dynasty[39]) and the peripheral societies is an institutionalized one of power and long duration.[40] The object of the relationship is the establishment of an imperial peace—never perfectly achieved—within the subordinated territories that allows the extraction of adequate resources from the peripheral societies to maintain the necessary political unity and military capacity to support the imperial ambitions of the ruler and his advisers. Their policies aim at maximizing their independence by freeing them from the restraints imposed by traditional elites and power structures and at gaining control over men, money, and resources.[41]

The survival of the political system of empires requires the continuous existence of a delicate balance between traditional and nontraditional elements and between the limited political participation of segments of the population—traditional aristocracy, some urban groups, religious groups, parts of the peasantry (in some cases)—and the noninvolvement of the majority.[42] Democracy and empire are incompatible. Empire, by definition, denotes a relationship of political inequality. Recognition of the political equality and sovereignty of the peripheral societies empowers the latter to act in opposition to the will of the center, or even to secede from the empire. At that point empire ceases to exist. There can be territorially discontiguous empires that can have democratic centers and undemocratic peripheries, but this cannot be the case with contiguous territorial empires. It does not seem possible to reconcile, in the same territorial entity, the absolutist intentions of imperial bureaucratic rule in the contiguous peripheral societies with political liberty and participatory government in the center.[43]

The central purpose of empire is expansion. The ruler and his advisers are animated by a religious or secular ideological doctrine, seen as embodying universal truths, whose spread they see as their historical mission. The Habsburg and Ottoman rulers saw themselves in that light in the period of the ascendancy of their empires, and even afterward. The Habsburgs legitimated their rule in terms of their family's historical role as the holders of the crown of the Holy Roman Empire and as the protectors of Catholic Christendom. The Ottoman rulers regarded themselves as torchbearers for Islam. Decay and decline occur when the historical mission encounters barriers to its expansion and the empire loses its universalistic credentials. At that point the empire turns from the offensive to the defensive. The Ottoman and Habsburg Empires reached that point in the eighteenth century. The view that the Ottoman Empire started to decline as early as the mid-sixteenth century seems controverted by the fact that the Ottoman state was still strong enough "to threaten Europe at the doors of Vienna" in 1683.[44]

Imperial decay is the erosion of the hegemonic center–periphery relationship. It inevitably sets in when the ruler, in order to preserve the integrity of his empire, accords to some or all of the peripheral territories a greater degree of autonomy vis-à-vis the center. This strategy, however, contradicts the absolutist basis[45] on which imperial rule rests and therefore ultimately backfires, increasing the regionalist self-identification of vassals, their claims on financial and material resources, and the demands of protonationalist regional elites. Maintaining the delicate balance of forces and interests necessary for the independence of the center becomes increasingly difficult. Together, these developments decrease the resources drawn from the provinces, weaken the independence of the center, delegitimate the imperial ideology, and accelerate imperial decay. Imperial decay leads to the weakening of the state's power and its capacity to compete internationally. The decay of state power, in turn, leads to territorial diminution by a process of attrition as rival powers pick off peripheral lands. The strategies of the ruler and his advisers to arrest decline all tend to be counterproductive and lead to crisis situations. Eventually the linked processes of imperial decay and decline result in the severing of the bonds between center and periphery as well as the emergence or re-emergence of previously subordinated historical-political entities.[46] This chain of events concisely describes what happened to the Habsburg and Ottoman Empires in the last one hundred years of their existences.

Decay and Decline of the Habsburg and Ottoman Empires

Like all empires, the Habsburg Empire was created—in the sixteenth and seventeenth centuries—largely by war and conquest, although the process was helped along by some brilliant marital contracts.[47] There are instances of what Karen Dawisha, in chapter 14, calls autocolonization, whereby a polity voluntarily subordinates itself to an external power for security or economic reasons,[48] but there is scarcely a major historical empire in which military force has not played a major role in its expansion. Again, like all empires, the internal confusion and weakness of the surrounding geographical area created a power vacuum that afforded the Habsburgs an opportunity for expansion. The collapse of the Bohemian and Hungarian kingdoms in the wake of the Ottoman advance into central Europe in the early sixteenth century provided that opportunity for the Habsburgs. By the end of the seventeenth century, the Habsburg Empire had emerged as a European great power following wars against Bohemia, Hungary, and the Ottoman Empire. However, the political unity of the empire was still tenuous despite some victories over internal feudal elements, such as the transformation of the dynasty's status from elected to hereditary rulers of Bohemia and Hungary, the development of some institutions of bureaucratic centralization, and the formation of a standing army. As R.J.W. Evans writes, Habsburg rule in Austria, Bohemia, and Hungary "subsisted on a community of interest between dynasty, aristocracy, and the Catholic church" and, as in the Holy Roman Empire in its entirety, of which the Habsburgs were perennially elected emperors, "loyalty became a calculation, not a sort of disembodied idealism." The Habsburg Empire, he writes, was "a complex and subtly balanced organism, not a 'state' but a mildly centripetal agglutination of bewilderingly heterogeneous elements." [49] As such, it was unable to compete with other centralized and protonational states in the more aggressive and competitive eighteenth-century international arena. Prussia's invasion and annexation of the rich Habsburg duchy of Silesia in 1740 was a herald of this new world. The response of the Habsburg dynasty was internal reform.

The Ottoman Route to a "Mildly Centripetal State"

Much of what is said in the previous paragraph about the Habsburg Empire can be said about the Ottoman Empire as well, although the process by which the latter became "a mildly centripetal state" at the end of the seventeenth century was somewhat different than that of the former. The Habsburgs started out from a feudal base and moved toward centralization. The Ottomans, in contrast, moved from a highly centralized state that coincided with the period of expansion to a more indirect but still centralized form of control. As in the Habsburg Empire, the Ottoman rulers exploited a power vacuum in their region: the fighting among the Balkan states to establish boundaries and the collapse of the Byzantine Empire in the mid-fourteenth century gave the Ottomans their opening. Through almost constant warfare since the fourteenth century, Ottoman rulers built a gargantuan empire spread over three continents—Europe, Asia, and Africa.

The Ottoman Empire reached the apex of centralized absolutism in the sixteenth century. However, the sheer size of the empire, together with economic adversity (devaluation of silver coins and a shift in trade routes), made direct control of the periphery increasingly difficult. Therefore, in the seventeenth century, the sultan and his advisers shifted to a method of indirect control that complemented centralization. They "combined a patrimonial system of rule with a brokerage style of centralization." [50] They bargained with and co-opted both the local Muslim notables (*ayans*) and the bandit/mercenary soldiers who challenged the authority of the center. The bargaining process was helped by the fact that the ayans held their lands as a form of prebend from the sultan and did not have roots in the areas in which they held land.[51] In essence "the state incorporated or legitimized these groups"[52] by offering them favors and rewards. The result was a system of indirect control based on local notables who became agents of the central government and saw their advantage in preserving the existing social order and not opposing the state apparatus.

Although it provides evidence of the flexibility of the Ottoman ruler and his advisers, this alliance of dynasty, local notables, and bandit/mercenary soldiers faced the same military, administrative, and financial pressures in the eighteenth century that the Habsburg Empire did. A series of lost wars and weakening control over peripheral areas to the advantage of the ayans brought the empire into a parlous state. The ayans had taken on the character of a hereditary, landed aristocracy permanently residing in their regions, who used private armies and their bargaining power with the government to acquire regional benefits and autonomy from the state.[53] The wake-up call for the Ottoman government was the disastrous 1774 Treaty of Küçhük Kaynarca that concluded a war with Russia. The treaty extended Russian territory along the Black Sea, which ceased to be an Ottoman lake, and recognized Russia as the protector of Orthodox Christians within the Ottoman Empire. Just as the loss of Silesia spurred Habsburg efforts at reform, the Treaty of Küçhük Kaynarca similarly catalyzed the Ottoman sultan and his advisers.[54]

Habsburg Strategies to Shore Up the Empire

In response to Prussia's grab of Silesia, the Habsburgs, from 1740 until 1848, vigorously pursued a policy of centralized royal absolutism and a German-speaking imperial administration as they strove to build a modern autocratic state. The abrogation of local governments and local privileges, which was a corollary of the policy, triggered a rebellion by the regional nobilities during the reign of Joseph II (1780–90) that took the form of protonationalism. Leopold II (1790–92), Joseph's successor, mollified the opposition by repealing or modifying some of his predecessor's more far-reaching reforms, but the general direction of Habsburg policy, underpinned by resistance to the French Revolution, remained the same.[55] Following the revolutions of 1848, the failure of neoabsolutism, the lost wars of 1859 and 1866, and the pressure of modernizing forces, the Habsburgs reversed course. In order to ensure the prolongation of their empire in increasingly difficult political circumstances, they inadvertently sponsored a degree of pluralism and diversity while continuing to rule over a hierarchical and undemocratic state. Their rule had become overextended and their ability to extract resources from the provinces had diminished. The loss of the rich provinces of Lombardy and Venetia—besides serving as a symptom of the empire's growing weakness—drained away manpower, money, and resources. Holding onto their possessions now compelled the Hapsburgs to decentralize their power.

In keeping with the new policy of limited decentralization, the Habsburg ruler and his advisers negotiated the Compromise of 1867 with the Magyar oligarchy, creating a quasi-federal structure consisting of two centralized, quasi-parliamentary states—"pseudo-democratic Hungary and half-democratic Austria"[56]—and three semi-absolutist joint ministries (war, foreign affairs, and finance). The compromise gave the Magyar oligarchy control over the other ethnic groups in the Hungarian kingdom and a virtual veto over all further efforts to remodel the empire.[57] In this limited sense, Habsburg leaders acknowledged that nationalism had grown in intensity since 1848; even in this limited degree, however, decentralization and recognition of nationalism led to the formation of national constituencies that vied with the Vienna imperial center for power and delegitimated the supranational imperial ideology, which further accelerated imperial decay.

The most obvious example of the empire's limited response to nationalism is, of course, the above-mentioned Compromise of 1867, which gave the empire a deceptive stability for fifty years, but at the price of alienating most of the Slavs, with the exception of the Poles in the Austrian part of the empire. In return for their acceptance of the compromise and their support in the Austrian Parliament, the Polish magnates were granted their own compromise with the Habsburgs in 1869. The compromise gave Galicia virtual autonomy and made Polish the official language there. The compromise also gave the Polish elite domination over the Ruthenians and the Jews, who together constituted the majority in the province. These favorable arrangements did not alter the fact that the Poles always aimed for secession and the reestablishment of an independent Poland.[58] Beyond the Compromise of 1867, the emperor and his advisers sought to preserve their independence by playing one nationality against another—that is, "to maintain a more-or-less balanced and equitable distribution of dissatisfaction."[59] So, for example, they helped nurture the Ukrainian nationality (Ruthenians) in Eastern Galicia to counter the Poles and to emphasize the differences between Ruthenians (in Ruthenian, Rusyn) and Russians.[60] That strategy, otherwise known as divide and rule, was counterproductive; the concession to nationalist aspirations on which the strategy was based strengthened national elites and stoked the fires of national rivalry, which later disrupted internal tranquillity.

Ottoman Strategies to Shore Up the Empire

In the mid-nineteenth-century Ottoman Empire, the sultan and his advisers were engaged in the same struggle as the Habsburgs. Roderic Davison, in his study of the midcentury (1856–76) reform efforts, writes:

> They [Ottoman statesmen] were struggling to keep the empire as a going administrative concern and as a territorial unit; looking for some centripetal force or form of organization, as also was the similarly heterogeneous Habsburg Empire in the same years.[61]

Earlier, in response to the challenge of Western military superiority in the eighteenth century, Ottoman leaders had taken a path of reform similar to that taken in the Habsburg Empire under Empress Maria Theresa (1740–80) and Emperor Joseph II. During the reigns of Sultan Selim III (1789–1807) and Mahmut II (1808–39), Ottoman officials redrew their institutions along lines of

Western enlightened absolutism.[62] Indeed, Ottoman bureaucrats at the end of the eighteenth century showed growing interest in Habsburg administrative systems.[63] Like Joseph II's centralizing measures, Selim III's efforts to regain control over local and provincial governments, to establish a new regular army, and to abolish tax farming led to a rebellion by groups whose power and privileges were threatened by these reforms: ayans; janissaries (military elite); *ulema* (doctors of religious law) who feared the influence of French revolutionary ideas; and conservatives in general. These groups succeeded in overthrowing Selim III in 1807. Nevertheless, his successor, cautiously at first, continued his policy of centralization and modernization.[64] However, as in the Habsburg Empire, adverse internal and external circumstances—rebellions by subject peoples, military defeats, lost territories, and pressure by the Great Powers to enact domestic reforms—compelled a change in policy.

The course that Ottoman statesmen adopted in the mid-century reform era, which followed Western lines, was similar to the one chosen by Habsburg policy makers: limited decentralization for areas still under direct Ottoman control, and broader autonomy for peripheral areas such as Lebanon, Syria, Egypt, Serbia, Montenegro, and the Romanian principalities, which already enjoyed varying degrees of self-government. Local and provincial councils were introduced into those areas still under direct control of the center. In an attempt to depoliticize national feeling, the sultan issued an edict in 1856 that proclaimed the equality of all subjects of the empire regardless of their ethnic or religious background. The supranational idea formed the basis of the concept of Ottomanism (Osmanlilik). A form of official nationalism, Ottomanism developed in reaction to the rise of popular national movements and defined a more modern and secular form of political allegiance based on common Ottoman citizenship in a common Ottoman community.[65]

The purpose of Ottomanism was to counter the growing nationalist and separatist tendencies in some of the millets, especially the Christian ones in the Balkans, which were abetted by the Great Powers (Austria-Hungary, France, Germany, Great Britain, and Russia). The logical result of the principles of equality and common Ottoman citizenship should have been the elimination of the millet system, which was based on religious communities; but the system was not abolished, rather it was reformed in the 1860s. The reforms strengthened the empire's centrifugal tendencies by diminishing the power of the clergy and increasing the influence of laypeople and the emphasis on secular education.[66] Taken together, the millet reforms reemphasized the lack of homogeneity and strengthened the separate identities of the Balkan peoples; both effects deepened nationalist feelings.[67] The reforms culminated in the Constitution of 1876, which was handed down from on high by the sultan and his advisers. The constitution created a central parliament based on a restrictive suffrage and left a great deal of appointive and decision-making power in the hands of the sultan and his officials.[68] The reforms failed to mollify the sultan's discontented subjects; the more the government conceded to its discontented people, the more their appetites were whetted. In all probability, there was nothing the Ottoman government could have done to lessen the desire of the Balkan peoples to secede. Four centuries of the millet system had preserved, at least in a dormant form, an awareness of distinct nationalities that was made more conscious by French revolutionary ideas of nationalism, which filtered into the Balkan Peninsula through various channels. In effect, the non-Turkish nationalities passed from a millet consciousness to a national consciousness without ever passing through an Ottoman consciousness. Be that as it may, the underlying motive of the reformers precluded any solution that might have gained the loyalty of the Balkan Christians and their acceptance of the Ottoman state. In the first place, most of the reforms were introduced to garner the goodwill of the Great Powers and/or to stave off their intervention in domestic affairs.[69] The Constitution of 1876 was promulgated after the rebellions in Bosnia-Herzegovina and Bulgaria, and was seen as a "device for turning the tables on the Great Powers by guaranteeing equality for all Ottomans, thereby blocking special reforms for particular ethnic and religious groups."[70]

It soon became apparent to the sultan that the constitution did nothing to deter the Great Powers from pressing for domestic reforms favorable to Ottoman Christians. The sultan next dissolved the parliament and suspended the constitution after several deputies criticized the government. The sultan then "gradually reinstated the neopatrimonial regime."[71] The sultan and his advisers, including most of the bureaucratic reformers, were not committed to constitutionalism and parliamentary government, which they saw as hazardous in a multireligious and multinational state. Their primary objective was preservation of the empire; that is, preservation of the unity and central control of the empire by the sultan and his government.[72] Consequently, the idea of a federal political organization, which was raised in some quarters, was never seriously considered for the same reason that the Habsburgs rejected genuine federalism: it ran counter to the bases of imperial rule.[73] The concept of Ottomanism, too, served the same primary objective of strengthening imperial rule, thereby vitiating its legitimating power.

The Problem of Legitimacy in the Habsburg and Ottoman Empires

After 1867, the Habsburg dynasty had a legitimacy problem of its own. The Habsburgs found it difficult to justify their ostensibly supranational rule vis-à-vis national elites and masses. Their supranational ideology was derived from their historical roles as Holy Roman Emperors and protectors of Christendom, but the dynasty itself "was in some irreducible sense German,"[74] and the members of the imperial elite, regardless of ethnic origin, felt themselves bound to the German *Kulturnation*. Consequently, the dynasty, the court, and the imperial government increasingly appeared German. Since the eighteenth century, the Habsburg ideal of government (sometimes referred to as the *österreichische Staatsidee*) was a centralized, unified state run by German-speaking bureaucrats and military leaders, though Emperor Francis Joseph I was forced to modify that ideal in the course of the nineteenth century to hold onto the dynasty's possessions. For the foregoing reasons, the concept of Austrianism (Österreichertum)—requiring patriotic allegiance to an Austrian fatherland rather than to a dynasty, and equivalent to Ottomanism as a form of official nationalism—made little headway outside of bureaucratic, military and court circles and among German-Austrians for whom Austrianism and Germandom (Deutschtum) became fused in a variant form of German nationalism. There was support for the concept of Austrianism among some minorities, such as the Jews, who sought Habsburg protection against strong nationalist groups. The dynastic supranational ideology was further weakened by the fact that, in practice, the Habsburgs' rule favored the Germans and the Magyars. The vital interests of the Habsburgs, preeminently the empire's designation as a Great Power, became intertwined with those of the two nationalities. Count Kálnoky, the Austro-Hungarian foreign minister, made that explicit in his memorandum of the 1880s:

> The governance of the empire, which is based on the one hand, on that nationality [the Magyars] whose interests are most securely tied to its continued existence and, on the other, on that nationality [the Germans] whose moral defection would involve the question of the very existence of the monarchy, is the logical justification for the dualistic system from the standpoint of foreign policy.[75]

Austrianism also was counterproductive. It alienated non-Germans and non-Magyars and strengthened demands for national autonomy.

As indicated earlier, the Ottoman Empire had a similar problem with legitimacy. It, too, failed to develop a sense of belonging in the minds of its subjects. The Osmanli dynasty, to paraphrase R.J.W. Evans's point about the Habsburgs, was in some irreducible sense Turkish. Submission to Islam, the caliphate, and the Ottoman sultan hid the reality that the Ottoman state "was in fact though not theory a Turkish state."[76] Turkish leaders were conscious of their ethnic individuality from early times. Many nineteenth-century statesmen who espoused the concept of Ottomanism as a new form of patriotism that focused on country rather than dynasty believed, for the most part, in a Turkish colorization of Ottomanism.[77] The exclusive use of Turkish symbols to promote Ottoman patriotism jarred many non-Turkish intellectuals.[78] For that reason, the concept of Ottomanism suffered the same fate as Austrianism. Some non-Turkish and non-Muslim groups that identified with Ottomanism—such as the Jews and Kutzovlachs, who had little hopes for a separate existence—were a quantité negligiable. Others saw Ottomanism as a useful weapon against rival national groups, without having the least interest in creating a hyphenated nationalism such as Greek-Ottoman or Macedonian-Ottoman. In the end, none of the non-Muslim nationalities, with the exceptions noted just previously, were prepared to identify with the Ottoman Empire and strongly support its continued existence. The Young Turk revolution of July 1908 did little to change that.

Nationalism and Empire in Young Turk Ideology

The revolution generated a great deal of optimism at first. The Constitution of 1876 was restored, and Balkan Christians, Kurds, Armenians, and other peoples of the empire believed that they would be granted broader self-government and recognition of their national rights. Arab leaders advocated the transformation of the Ottoman Empire into a dual Arab-Turkish state, similar to Austria-Hungary. The optimism lasted for only a short time. The restoration of the 1876 constitution did not really mean the advent of representative government or an end to the millet system. This would have been the case even if the pressure of external events, such as Austria-Hungary's annexation of Bosnia-Herzegovina in October 1908, could be seen to justify an authoritarian regime.

The Young Turk ideology, rooted in the antidemocratic theories of Gustave Le Bon, was elitist and antithetical to constitutionalism and parliamentary government.[79] Like mid-nineteenth-century Ottoman reformers, the Young Turks "considered the constitution, as a useful tool in fending off the intervention of the Great Powers in Ottoman politics."[80] The Young Turk revolution was nationalist in essence and called for a central authority and Turkish domination of the empire.[81] As the British ambassador reported to the foreign office, "Ottoman means Turk."[82] The strong Turkish nationalism of the Young Turks developed several years before the revolution, in response to the Great Powers' economic penetration and political intervention in the empire.[83] The ultimate and desperate concern of the Young Turks was the survival of the empire. They were determined not to weaken it or their hold over it. Like Kálnoky, the Habsburg foreign minister who believed that the Germans and Magyars should be favored because they offered the strongest support for the international position of the Habsburg Empire, so the Young Turks believed that the control of the Ottoman Empire should be in the hands of the Turks, who were numerically the most significant nationality in the empire.[84] Consequently, the period of Young Turk rule turned the Ottoman Empire into an arena of bitter nationalist struggles. While these struggles contributed to the end of the empire, the Turkish nationalist slant of Ottomanism and Young Turkism also prepared the ground for the modern Turkish nationalism that became the foundational ideology of the Turkish republic in 1923. The republic, shorn of most of its non-Turkish provinces, emerged out of defeats in World War I only after Young Turk dreams of a Pan-Islamic or Pan-Turanan empire—the latter incorporating the Turkish people who inhabited territories extending from Europe to the Pacific—"proved to be merely dreams."[85]

Decay of the Center–Periphery Relationship and Decline of Habsburg and Ottoman State Power

By 1914, Vienna was declining as an imperial city: the policies of the emperor and his advisers no longer represented the whole empire or even the Austrian part of it, except in military and foreign affairs, and not even in those areas completely. So, for example, the right conceded to the Hungarian government by the emperor, in 1902, to sign international treaties in its own name, compromised the formerly exclusive monarchical prerogative of representing the entire empire in international affairs.[86] Other than Budapest, power had shifted to the peripheries of the empire, to new nationalist political forces in the new power centers of Prague, Kraców, Zagreb, and Lvov, which were pulling away from the center, that is, from Vienna and the Habsburg hereditary lands. The emperor and the court became more and more unable to relate to the most important conflicting forces in the empire. The imperial state became an abstraction, and the emperor's strength more symbolic than real.

The relative economic backwardness of the Habsburg Empire compared to the other great powers made it difficult to draw subsidies from the periphery to serve the center, and the organizational inefficiency of the imperial structure diminished its military capacity and undermined its prestige as a great power. From the point of view of the emperor and his advisers, the ability of the empire to play the role of a great power was the sole justification for its existence, even though it lacked the requisite political and economic conditions. Any other policy, such as withdrawal or disengagement—that is, accepting the status of a middling power, which would have accorded with perceptions of it within the European concert—was rejected, because such moves would be a sign of weakness and would convey the wrong signal to all of the domains under Habsburg control. It was the determination of the ruler and his advisers to preserve the shaky imperial structure and restore the empire's reputation as a great power that motivated them to seek salvation in war in 1914, as they had done in 1859 and 1866. In that sense, the war was not an accident, of which the collapse of the Habsburg Empire was an unfortunate by-product; rather it was a symptom of the systemic crisis of the imperial structure.

If anything, the Ottoman Empire, in 1914, was far more economically backward, militarily incapable, and organizationally inefficient than the Habsburg Empire, and it had lost the bulk of its European territories as well. The new frontiers established after the Balkan Wars of 1912–13 were vulnerable to Greece and Bulgaria. True, the Ottomans still had a large empire in the Middle East, but even there the center's control over the periphery was weakening, as the idea of nationalism had emerged as an animating political force among the Arabs in the two decades before the wars.[87] Enver Pasha, the Young Turk leader and influential minister of war, and those in his circle saw the situation as so threatening that they persuaded themselves that it had to be changed, by force if necessary. Enver Pasha and his faction realized that this could lead to a European or world war. In such a war, they concluded that the interests of the Ottoman Empire would lie on the side of the victory of Germany and Austria-Hungary.[88] While the war might be European or worldwide in scope, the Ottoman government planned to fight a strictly Balkan war against Russia. In addition to recovering western Thrace, the Young Turk leaders, who still harbored dreams of imperial expansion, hoped to eject Russia from the Caucasus and perhaps from territory beyond.[89] On the insistence of Enver Pasha and other influential Young Turk leaders, the Ottoman government concluded a secret treaty with Germany on August 2, 1914. Two months later, on October 29, the Ottoman navy, under the command of a German admiral, deliberately launched an attack on Russian Black Sea ports, which provoked the Triple Entente powers into declaring war on the Ottoman Empire in November of the same year. The Ottoman Empire did not stumble into war, and it was not an accident, a stroke of fate, or a product of drift, as some historians maintain.[90] It was the outcome of a decision by Ottoman leaders who, like those in Vienna, sought to save their decaying empire by going to war.

The Final Disintegration of the Habsburg and Ottoman Empires

The decay of the center–periphery relationship and the attendant decline of state power would have led in time to the demise and eventual disappearance of the Habsburg Empire through a gradual process of territorial attrition. That was the fate suffered by the Ottoman Empire and all previous historical empires, including the British and French overseas empires. The Habsburg Empire, as Count Kálnoky noted, was surrounded by nationally homogeneous states that would have liked to strengthen themselves by incorporating Habsburg territories inhabited by their conationals.[91] Some attrition had taken place in the nineteenth century; Lombardy and Venetia were lost to the new Kingdom of Italy. The process, however, was held in check by the operation of the international system. As Hans Mommsen states:

> Without some impulse from without, that is, without some change in the European power constellation which set aside the foreign policy compulsion to preserve the dualistic state, no resolution of the nationalities problem was possible." [92]

The international system "sheltered"—to use Alexander Motyl's term—the Habsburg Empire from the worst consequences of its political and military weaknesses.[93] As a result the Habsburg Empire, along with the tsarist Russian and Soviet empires,[94] underwent a unique twentieth-century imperial experience: the sudden and swift collapse and complete dismantling down to its core land.

On its own, the Habsburg Empire would not have been able to survive in the competitive world of Great Power politics, but it was not on its own. Its continued existence was considered a necessity for the proper functioning of the balance-of-power system, and to prevent a power vacuum in east-central Europe, which could lead to a war among the Great Powers to fill it. After 1815, Russia provided support for the security of the Habsburg Empire, but withdrew it as a consequence of Habsburg policy during the Crimean War. The Habsburg Empire was defeated by France (and Sardinia-Piedmont) in 1859 and by Prussia in 1866, but in neither case was its continued existence as a state at issue. Bismarck eschewed marching into Vienna and showed no interest in incorporating the Habsburg Empire's nine million Germans into the new German state. The preservation of the Habsburg Empire was more useful to Bismarck than the annexation of its German inhabited territories. The alliance with Germany in 1879, while not unproblematic, protected the Habsburg Empire from the thrust of imperialist pan-Slavism under the aegis of the tsar. When, in the last quarter of the nineteenth century, Bismarck proved unwilling to provoke Russian ill-will by supporting Vienna's more aggressive anti-Russian Balkan policies, England came to the aid of the Habsburgs against Russian designs in Bulgaria and Constantinople. In short, the Habsburg Empire depended for its security on other great powers, and throughout the nineteenth century it received the support of at least one of them.[95]

The Changing Role of the International System

The European international system underwent a significant change after 1900. The fluidity and flexibility that had characterized international relations was replaced by a more rigid system of alliances. The policy of Great Britain also changed drastically. Traditional British policy after 1815 had eschewed assuming any obligations in Europe. A free hand and the control of the balance of power were considered the best means to protect British interests. England, however, could not but regard the buildup of the German navy as a direct challenge to its security. In response, Great Britain moved closer to France and Russia—its traditional enemies—and assumed obligations in Europe. Increasingly, England and its allies viewed the Habsburg Empire as a German satellite, and were no longer as thoroughly convinced that Austria-Hungary's existence was a European necessity as they had been before 1900. The Habsburg leaders' reckless choice of war to restore the prestige of the empire as a Great Power proved as counterproductive as did their domestic policies to prevent imperial decay and state decline.

The decision for war against Serbia precipitated the crisis that led to the collapse of the empire. It lost its sheltered position and became expendable "when the specter of a German dominated Europe began to haunt the allies in 1916. At that time plans for a 'new' East Central Europe replacing Austria-Hungary received serious consideration."[96] What that meant in practice was that the Allies would allow events to follow a more or less natural course as the empire began to break up in the fall of 1918.[97] Paradoxically, the complete dismantling of the imperial relationship between core and periphery was conditioned by the sheltered international position that the Habsburg Empire enjoyed for a hundred years. Only that protected status allowed the decay and decline to develop to such a degree that the imperial state no longer had sufficient strength to resist the political defection that came from all sides in the last month of the war.

The disintegration of the Ottoman Empire, unlike that of the Habsburg Empire, was the result of a slow process of attrition during which it lost vitality and provinces on the way to its disappearance. Still, the international system played a role in allowing the Ottoman Empire to last as long as it did, but it was not sheltered to anywhere near the same extent as was the Habsburg Empire. The latter clearly was regarded as part of Christian Europe, while the Muslim Ottoman Empire clearly was not. There was a sense among Europeans that it was not appropriate for Muslim rulers to govern Christian subjects. This attitude informed repeated interventions by European governments in favor of granting independence to the Balkan states, which accelerated the process of disintegration. Austria-Hungary faced no such interference in its internal affairs or disregard for its territorial integrity.

Like the Habsburg Empire, the Ottoman government was not capable of defending its territorial integrity or maintaining its political independence without outside help. That support was assured by the strategic position of the Ottoman lands and their vital significance for the expanding European imperial states. The vulnerability of the Ottoman Empire encouraged the European Great Powers to think in terms of eventual partition, but mutual fears of one power gaining too great a share worked against active support for partition, although, as pointed out just previously, such fears did not prevent them from aiding the secession of Balkan Christians or from picking off some peripheral areas themselves. Thus, British fears of a Russian takeover of Ottoman lands influenced Britain throughout the nineteenth century to keep the Ottoman Empire as much as possible intact. At the time that Russia was preparing for war against the Ottoman Empire in November 1876, "Disraeli made it clear that the British government would not acquiesce in the partition of the Ottoman Empire."[98] For its part, France opposed partition because it feared that the entire area would fall under British or Russian control; the French government preferred to maintain the status quo for as long as possible. The Habsburg Empire took a similar stance. By the beginning of the nineteenth century, Habsburg leaders came to doubt the wisdom of collaborating with Russia in wars against the Ottoman Empire, which had clearly ceased to be an expansionist power. They came to see that their chief threat was the same Balkan nationalism that was undermining the Ottoman Empire.[99] Therefore, they could win little by a change in the condition of the Ottoman Empire, although the 1908 annexation of Bosnia and Herzegovina (occupied by Austria-Hungary since 1878) weakened the Ottoman status quo, which encouraged Italy in 1911 and the Balkan states in 1912 to claim their shares of the Turkish inheritance.

What little sheltering the Ottoman Empire enjoyed in 1914 was withdrawn during the war. In its efforts to keep the Ottoman Empire out of the war, Britain offered to guarantee the empire's independence and integrity if it remained scrupulously neutral.[100] After failing to prevent the Turks from entering the war, England and Russia sought to enlist the support of discontented Ottoman subjects; England concentrated on the Arabs and Russia on the Armenians. At the war's end, the Anatolian core of the Ottoman Empire lay bare as the exposed and stripped center of a once immense imperial edifice. A revolution from above, led by Mustafa Kemal, then took place to salvage what was left.

After the Fall

The aftermath of the disintegration of the Habsburg and Ottoman Empires is the subject of another paper in this volume. The following observations in this regard are intended to round off the analytical framework presented here. The disintegration of the Habsburg and Ottoman Empires, along with the similarly multinational tsarist Russian Empire, led logically to Balkanization in east central and southeastern Europe—the other side of nation-state building. As stated previously, in the section "Pattern of Empire," imperial orders do not cause subordinated states to disappear, nor do they resolve conflicts among the disparate nationalities forced by overriding authority into political unity; the ruler and his advisers merely suppress and/or manipulate such conflicts for the purpose of enforcing an imperial peace as a foundation for their political ambitions.

With the collapse of the imperial order, the old historical structures and the suppressed conflicts reemerge, modified by factors associated with the extinct empire. Not the least of these factors is empire itself, that is, the persistence of empires in east-central and southeastern Europe until well into the twentieth century (assuming that the defunct Soviet Union had some key structural features of an empire). The persistence of empires interrupted, delayed, and aggravated the process of state and nation building and the development of nationalism in both regions. Foreign overlordship, as George Schöpflin points out, blocked the state and the cultural community from developing more or less coextensively. The separation of "the civic and ethnic elements from one another precluded the continuous interrelationship between the two that proved to be so significant in the evolution of nations in the West."[101] Consequently, nationalism in east-central and southeastern Europe developed a predominantly ethnic/religious content that was exclusive, as opposed to the inclusive political nationalism of the West.

To be sure, there were positive aspects of the Habsburg and Ottoman imperial legacies—more so in the Habsburg case—although they were not the same for all the successor states. Czechoslovakia, for example, inherited the industrial heartland of the Habsburg Empire, which provided it with the necessary economic foundations to become the most politically and socially stable state in interwar East-Central Europe, as well as an exception to the region's aggressive nationalist and authoritarian trends. All of the successor states benefited to some degree from the modernizing policies that characterize all empires, even if these were undertaken for the benefit of the center. The ability cf the East-Central European states to legitimate their sovereign existences, despite internal weaknesses and external vulnerabilities, was due partly to inherited bureaucratic institutions, a body of experienced bureaucrats and political leaders, educational institutions, and a fair number of professionals. This was truer of the Habsburg successor states—especially Czechoslovakia, Hungary, and Austrian Galicia (which became part of a resurrected Polish state)—than of those that emerged from the Ottoman Empire. The chief beneficiary of the Ottoman legacy of imperial bureaucracy was the former core land of the extinct empire, the new Turkish republic, for which it provided a firm governmental structure.

On balance, though, it was the negative sides of the imperial legacies that were more telling. Many of the lamentable aspects of the behavior of the successor states after they gained their independence can be traced back to their "mother" empires. The frequents shifts in imperial borders, as Dankwart Rustow points out in chapter 7, made it extremely difficult for the postimperial nation-states to defend their borders or even their basic identities. As a result, the Habsburg and Ottoman successor states in east-central and southeastern Europe were just as heterogeneous ethnically and/or religiously as the empires from which they had emerged, reproducing in miniature the agonies of those empires in decline. The manipulative practice of juggling nations and nationalities for imperial ambitions, and the subordination of some nationalities to others sharpened national rivalries. Politics in the former empires and in the successor states became equated with ethnic politics. The underlying authoritarian and hierarchical social and political structures of both empires perpetuated social cleavages that carried over into the successor states. The revolutions, if they can be called such, that dismantled the Habsburg Empire in 1918 were national rather than social in their content, in that they were most often led by elites who saw national revolution as a strategy to prevent substantive social change. The struggle of the East-Central European states to establish identities, the many irredentist disputes, and the debilitating socioeconomic weaknesses rendered them unstable inside and outside and effectively undermined parliamentary institutions. Those conditions fueled extreme ethnic nationalisms, often manipulated by political elites to deflect popular resentment. That led to intolerance toward minorities and made much needed economic cooperation nearly impossible.

Interwar East-Central Europe, with its conflicts and disharmony, is a classic example of the power vacuum created by collapsed empires. In the past, the power vacuum had been filled by a new or reconstituted empire. That seemed unlikely in the 1920s. Austria and Turkey were both too small in size and population and too economically weak to bear the costs of imperial expansion; Germany was exhausted by war, and Russia by revolution. In the absence of empires and with economic aid, the successor states, in time, might have developed stronger economies, reduced glaring social imbalances, and lessened ethnic and irredentist tensions. Unfortunately, they were granted neither freedom from external pressures nor adequate time. The exhaustion of Germany and Russia proved temporary; both countries rapidly revived in the 1930s. With the abdication of the Western powers, especially France, of their security responsibilities in east-central Europe, Germany and Russia divided the region between themselves in 1939. After the defeat of Germany, the USSR incorporated most of the successor states into its expanded empire.

The collapse of the USSR raised anew the question of the future of East-Central Europe. The post-communist successor states are now more thoroughly modernized than they were before the World War II and they are more national than they were in 1918. The terrible splintering of Yugoslavia represents one of the final steps in the process of nation-state formation in the region. There are, however, tensions and conflicts arising from economic disparities and competition that could result in the formation of a new power vacuum. As after World War I, there seems little threat of imperial takeover by an outside power; neither Germany nor Russia—the past exploiters of power vacuums in east-central Europe—appear to harbor imperial ambitions. However, it would be rash to assume that the cycle of great-power hegemony and empires has been broken in the absence of some international mechanism to prevent its resumption. For east-central and southeastern Europe, the most promising mechanism for restraining imperial ambitions would be a pan-European federation or confederation of equal states—precisely what empires are not.

Notes

1. The three earlier conferences are: 1898, Center for Austrian Studies, University of Minnesota; 1993, Norwegian Nobel Institute, Tromso, Norway; and 1994, Harriman Institute, Columbia University. A volume of essays from each conference has been published. They are respectively: Richard L. Rudolph and David F. Good, eds., *Nationalism and Empire: The Habsburg Monarchy and the Soviet Union* (New York: St. Martin's Press, 1991); Geir Lundestad, ed., *The Fall of Great Powers: Peace, Stability, and Legitimacy* (London: Oxford University Press, 1994); and Karen Barkey and Mark von Hagen, eds., *The End of Empire: Causes and Consequences* (Boulder: Westview Press, forthcoming, July 1997). This chapter draws on an earlier essay that will be published under the title "The Collapse of the Habsburg Empire: The Imperial Factor," in Barkeley and von Hagen, eds., *The End of Empire.*

2. Michael W. Doyle, *Empires* (Ithaca: Cornell University Press, 1986); Paul Kennedy, *The Rise and Fall of the Great Powers* (New York: Random House, 1987); Alexander J. Motyl, "From Imperial Decay to Imperial Collapse: The Fall of the Soviet Empire in Comparative Perspective," in Rudolf and Good, pp. 15–43; Motyl, "Imperial Collapse and Revolutionary Change: Austria-Hungary, Tsarist Russia, and the Soviet Union in Theoretical Perspective," in Jürgen Nautz and Richard Vahrenkamp, eds., *Die Wiener Jahrhundertwende: Einflüsse-Umwelt-Wirkungen* (Vienna: Böhlau Verlag, 1993), pp. 813–32; William McCagg, "The Soviet Union and the Habsburg Empire: Problems of Comparison," in Rudolf and Good, pp. 45–64; Imanuel Geiss, "Great Powers and Empires: Historical Mechanisms of Their Making and Breaking," in Lundestad, pp. 23–43; S.N. Eisenstadt, ed., *The Decline of Empires* (Englewood Cliffs, NJ: Prentice-Hall, 1967);

and S.N. Eisenstadt, *The Political System of Empires* (New York: Free Press, 1963).

3. Geir Lundestad, "The Fall of Empires: Peace, Stability, and Legitimacy," in Lundestad, pp. 383–402; quotation on p. 393.

4. Cemal Kafadar, *Between Two Worlds: The Construction of the Ottoman State* (Berkeley and Los Angeles: University of California Press, 1995), p. 8.

5. I have relied mostly on the following: Bernard Lewis, *The Emergence of Modern Turkey* (London: Oxford University Press, 1961); Roderic H. Davison, *Reform in the Ottoman Empire, 1856–1876* (Princeton: Princeton University Press, 1963); Davison, *Essays in Ottoman and Turkish History, 1774–1923: The Impact of the West* (Austin: University of Texas Press, 1990); Karen Barkey, *Bandits and Bureaucrats* (Ithaca: Cornell University Press, 1994); Kemal H. Karpat, ed., *The Ottoman State and Its Place in World History* (Leiden: E.J. Brill, 1974); Peter F. Sugar, *Southeastern Europe Under Ottoman Rule, 1354–1804* (Seattle: University of Washington Press, 1977); Charles and Barbara Jelavich, *The Establishment of the Balkan National States, 1804–1920* (Seattle: University of Washington Press, 1977); and Sükrü Hanioğlu, *The Young Turks in Opposition* (New York: Oxford University Press, 1995).

6. Lewis, p. 38, emphasis in the original.

7. Ibid., p. 351.

8. Alan Sked, *The Decline and Fall of the Habsburg Empire, 1815–1918* (London: Longman, 1989), p. 187.

9. Ibid., p. 264. See also Istvan Deak, *Beyond Nationalism: A Social and Political History of the Habsburg Officer Corps, 1848–1918* (New York: Oxford University Press, 1990), pp. 3, 8–9.

10. See Solomon Wank, *The Nationalities Question in the Habsburg Monarchy: Reflections on the Historical Record* (working paper no. 93–3, University of Minnesota Center for Austrian Studies, 1993); and Wank, "The Collapse of the Habsburg Empire: The Imperial Factor." As evidence of the instability, one can point to the suspension of the constitutions of Istria, Croatia, and Bohemia in 1910, 1912, and 1913, respectively, and the dissolution of the Austrian parliament in March 1914, with no intention of reassembling it any time soon.

11. Quoted in H. Gordon Skilling, "T.G. Masayrk, Arch-Critic of Austro-Hungarian Foreign Policy," *Cross Currents: A Journal of Central European Culture* 11 (1992): 213–33. Quotation on p. 214.

12. The attitudes of the Poles and the Italians are enlightening in regard to the distinction between resignation and acceptance. Despite the fact that both nationalities were well treated, neither regarded their existence in the Habsburg Empire as permanent. They looked forward, respectively, to the resurrection of an independent Polish state and to joining the Kingdom of Italy.

13. Diary entry, July 24, 1914. Quoted in vol. 1 of Josef Redlich, *Schicksalsjahre Österreich. Das politische Tagebuch Josef Redlichs*, Fritz Fellner, ed., 2 vols. (Graz: Böhlau Verlag, 1953–1954), pp. 238–39. On Hoyos, see Fritz Fellner, "Die Mission Hoyos," in Heidrun Maschl and Brigitte Mazohl-Wallnig, eds., *Vom Dreibund zum Volkerbund: Studien zur Geschichte der internationalen Beziehungen, 1882–1919* (Vienna: Verlag fur Geschichte und Politik, 1994), pp. 112–41.

14. Baron Leopold von Andrian-Warburg, 1916 memorandum, in John Leslie, "Österreich-Ungarn vor dem Kriegsausbruch: Der Ballhausplatz in Wien im Juli 1914 aus dem Sicht eines osterreichisch-ungarischen Diplomaten," in Ralph Melville et al., eds., *Deutschland und Europa in der Neuzeit: Festschrift für Karl Otmar Freiherr von Aretin zum 65. Geburtstag* (Stuttgart: Franz Steiner Verlag, 1988), pp. 663–84. Quotation on p. 675.

15. See Michael R. Gordon, "Domestic Conflict and the Origins of the First World War: The British and the German Cases," *Journal of Modern History* 40 (1974): 191–226.

16. On the Austro-Hungarian decision for war, see Samuel R. Williamson, Jr., *Austria-Hungary and the Origins of the First World War* (New York: St. Martin's Press, 1991), p. 191. See also Solomon Wank, "Desperate Counsel in Vienna in July 1914: Berthold Molden's Unpublished Memorandum," *Central European History* 26 (1993): 281–310.

17. Sked, pp. 54–56; F.R. Bridge, *The Habsburg Monarchy Among the Great Powers, 1815–1918* (New York: Berg, 1990), pp. 336–38; Istvan Deak, "The Fall of Austria-Hungary," in Lundestad, pp. 82–83.

18. Otto Brunner, "Das Haus Habsburg und die Donaumonarchie," *Südostforschungen* 14 (1955): 123–24, 126–27, 140–44. Had they wanted to reorganize along federal lines, the emperor and the archduke would have met stiff resistance from the Magyars, the Germans, and Germany. The latter based its adherence to the 1879 Austro-German alliance on the predominance of Germans and Magyars in Austria and Hungary respectively. The emperor and his advisers accepted these constraints because the Magyars, the Germans, and Germany supported the continuation of the Habsburg dynasty as an imperial power.

19. Davison, *Reform in the Ottoman Empire*, p. 5.

20. Sked, p. 187.

21. Ibid., p. 259. F.R. Bridge, in his authoritative diplomatic history of the Habsburg Empire, states that during the course of the war, Germany reduced the monarchy to the position of "a helpless satellite" for whom a German victory would have meant the end of its existence "as an independent Great Power." Bridge, pp. 341, 380.

22. Andrej Mitrović, "Die Kriegsziele der Mittelmächte und die Jugoslawienfrage 1914–1918," in Adam Wandruszka, Richard G. Plaschka, and Anna M. Drabek, eds., *Die Donaumonarchie und die südslawische Frage, 1848 bis 1918* (Vienna: Verlag der osterreichischen Akademie der Wissenschaften, 1978), pp. 153–57, 160–62, 164.

23. Andrej Mitrović, "Die Balkanpläne der Ballhausplatz-Burokratie im Ersten Weltkrieg (1914–1916)," in Ferenc Glatz and Ralph Melville, eds., *Gesellschaft, Politik und Verwaltung in der Habsburgermonarchie 1830–1918* (Stuttgart: Franz Steiner Verlag, 1987), p. 370.

24. Doyle, pp. 35–36.

25. Ibid., p. 42.

26. Davison, *Essays in Ottoman and Turkish History*, p. 87.

27. William H. McNeill, "The Ottoman Empire in World History," in Karpat, *The Ottoman State and Its Place in World History*, p. 37.

28. Gustav Graf Kálnoky, *Memorandum: Die Nationalitätenfrage in Oesterreich-Ungarn in ihrer Rückwirkung auf die aeussere Politik der Monarchie*. The memorandum is printed in two places: Barbara Jelavich, "Foreign Policy and the National Question in the Habsburg Empire: A Memorandum of Kálnoky," *Austrian History Yearbook* 6–7 (1970–1971): pp. 147–59; and in Ernst Rutkowski, ed., *Briefe und Dokumente zur Geschichte der österreichisch-ungarischen Monarchie*, pt. 1 (Munich: Oldenbourg Verlag, 1983), pp. 490–500. The memorandum is discussed in Solomon Wank, "Foreign Policy and the Nationality Problem in the Austria-Hungary, 1867–1914," *Austrian History Yearbook* 3, pt. 3 (1967): pp. 38–41, 45.

29. Motyl, "Imperial Collapse and Revolutionary Change," p. 816. Medieval France and England are examples of the successful transformation of imperial systems into state monarchies based on the fusion of territorial nationalities into a state nationality. Ibid., p. 813. See also Jenö Szücs, *Nation und Geschichte: Studien* (Budapest: Corvina Kiadó, 1981), pp. 26–28.

30. On population statistics 1880–1910, see Robert A. Kann, *The Habsburg Empire, 1526–1918* (Berkeley and Los Angeles: University of Calfornia Press, 1974), pp. 605–8

and A.J.P. Taylor, *The Habsburg Monarchy* (London: Hamish Hamilton, 1948), pp. 263–69. The ratio between Germans and Czechs in Bohemia also was relatively stable, but with a considerable numerical disparity in favor of the Czechs due to the higher Czech birthrate. Between 1880 and 1910, the total population of Bohemia grew from 5.5 million to 6.7 million. The German share of the population was 36.9 percent in 1880 and 36.4 percent in 1910. The Czech shares were 62.4 and 62.6 percent respectively. See Bruce M. Garver, *The Young Czech Party, 1874–1901 and the Emergence of a Multi-Party System* (New Haven: Yale University Press, 1978), pp. 323, Table 1. In addition to being outnumbered, Germans in Bohemia felt threatened by the strong Czech challenge to their hegemonic position.

31. On the evolution of and problems associated with Ottoman censuses see Kemal Karpat, *Ottoman Population, 1830–1914: Demographic and Social Characteristics* (Madison: University of Wisconsin Press, 1985), pp. 3–11.

32. Karpat, *Ottoman Population*, p. 116, Table I.2 and p. 117, Table I.6.

33. Justin McCarthy, *Muslims and Minorities: The Population of Anatolia and the End of the Empire* (New York: New York University Press, 1983), p. 109. McCarthy sets the population of Anatolia at 17.2 million. If one subtracts non-Turks, identifiable by religion or area of settlement, one arrives at a figure of about 12.5 million Turks.

34. Karpat, *Ottoman Population*, p. 56, Table 3.7. Estimates of the total population of the Ottoman Balkans in the second half of the nineteenth century are 10–14 million (ibid., p. 45). The figure of 11 million seems to comport best with the information in Table 3.7.

35. See Karpat, *Ottoman Population*, pp. 162–69 and 174–89 for the census reports. The census reports are usefully summarized in Stanford J. Shaw, "The Ottoman Census System and Population, 1831–1914," *International Journal of Middle East Studies* 9 (1978), pp. 325–38.

36. Karpat, *Ottoman Population*, p. 189.

37. The Turkish majority was probably smaller than the data indicates because of undercounting, especially in the Middle Eastern provinces. There also was a relatively large nomadic population that eluded the census takers.

38. Motyl, "From Imperial Decay to Imperial Collapse," p. 19.

39. As used here, the term covers substantially the same area as the present-day Republic of Austria. Since there is no consistency in the use of Constantinople and Istanbul in the literature, I have chosen to use the former throughout this paper.

40. By Motyl's definition, the Napoleonic and Nazi empires were military occupations, rather than genuine imperial structures.

41. Eisenstadt, *The Political System of Empires*, pp. 116–19.

42. Ibid., pp. 199, 132–37.

43. On the incompatibility of democracy and empire, see Doyle, pp. 34, 36, 64, and 137 and Motyl, "From Imperial Decay to Imperial Collapse," pp. 19–20.

44. Barkey, p. 17.

45. In practice, absolutist governments are never absolute. Constraints are often imposed by the rebellion or threat of rebellion by regional elites and ethnic or religious groups.

46. For some suggestive reflections on this point, see Imanuel Geiss, "Decolonisation et conflits post-coloniaux en Afrique: Quelque Reflections," in *Colloque international: Les deux guerres mondiales; les analogies et les différences,* September 12–14, 1984 (Warsaw: Comité des Sciences historiques, 1985), pp. 1–22. See also, Geiss, "Great Powers and Empires," pp. 38–42.

47. See in general, Charles Ingrao, *The Habsburg Monarchy, 1618–1815* (New York: Cambridge University Press, 1994), pp. 2–22 and R.J.W. Evans, *The Making of the Habsburg Monarchy, 1550–1700* (London: Oxford University Press, 1979).

48. Doyle, pp. 80, 162.

49. Evans, pp. 240, 307, 447.

50. Barkey, p. 14.

51. Ibid., p. 240; Lewis, p. 33.

52. Barkey, p. 2.

53. Ibid., p. 240; Lewis, p. 38.

54. Lewis, p. 38; Davison, *Essays in Ottoman and Turkish History,* p. 21.

55. Oscar Jaszi, *The Dissolution of the Habsburg Monarchy* (1929; reprint, Chicago: University of Chicago Press, 1961), pp. 61–73.

56. Robert A. Kann, "Zur Problematik der Nationalitätenfrage in der Habsburger-monarchie, 1848–1918: Eine Zusammenfassung," in *Die Habsburgermonarchie, 1848–1918,* Vol. III, *Die Völker des Reiches,* Adam Wandruszka and Peter Urbanitsch, eds., 2 pts. (Vienna: Verlag der österreichischen Akademie der Wissenschaften, 1981), pt. 2, p. 1323.

57. Jaszi, pp. 106–18.

58. Piotr Wandycz, *The Lands of Partitioned Poland, 1795–1918* (Seattle: University of Washington Press, 1974), pp. 219–28.

59. Dennison Rusinow, "Ethnic Politics in the Habsburg Monarchy and Successor States: Three Answers to the National Question," in Rudolph and Good, quotation on p. 254.

60. Ivan L. Rudnytsky, "The Ukrainians in Galicia under Austrian Rule," in Andrei S. Markovits and Frank E. Sysyn, eds., *Nationbuilding and the Politics of Nationalism: Essays on Austrian Galicia* (Cambridge, MA: Harvard University Press, 1982), pp. 31, 57, 61. In the same volume, see Markovits's introduction, esp. p. 16.

61. Davison, *Reform in the Ottoman Empire,* p. 5.

62. Şerif Mardin, "Civil Society and Islam," in John A. Hall, ed., *Civil Society: Theory, History, Comparison* (London: Polity Press, 1995), p. 292.

63. I am grateful to Şerif Mardin for allowing me to cite this piece of information from a draft of his paper, "Some Consequences of the Demise of the Ottoman Empire." It will be published in *The End of Empires: Causes and Consequences,* cited above, n. 1.

64. Davison, *Reform in the Ottoman Empire,* pp. 25–36.

65. Ibid., pp. 3, 8, 55–56, 194; Roderic H. Davison, *Essays in Ottoman and Turkish History,* pp. 114–19, 127–28. On official nationalism see Eric Hobsbawm, *Nations and Nationalism Since 1750: Programme, Myth, Reality* (Cambridge: Cambridge University Press, 1990), pp. 80–100.

66. On millet reform, see Davison, *Reform in the Ottoman Empire,* pp. 115–32.

67. Ibid., p. 132.

68. On the 1876 Constitution see ibid., pp. 358–90; Davison, *Essays in Ottoman and Turkish History,* p. 87. Lewis, pp. 161–64.

69. Lewis, pp. 160–62; Davison, *Reform in the Ottoman Empire,* p. 369.

70. Hanioğlu, p. 30.

71. Ibid. and Lewis, pp. 163–66.

72. Davison, *Reform in the Ottoman Empire,* p. 5.

73. Ibid., p. 8. In the late 1860s, the more moderate wing of the Bulgarian national movement floated the idea of a Bulgarian-Turkish dualism analogous to the Compromise of 1867 between the Magyars and Emperor Francis Joseph I. The Ottoman government opposed the proposal and it came to nothing. Among other things, the plan called for a Christian vice king (*Vizekönig*) who would exercise the administrative, judicial, and executive power and command a Bulgarian national army. Next to the title of emperor of the Ottomans, the sultan would assume the title king of the Bulgarians. Friedrich Gottas, "Die Bulgarische Nationale Bewegung in den Jahren, 1867 und 1868," in Christo Choliocev, Karlheinz Mack, and Arnold Suppan, eds., *National-Revolutionäre Bewegungen in Südosteuropa im 19. Jahrhundert* (Munich: R. Oldenburg Verlag, 1992), pp. 89–90.

74. Evans, p. 275.

75. Kálnoky, *Memorandum.*

76. Lewis, p. 1.

77. Davison, *Reform in the Ottoman Empire,* p. 408.

78. Hanioğ lu, p. 215.

79. Ibid., p. 32.

80. Ibid., p. 31.

81. Lewis, p. 209.

82. Ibid., p. 214.

83. Hanioğ lu, p. 210.

84. See the population statistics given earlier in the section "Pattern of Empire."

85. Feroz Ahmad, *The Young Turks: The Committee of Union and Progress in Turkish Politics, 1908–1914* (Oxford: Clarendon Press, 1969), p. 155.

86. The 1902 concession was formalized in 1907. See Éva Somogyi, ed., *Die Protokolle des gemeinsamen Ministerrates der österreichisch-ungarischen Monarchie, 1896–1907* (Budapest: Akademiai Kiado, 1991), p. 507, doc. no. 73, October 9, 1907.

87. Albert Hourani, *A History of the Arab Peoples* (New York: Warner Books, 1991), p. 309.

88. F.A.K. Yasamee, "The Ottoman Empire," in Keith Wilson, ed., *Decisions for War* (London: University College of London Press, 1995). p. 234.

89. Ibid., pp. 228, 234.

90. See, for example, Lewis, p. 233.

91. Kálnoky, *Memorandum.*

92. Hans Mommsen, "Die Arbeiterbewegung in Deutschland und Österreich: Eine Vergleichende Betrachtung," in Robert A. Kann and Friedrich E. Prinz, eds. *Deutschland und Österreich: Ein bilaterales Geschichtsbuch* (Vienna and Munich: Jugend und Volk, 1980), p. 437.

93. Motyl, "Imperial Collapse and Revolutionary Change," pp. 816–19.

94. The evidence of World War II and the Cold War would seem to controvert sheltering in the Soviet Union's case. However, I think that the essential freezing of the geopolitical balance after 1945, based on a tacit agreement between Soviet and American elites, sheltered the Soviet Union from attrition. As long as that agreement held, national liberation struggles in the periphery could not succeed (e.g. Hungary, 1956; Czechoslovakia, 1968; and Poland, 1981).

95. The dependent international position of the Habsburg Empire is the underlying theme of F.R. Bridge's masterly analysis of Habsburg foreign policy, *The Habsburg Monarchy Among the Great Powers.*

96. Piotr Wandycz, *The Price of Freedom: A History of East Central Europe from the Middle Ages to the Present* (New York: Routledge, 1992), p. 196. See also Henry Cord Meyer, *Mitteleuropa in German Thought and Action, 1815–1945* (The Hague: Matinius Nijhoff, 1955), pp. 215, 240, 250–51.

97. Fritz Fellner, "The Dissolution of the Habsburg Monarchy and its Significance for the New Order in Central Europe: A Reappraisal," *Austrian History Yearbook* 4–5 (1968–69): 3–27, esp. pp. 8–9, 10–12.

98. Lewis, p. 161.

99. F.R. Bridge, "Austria-Hungary and the Ottoman Empire in the Twentieth Century," *Mitteilungen des Österreichischen Staatsarchivs* 34 (1981): 234–37.

100. Yasamee, p. 247.

101. George Schöpflin, "Nationalism and Ethnicity in Europe, East and West," in Charles A. Kupchan, ed., *Nationalism and Nationalities in the New Europe* (Ithaca: Cornell University Press, 1995), p. 49.

5

Decolonization
Britain, France, and the Cold War

Michael Graham Fry

Introduction

The British and French empires of the nineteenth century, in the age of industrialization, were marked by diversity. Empire was formal and informal, rule direct and indirect, policy controlled and influenced. Trade, investment opportunities, and strategic reach frequently substituted for colonization. White, Anglo-Saxon, and Protestant dominions, India and Egypt, colonies and protectorates all found a place, for example, in the British Empire. Possession of empire was the mark of status, the test of greatness for Britain and France. But it was not paradoxical for Britain, at the zenith of its power, to concede virtual independence to its ethnically white dominions. Enhanced economic, strategic, and diplomatic benefits would flow from relinquishing sovereignty; institutionalized freedom, generously granted, would increase imperial unity. At the same time, the imperial mind of the nineteenth century found moral purpose in formal empire, in benefits generously bestowed on native peoples by charismatic leadership, administrative skill, and institutional growth, in the spreading of the majestic governing art.[1]

Imperial policy was always part of foreign policy and of grand strategy, if only because empire was maintained in a hostile and competitive international climate. Russia, France's ally by the end of the century, presented the greatest strategic threat to the British Empire. Britain and Germany challenged the French Empire. The threats to both empires were resolved through diplomacy, as the labile, aspiring hegemon that was united Germany undermined the Concert of Europe. U.S. preferences in these contests were largely irrelevant, and where germane, appeasable.

World War I demonstrated the value of the empires in action, just as it squandered British and French resources. The peacemaking of 1919–1923 gave the empires their greatest territorial dimensions and added to their complexity. Differentiated mandates, A Class for the Middle East, B Class for Africa, C Class for Asia-Pacific, were distributed under League of Nations auspices between Britain and France, as they partitioned the German and Ottoman empires. As always, war and diplomacy were the powerful engines of change, beliefs and values its influential representatives. Postwar recovery and the possibility of enduring prosperity seemed to rest substantially on summoning the empire's resources, yet beliefs and values were in transition. The principle of national self-determination—contested in its meaning, explosive in its consequences, likely to bring about, as Woodrow Wilson finally realized, "a tragedy of disappointment"—knew no racial or geographic boundaries. What transplanted white Europeans had achieved, Arab elites coveted; what eastern Europe had been granted in 1919, African and Asian, and particularly Indian, nationalists came to expect. While imperial trade and investment flourished in an increasingly hostile international economic environment, France rested its imperial future on centralization and direct rule; Britain chose to accommodate client rulers and collaborators in profit- and power-sharing, in economical empire. Both brought their A Class mandates, Syria and Iraq respectively, to the point of independence, following Egypt's emancipation, in ways that preserved British and French influence. Transjordan's independence from Britain waited until after World War II. India could not long be denied the same treatment as the Arab Middle East had received. The Soviet Union, as it entered the world, threatened the British and French empires, ideologically if not strategically. Italy and Japan presented more formidable strategic problems, harnessed to those from Nazi Germany. Diplomacy, appeasement, and deterrence were to counter these threats, as they had before 1914. Atlanticists in Britain, both ideologues and those who looked to the United States merely to behave as a normal state, had thought in terms of a Pax Anglo-Americana. This scheme, with its logic, its prescience, and its naïveté, assumed that the United States, in partnership, would underwrite the maintenance of the British Empire. France harbored no such illusions, but, for France as much as Britain, the imperial future would be bound up principally with U.S. policy, and with that of the Soviet Union.

World War II provided the test. Britain, mobilizing the empire yet again, met the test more successfully than France, as its Vichy government grappled with its competitors. Again, however, world war sapped their resources and loosened their grip on empire, physically if not psychologically. The United States and the Soviet Union emerged victorious, unequally formidable, and, each in its own way, hostile to empire. Nationalists in the imperial possessions sensed the opportunity to bring about significant change, even to create independent states. Fatigue, if not exhaustion, at the core met revolt at the periphery. Two maps, drawn simultaneously after 1945—that of the Cold War and that of the United Nations—came to represent the meaning of World War II. The former captured the bipolar world that arose from the defeat of the Berlin-Rome-Tokyo axis; the latter, the processes of decolonization. The former did not provide the essential context for the latter. Rather, each was part of the explanation of the other, if not equally so. Both maps had their own historical logics. The Cold War map reflected a line of reasoning stretching from Alexis de Tocqueville to the declinists, who had predicted the rise of the United States and Russia to the relative detriment of Europe. The UN map was drawn as the age of empire gave way to decolonization.

There was something logical, even morally comforting, to all critics of empire about the latter trend. The tale was being told as it should, a process was being completed, linear trends were reaching their allotted maturity. Henri Labouret identified the progression in 1952: colonization, colonialism, and decolonization. As Felipe Fernandez-Armesto, in his *Millenium,* described it, "the tectonic plates of world history" had shifted as they should. Empires rise and fall. But there was more. Ingenuity could counter fatigue. A case would be made that Asia and, especially, Africa still needed moral and material British and French leadership. The Cold War could, in Roger Louis's and Ronald Robinson's phrase, provide for a renewal of imperialism, for the imperialism of decolonization and for the dependence of interdependence. That is why the yet-to-be-constructed narratives of the Cold War will find, in abundance, uncertainty and contingency, nonlinearity and paradox, ideological imperatives and pragmatism, illusion and reason, in that element of the Cold War that was the contest over and for the decolonizing world—which was itself a part of, though less than, the Third World.[2] The Cold War made decolonization a triangular process: the United States and the Soviet Union as one apex; the imperial powers, principally Britain and France, as the second; and nationalist leaders in Asia, Africa, and the Middle East as the third. Three layers of transactions between these actors were unavoidable, as was the exposure of their policies to and in the United Nations. Two of the triangle's points—the United States–Soviet Union relationship and the nationalist movements—represented profound divisions in and of themselves.[3]

The issues and themes of the analysis are thus set: (1) the historical diversity of empire geographically, constitutionally, and in terms of its governance processes and distributions of power between the metropoles and the overseas territories; (2) the importance of beliefs and values; (3) the meaning of empire to France and Britain, and its role in their claims to world power; (4) imperial policy as a component of grand strategy in the face of threats from international actors; (5) British and French determination, born of conviction and necessity, to retain the assets and resources of empire while transferring sovereignty to nationalist elites; (6) ingenuity, diplomacy, and the intangibles of power as compensation for loss of tangible resources; and (7) the presence of paradox.

Vocabularies of Decolonization

Decolonization, in the broadest sense, was a process of social transformation marked by the dispersal of power, state creation, and nation building, which took place between 1945 and 1970 in that part of the Third World still subject to Japanese and European imperialism. It encompassed, unevenly, political, economic, cultural, and racial change. Just as the creation of the state of Israel was viewed as an act of imperialism by Palestinians and an act of decolonization by Israelis, so too does decolonization have several vocabularies. *Political decolonization* is both the transfer of sovereignty and the granting of independence, and the end of political repression orchestrated by imperial powers with colonial collaborators who had sought to perpetuate traditional sources of authority. It has a strategic dimension, as the imperial center ceases to use colonies as bases from which to project military power. *Economic decolonization* is both the careful, imaginative reordering of established economic relationships and the end of economic exploitation and gross inequality, as preferential trade and investment relationships gave way to more regulated systems aiming at national economic development. A symbol of the latter was the triumphal nationalization of, for example, the assets of the Anglo-Iranian Oil Company in 1951 and of the Suez Canal Company in 1956. *Cultural decolonization* is, for example, both the legacy of the *mission civilatrice*—after the French confrontation with Arab culture in North Africa—and the regeneration of indigenous customs, practices, arts, and values. Cultural decolonization allows formerly colonial people to question whether economic growth must rest on the foundation of European culture and to challenge the Western version of human rights. As native cultures grew in self-esteem all things Western could be made suspect, perhaps to the point of producing a crisis for Western culture itself. *Racial decolonization* is the payoff from education and training, as businesses, for example, are transferred to indigenous entrepreneurs and technicians, as well as the end of paternalism, of white rule over black peoples, and the restoration of dignity. Some would add a fifth, demographic theme, in that decolonization put an end to the white settler phenomenon, thus closing the European frontier. In any case, the four themes and the triplice of actors—Cold War protagonists, the imperial powers, and local elites—give the process of decolonization its complexity and its fascination.

Structures

Beliefs, Values, and Norms

Both of the "global theologians," the United States and the Soviet Union, laid claim to the moral high ground as they competed for the soul of nationalism, rather than making the claim to common ground a source of cooperation. Lenin, in his confrontation with Woodrow Wilson, had declared the world to be ideologically bipolar. Capitalism and imperialism threatened a temporarily vulnerable communism and suppressed nationalisms, but would be defeated when the latter two forces united. There was every reason for Josef Stalin and Foreign Minister Vyacheslov Molotov to retain these themes in Soviet policy, although

Stalin, seeing the resilience of capitalism and respecting the reach of U.S. power, was cautious. Decolonization, surely, would weaken the West, even as the Soviet Union consolidated its own empire. Stalin's successors after 1953 spoke of natural alliances to be forged with the forces of progress. Opportunities for the Soviet Union would present themselves in specific states (e.g., in the national democracies of Cuba and Ghana), regionally (as Pan-Arabism and Pan-Africanism surfaced), and globally.

History, tradition, conviction, self-interest, and the diplomacy and rhetoric of World War II—the Atlantic Charter, the Four Freedoms, the UN Charter—cast the United States as the champion of national self-determination and freedom and as the foe of the repression, inequality, and darkness that was empire. In practical terms, that meant at the very least demanding from the imperial powers constitutional reform and self-government for many of their colonial possessions, and dominion status and cultural freedom for India. The war against the Axis, particularly Japan, had not been fought to preserve the British and French empires in Asia, Africa, and the Middle East, empires that were not only anachronisms, but also threats to the effective prosecution of the war. Oppressive, inefficient, and insulting colonial rule—the sheer folly of it—must end. There could not but be tension in Anglo-American and U.S.-French relations. One side saw oppression, the other necessary obligation; one ally saw urgency, the other the imperative of measured, careful change. The negotiations on the Joint Declaration on the Colonies, from 1942 to 1944, captured and foundered on these tensions. After the war a U.S. congressman, seeking prominence on the "Palestine question," could summarize the British problem, without fear of contradiction from other than the Joint Chiefs of Staff, as "too damned much socialism at home and too much damned imperialism abroad." It was not difficult for U.S. officials to extend the diatribe to France—the France of socialist governments and Gaullist pretensions—and add a layer of distrust mixed with contempt. Roosevelt disapproved of French rule in Indochina and supported France's ejection from Lebanon and Syria, attitudes that were reflected in his pointed warning to Charles de Gaulle that he must not expect to exercise power in France or over the French Empire without the legitimacy of elections and consent. In any case the consequences of this post–World War II policy for the United States in the Cold War–era seemed clear enough—U.S. policy must not be tainted with imperialism, inequality, exploitation, or repression, or with the unacceptable faces of capitalism. Decolonization, most emphatically, must not be a triumph for Soviet policies, a threat to Western interests, or a choice for Soviet over American "theology." [4]

It was not surprising that *enragés* in Britain and France detected a U.S. conspiracy, misguided, naive, disingenuous, and frankly dangerous, against empire. They came to expect nothing less of the Soviet Union. Some French officials saw the UN trusteeship scheme as a U.S. ruse to extend U.S. influence at France's expense and as a threat to the French Union. But officially, publicly, there could be no effective campaign against the ethics and historicism of the beliefs and values that underpinned the challenge to—even the armed revolt against—empire. The use of force to counteract the challenge had its advocates, and even merit. On occasion it was tried but ultimately was found wanting. There were Labor-Conservative and Socialist-Radical-Gaullist perspectives on the predicament, idealism facing nostalgia, paternalism and authoritarianism, but no matter. Britain's declaratory policy was voluntarily to transform empire through the creation of a system of independent, self-governing states, new nations that would be able to institute social reform, enjoy economic growth, and be free of oppression. Freedom would breed cohesion, as it had in the past, and cohesion would enhance British prestige. The new states would enter the United Nations and the British Commonwealth, and transform them. France's declaratory policy was wrapped in the calculated ambiguity of the French Union, in that overseas territories could achieve emancipation by remaining French. But declaratory policy, by definition, commits. It demands legitimation. Successive British and French governments calculated the political consequences at home of committing to or opposing decolonization. Those consequences were marginal in Britain for both parties, crucial in France for Socialists and Gaullists alike.[5]

The indigenous elites of decolonized lands were, necessarily, as different as the empires in Africa, Asia, and the Middle East were diverse. Some were survivors of the war, others products of it, and thus they were old, transitional, and new. Politically and ideologically, conservatives, notables, and moderates competed with radical nationalists, who were themselves divided ideologically and varied in their extremism and sense of grievance. Conservatives and moderates, in sub-Saharan Africa, saw distinct benefits—economic, financial, strategic, and diplomatic—in neo-empire, and found satisfaction in power and profit sharing. Sheikhs of the oil-producing Gulf states wanted British protection against local and regional rivals as much as self-government, to the point where the status quo was eminently preferable to strategic uncertainty. Britain left the Gulf in 1970, but was not forced out. Some elites were anxious to be British and French; others saw assimilation as ridiculously arcane.

Indigenous elites differed in their skills, in their standing both locally and in London and Paris, in their educational roots, and in the resources available to them, whether ideological, military, organizational, or political. Some faced entrenched white settlers, backed or not by France and Britain. Radicals were more impatient and thus more acceptant of risk—of confrontation with powerful security forces, of war, of civil unrest that might backfire and make moderate elites and continued British or French presence more attractive to the local peoples— than were conservatives and moderates. The latter faced other forms of risk—the risk that caution would mean loss of influence, that compromise and the invitation of neo-empire would discredit them. There were always rivals, even if civil war did not lurk in every independence movement as Tony Smith claimed. The trend over time—uneven, not always linear—was to settle not for mere reform but for nothing less than political sovereignty.

Elites were poised to mobilize protonationalisms and direct liberation movements in such a way as to ensure that their preferences became popular expectations in rural and urban areas. Buoyed by the world war and then by the examples of India, China, and Indochina, they opposed foreign control, be it Japanese or European. The status of collaborator would become a historical artifact as they forced or negotiated the end of white rule, whether doing so as irrepressible opponents or as equal partners. They led revolutionary movements to create states that were emancipated, not subservient and dependent. Those states, once established would, as they had since 1919, create nations. The fact that quintessential collaborators such as the Hashemites of Iraq and Transjordan had tried and failed to create nations did not discredit the quest. There was little reason to dwell on a "modernist fallacy"—that states and the nations they create out of ethnic, religious, and tribal groups are mere transitional phenomena en route, via regional arrangements, to a global society. States, as optimal social arrangements, as the logical response to the end of traditional society, offered the most promising basis for order. States, more daily plebiscites than imagined communities, create nations by building identities, fostering healthy patriotism, and institutionalizing ideologies. The development of symbols, the provision of security against domestic and international threats, and the stimulation of economic growth and social progress are the tests of a state's success at nation building. These are Yasir Arafat's formidable challenges. The tragedy of Yugoslavia demonstrated how nationalism can destroy states. Yugoslavia was an ethnic absurdity; its successors may turn out to be absurdities as political economies, as viable strategical entities, and as systems of transportation and communication.[6]

In the process of state creation and nation building, nationalist leaders were comforted by the sense that history and ethics were on their side and that what was sociologically inevitable was entirely defensible morally. The superpowers, the remaining imperial powers, the United Nations, the emerging international organizations all acknowledged the same norms as they adopted the vocabulary of self-determination, human rights, racial equality, modernization, development, and dignity. Industrial and agrarian, Western and non-Western societies all agreed that they were participating in what was surely a turning point in the moral history of humanity. Empires would not succeed empires; there was no question of merely changing imperial masters, even if the contenders were the United States and the Soviet Union. Wars of emancipation that were being lost on the ground could be won in the arena of global values. But beyond the oratory and because of their commitment, nationalist elites faced dramatic challenges along with internal struggles—to reconcile rural and urban expectations; to use judiciously the weapons of nationalization and restriction of foreign capital and imports; and to meet the expectations of disgruntled domestic traders, investors, and peasant farmers. They must demonstrate that decolonization would lead to something other than excesses of nationalism, corruption, incompetence, conflict, and military rule. They must avoid resurgences of tribalism and fundamentalism and foil extensions of imperialism. Nationalist leaders must prove that they could manage the choice between the United States and the Soviet Union without resorting to mere opportunism (Egypt's Gamal Abdel Nasser passed the test; Jomo Kenyatta, willing to bargain with anyone to advance his cause, failed it) and show that they were worthy and legitimate successors to British and French rule. It was a case, as Joseph Chamberlain warned in an entirely different context, that if one sups with the devil one needs a long spoon.

The Relative Distribution of Power

There is no reason to dwell on the tangibles of Anglo-French decline, which was dramatized by World War II and confirmed by postwar economic problems. The statistical evidence is incontrovertible, starting as early as the 1890s in some cases. In 1870, Britain controlled 24 percent of world trade, in 1914 15 percent; and by 1928 it controlled only 9.3 percent. Its industrial monopoly had evaporated. Britain had lost markets and the trend toward net debtor status had set in. Britain liquidated £4.2 billion of foreign assets during World War II. The USSR may initially have been in even more dire economic straits than either Britain or France, but the United States, without having shed the fear of postwar depression, had emerged in 1945 as the foremost industrial and trading state, the financial master of the Western world, the giant creditor nation, in de facto control of the World Bank, the International Monetary Fund, and its own Export-Import Bank.

   Britain's postwar economic problems, largely inherited but partly self-imposed, were formidable. It faced debtor status, a dollar shortfall, and balance-of-payments deficits with the United States. Imperial commitments and Britain's role in the German occupation had exacerbated its balance-of-payments problems and indebtedness (e.g., with Canada, India, and Egypt). Exports were stagnant and trade deficits persisted. As the principal beneficiary of the Marshall Plan, Britain received $2.7 billion of the total $13 billion and was thus, despite the cancellation of its Lend-Lease Agreement debt, ever dependent on U.S. loans and aid. Its gold and dollar reserves hovered perilously close to the waterline of $2 billion, while it attempted to maintain sterling as an international reserve and trade currency and to weather devaluation and energy crises. Domestically, Britain needed to cut £700 million from a defense budget that was consuming 8 percent of GNP. In 1950 it invested only 9 percent of GNP in modernizing its industrial infrastructure; and it was faced with the challenge of financing the pursuit of full employment, social welfare, and nationalization with revenues yet to be earned.[7]

   France's economic condition, after a brief upturn in 1945–46, was equally perilous as it freed itself from the Nazi European economy and resisted German economic revival. It had lost overseas investments and neglected its industrial infrastructure. Food shortages worsened because of the disastrous 1947 harvest. Exports were low and imports excessively high. A dollar shortage hindered food and raw material purchases. Gold and dollar reserves shrunk while balance-of-payment debts and budget deficits increased. France embarked on an ambitious plan to fund socialist reform plans and industrial modernization programs, but had an inadequate and regressive tax system, faltering economic performance, and chronic labor problems, which were brought on by declining real wages (a consequence of the failure to curb inflation). All these problems, compounded by political instability, threatened France with the prospect of an embarrassing degree of policy dependence on the United States.[8]

The statistics and the gloom of relative decline, must not, however, mask their significance for decolonization. The issue for British and French policy was not their decline per se, but rather ensuring that the gap between resources—in other words, mobilizable and projectable power in all its tangible and intangible forms—and necessary commitments was not a chasm. Providing such assurance presented a formidable challenge, for empire was measured in terms of both assets and obligations, of both potential and burden. In two periods, Britain's empire, for example, had been pivotal to its economic well-being. The first instance lay in the distant past of the mercantilist arrangements of the late eighteenth and early nineteenth centuries. The second period of economically beneficial empire began as early as the 1890s and matured in the 1930s. In this period, preferential trading schemes, intra-imperial trading, and regional trading blocs—created by reducing colonial tariffs on British exports, discriminating against nonimperial products, and denying colonies the protection of tariff walls for their infant industries—became the empire of the sterling area and imperial preference. The trend followed from the surrender of industrial leadership, the unraveling of free trade, the loss of faith in international economic liberalism, the economic consequences of war, and depression. In such circumstances, Britain looked to empire. In both of these periods, trade with and investment in the empire as a percentage of Britain's total trade and foreign investment rose. In 1939, for example, the empire provided almost 40 percent of Britain's imports and absorbed 49 percent of Britain's exports. In the second period, emigration to the empire's dominions constituted a majority of total emigration. In between these two periods, for the bulk of the nineteenth century, however, in the decades of free trade and investment, the empire was not the principal target of overseas investment (it absorbed between 25 percent and 39 percent), and it could not match the United States as a magnet for emigration (62 percent of emigrants went to the United States). The empire was neither Britain's principal market for exports (it absorbed between 25 percent and 33 percent), nor was it the major source of imports (it provided between 20 percent and 25 percent). Imperial investments did not produce rents comparable to those from investments at home or in the United States.[9]

The United States, after World War II, seemed bent on re-creating the economic world of the nineteenth century—the world of international economic liberalism. That challenge must be finessed, along with many others. The sterling area, French currency arrangements, and imperial preference must be maintained. The sterling area was an efficient mechanism to generate dollars by exporting food, minerals, and raw materials from the colonies to the United States. The dollars earned were deposited in sterling accounts in London. Malaya was a major dollar earner for Britain, Indochina for France. Increasing metropole as well as colonial dollar-earning exports and reducing imports would further enable them to meet the challenge presented by U.S. policy. Overseas possessions were also necessary sources of cheap imports, of food, fats, and raw materials that could be purchased at low prices through monopoly arrangements. They were also lucrative markets, because imperial exports profited from controls placed on competitive imports. Even as imperial commitments were reduced, the empires would provide increased resources and would contribute to economic recovery.

Statecraft

The United States and the Soviet Union

U.S. postwar policies toward Western Europe and the Third World were essentially a function of its Russian policy. Secretary of State John Foster Dulles, during the Suez Crisis of 1956, captured the consequences—the United States had been "walking a tightrope," balancing between resurgences of European imperialism and decolonization. President Eisenhower put his finger on the immediate issue: to support Britain and France was to lose the Arab world.

Containment determined that the United States give priority to the political and economic resuscitation of Britain, France, and West Germany, and then of Japan. The United States needed to create and lead a West European alliance of vigorous, progressive, capitalist, industrially modernized, politically stable, and economically prospering states. That was the mandate of the U.S. Economic Cooperation Administration set up to administer the Marshall Plan. The alliance's member states must be invulnerable to communist influence and rearmed; NATO must be robust and credible. It came to be assumed that Britain and France could not fulfill their roles in containment if they were deprived of the benefits of empire. In pursuing these postwar policies, the United States risked the consequences—though they were not great until West European disillusionment born of recovery set in—of left-wing and Soviet charges of U.S. imperialism. The scholarly debate on these questions rests partially on examining the degree to which U.S. corporate interests fueled the creation of an informal American empire, perhaps by invitation, or an analog of empire, in Western Europe.[10]

World War II prompted Roosevelt's vision of an international order susceptible to U.S. power and leadership. The dogmas of liberal internationalism, free trade, open markets, and convertible currencies demanded that the United

States—industrial powerhouse, global trader, banker, and investor—have access to the food, raw materials and minerals, and the markets and investment opportunities in the Third World. The Cold War mandated that these resources be denied to the Soviet Union. The emerging states of the Third World, beginning to enjoy economic growth, social progress, and self-government, had to opt for cooperation in the Western international economy. But on what terms would Britain and France, the indispensable allies, participate in the new order and prosper because Middle East oil, for example, flowed cheaply and predictably to Western Europe? Regional trading arrangements, imperial preferences, practices that inflated, for example, the price of U.S. imports of rubber and tin, the sterling area, and nonconvertible currencies were at odds with the new order.

Strategic considerations, since the United States supplied and dispensed security, were the source of further dilemmas. A bureaucratic debate within the Roosevelt administration during World War II had revolved around the preference of the Joint Chiefs of Staff to restrict UN trusteeship to the mandatory territories and captured Japanese colonial possessions. Containment, deterrence, and the protection of trade routes necessitated the establishment of a web of strategic bases, many of them in imperial hands. The spread of the Cold War from the eastern Mediterranean and the northern tier states to the global arena, by way of the Korean War, demanded ad hoc defense arrangements, formal defense schemes, and ultimately security alliances such as the Baghdad Pact, the Central Treaty Organization (CENTO), ANZUS, and the South East Asia Treaty Organization (SEATO). Could it be wise, therefore, to jettison strategic assets still under British and French control? Surely it would not be wise to do so if, for example, Britain remained vital to the defense of the Middle East.[11]

It was not as if the Soviet Union was in retreat—quite the reverse. Stalin, for all his caution, was like Lenin in that he saw loss of empire as a potentially fatal blow to Western capitalism. Because the West needed, for example, the resources and base facilities of the Middle East more than did the Soviet Union, which controlled East European coal and oil, Soviet policy called for denying these assets to the United States and its allies. The Soviet Union expected to exploit Middle East stability and instability, and use both for Soviet purposes. It planned to manipulate Arab and Zionist clients to destroy British leadership and French interests, to sponsor Middle East communist parties, undermine Western unity in the Middle East, and ensure that the northern tier did not become NATO's southern flank. Molotov articulated the threat to a Europe in need of reconstruction of U.S. capital and culture, of a hegemony that would suffocate freedom. The United States, unless countered, could achieve monopoly power and enslave and dominate European states devastated by war. They would become subject to the arbitrary behavior of U.S. corporations and banks. After 1953, the Soviet Union turned more decisively to harnessing Third World nationalism with communism. Impressive economic growth and dramatic technological achievements gave credibility to Soviet diplomats who preached the merits of command economies as models for modernization and development. The Marxist-Leninist version of human rights—for groups instead of individuals, for exploited peoples, for races subject to discrimination, for a global proletariat denied justice by capitalistic imperialism—measured up favorably against the Western, liberal model of individual rights and freedoms when the two systems were compared by indigenous elites. Soviet arms transfers were portrayed as indispensable for the consolidation of revolutionary regimes, strategic security, and even survival in the face of a reviving, menacing, and even rampant, Western imperialism.[12]

As Nikita Khrushchev confronted John Kennedy, U.S. officials had little difficulty concluding that decolonization could threaten U.S. interests (e.g., through a loss of strategic reach or intelligence capability), constitute a setback to U.S. credibility, and could therefore benefit the Soviet Union. The preservation of aspects of, rather than wholesale dismantling of, empire—retaining the assets of neoempire while serving the expectations of decolonization—would surely better serve U.S. interests. Permitting U.S. behavior to contradict declaratory policy was not sufficient. Difficult choices must be made; whether to use threats of economic reprisal and foreign aid as weapons of statecraft; whether to intervene in threatening situations, by covert operations or military intervention; and whether to permit Britain and France similarly to intervene.[13] The United States must decide how to manage arms transfers so as to induce cooperation. It must fathom the contradictions implicit in global, as opposed to regional, strategies, knowing that Cold War necessities could not always justify insensitivity to regional realities, and that the Soviet Union would pounce on evidence of U.S. hostility toward nationalist liberation movements. The United States must identify enemies, real and imagined, and allies, populist leaders or autocratic enemies of reform. Each U.S. administration must learn to balance respect for private property rights against acts of nationalization, with due regard for U.S. interests in canals and oil, while debating Henry Kissinger's interminable obsession with the national interest. They must grapple with the phenomena of revolution and tottering dominoes, the former problem being bound up with U.S. repugnance for any revolution that strayed beyond the boundaries of its own. All these decisions had to be faced without precise understanding of the relationship between communism and revolutionary nationalism, without knowing just how vital Third World resources were, and being unaware of what benefits might accrue to the United States when the Soviets stepped into colonial quicksands.

It is possible to identify the components of a U.S. grand strategy here. First, assist the economic recovery and political stability of Britain and France, and assure them continued access to imperial assets, while tolerating the blemishes, the discriminatory features, of empire. Second, ensure U.S. imports of Third World strategic and nonstrategic minerals (oil, tin, and copper), food, fats, and raw materials (rubber); and protect U.S. access to investment and market opportunities. Third, support the development of representative government in the

Third World and have these governments—conservative, even authoritarian, prudent, and anticommunist—as allies (i.e., South Vietnam, South Korea, Taiwan, and Iran). Fourth, deny influence in the Third World to the Soviet Union. Finally, create economic interdependence and political harmony between the United States, Western Europe, the Third World, and Japan (U.S. aid to and the resources and markets of Vietnam, Indonesia, Taiwan, and Burma would help ensure the recovery and integration of Japan). In implementing this grand strategy the United States would create alternatives to chaos and communism in Asia and Africa, effectively counter the Soviet threat, foster security, and promote peace.

But the devil was in the detail, region by region, state by state, case by case. How could the record of U.S. policy be anything but checkered; the research challenge to scholars anything but formidable?[14] In the United States' dealings with Britain and France, there was neither a conspiracy against empire nor a willingness to permit the Cold War merely to salvage their empires and taint the United States with imperialism. An outright anti-imperial strategy would have invited chaos, revolution, and communism, weakened NATO, and threatened containment policies. The latter would have presented opportunities for indigenous extremists and the Soviet Union, meant loss of global influence (manifest in the United Nations and the corridors of Pan-Africanism and Pan-Arabism), and would have put the United States out of step with the march of history. The United States, therefore, chose the difficult middle ground whereby decolonization, in reducing the burden and ending the pretense of traditional empire but fostering neoempire, would serve Western and not Soviet purposes. If further strategic choices had to be made, decolonization would be forfeit to Cold War necessities.

The United States did not pretend to treat Britain and France equally. The British Commonwealth, in conception and action, and in its range of activity, initially seemed more valuable than the French Union. After the 1957 Anglo-American Bermuda Conference, Britain settled into the position of junior partner in the "special relationship." It joined in security arrangements, helped defend the Middle East, collaborated in meeting the triple challenge in the Middle East in 1958, and received U.S. financial support. From 1958, in contrast, the France of de Gaulle went its own way and distanced itself from the United States' Western bloc. In the process, France complicated European integration and undermined NATO. The United States addressed itself more seriously to preserving Britain's economic and strategic assets in the newly negotiated informal neoempire than it did to preserving French interests, at least until the benefits of the narrower French Union, in sub-Saharan Africa, became apparent. U.S. leadership meant that it decided whether Britain and France could use coercion and force, not diplomacy, in Malaya and Cyprus, for example. At one critical point during the 1956 Suez Crisis, the United States brought both countries to heel via financial and diplomatic pressure, following their aggression, in collusion with

Israel, against Egypt. There was no paradox in the fact that Britain was more vulnerable to U.S. pressure than France, but Anglo-American differences (for example over Red China, Iran, and the Buraimi oasis) were less bitterly contested and more promptly resolved than those differences that endangered accord between the United States and France. On rare occasions, as in the 1957 affair over Gaza and Sharm-el-Sheikh, the United States' acceptance of French leadership, itself the product of Franco-Israeli cooperation, was decisive. In the Lebanon-Iraq-Jordan crisis of 1958, however, the United States kept France at arm's length.[15]

Specifically, along with its own act of decolonization in the Philippines in 1946, which preserved U.S. economic and strategic assets, the United States attempted to find a way across the middle ground of decolonization. This was done in two stages: the position taken on and involvement in the granting of independence, and the United States' subsequent behavior toward the operation of informal neoempire. The United States, condemned by the Soviet Union for wavering on the UN decision to create an Israeli state, helped ease a willing Britain out of Palestine in 1947–48, after the joint Anglo-American effort to eject France from Lebanon and Syria. However, the United States looked to Britain—with its string of bases from Gibraltar to Singapore, and especially dense in the Middle East—to help defend the Middle East and the northern tier under the aegis of the Truman Doctrine and a U.S. strategic presence in the eastern Mediterranean. Both Britain and France could contribute to the security of South and Southeast Asia, but only at the margin. The United States had effective control of Saudi Arabia's oil development, and secured a 33 percent stake in Iranian oil in 1954, but left Britain's preserve in Iraq and the Persian Gulf untouched.

The United States applauded the independence of India, Pakistan, and Burma—if not the process—and supported the entry of the former two into the Commonwealth. It had wanted orderly change and a peaceful transfer of power in the Indian subcontinent as well as the advent of moderate government. As secondary goals, the United States hoped to play a role in India's development and locate strategic bases there. A minor benefit from the Korean War would be to bolster French morale in Indochina. (It has been argued, however, that the peace settlement in Korea enabled the Chinese communists to focus their attentions on Indochina, thereby dooming the French empire in Southeast Asia.) Under Eisenhower, the United States, having failed to convince France to do in Indochina what Britain had done in India, refused to contribute U.S. forces to assist France in its Indochina war. France, the United States felt, could no more win the war than could the Dutch in Indonesia. The U.S. view was that France should end the conflict and return its forces to Europe. Financial assistance, direct and through the Marshall Plan was the extent of U.S. support. The United States attended the Geneva Conference of 1954 but refused to sign the Final Declaration, which it condemned as a flawed Anglo-French-Chinese compromise that favored the Communists. Its military aid and financial assistance to the government of South Vietnam, even as it conspired against free elections, then set the United States on the path to the Vietnam War, a path that France refused to tread. The United States financed the British campaign against insurgency in Malaya.

Eisenhower initially gave tacit support to France in its Algerian crisis, but starting in 1957, the United States withdrew into studied detachment, and neither recognized the Algerian rebel government nor supported French policy. The United States did little more than acknowledge the 1962 settlement. By then, Africa was the focus of decolonization. The extent to which President Kennedy chartered a new course toward Africa remains controversial. As senator and candidate he had excoriated Eisenhower over Algeria and sub-Saharan Africa. Oratorically, he was Roosevelt's heir, or even Truman's, when he spoke out against neocolonialism in Africa. He knew the politics of the U.S. civil rights movement. He understood the argument that, in Africa, the struggle against communism was better fought in alliance with nationalism than with the European powers. He could also see, however, merit in British and French plans for Africa, in that a combination of political independence and economic dependence might result in politically stable states allied to the West and receptive to U.S. economic and military assistance. Perhaps there was more—the Kennedy administration furthering U.S. business interests in the Congo, Gabon, Guinea, and Ghana; preserving a united Congo (instead of supporting Katanga's secession) in 1961–1962, amid criticism from France and Belgium but in alliance with the United Nations; and crafting a policy that would expand U.S. influence in Africa. But neither Kennedy nor his successor acted in Africa to the extent of depriving Britain and France of the benefits of neoempire, although U.S. officials took enough action to outrage their French and British colleagues.[16]

Britain and France

Decolonization must be seen as part of foreign policy, indeed of grand strategy. As Britain and France redefined their functions as great powers and searched for a place in the postwar constellation, it was difficult for either to envisage identity and role distinct from empire. This may have been more the case for France than for Britain. Whether they were destined to be Atlantic or European states, or hybrids, world power was bound up with the preservation of empire. Empire was not a third option in itself, through which to gain independence from the United States and the Soviet Union, any more than cooperation with the Soviet Union at the expense of the United States was an option. Rather, empire was a source of postwar economic revival, diplomatic influence, political status, and strategic reach. Yet the fact that the United States, in partnership with them to contain the Soviet Union, would not countenance the perpetuation of empire in its current forms, was incontrovertible by the summer of 1945. This attitude, to say the least, made the United States a difficult ally, particularly in the person of James Byrnes, Truman's secretary of state. Sir Orme Sargent, serving with Ernest

Bevin at the British Foreign Office, captured the moment: Britain, one of the world's three great powers, must assert itself, enroll the Dominions, France, and the lesser European powers as collaborators, and not allow the United States to treat Britain as Britain had dealt with France after World War I.[17]

The answer lay in bold statecraft, in acts of European diplomatic brilliance, in the fact that Britain and France were indispensable allies of the United States as it balanced between containment and decolonization. They could use the Cold War to their advantage, although they would risk contributing to its intensity and incurring increments of Soviet hostility. De Gaulle and his socialist successors knew that France, in Germany's partial absence, would unavoidably play a crucial role in European integration. Surely it was not beyond the wit of French diplomacy to invite U.S. assistance, pocket U.S. dollars, and spend some of them on colonial development or use them to free up domestic assets for the same purpose. The United States could help France refashion its empire to its own advantage. Surely, even U.S. officials, their confidence matching their inexperience, could be educated and convinced that the benefits of empire must continue to flow to the imperial powers. The United States must be called on to provide Britain with generous economic and financial assistance. Yet, the very purpose for Britain of U.S. aid—social welfare and economic recovery, in which the empire and its development would assist—was to reduce the extent of dependence on the United States and avoid a status of permanent subordination. In short, the intention was for the United States to underwrite British and French recovery in order to enable them to achieve effective distance from the United States. Foreign policy independence would follow, necessarily, from economic and financial autonomy. Everyone would benefit; the United States would pay. It was a scheme worthy of the arrogance and determination of the British foreign office.[18]

Planning the future of empire lay at the core of this strategy for recovery and social reform. It would be, therefore, singularly inappropriate to apply John Seeley's aphorism—that nineteenth-century empires were obtained in a fit of absentmindedness—to the processes of Anglo-French decolonization. It was one thing, as Bernard Potter observed, to be wrongheaded, quite another to be empty-headed. Success rested, in the first instance, on holding the collective nerve, demonstrating that appetite for leadership was not dulled, that courage and faith in self had not evaporated, that despair had not set in, that there would be no pusillanimous response to nationalist pressure, that relative decline did not mean decadence. These instincts, these first principles, reinforced a determination to not scuttle the empire, a decision that rested on tangible and psychological sunk costs and on the calculation that to scuttle would be electoral suicide. To scuttle would mean to abandon empire precipitately, prematurely, and without due preparation. It became the rallying cry of those who resisted decolonization—of white settlers in Rhodesia, Indochina, and Algeria, of French colonial bureaucrats and military officers, of entrenched economic interests, of the British Sudan political service, of Colonial Office officials in Aden, and of Foreign Office representatives in the Persian Gulf. Resistance to decolonization was, however, less virulent in the British than in the French case. British governments overcame it, therefore, more easily.

Both empires were still marked by diversity—constitutionally, culturally, and economically—not uniformity. France had its associated states, territories, and departments, Britain its mandates, protected states, protectorates, and colonies, spread across Asia, Africa, and the Middle East. India, united or divided, had already moved toward independence. France's possessions in Southeast Asia expected independence just as promptly. But was it time for black Africa to overcome what was deemed to be a chronic incapacity to govern itself (see Appendix A, p. 146). The range of the agenda was breathtaking, but some of it was distinctly urgent, even undeniable. The speed of the process of decolonization thus became crucial. Was calculated delay or acceleration wise, and which strategy would incite violence, extremism, and chaos? What timely concessions and adjustments could be used to counter all three effects? Cumulative trends had their impact, inspiring indigenous elites, angering white settlers, making the Mahgreb more controversial for French governments because of the loss of Indochina, warning Britain of the risk of their own "Algeria" in Central Africa. Calculations about the use of force were also critical. It was one thing to use force, with or without U.S. aid, to prevent radicals and communists from securing control of newly emerging states and allying with the Soviet Union, although in some instances the use of force could bring on exactly what it was meant to prevent. It was quite another scenario to risk protracted warfare in an attempt to retain empire by force in alliance with white settlers. What legitimacy could there be in such a gamble? Decolonization in Malaya and Rhodesia for Britain, and in French Indochina and Algeria, tested both nerve and ingenuity. Such reasoning about range, speed, and method of decolonization rested on a single naive assumption—that Britain and France could actually control the expectations of nationalism, could control the timing, rate, and predictability of decolonization. At most they could ameliorate the potential for exploitation of the process by extremists of all races.

The value of the Robinson thesis, scarcely a formal theory, lies less in its pericentric emphasis and more in its insistence that the creation of empire was an act of bargaining with indigenous elites, identified invariably as collaborators. According to Robinson, empire, formal and informal, functioned as a contractual relationship that distributed power, determined policy control, shared benefits, and served interests, all unequally, all in favor of the imperial power, and sometimes grossly so. The processes of decolonization should be seen in the same way, though not to the extent of deeming decolonization an elaborate charade that masked the nominal transfer of power to a new generation of trusted collaborators. Decolonization would rest on a second act of European diplomatic brilliance, which arose out of a subtle distinction between British and French arrogance. Colonized peoples could not expect to become British and would settle for a reflection of the real thing; how could foreigners, on the other hand, want to be anything but French? Though their colonial legacy was unevenly marked by paternalism and exploitation, although the surviving collaborators were ill-prepared and ill-positioned for self-rule, and despite the fact that nationalists were prepared to challenge rather than merely protest imperial authority, British and French officials found reasons for confidence. Revised contractual relationships could be engineered; moral victories were within reach. France, for example, had so stamped the colonies with its beliefs, institutions, and "civilization," and had so well trained people in French ways, that the new states would behave like the former colonies had—loyally. By dividing the empire into small, manageable states that were still dependent on France for security and for economic and diplomatic support, France would be able to retain control more easily. In any case, Africa needed France; without France, there would be no security.[19]

The French Union

France, its rule reconstituted by de Gaulle in Indochina and North Africa, wanted to retain the essences of empire through processes of decolonization, but did not have a single plan. Schemes were floated, pursued, discarded, and followed by revised schemes as Gaullists and Socialists—united at least in a vision of state and empire—settlers, business interests, the military, and colonial administrators all set out to determine policy. French planning initially embraced Southeast Asia, Africa, and the Pacific and Caribbean colonies. With the loss of Indochina in 1954, the Mahgreb became the focus. From 1958, under de Gaulle, French plans settled on black Africa. In January 1944, French colonial administrators met at Brazzaville in French Equatorial Africa, to discuss ways to reform the empire so as to retain it, and preserve the administrative autonomy they had enjoyed during the war. They ruled out independence for the African colonies and Madagascar,[20] although greater political authority would be vested in local, elected councils. They proposed a range of educational, social, economic, and administrative reforms. Many of these reforms were not implemented, but the worst abuses of colonial rule—forced labor, for example—were ended. The colonies were to send elected representatives to a Constituent Assembly in Paris, convened to write a new constitution and create the nucleus of a global French Union. The collaborators would play their allotted roles by deflecting radical dissent in the colonies and by seeking to influence French policy while endorsing it.

In the first Constituent Assembly, in Paris, convened in late 1945, Socialists, who favored union through a democratic federation of equal states, confronted Gaullists, who preferred a French-dominated federation. They agreed that France must retain the most important parts of empire, such as Algeria, but could relinquish other territories, such as Laos and Cambodia. Thirty-eight of the sixty-four seats in the Assembly were held by representatives from the colonies; half of them were French residents, the other half were indigenous elites. The latter had an opportunity to air grievances against, and to demand greater political, social, and economic autonomy within, the empire. The draft constitution proposed a French Union that could be joined by consent and with the right of secession, that granted greater freedoms and political powers to the colonies, but that also extended French law to the empire. All the subjects of the empire would become French citizens. The draft constitution was approved by colonial voters, but was rejected in May 1946 by the electorate in France. Reform had collapsed.

Conservatives, encouraged by rejection of the constitution, argued that France must allow its colonies neither significant political autonomy nor excessive authority in a federation. They preferred a French-dominated federation instead of a federation of equals, one that would permit France to control its empire, not be controlled by it. Their goal became, therefore, to turn France's colonies, territories, and departments into extensions of France in a global, powerful French Union.

In 1946, the second Constituent Assembly, with sixty-four delegates elected from France and from the colonies, drafted a constitution that created a federal French Union of unequal states. The French Union, to be created on October 27, 1946, after a constitutional referendum, would be composed of autonomous states, with France first among equals and retaining control over high policy. The Socialists, who were in office, viewed the new constitution as a defeat because the proposed French Union was heavily centralized, called for assimilating the colonies into France, and was not a federation of equal, independent states. In fact, the new constitution was a series of compromises between federalism and assimilation, between equality and the attempt to ensure that France led the Union.[21] France and the colonies were indivisible, yet the colonies were autonomous. Although it ruled out independence for the colonies, the constitution permitted the organization of political parties and extended freedoms of speech and of the press, thus granting legitimacy to local political groups. But policy control remained in Paris.[22]

The French Union was comprised initially of associated states—that is, Tunisia, Morocco, Vietnam, Cambodia, and Laos—and associated territories—that is, Togoland and the Cameroons. Overseas departments, including Martinique, Guadeloupe, French Guiana, and Reunion, were designated as units of the French Republic, as were the overseas territories of French West Africa (Senegal, Mauritania, Sudan, Guinea, Ivory Coast, Upper Volta, Dahomey, and Niger), and of French Equatorial Africa (Gabon, Middle Congo, Unbagi-Shari, and Chad). Algeria was divided into three overseas departments administered as units of the French Republic.[23] The loss of Indochina and the Mahgreb made the French Union, by 1960, essentially an arrangement for west and equatorial Africa.[24] (See Appendix B, p. 147.)

War or Negotiation?

After World War II, undeniable nationalist aspirations emerged in the colonies, and France faced a choice between war and negotiation. In colonies where white settlers were numerous or influential, and were supported by the colonial bureaucracy, entrepreneurs, and the army—such as in Indochina and Algeria—successful negotiations proved impossible. Fearful of losing their privileges, the traders, merchants, and planters who formed the French colony in Indochina urged the local French military and colonial administrators to fight Ho Chi Minh and the communists, igniting almost a decade of war.[25] In Algeria, the French had never created an indigenous elite; instead, white settlers had filled the key positions in government and business. Therefore, there was no indigenous elite with whom to strike a bargain on decolonization. The Algerian radical nationalists rejected the French offer of union, and revolt erupted in 1954. The settlers—their identity tied to empire and dependent on its perpetuation—sought to keep Algeria in the French Union as an integral part of France. Settlers feared losing their lives, careers, influence, social standing, homes, land, and businesses if independence was granted. There was also great uncertainty about what would happen after independence, particularly if the newly independent state was dominated by radicals, nationalists, socialists, and communists. In Algeria, in contrast to Tunisia and Morocco, settlers made up 12 percent of the population and most of them were poor. They could not afford to return to France, even if they had wanted to leave the colony, which was their birthplace and birthright.[26] Settlers believed they had created Algeria, and they would make trouble rather than leave. The empire, and Algeria specifically, *was* France. The settlers believed that it would be a tragic mistake and morally wrong of France to abandon Algeria, if it cut the constitutional, economic, social, cultural, and military ties. But war brought failure in Algeria, as it had in Indochina.

While war waged in Vietnam and in Algeria, the French, in order better to focus their resources, granted relatively peaceful independence to their neighbors. To reduce its commitments and to concentrate on Vietnam, France granted Laos autonomy in 1946 and independence in 1949, although it remained an associated state of the French Union until a 1953 treaty granted full independence. Cambodia gained independence in 1954. The French were just as eager to focus attention on Algeria. Tunisia was granted internal independence in 1955 and full independence in 1956, the same year as Morocco. Both bargains were struck with conservative nationalists, in a process relatively free of white settler influence.

In the midst of the Algerian war, while its costs mounted, de Gaulle negotiated independence with colonies with far smaller settler populations and, therefore, with far less political influence in Paris. Fifteen French colonies gained independence in 1960. Although in some cases, such as Madagascar, the transition was violent, none approached the magnitude of Algeria or Vietnam. In black Africa, the indigenous elites were nurtured and aided by the French. These elites were not destroyed during World War II, as they had been in Indochina; nor had there been enough white settlers in black Africa to fill the colonial administration, as there had been in Northern Africa. The black African elites, reliant on the

French for power, peacefully negotiated independence. France could create neo-empire by consent.

Postindependence: Benefits and Responsibilities

The benefits that France retained after decolonization and from neoempire varied greatly. The war in Indochina had so soured Vietnamese-French relations that independence meant virtually the total loss of French economic, political, strategic, and cultural interests. France lost, for example, a significant source of U.S. dollars from the exports of the region. By contrast, however, Franco-Algerian postindependence relations were promising and productive because of the settlement that de Gaulle engineered. French economic aid flowed in, and French forces continued to use bases in Algeria. Economic, political, and cultural relations flourished. The benefits to France from decolonization in Tunisia and Morocco, for example, were also significant. Such was not the case, however, in Laos and Cambodia, where war soon flared anew and communist governments were destined to rule.

The benefits of decolonization were most apparent in France's postindependence relations with black Africa. After granting independence, France maintained close economic, political, cultural, social, and military ties with its former colonies, under the auspices of both the French Union and the transitory Franco-African Community. Relations with Guinea and Mali, though strained for brief periods, were excellent overall. The French managed the currencies, central banks, fiscal policies, and treasuries of all but two of the newly independent states through the Franc Zone, which was created on March 12, 1962, and comprised Benin, Burkino Faso, Ivory Coast, Mali, Senegal, Togo, Cameroon, Chad, the Central African Republic, Congo, Gabon, Equatorial Guinea, and the Comoro Islands. France also negotiated preferential trade arrangements with its former colonies, and paid higher than world prices for raw materials from Africa.[27] French investment flowed to these states, as did targeted financial aid, as France took on burdens that Britain refused to shoulder.

The central African states also relied on France for military and political support. France kept about four thousand troops in Djibouti, and fewer numbers in Senegal, Gabon, Chad, and the Central African Republic. Almost two thousand African officers trained in France each year, and France sent one thousand military advisers to twenty-three African states. France negotiated defense agreements with eight African states and military assistance agreements with twenty-two African states.[28] Intelligence cooperation became the norm between France and its former colonies in Africa. France intervened in the Central African Republic, the Congo, Gabon, Chad, Niger, and Mauritania to preserve friendly governments against internal threats, and in Chad to protect it from Libya. Most recently, in 1995, the French intervened in the Comoros.[29] Diplomatically, France and its former African colonies cooperated at the United Nations and held summits together to coordinate policies.

The French Union, focused in black Africa, provided France, therefore, with a flourishing neo-empire. In his pursuit of French greatness, de Gaulle found alternatives for France to empire: as a leader of Europe in harness with West Germany, as an independent nuclear power, and as a third force free of U.S. domination and able to deal independently with the Soviet Union. This creativity was matched by his courtship of the Arab world as de Gaulle reversed the Fourth Republic's preference for Israel. Neo-empire remained, but the foundations of France's world status were irrevocably transformed.

Britain: Calculated Decolonization

In 1948, the Labour government of Clement Attlee, secure in its parliamentary majority, completed a first, urgent phase of decolonization in South Asia and, tangentially, the Middle East; World War II had already ended Britain's role as a major Asian power. The Conservative governments of Anthony Eden and Harold Macmillan launched a more protracted, but no less calculated, phase of decolonization in 1957, focusing on Africa and lasting into the 1970s.[30] Decolonization in both phases was meant to be a process of orderly, timely change based on negotiation, avoiding conflict, and contributing to British postwar recovery and influence. Britain intended to use force only to counter extremism. There was, in the unavoidable reordering of empire, in the rewriting of the imperial contract, in the discourse, a vision of influence perpetuated, of assets retained, and the provision of moral leadership. The government must provide as little ammunition as possible for those who would cry scuttle, and as much comfort as possible for those who wanted inexpensive, neoempire. In contrast to France, the phases of British decolonization reflected more bureaucratic and governmental decisions than political bargaining.[31]

By 1948, Britain had shed politically and financially untenable situations, at the insistence of the Treasury, and had disgorged indefensible positions. It granted independence to India, Pakistan, Burma, Borneo, and Ceylon, and made Palestine a ward of the United Nations and then a land divided between Israel and Transjordan. Britain also divested itself of strategic responsibilities in Iran, Cyrenaica, Eritrea, and Somalia. However, in the face of the Soviet threat to the eastern Mediterranean and the Middle East and by extension to East Africa, and given U.S. preoccupation elsewhere, Britain attempted to transform a facade of control left over from the war into a Middle East security system. Two existing options—a dense pattern of treaty-protected bases in Egypt, Jordan, and Iraq, and a sprawling defense arrangement stretching from Libya through the Sudan and eastern Africa to the Gulf States—could not be sustained. India was not on call from 1947. Two other options—a retreat to Africa (the Lagos-Kenya line) and a Commonwealth plan (Australia and New Zealand, consuming U.S. security in ANZUS, and South Africa, despite the consequences of the Boer nationalist victory in the 1948 elections, were to contribute) were explored at length but inconsequentially. Logically, unavoidably, the United States orchestrated alternative arrangements in the Middle East in the 1950s, as radical Arab nationalism and Nasserism seemed to exacerbate the Soviet threat, resulting in the Baghdad Pact and then the establishment of CENTO. In any case, the territorial extent of Britain's empire was substantially reduced. By 1950, beyond the dominions, it embraced black Africa; remnants in South Asia, Caribbean, Pacific, and Mediterranean possessions; Aden; Kuwait; and the Persian Gulf states.

The transfer of sovereignty in South Asia was not to be the equivalent to abdication. The Indian subcontinent, to whose independence the Labour party had been committed since the 1930s, was to remain unpartitioned, free of civil war, a member of the Commonwealth, and certainly not nonaligned. Ideologically based cooperation and Commonwealth membership would follow from decolonization if the newly sovereign states, led by long-standing collaborators, adopted participatory government and the rule of law and retained their inherited British institutions. A degree of strategic interdependence might be created. The sterling area should flourish, as exports to dollar markets expanded and nonconvertible sterling balances accumulated. Undifferentiated trade statistics substantiated the claim that the empire as a whole continued to make a necessary contribution to Britain's economic recovery. Between 1945 and 1949, the empire provided 48 percent of British imports and absorbed 57.5 percent of British exports. The figures for the period from 1950 to 1954 were 49 percent and 54 percent, respectively. Both sets of figures exceeded those of 1939, reflecting economic recovery and trade revival. At the same time, Britain, at the Treasury's insistence, avoided taking on untenable economic aid and financial burdens, and refused to guarantee private investments in colonial development.

Conservative governments of the early and mid 1950s were publicly committed to the established policy of guiding colonial possessions toward self-government within the British Commonwealth. These governments had additional incentives to use imperial holdings to assist Britain's recovery and to confirm its status as a global power. U.S. financial assistance lessened, and financial and strategic retrenchment was still necessary. Britain remained in debtor status, and experienced only temporary respite from balance-of-payment deficits. The Suez Crisis of 1956 dramatically demonstrated sterling's subservience to the dollar and mapped out Britain's future as the junior partner in the Anglo-American special relationship. By 1957, black Africa was Britain's central concern. Conservative talk of tightening British political control, defying nationalist leaders, and using force to deny them independence stopped. Insistence that parts of Africa—Kenya, Tanganyika, Uganda, Sierra Leone, and Somaliland—were still not ready for independence ceased. The schemes to rally to the white settlers and retreat into a "satellite world," to use Eric Hobsbawn's phrase, were put to rest. Such strategies would merely invite armed revolt, which could be put down, as it was in Kenya and in Malaya, but armed revolt would be led and exploited by extremists. Such situations would undermine the influence of indigenous moderate realists, with whom bargaining would be conducted and on whom cooperation depended. Violence in Malaya, Kenya, and Cyprus both consumed resources and warned that premature transfer of sovereignty, as in the case of the Gold Coast, might be more prudent than to delay and invite conflict.

In January 1960, Macmillan toured southern Africa to make points that needed to be made, to speak of history on the march. Britain supported the principle of black majority rule; indigenous political parties were authentic and legitimate. Macmillan warned white leaders of the "winds of change" from the north. He dismissed charges of British appeasement of black majorities. He promised that astute management of decolonization could reconcile political independence with profitable, economic interdependence and dependence. After all, political stability remained the necessary condition of trade and investment. A string of alliances between Britain and the African states could be negotiated. He would demonstrate to African nationalist leaders that they must cast their lot with the West.

From 1957, beginning with Ghana and focusing first on Western and then on Eastern Africa, sovereignty was vested in new states, and political decolonization went forward, initially with even higher expectations of what the renegotiated contract could offer. Strategic interdependence, ideological compatibility, and commonwealth membership were to bring about partnerships in Africa between nominal equals that were, in fact, compliant allies of Britain, even client states. Economic complementarities would be drawn more finely and deeply, and would provide benefits for both parties when the new states were integrated into the Western economy. Economic development, profit sharing, and reform would both deny the cause of exploitation of labor and of the landless to radicals, and would increase economic growth, indigenous incomes and savings, and state revenues. The new African states' continued membership in the sterling area would maintain the flow of U.S. dollars to London, but not, it must be conceded, provide adequately compensating benefits for the newly independent states. They would develop further, however, as markets for and sources of raw materials, food, and minerals, and would provide investment opportunities. Economic diversification could follow; British investment could exit weak markets and enter those with significant potential (e.g., Nigerian oil). Industrial development in certain African states would reflect increased British investment and export of industrial equipment and capital goods. Partnerships and joint ventures could stimulate the Africanization of business and commerce. These were the high expectations of Britain in postcolonial Africa. There proved to be limits, however, to the maintenance of a neoempire in Africa, which rapidly became apparent. Preferential trading and investment arrangements, for example, became increasingly difficult to maintain. As the dollar gap narrowed, sterling approached convertibility but was rarely strong and free of crisis. Newly independent states found economic alternatives to Britain—the United States, for example, or India in the case of Nigeria. Britain turned more toward Europe to find its economic future, and struggled to prosper amid freer trade patterns in a global market. There had to be and were alternatives to empire, among them the special relationship with the United States, and nuclear status. The dark side of African decolonization was Britain's failure to satisfy the white community in Rhodesia and its illegal defiance of change, and the violent confrontation between the white minority and black majority in Kenya. The violence in these two situations more than matched that in Malaya and Cyprus, but never approached the magnitude of the French experience in Vietnam and Algeria.

The disillusioned and the nostalgic found evidence of scuttle in the political records of both Labour and Conservative governments, in the loss of India, Palestine, Aden, and the Gulf States—losses that stood out when only the *rentier* Hashemite kingdom of Jordan survived to remind imperialists of Britain's moment in the Middle East. As a decolonizer, Britain avoided high defense and development costs and had rarely indulged in military intervention. But that had meant that African elites, for example, judged Britain to be a weak patron, with less leverage in Europe than France, and with less security to supply than the United States. There are grounds here for a favorable contrast of the French Union in Africa with the British Commonwealth, but the comparison of a global, diplomatic enterprise with a functioning neo-empire in Africa is somewhat misplaced. Indeed, weighing costs and benefits, some may change the verdict on the outcomes of British as compared to French decolonization.

In any case, by 1970, British decolonization had spawned thirty independent states, home to some 750 million people (see Appendix B, p. 147). Only 5.5 million were left under British rule; 4.0 million resided in Hong Kong, and 0.5 million in Fiji. Such was the magnitude of the process, of the accomplishment, as the UN map took shape, and as complex interdependence prevailed. The task was completed with indispensable U.S. support and tolerance, which tainted the process somewhat in the eyes of some nationalists, but Britain also decolonized with a certain élan and subtlety. British decolonization, furthermore, did not bring about unequivocal, demonstrable, and permanent benefits to the Soviet Union.

Reflections: Nostalgia or Realism

Lord Beloff, heir to those who warned against precipitate decolonization in Africa, has argued that decolonization after World War II was a catastrophe—bringing chaos, war, famine and deprivation, military coups, and dictatorial regimes. These dangerous and deplorable consequences resulted largely from a U.S. failure to fill the vacuum left by Britain, a vacuum that was created in part by U.S. pressure on Britain to dissolve its empire. The American failure was one either of will or intellect, or of some combination of them. The United States, Beloff suggested, became a de facto imperial power that could not accept its own imperial role. Nor was it fit to do so, misled as it was by neo-Wilsonianism and by the lure of "traditional simplicities of a less complex past." Obsessed with the Soviet threat, the United States turned regional issues into a bipolar, zero-sum strategic contest. Enamored of informal empire that could be maintained through indirect rule and dubious clients, the United States was unable to solve the contradictions emanating from the juxtaposition of an anti-imperial doctrine with support for nationalism, independence and equality, and global power. The United States failed the world—it was made responsible for events even when it was not responsible and it floundered on, omnipotent but defensive, and embarrassed by being indicted as the new imperial, even satanic, power. The occasions on which the United States recognized the value of the British Empire and sought its aid were all too infrequent.[32] Beloff is not alone. The UN Development Program, in its *Human Development Report* of 1991, suggested that developing countries had primarily themselves to blame for their enduring poverty. They were wasting resources and opportunities on rearmament; greedy and vain elites squandered funds on inefficient and prestigious projects, and ignored basic human needs. Third World states were unable to rid themselves of corruption. Lack of political will, not of financial resources, was at the root of the tragedy.[33]

Critics of the Beloff thesis, such as the late Hedley Bull, deny that decolonization was a catastrophe, and insist that what was needed in the wake of empire was not more U.S. imperialism, but a reconstituted, stable world order. The Third World existed; it functioned. An explicit, overt U.S. imperialism was neither preferable nor feasible. Indeed, Roger Louis argued that an imperialist role would sacrifice "the central values of the American democracy." One might point out, in addition, that the British and French empires did not collapse in chaos. The process of decolonization, for all its violence and uneven consequences, proceeded with a degree of order and design that compares favorably to similar processes marking the end of the Soviet empire.

Appendix A: Independence

Independence, a seemingly elementary matter, is in fact a complicated question and proves elusive in so much of the literature. Autonomy, independence in external as well as internal policy matters, within a federal or confederal framework, and independence coupled with freedom from either kind of framework are all distinct stages. These contractual arrangements, in modus vivendi, conventions, and treaties, may be made sequentially or in one final act. The contractual arrangements could be made under one government but implemented under another, with or without amendments. Such scenarios bring into question claims that, for example, more French colonies achieved independence under Gaullist than under Socialist governments. Given the speed with which French governments in the Fourth Republic rushed in and out of office, it would have been remarkable had any one government actually begun the bargaining, negotiated the contract, and implemented the agreement in its term of rule.

French Guinea and Madagascar negotiated self rule with a Socialist government but achieved independence while a Gaullist government was in power. In 1946, indigenous elites were granted a limited role in a number of nominally autonomous states (e.g., in the Ivory Coast). In 1958, the Gaullist government of Michel Debré offered autonomy within the Franco-African Community to the Ivory Coast and six other states. In March 1959, the Ivory Coast adopted its first constitution as a self-governing republic. Early in 1960, the Debré government offered independence and membership in the French Union. The Ivory Coast rejected the offer, withdrew from the French Union, and became independent in August 1960. Kenya, from 1952 to 1963, and Ghana, from 1946 to 1957, provide examples of similar protracted independence processes in the British empire.

Finally, the various agreements, conventions, and treaties which embody the contractual arrangements of decolonization have not received careful enough scrutiny for what they contain and what was left to supplementary arrangements, informal undertakings and, simply, the future. They capture constitutional arrangements more clearly than economic, strategic and cultural expectations, and yet the latter were the stuff of neo-empire, interdependence and influence retained.

Appendix B: Postwar Decolonization

Francea

Governments	Colony and Year of Independence
Center Socialist President Vincent Auriol (1947–54)	*Region: Southeast Asia* Cambodia 1954 Laos 1954 Vietnam 1954 (conflict then internationally negotiated settlement)
Center Socialist President Rene Coty (1954–58)	*Region: Northern Africa* Morocco 1956 (limited conflict followed by negotiation) Tunisia 1956 (limited conflict followed by negotiation)
Right Gaullist President Charles de Gaulle (1958–69)	*Region: Africa and Northern Africa* Guinea 1958 Benin 1960 Burkino Faso 1960 Central African Republic 1960 Chad 1960 Congo 1960 Gabon 1960 Ivory Coast 1960 Madagascar 1960 (limited conflict followed by negotiation) Mali 1960 Mauritania 1960 Niger 1960 North Cameroon 1960 Senegal 1960 Togo 1960 Zaire 1960 Algeria 1962 (conflict followed by negotiated settlement)

(continued)

Appendix B *(continued)*

Right
Gaullist President
Georges Pompidou
(1969–74)

Right   *Region: Indian Ocean, Eastern Africa, Pacific Ocean*
Gaullist President   Tonga 1970
Valery Giscard d'Estaing   Comoros 1975
(1974–81)   Djibouti 1977
                                    Vanuatu 1980

United Kingdom[b]

Governments   Colony and Year of Independence

Labour   *Region: South Asia, Middle East*
Prime Minister   Bhutan 1947
Clement Attlee   India 1947 (negotiation followed by civil war)
(1945–51)   Pakistan 1947
                                    Borneo 1948
                                    Burma 1948
                                    Ceylon 1948
                                    Palestine 1948 (UN settlement preceded and followed
                                        by violence)

Conservative Prime Minister
Winston Churchill
(1951–55)

Conservative   *Region: Africa, South Asia*
Prime Minister   Sudan 1956
Anthony Eden   Ghana 1957
(1955–57)   Malaya 1957 (negotiation followed by conflict)

Conservative   *Region: Mediterranean, Middle East, Caribbean, South
Prime Minister   Asia, Pacific Ocean, Africa*
Harold Macmillan   Cyprus 1960 (negotiated settlement preceded and
(1957–63)   followed by conflict)
                                    Somaliland 1960
                                    Kuwait 1961
                                    Sierra Leone 1961
                                    South Cameroon 1961
                                    Jamaica 1962
                                    Kenya 1962 (conflict followed by negotiated settlement)
                                    Solomon Islands 1962
                                    Trinidad-Tobago 1962
                                    Uganda 1962
                                    Singapore 1963
                                    Tanzania 1963

Conservative   *Region: Africa, Mediterranean*
Prime Minister   Malawi 1964
Alexander Douglas-Home   Malta 1964
(1963–64)   Zambia 1964
                                    Zanzibar 1964

(continued)

Appendix B *(continued)*

Labour
Prime Minister
Harold Wilson
(1964–70)
	Region: Africa, Caribbean, Indian Ocean, Middle
	    East, Latin America, Pacific Ocean
	The Gambia 1965
	Maldives 1965
	Rhodesia 1965 (illegal independence followed by
	    conflict)
	Barbados 1966
	British Guiana 1966
	Aden 1967 (conflict before and after independence)
	West Indies Associated States 1967
	Mauritius 1968
	Fiji 1970

Conservative Prime Minister Edward Heath (1970–74)	*Region: Middle East, Caribbean* Bahrain 1971 Qatar 1971 United Arab Emirates 1971 Grenada 1974
Labour Prime Minister Harold Wilson (1974–76)	*Region: Indian Ocean* Seychelles 1976
Labour Prime Minister James Callaghan (1976–79)	*Region: Caribbean, Pacific Ocean* Dominica 1978 Tuvalu 1978 Kiribati 1979 St. Lucia 1979 St. Vincent and the Grenadines 1979
Conservative Prime Minister Margaret Thatcher (1979–1990)	*Region: Caribbean, Pacific Ocean, South Asia* Vanuatu 1980 British Honduras 1981 St. Kitts-Nevis 1983 Brunei 1984
Conservative Prime Minister John Major (1990–)	*Region: South Asia* Hong Kong 1997

Note: Unless indicated otherwise, independence came by negotiation, unmarred by
    conflict before or immediately after.
[a]France still rules Martinique, Gaudeloupe, French Guiana, and Reunion in the
    Caribbean; the Society Islands, Marquesas Islands, and Tuamotu Archipelago in
    the Pacific; and St. Pierre and Miquelon in the Atlantic; and Kerguelen Archipelago
    and the Crozet Islands near Antarctica.
[b]The United Kingdom still rules Anguilla, Bermuda, the Bahamas, the British Virgin
    Islands, Cayman Islands, Falklands, Gibraltar, Montserrat, Northern
    Ireland, Pitcairn Island, Saint Helena, and Turks and Caicos.

Notes

1. John Field, *Towards a Programme of Imperial Life: The British Empire at the Turn of the Century* (Westport: Greenwood, 1982); Kathryn Tidrick's quite brilliant *Empire and the English Character* (London: Tauris, 1989), revealing the beliefs of the colonial official in the field; Wolfgang J. Mommsen, "The Slow Death of Imperialism," in Nobutoshi Hagihara et al., eds., *Experiencing the Twentieth Century* (Tokyo: University of Tokyo Press, 1985), pp. 77–100; and Michael Howard, "Empire, Race and War in pre-1914 Britain," in Hugh Lloyd-Jones, Valerie Pearl, and Blair Worden, eds., *History and the Imagination* (New York: Oxford University Press, 1982). Business history, particularly because it explains how informal empire actually ran, how decolonization could threaten it, and how the threat could be finessed, provides another approach. See, for example, David K. Fieldhouse, *Merchant Capital and Decolonization: The United Africa Company, 1929–1987* (Oxford: Oxford University Press, 1994).

2. The British and Soviet evacuation from Iran in 1946 need not be included in the history of decolonization. Latin America was part of the Third World, but the only reasons to include it in the processes of decolonization would be to emphasize British divestment from the region to define the process as emancipation from an informal U.S. empire. Similarly, the violence that marked aspects of decolonization was a function of the one hundred or more "low-intensity" wars that ravaged the Third World after 1945, resulting in more than twenty million deaths and the refugee tragedy. Some attribute coinage of the term *decolonization* to Moritz Bonn in the 1930s. Moritz Bonn, *Economics and Politics* (Boston: Houghton Mifflin, 1932); and *The Crisis of Capitalism in America,* translated by Winifred Ray (New York: John Daz, 1932). Also see the work of Henri Brunschwig, "Preface" in Winifried Baumgart, *Imperialism: The Idea and Reality of British and French Colonial Expansion, 1880–1914* (New York: Oxford University Press, 1982); and Rudolf von Albertini, *European Colonial Rule, 1880–1940: The Impact of the West on India, Southeast Asia, and Africa,* trans. by John G. Williamson (Westport, CT: Greenwood, 1982; and *Decolonization: The Administration and Future of the Colonies, 1919–1960,* trans. by Francisca Garvie (Garden City, NY: Doubleday, 1971).

3. There were no significant Anglo-French tensions after the Lebanon-Syria affair in World War II that materially affected decolonization. On that episode see Ariel Roshwald, *Estranged Bedfellows: Britain and France in the Middle East During the Second World War* (New York: Oxford University Press, 1990). The British authorities, in liberating Saigon from Japanese rule, favored the French over the Viet Minh, and then used the Japanese against Vietnamese nationalists. Ernest Bevin, the Labour foreign secretary, found merit in Anglo-French cooperation in African development, but also found much to dislike in French visions of Europe's future (i.e., the Schuman and Pleven plans), and in the French threat to an emerging Atlantic community and Anglo-American cooperation. Britain and France watched each other in the process of decolonization and weighed the cumulative effects of each others' experience. Their collaboration in the Suez Crisis of 1956 was an aberration and a warning against further such escapades.

4. Max Beloff, *Imperial Sunset,* vol. 2 of *Dream of Commonwealth, 1921–42* (Dobbs Ferry, NY: Sheridan House, 1989); J.E. Williams, "The Joint Declaration on the Colonies: An Issue in Anglo-American Relations, 1942," *British Journal of International Studies* 2 (1976): 267–92; William Roger Louis, *Imperialism at Bay, 1941–1945* (Oxford: Clarendon, 1977) and William Roger Louis, *The British Empire in the Middle East, 1945–1951* (Oxford: Clarendon, 1984); Mario Rossi, *Roosevelt and the French* (Westport: Praeger, 1993); Hugh Ragsdale, ed., *Imperial Russian Foreign Policy* (New York: Cambridge University Press, 1993); Alexei Vassiliev, *Russian Policy in the Middle East* (New York: Ithaca, 1993); and Dominic Lieven, "The Russian Empire and the Soviet Union as

Imperial Politics," *Journal of Contemporary History* 30, no. 4 (1995): 607–36. Despite several informative studies of Soviet policy toward the Middle East—for example, Oles M. Smolansky and Bettie M. Smolanski, *The U.S.S.R. and Iraq* (Durham: Duke University Press, 1991); Efraim Karsh, *Soviet Policy Toward Syria Since 1970* (New York: St. Martin's, 1991) and Galia Golan, *Soviet Policies in the Middle East from World War II to Gorbachev* (Cambridge: Cambridge University Press, 1990)—Sovietology trails far behind scholarship on U.S. policy.

5. Labour found a degree of party unity in espousing decolonization, whereas the Tories gained only limited and transitory electoral advantage by protesting it. Both parties recognized that it would be damaging politically to indulge in scuttle. Conservative nationalists in France made a cause out of empire generally and of Algeria specifically, in league with white settlers, colonial bureaucrats, and military officials: Socialists saw scant political advantage in decolonization. De Gaulle, in the wake of the Algerian War and the demise of the Fourth Republic, took decolonization out of French politics as a way to consolidate the Fifth Republic. On these and related issues see David Goldsworthy, *Colonial Issues in British Politics, 1945–1961: From Colonial Development to Winds of Change* (Oxford: Clarendon, 1971) and Miles Kahler, *Decolonisation in Britain and France: The Domestic Consequences of International Relations* (Princeton: Princeton University Press, 1984).

6. Tony Smith, *The Pattern of Imperialism: The United States, Great Britain, and the Late-Industrializing World Since 1815* (Cambridge: Cambridge University Press, 1981); Michael H. Hunt and Steven I. Levine, "The Revolutionary Challenges to Early U.S. Cold War Policies in Asia," in Warren Cohen and Akira Iriye, eds., *The Great Powers in East Asia, 1953–1960* (New York: Columbia University Press, 1990). World War I and the peacemaking of 1919, the master organizing principle of the latter being national self-determination, brought sociology back into international relations. The literature, now couched in terms of culture and identity, is vast. One might begin with Willard A. Mullins, "On the Concept of Ideology in Political Science," *American Political Science Review* 66, no. 2 (1972): 498–510; William Bloom, *Personal Identity, National Identity, and International Relations* (Cambridge: Cambridge University Press, 1990); Eric Hobsbawm, *Nations and Nationalism Since 1780: Programme, Myth and Reality* (Cambridge: Cambridge University Press, 1990); and Anthony Smith, *Nations and Nationalism in a Global Empire* (Cambridge: Polity, 1994). For the state of debate in international relations aound these topics, see Yosef Lapid and Frederick Kratochwil, eds., *The Return of Culture and Identity in International Relations Theory* (Boulder, CO: Lynne Rienner, 1996). See also Robert H. Jackson, "The Weight of Ideas in Decolonization: Normative Change in International Relations," in Judith Goldstein and Robert Keohane, eds., *Ideas and Foreign Policy: Beliefs, Institutions, and Political Change* (Ithaca: Cornell University Press, 1993), pp. 111–38.

7. The record of the Labour government cannot but be controversial, attacked as it was from the disillusioned Right, which spoke of avoidable decline and wrong policy choices (i.e., the welfare state), and from the Little Englander Left, which blamed precipitous decline on the foolish pursuit of great-power status and prestige. See, for example, Correlli Barnett, *The Pride and Fall: The Dream and Illusion of Britain as a Great Nation* (New York: Free Press, 1986); Correlli Barnett, *The Lost Victory: British Dreams, British Realities, 1945–1950* (London: MacMillan, 1994); and Michael Blackwell, *Clinging to Grandeur: British Attitudes and Foreign Policy in the Aftermath of the Second World War* (Westport: Greenwood, 1993). Barnett lambastes the Labour government for chasing global ambitions and inviting "total strategic over-stretch."

8. Irwin Wall, *The United States and the Making of Postwar France, 1945–1954* (New York: Cambridge University Press, 1991); Michael J. Hogan, *The Marshall Plan:*

America, Britain, and the Reconstruction of Western Europe, 1947–1952 (New York: Cambridge University Press, 1987); and William Burr, "Marshall Planners and the Politics of Empire: The United States and French Financial Policy, 1948," *Diplomatic History* 15, no. 4 (1991): 495–522. There is no need here to join the debate in response to Alan Milward on the central or marginal role of the Marshall Plan in European recovery.

9. See Lance Davis and Robert Huttenbach, *Mammon and the Pursuit of Empire: The Political Economy of British Imperialism, 1860–1912* (New York: Cambridge University Press, 1986) and P.J. Cain and Anthony S. Hopkins, *British Imperialism*, 2 vols. (London: Longman, 1991). In the nineteenth century, rising defense costs necessitated increased taxation, which provided ammunition for the radical critique that empire was a waste of public and national resources.

10. The state of the debate between the principal participants is nicely summarized in Burr, "Marshall Planners and the Politics of Empire."

11. Robert E. Wood, *From the Marshall Plan to Debt Crisis: Foreign Aid and Development Choices in the World Economy* (Berkeley and Los Angeles: University of California Press, 1986); Robert J. McMahon, "Credibility and World Power," *Diplomatic History* 15, no. 4 (1991): 455–71; Robert J. McMahon, "Interpreting America's Failures in the Third World," *Diplomatic History* 15, no. 1 (1991): 131–36; Dennis Merrill, "America Encounters the Third World," *Diplomatic History* 16, no. 2 (1992): 325–30; Cary Fraser, "Understanding American Policy Toward the Decolonisation of European Empires, 1945–1964," *Diplomacy and Statecraft* 3, no. 1 (1992): 105–25; David S. Painter, "Explaining U.S. Relations with the Third World," *Diplomatic History* 19, no. 3 (1995): 525–48. It would be an error to ignore Gabriel Kolko, *Confronting the Third World: United States Foreign Policy, 1945–1980* (New York: Pantheon, 1988); one can safely dispense, however, with Noam Chomsk, *Deterring Democracy* (London: Verso, 1990). The domestic significance of the United States' inability to espouse imperialism for itself, to champion the imperialism of its allies, and the embarrassment of the racial and other blemishes on U.S. society, as the United States searched for its identity after World War II, are approached in David Campbell, *Writing Security: U.S. Foreign Policy and the Politics of Identity* (Minneapolis: University of Minnesota Press, 1992).

12. Roger Kanet, ed., *The Soviet Union and the Developing Nations* (Baltimore: Johns Hopkins University Press, 1974); Peter Shearman and Phil Williams, eds., *The Superpowers, Central America, and the Middle East* (London: Brassey's Defence Publishers, 1988); Edward A. Kolodziej and Roger Kanet, eds., *The Limits of Soviet Power in the Developing World* (Baltimore: Johns Hpokins University Press, 1989); Alvin Z. Rubinstein, *Moscow's Third World Strategy* (Princeton: Princeton University Press, 1988); and Mark N. Katz, ed., *The U.S.S.R. and Marxist Revolution in the Third World* (New York: Cambridge University Press, 1990).

13. For British and U.S. decisions about military intervention in the Third World, see Scot Macdonald, "Historical Analogies and Learning: The Influence of Historical Analogies and Learning on Decisions to Use Military Force" (Ph.D. diss., University of Southern California, 1996).

14. Historians and others have made an impressive start, particularly those who weave command of the U.S. archives with an understanding of Third World politics and culture. It is not surprising, however, that few scholars go beyond a regional mandate—in other words, U.S. policies toward Korea, the Middle East, southern Africa, and South Asia—to work comparatively toward a grand synthesis. See, for example, Robert J. McMahon, "Toward a Post-Colonial Order: Truman Administration Policies Toward South and Southeast Asia," in Michael J. Lacey, ed., *The Truman Presidency* (New York: Cambridge University Press, 1989); Michael J. Lacey, ed., *The Cold War in the Periphery: The United States, India, and Pakistan, 1947–1965* (New York: Columbia University

Press, 1992); Bruce Cumings, *The Origins of the Korean War*, 2 vols. (Princeton: Princeton University Press, 1981 and 1990); Hunt and Levine, "The Revolutionary Challenges to Early U.S. Cold War Policy in Asia"; Douglas Little, "Gideon's Band: America and the Middle East Since 1945," *Diplomatic History* 18, no. 4 (1994): 513–40; Dennis Merrill, "The United States and the Rise of the Third World," in Gordon Martel, ed., *American Foreign Relations Reconsidered, 1890–1993* (London: Routledge, 1994); Lawrence Kaplan, Denise Artaud, and Mark Rubin, eds., *Dien Bien Phu and the Crisis of Franco-American Relations, 1945–1955* (Wilmington, DE: SR Books, 1990); Peter Hahn, *The United States, Great Britain, and Egypt, 1945–1956* (Chapel Hill: University of North Carolina Press, 1991); Mark Gasiorowski, *U.S. Foreign Policy and the Shah: Building a Client State in Iran* (Ithaca: Cornell University Press, 1991); and David L. Anderson, *Trapped by Success: The Eisenhower Administration and Vietnam, 1953–61* (New York: Columbia University Press, 1991).

15. Randall B. Woods, *A Changing of the Guard: Anglo-American Relations, 1941–1946* (Chapel Hill: University of North Carolina Press, 1990); Robert A. Pollard, *Economic Security and the Origins of the Cold War, 1945–1950* (New York: Columbia University Press, 1985); Melvyn P. Leffler, "The American Conception of National Security and the Beginnings of the Cold War, 1945–48," *American Historical Review* 89 (April 1984): 346–81; Melvyn P. Leffler, *A Preponderance of Power* (Stanford: Stanford University Press, 1992); William Roger Louis and Ronald Robinson, "The Imperialism of Decolonization," *Journal of Imperial and Commonwealth History* 22, no. 3 (1994): 462–511; and Michael Fry and Miles Hochstein, "The Forgotten Middle Eastern Crisis of 1957: Gaza and Sharm-el-Sheikh," *International History Review* 15, no. 1 (1993): 46–83.

16. Thomas Borstelmann, *Apartheid's Reluctant Uncle: The United States and Southern Africa in the Early Cold War* (New York: Oxford University Press, 1993); and David N. Gibbs, "Political Parties and International Relations: The United States and the Decolonization of Sub-Saharan Africa," *International History Review* 17, no. 2 (1995): 300–327. Gibbs finds a pattern of change rather than of continuity in U.S. policy as different presidents occupy the White House. Roosevelt and Truman, preoccupied by global war and the emerging Cold War, substantially left Africa—despite their oratory—to the European colonial powers. Their administrations railed against Anglo-French policies that discriminated against U.S. trade, in part through commercial shipping monopolies, and U.S. oil interests. Truman particularly wanted Africa to remain loyal to Western Europe, and Western Europe to benefit from continued imperial links. The United States needed the uranium and minerals of South Africa even as apartheid flourished. Eisenhower, deeply skeptical of black nationalism, disinterested in Africa, and unimpressed with U.S. trade and investment opportunities, looked to Britain and France to guide Africa toward a better, noncommunist future. Revolutionary nationalism seemed to him so implausible that he applauded even Belgian and Portuguese policies. See also William Minlev, "Cold War, Racism, and Uranium," *Diplomatic History* 20, no. 1 (1966): 133–37.

17. Orme Sargent memorandum, July 11, 1945. Quoted in Rohan Butler, M.E. Pelly, and H.J. Yasamee, eds., *Documents on British Policy Overseas*, ser. 1, vol. 1, no. 102 (London: Her Majesty's Stationery Office), pp. 181–87.

18. John Kent, *British Imperial Strategy and the Origins of the Cold War, 1944–1949* (London: Leicester University Press, 1993); Anne Deighton, ed., *Britain and the First Cold War* (New York: St. Martin's, 1990); and R. Aldrich, *British Intelligence, Strategy, and the Cold War, 1945–1951* (London: Routledge, 1992). More generally, see Henri Grimal, *La Décolonisation, 1919–1963* (Paris: A. Colin, 1965); and Wyndraeth H. Morris-Jones and Georges Fischer, *Decolonisation and After: The British and French Experience* (London: F. Cass, 1980).

19. One must emphasize, however, that the archival research necessary to examine

these assertions for the late 1950s and 1960s could not be attempted until recently because of the 30-year rule. The French archives are never the easiest shale to quarry. John Chipman's admirable monograph rests on interviews, public documents, and secondary sources. Roger Louis and Ronald Robinson have begun to show what careful and detailed research must be done if one is to grasp the nature of the bargaining that constituted decolonization. There are even more elementary, definitional problems to be resolved, which are identified in Appendix A.

20. D. Bruce Marshall, *The French Colonial Myth and Constitution-Making in the Fourth Republic* (New Haven: Yale University Press, 1973), pp. 102–15.

21. Hubert Deschamps, *The French Union* (Paris: Berger-Levault, 1956).

22. Marshall, *The French Colonial Myth,* ch. 6.

23. Deschamps, *French Union.*

24. See Appendix B.

25. Stanley Karnow, *Vietnam: A History* (New York: Penguin, 1984), ch. 4.

26. Alistair Horne, *A Savage War of Peace: Algeria, 1954–1962* (New York: Macmillan, 1978), pp. 545–47.

27. Richard Adloff, *West Africa* (New York: Holt, Rinehart, and Winston, 1964); William J. Foltz, *From French West Africa to the Mali Federation* (New Haven: Yale University Press, 1965); John D. Hargreaves, *West Africa: The Former French States* (Englewood Cliffs, NJ: Prentice-Hall, 1967); Patrick Manning, *Francophone Sub-Saharan Africa, 1880–1985* (New York: Cambridge University Press, 1988); Virginia Thompson and Richard Adloff, *French West Africa* (Stanford: Stanford University Press, 1957); and Horne, *A Savage War,* pp. 539–44.

28. John Chipman, *French Power in Africa* (Oxford: Oxford University Press, 1989), pp. 118, 131–32.

29. Dominique Moisi, "Intervention in French Foreign Policy," in Hedley Bull, ed., *Intervention in World Politics* (Oxford: Oxford University Press, 1984), pp. 67–77.

30. See Appendix B.

31. Central Office of Information, *Britain and the Process of Decolonization* (London: Her Majesty's Stationery Office, 1970); Ronald Hyam, ed., *The Labour Government and the End of the Empire* (London: Her Majesty's Stationery Office, 1991); David Goldsworthy, ed., *The Conservative Government and the End of Empire, 1951–1957* (London: Her Majesty's Stationery Office, 1994); Stephen Howe, *Anticolonialism in British Politics* (Oxford: Clarendon, 1993); Allister E. Hinds, "Sterling and Imperial Policy, 1945–51," *Journal of Imperial and Commonwealth History* 15 (1987): 148–69; John Darwin, *Britain and Decolonisation: The Retreat from Empire in the Post-War World* (New York: St. Martin's, 1988); Glen Balfour-Paul, *The End of Empire in the Middle East* (Cambridge: Cambridge University Press, 1990); Prosser Gifford and William Roger Louis, eds., *The Transfer of Power in Africa: Decolonization, 1940–1960* (New Haven: Yale University Press, 1982); Prosser Gifford and William Roger Louis, eds., *Decolonization and African Independence: The Transfer of Power, 1960–1980* (New Haven: Yale University Press, 1988); and H. Rahman, *A British Defense Problem in the Middle East: The Failure of the 1946 Anglo-Egyptian Negotiations* (Reading, UK: Ithaca, 1994).

32. Michael Fry, "The Special Relationship," *Review of International Studies* 14 (1988): 237–45.

33. Anatole Kaletsky, "In Praise of Imperialism," *The Times* (London), June 3, 1991.

III

Peripheral Successor States and the Legacies of Empire

6

State Building in the Shadow of an Empire-State

The Soviet Legacy in Post-Soviet Politics

Mark R. Beissinger

Introduction

Like old soldiers, empires never really die; at most they fade away. The consequences of empires usually live on for generations beyond their institutional lives, and well after actual relationships of imperial domination have ceased. Indeed, long beyond the dissolution of empires, many of the legacies of imperial domination remain so embedded in everyday existence as to be practically prosaic.

How then should one conceptualize the legacies of four hundred years of Russian Empire for state building in a region widely known as home to the world's "last empire"? The tsarist legacy itself continues to exert a significant influence on current politics, often in subtle ways. Given the enormous political upheavals, social engineering, and societal transformations of the Soviet period, the social, economic, political, and environmental consequences of empire in Eurasia begin to approach the impenetrable. To make the task more manageable, I will address primarily the legacies of the Soviet empire for post-Soviet state building and will confine my analysis to state building in the non-Russian post-Soviet states, although one could easily pose these same questions for Russia and the republics of Russia as well.

Of course, in every respect, it is much too early to take stock of the legacies of Soviet rule for post-Soviet state building. Within a short period of time, a number of aspects of the Soviet legacy have been shed, while many others persist. But the real legacies of empires are only visible over the course of decades. It is an axiom throughout the region that post-Soviet states are supposedly endeavoring to overcome the legacies of totalitarianism and empire and to remake their states and societies in a new image. Yet, in a number of cases this struggle remains little more than a constitutive myth, and elites have already accepted—or at least come to terms with—a number of critical aspects of the Soviet legacy. Certainly, from what we know about other postcolonial situations, this result seems likely. Also, we cannot possibly know the outcome of post-Soviet state building; it is impossible to forecast whether true stateness will congeal in Eurasia, or whether Eurasian states will become, like many states in Africa, states in name only.[1]

One need merely recall how the euphoria that accompanied decolonization in many parts of the world in the 1950s and 1960s gave way to despair by the 1970s and to generalized crisis by the 1980s. Georgian leader Zviad Gamsakhurdia, himself a victim of persecution by the KGB, is said to have told his followers: "We are being robbed by the Soviet occupiers; if we get rid of them, we will live well."[2] Yet, having attained power, Gamsakhurdia imitated his former tormentors, imposing a terror on his fellow Georgians that rivaled that of the Soviet secret police and unleashing a wave of interethnic violence that turned Georgia into a mere shell of a state. Georgia perhaps represents the extreme of failed state building among the newborn states of the former USSR; certainly, it is not the only case. Yet, the example of Gamsakhurdia starkly illustrates not only how naive assumptions underlie early understandings of the transcendence of empires, but also how postindependence leaders are at times drawn to reproduce the very patterns of behavior against which they rebelled.

There is a large and varied body of theoretical literature addressing the legacies of imperialism for state building, the vast majority of which focuses on European overseas empires. While a first wave of scholarship, under the influence of modernization theory, directed its attention to the cultural implant of modernity bestowed through prolonged contact with European colonizers, a second wave concentrated instead on the political, social, and economic implications of continuing transnational economic control in the wake of decolonization. More recent work has focused on the institutional and political dynamics of colonial government and its role in remaking colonial societies: establishing structures and roles into which postcolonial behavior flowed, defining new cultural identities, and demarcating what would become postcolonial space. As René Lemarchand has written with regard to Africa, "the colonial state . . . must indeed be viewed as the single most powerful agent of societal transformation in the history of the [African] continent."[3] Crawford Young, in his monumental work on the African colonial state, gives the following assessment of the impact of colonial institutions on postcolonial African politics:

> The colonial state in Africa lasted in most instances less than a century—a mere moment in historical time. Yet it totally reordered political space, societal hierarchies and cleavages, and modes of economic production. Its territorial grid—whose final contours congealed only in the dynamics of

decolonization—determined the state units that gained sovereignty and came to form the present system of African polities. The logic of its persistence and reproduction was by the time of independence deeply embedded in its mechanism of internal guidance.

As Young argues, once institutionalized, a state "has a formidable capacity for its own reproduction across time and in the face of systematic efforts by a new regime to uproot prior forms." [4]

I take this as an important starting point for investigating the legacies of Soviet rule for post-Soviet state building. If indeed, as Young argues, the legacies of imperialism are inseparable from the ways in which imperial control is crystallized in institutions,[5] then any attempt to penetrate the legacies of imperialism for Eurasian state building must begin with an understanding of the specific ways in which the Soviet empire-state institutionalized domination across its expanse. The major political issue confronting the newly independent Baltic states in the 1920s, for instance, was land reform: breaking up the large estates owned by the German, Polish, and Russian nobility through which tsardom had exercised its domination over the region; and creating a landed peasantry capable of acting as a bulwark against the threat of Russian communism.[6] In the 1990s, by contrast, the large Russian-speaking minority that was settled into the region as part of the Soviet government's efforts to establish control is widely understood to be the region's most significant political issue, as well as the most serious threat to Baltic sovereignty. This is not to say that a minority issue was not present in the 1920s, nor a land issue in the 1990s; but in the 1920s, minorities in the Baltic were accommodated within state structures and afforded a considerable degree of autonomy (policies that were ultimately abandoned in the 1930s with the rise of authoritarian regimes), while the breakup of collective farms in the Baltic in the 1990s has largely created thorny issues of state subsidy, not of sovereignty and social equality.

The character and larger meaning of postcolonial politics in the Baltic states changed dramatically over the span of the twentieth century, largely as a result of the very different institutional legacies of Soviet and tsarist rules. Certainly, while one can find commonalities of institutional forms across empires, particularly if one deals with them at a relatively high level of abstraction, Soviet institutions stand out in so many respects from the institutions of other empires, including those of tsarism. As we shall see, the specific way in which Soviet institutions had crystallized on the eve of the demise of the Soviet state not only bequeathed a unique set of problems to post-Soviet state builders, but also accounts for many of the variations in state building that one finds in the successor states.

A consideration of the institutional differences between Soviet and other patterns of imperialism leads us toward a second perspective from which to approach the issue of the legacies of empire for post-Soviet state building. If understanding of postimperial legacies derives to a large extent from an understanding of the political dynamics of imperial domination, then we must recognize that, in sharp contrast to overseas empires, empire building and state building in Eurasia have been profoundly ambiguous enterprises. The Soviet Union always straddled the divide between empire and state. This ambiguity has important implications for the study of imperial legacies. One cannot easily separate the Soviet imperial legacy from the Soviet state-building legacy. Indeed, the inability to make this distinction clearly was one of the conditions that prevented Soviet reformers from averting disintegration and collapse.[7] One cannot treat empire and its legacies in the Soviet case as having merely an institutional dimension. Rather, the Soviet legacy is read as imperial, an act that speaks as much about the nature of identities and authority relations as it does about those who do the reading.

The constructed nature of the Soviet imperial legacy raises questions about the tendency in much of the scholarship on imperialism to treat empires as things, that is, as structural entities of external control composed of an exploitative center and an exploited periphery. It is understandable why such a structural understanding might be attractive in studying overseas empires. The boundaries between center and periphery seemed obvious; they were demarcated not merely by differences in power and culture, but also were palpable geographically and physically, were institutionalized in colonial legal codes, and usually were visibly marked by race. Most overseas empires did not seriously seek to legitimate themselves within the societies that they dominated; coercion and submission were enough. Efforts to legitimate colonial rule were aimed instead at metropolitan populations; and only when direct domination was difficult did overseas imperial powers introduce into peripheral societies modes of indirect rule and noncoercive ideologies of colonial legitimation. Extraction of wealth and resources for overseas empires was a proclaimed goal. In a world in which multiple self-avowed empires openly vied for domination with the expressed purpose of benefiting an imperial core, a structural understanding of empires made a great deal of sense.

But the Soviet empire-state did not inhabit such a world. With the exception of the first several decades of the Soviet state, when the USSR defined itself in opposition to the norms of the European imperial system, the USSR inhabited instead a world of states, a world in which empires came to be universally recognized as illegitimate. In a world of states, in which no political entity acknowledges itself to be imperial, in which political power rests on legitimacy at least as much as (if not more than) it rests on coercion, and in which a profound uncertainty often hangs between domination and consent, a structural understanding of empire makes much less sense.

Michael Doyle began his study of empires with a quote from Lord Hailey that "imperialism is not a word for scholars." Fortunately, this did not dissuade Doyle or other scholars from studying the subject. But in contrast to empires of the past, which unabashedly wore the imperial badge, in the late twentieth century "empire" is not considered a polite term for states. The reasons are clear. Ian Lustick has pointed to the powerful effects that images of state and empire have upon those to whom they are addressed. He notes that "in the modern world, empires are expected to break apart," and secession and decolonization have been turned into categories used by politicians "to label what they do to prevent or achieve changes in the shape of a state."[8] In a universe of mass politics in which, in Murray Edelman's words, "government affects behavior chiefly by shaping the cognitions of large numbers of people in ambiguous situations,"[9] states seeking to establish their claims to territorial control utilize the norms of the state system to shape expectations and cognitions. They do not take kindly to an anti-imperial rhetoric challenging these claims. Nevertheless, in the minds of many, empires do persist in a world of states,[10] in large part because imperial subjugation remains one of the few legitimate norms for challenging state boundaries. Empires in the late twentieth century have come to represent the antithesis of the modern state system. They have become one of several alter egos for polities claiming the status of states, embodying an essential rejection of the norms and practices of dominant groups within these states and constituting a term of opprobrium by those claiming the status of nation and seeking a major alteration in state boundaries.[11]

This has important implications for how one probes the legacies of the Soviet empire-state for post-Soviet state building. The constructed character of many of these legacies means that how one reads these legacies depends to a large extent on where one situates oneself in relationship to the former USSR and to the post-Soviet state system. The ambiguity that hangs over Russia's diaspora in the post-Soviet states is a case in point. Does the diaspora represent a repressed minority or a potential fifth column of the former occupying power? Many aspects of post-Soviet reality contain similar ambiguities and can be read through the lens of the Soviet imperial legacy. Is Russian the language of a cultural minority or the language of occupation? Are ethnic conflicts in post-Soviet societies the products of Soviet imperialism or postimperial phenomena? Are the economic convulsions brought on by "shock therapy" the result of the Soviet legacy of central planning or the design of post-Soviet officials and economists? These are the issues that engender controversy in post-Soviet politics, being part of the larger contest of politics and subject to interpretation. In the post-Soviet case, the Soviet state-building legacy and the physical proximity of the former dominating power inject a particular dynamic and an uncertainty into postimperial politics that were less salient in the cases of overseas empires. For the successor states, state building must occur in the shadow of their former occupier, an occupier that, for the most part, denies the legitimacy of the collapse of its past state-building projects, seeks to extend its influence over the new system of states, and even openly seeks to reintegrate these new states under its lead.

The constructed character of the Soviet imperial legacy pushes us to look beyond mere institutional structures and to probe the deeper cognitions, expectations, norms, and behaviors that underlie the state and interact with state structures. For both empires and states are much more than formal institutions or systems of ethnic stratification. James Rosenau, in a review of recent scholarship on the state, has called the state a "wavering" and "elusive" concept, one that is mired in ambiguity. Yet, "the reality of our analytic world is that the state is deeply embedded in our terminology and is unlikely to yield to efforts to replace it."[12] The state may be, as Rosenau notes, "a fictional abstraction, but as such it is a serious fiction and, like all fictions that are so serious as to create their own reality, cannot be ignored."[13] Much the same must be said about empires in a world of states. Just as, in Rosenau's words, "the state finds expression in those individuals who act on its behalf, employing its force and applying its laws so as to preserve and enhance the norms, habits, and practices of the collectivity,"[14] so too do contemporary empires find meaning in those individuals who would reject those norms. This is not to deny in any respect the authenticity or tangibility of contemporary empires. The behaviors and acts that give cause for large numbers of people to regard a polity as an empire are real enough. Indeed, for the most part, post-Soviet states remain haunted by the nightmares of their imperial pasts, a past that has been disfigured into the somber realities of everyday life. But the legacies of empires must be understood not only in terms of the physical scars that occupation inflicts on society and the human and material resources available for building viable state structures, but also as a way of thinking about authority.

Old structures of central domination may disappear, and former peripheries may constitute themselves as new centers. People, however, remain, and it is partly here that the legacies of past institutions endure: the relationship between state and society is defined in critical measure by ways of behaving and thinking in interaction with the state, and not just by the physical and material conditions left behind by external domination. It is not merely the question of whether states are congealing that interests us here, but also what kind of states appear to be congealing. Much as one can speak of an "African post-colonial state" in the sense of a political legacy deriving from colonialism that structures politics in significantly similar ways, we can also speak of a "Soviet postcolonial state," a powerful set of structures, constraints, and embedded ways of thinking and behaving that are likely to color post-Soviet politics for many years to come.

The following discussion begins with an examination of some of the institutional legacies of Soviet rule. The politics of identity in the post-Soviet era has been irrevocably altered by Soviet ethnofederalism, and I devote some attention to the ways in which Soviet policies in this realm have structured post-Soviet attitudes and behaviors. I then go on to examine how various crystallizations of the state across the expanse of Soviet territory have reproduced themselves in the post-Soviet era, as well as how the specific organization of the state on the eve of Soviet collapse determined the distribution of resources available for state building in the post-Soviet era. After discussing some of the shared cultural legacies of Soviet rule (manifested in particular in styles of governance, ways of interacting with the state, and popular attitudes towards authority), I conclude with some thoughts about the implications of state building in the shadow of one's former occupier, and how this condition, in interaction with the Soviet legacy and the parameters of the international system, extends a pale of uncertainty over the state-building projects of post-Soviet Eurasia.

Ethnofederalism and Identity Politics in Post-Soviet Politics

Let me begin with the most basic structural parameter within which state building is contained. It is well known that the borders that bind the post-Soviet state are little more than the republican borders of the Soviet federal system—an invention that for the first time formally divided political space in Eurasia and infused a sense of territoriality into nationality politics in the former USSR. The federal boundaries of the USSR were more than mere lines on a map. They established expectations around which behavior coalesced, determined flows of resources and access to cultural amenities (including native-language schooling and mass media), defined the contours of elites and bureaucracies, and consolidated identities around political-territorial units.[15] The invention of language-based nationalities in Central Asia was the result of the imposition of a federal structure across this territory.

In many ways, the breakup of the USSR itself can be rightfully understood as a child of Soviet ethnofederalism. Ron Suny has noted the ephemeral character of nationalism among non-Russians in the post-1917 period relative to the strength of local and social identities.[16] These patterns contrast sharply with those of the late 1980s, when national rather than class identities became the focus for mobilization. The relative weakness of nation in 1917 and its relative strength in 1989 were due in large part to the impact of ethnofederalism and the specific policies of national consolidation that it promoted. But, even among groups with union republics, the nation remained a weak category for mobilization and consciousness in the 1980s and 1990s in those cases in which Soviet policies fostered linguistic assimilation as part of a strategy for creating a non-Russian social base (e.g., in Belarus and eastern Ukraine), and in those cases in which strong local social bonds, reinforced by clientelistic relationships, tempered nationalist consciousness (as in Central Asia).

Statistical analysis of 1,320 secessionist demonstrations in the USSR from January 1987 through December 1991 among 40 different nationalities (excluding Russians) shows the important role played by the federal structure of the USSR and policies of linguistic assimilation in structuring nationalist consciousness. Controlling for population size and a host of other factors, the degree of linguistic Russification (measured as the percent of a nationality claiming Russian as its native language) had a strong negative relationship ($r = -.61$, significant at the .0001 level) with the frequency of efforts at secessionist mobilization. The federal unit of a nationality also had a substantial independent effect on secessionist mobilization. Even controlling for population size and other variables, groups within units lower than a union republic engaged in significantly less secessionist protest than did those with union republics (r = −.45, significant at the .01 level), and groups with no federal unit whatsoever engaged in even less frequent secessionist mobilization (r = −.49, significant at the .01 level).[17] In short, the varied crystallization of the Soviet state across its expanse accounts to a large extent for the manner and degree to which national consciousness materialized among post-Soviet nations. Colonial boundaries in Latin America, Africa, and Asia provided the basis for anticolonial mobilizations and eventually for the postimperial state system.[18] Similarly, the hierarchy of the Soviet federal system has shaped in significant ways the pressing of claims to independent statehood by Soviet nationalities, their recognition by the international community, and the degree to which post-Soviet states command social support within their populations on the basis of national identity.

The drawing of boundaries across Eurasia in the 1920s was a politicized act meant to advantage Soviet power by consolidating its control over these regions, but it was accomplished with extraordinary indifference to local circumstances. The central authorities never really took these borders as serious objects of meaning; after all, they had acceded unwillingly to federalism, and in any case it was believed that boundaries under Soviet socialism would eventually fade away. How else can one explain how nonchalantly this complex territory was carved up (i.e., the transfer of the Crimea from Russia to Ukraine in 1954, or the way in which the Amu Darya cuts across territories in Central Asia, creating a competition over who can siphon off more water earlier)? Local groups often understood the local political meaning of these lines and lobbied accordingly, freezing a particular moment's constellation of power into boundaries. The result was a remarkable patchwork of irrationality that continues in many ways to define the politics of the region. As in Africa, most ethnic groups straddle boundaries. Some, such as the Ossetians or the Armenians, were given two units within separate republics. Numerous territorial enclaves exist that are not visible on most maps. Thus, the origins of violence between the Kyrgyz and Tajiks over control of local land and water resources in the summer of 1989 in the Batken-Isfara region can be traced to the drawing of borders in the 1920s between what was then Uzbekistan and the Russian republic, but only subsequently separated out as Tajikistan and Kirgizia.

One glance at a detailed map of Batken-Isfara reveals an amazing archipelago, in the words of one journalist, "a complete jumble of scraps, corridors, and enclaves, many of them so small that they simply cannot be marked on large-scale maps."[19] To travel from Batken to Isfara, it is necessary to cross republican borders several times. In the days when republican borders were treated simply as internal administrative delineations, "the local authorities on both sides were even proud of this imprecise boundary as evidence of good relations between neighbors."[20] As another journalist noted, "for many years, no problems arose at all, and no one paid attention to who was building where, on Tadzhik or Kirgiz territory."[21] All this changed, however, as decentralization of authority (and eventually, independence) imbued administrative borders with new meaning. A similar situation exists along the Armenian-Azerbaijani border, the Kyrgyz-Uzbek border, and the Tajik-Uzbek border.

As much as post-Soviet interethnic violence has a dynamic of its own, it cannot be understood outside of tsarist and Soviet experiences. Major waves of violence broke out between Azerbaijanis and Armenians in 1905, 1918, 1920, and 1922—part of the larger conflict between Armenian and Turk that accompanied the breakdown of the Ottoman Empire and Russia's incursion into the Transcaucasus. The current struggle, however, traces itself to the drawing of borders across Transcaucasia in 1921, when large minorities of both groups were placed inside the titular republic of the other. Tensions between Abkhaz and Georgians intensified particularly after the 1870s, when the tsarist government brutally suppressed an Abkhaz revolt, sent two hundred thousand Abkhaz into exile abroad, and settled large numbers of Georgians, Mingrelians, and other groups into the region. Under the influence of Lavrentii Beria, a Mingrelian born in Abkhazia, a policy of Georgianization was pursued during the Stalinist period, and Abkhazia was incorporated into Georgia as an autonomous republic. It is not against Russian rule that the Abkhaz fight today, but rather against Georgian domination—a result largely of the ways in which tsarist and Soviet occupational policies crystallized in the region.

The roots of the Pridniestr–Moldova conflict can be traced to the use of migration by the tsarist and Soviet governments as a means for establishing control over territories. Tiraspol', which had been a predominantly Romanian and Jewish city in 1800, was transformed by 1900 into a city with significant (35 percent) Russian and Ukrainian minorities.[22] By 1989, Russians and Ukrainians together comprised 74 percent of the population of the city.[23] Russian migrants enjoyed an almost caste-like dominance over public life in Moldova in the Soviet period, reinforced by the low level of education within the Moldovan population, the dominance of Russian and Russified cadres in most major institutions, and the near-universal use of Russian as the language of official business in the republic. With the rise of the Moldovan independence movement in 1989 and 1990 and with encouragement from the USSR government, the Slavic population of the Pridniestr sought separation from Moldova. Local residents of the left bank have viewed the entire conflict through the prism of World War II, portraying Moldovan rule as a new Romanian "fascist occupation" and brandishing images of partisan warfare and the planting of the red flag over the "Reichstag" of Dubossary.[24] Numerous other examples could be added here. The key point, however, is that just as the contours of postcolonial "tribalism" in southern Africa precipitated in significant ways from the occupational policies of European colonial governments,[25] so too does the physiognomy of post-Soviet nationalisms have deep roots in the legacies of tsarist and Soviet rule.

In spite of the breakup of the USSR, ethnofederalism as an institution lives on in post-Soviet politics. If Poles in Lithuania, Russians in Crimea, northern Estonia, the Donetsk region, and Pridniestr, Ukrainians in Transcarpathia, and Gagauzy in Moldova (not to speak of the situation in Russia proper, where ethnofederalism, combined with a crippling crisis of politics in the center, nearly brought about the breakup of the first post-Soviet Russian republic) believe that they should have their own political units, it is because the norms of Soviet ethnofederalism continue to act as a source of political expectations and ambitions in post-Soviet politics. In addition to union republics, a number of other federal subunits of the former USSR (including Chechnia, Abkhazia, and Nagorno-Karabakh) have declared state independence, although these claims have not been widely recognized by the international community. "Sovereignization" emerged as the alter ego of Soviet hypercentralization. In this sense, if ethnofederalism was a tool for domination in the Soviet period, with the collapse of the Soviet order it has become a primary factor undermining consolidation of authority and instilling an essential "softness" into many post-Soviet states.

One of the subtle residues of ethnofederalism is a widespread belief within the majority populations of post-Soviet states that these states should represent the aspirations of the ethnic groups that gave them their names, even if their elites claim that these states are seeking to incorporate other groups living on their territories, and even if elites openly define these states as civic rather than ethnic polities. Indeed, this distinguishes post-Soviet states from those of Africa, Latin America, or the Middle East, whose boundaries were based not on ethnofederalism but on imperial administration and the rush to conquest. The widespread perception that politics in Uzbekistan should favor Uzbeks or that Ukraine should provide certain advantages for Ukrainians is fundamental to ethnic majorities of the region. In this sense as well, ethnofederalism generated expectations that live on in the post-Soviet period. The political nation remains an artificial category in post-Soviet politics, imposed by the state on society largely for the sake of placating restive minorities, but widely suspected by minorities to be bereft of substance. Indeed, significant minority populations continue to identify not as citizens of the new states, but as displaced persons left behind by the wreckage of their former homeland. A survey conducted in 1992 and 1993, for instance, showed that the majority of Russians living in Kyrgyzstan, Moldova, and Lithuania still viewed the USSR, not Russia, as their homeland, although the vast majority favored the introduction of some form of dual citizenship for themselves with Russia.[26]

A sense of lost statehood encompasses not only ethnic Russians, but also large numbers of Ukrainians, Belorussians, Jews, Armenians, and others who find themselves on foreign soil as a result of the combined effect of successive waves of migration during the tsarist and Soviet periods and the breakup of the

USSR. Not all of these populations are actually Russian-speakers in the sense that their native language is Russian. Significantly, the Russian law on citizenship does not define the potential citizens of Russia as those who speak Russian or who bear Russian ethnicity on their passports; anyone who was a citizen of the former USSR can qualify. One assumes that this is in part a generational phenomenon, and that intergenerational transmission of a Soviet identity in the absence of a Soviet state is unlikely. Nevertheless, it is uncertain whether new generations of minorities within post-Soviet states will come to identify themselves as full-fledged members of their political communities, particularly given their long-standing association with the former occupying power, the pervasive distrust that this generates, and the widespread majority attitude that the state is essentially an ethnic state.

Crystallizations of Soviet Institutions and the Reproduction of Politics

In a recent study of post-Soviet Ukraine, Alexander Motyl argues that post-Soviet societies "are so atomized that the challenge before them is not the radical and rapid *transformation* of existing social, political, and economic institutions, but their wholesale *creation.*" Ukraine, he writes, "is a land of people and things, but the organization of the people and things, the administration and arrangement of them, the relations between and among them, are still for the most part missing or undefined."[27] This is, in many ways, the standard argument about postcommunist politics, what Joseph Berliner has called "an unprecedented void in the kinds of controls that make social life possible."[28] Of course, this characterization contains an important kernel of truth. Soviet rule ended as the result of an institutional collapse. Moreover, the effort to traverse the divide between central planning and the market has led to great social upheaval and enormous dislocation. If one accepts the teleology of transitology and judges the Soviet legacy by the criteria of the development of liberal capitalism, then it is obvious that the institutional development of post-Soviet states is largely defined by what they are not, as these states face enormous tasks of inventing market economies, functioning democratic institutions, and civil societies where they hardly existed before.

At the same time, there is no reason to assume that market economies, effective democratic institutions, or civil societies in the same sense as we think of them in the West are indeed the logical outcomes of current transitions. In many instances, contemporary efforts at state building are being grafted onto older forms of social relationships that appear to retain a peculiar vibrancy. The collapse of the USSR was in many ways very much of an "unfinished revolution," one that altered the forms of legitimation and in some cases pushed aside old structures, but left many embedded relationships intact. In many cases, even old structures have been left intact, and the people manning those structures often remain as well. In this respect, it is not so much the absence of social relationships but rather their pervasive presence that defines the character of postcommunist societies. Indeed, were it not for the continued presence of old structures, ways of behaving, and ways of thinking, the creation of market economies, democratic polities, and cohesive nation-states would hardly present the difficult problems that they do.

Successor governments, in building new states, have faced choices of how to react to the legacies of the past, and they have differed in the extent to which they have sought to overcome them. It would be absurd to deny that significant elements of the Soviet legacy have been dismantled in a short period of time in a number of the former republics. Elimination of price controls and denationalization of property have often been the easiest of these legacies to tackle, in spite of the enormous disruptions in politics that these changes have engendered. But even in cases in which we have seen clear efforts to escape Sovietism through a kind of revolution from above, old patterns and interests have often resurfaced with startling speed. Anatol Lievan recently remarked that radical nationalism in the Baltics has been a form of "restorationism" whose proponents "are committed to restoring as far as possible the forms of the Baltic States as they existed prior to Soviet annexation in 1940, including a return to their former ethnic balances and social structures."[29] This project has turned out to be no less utopian a project than those of the communist past. Complaints abound that change has been halfhearted, and, as Andrejs Plakans notes, "chagrined reformers have had to admit that these so-called 'remnants' [of the Soviet period] have had a much greater staying power than the euphoria of the 'third national awakening' envisioned."[30] In a number of new states the downfall of the first cohort of post-Soviet elites—the leaders who brought their new countries to independence—has led to the rise of new elites often more closely connected with the old Communist regime and less concerned with nationalizing projects than with managing public disaffection left in the wake of earlier attempts at revolution from above.

The sources of this reproduction of politics can be found deep within the operational mechanisms of the Soviet state. The linchpin of the institutionalization of Soviet control over the non-Russian territories was, of course, the Communist Party of the Soviet Union (CPSU). It is here that we see perhaps the most visible continuities with the Soviet past, as well as some of the most important variations in the Soviet legacy. Although the CPSU and its ruling ideology died when the state representing its last two initials expired, former Communist officials remain in power as the leaders of well over half of the post-Soviet states. This group includes four former members of the Politburo. Altogether, renamed republican communist parties act as ruling parties in five of the post-Soviet states. In another three states, they continue to attract significant numbers of voters, although they are not formally in power. But these figures hardly capture the pervasive role that Communist elites continue to play in the legislatures, central bureaucracies, and local governments of the post-Soviet states. In this respect, the former USSR presents an interesting case of postimperial politics, one in which groups intimately connected with occupation continue to play a dominant role in politics even after imperial dissolution. The extent to which white settlers remained involved in postindependence African administration pales in comparison to the pervasive presence of former Communist officials in all aspects of post-Soviet political life. The vast majority of current political leaders who have previous administrative expertise are former Communist officials. Communist parties and their successors have also been among the most organized political forces in postcommunist societies, usually commanding significantly larger memberships than most other political organizations. One can expect that the influence of officials from the Communist period will gradually wane as power passes from the current generation to the next. But nevertheless, the basic modes of operation, political styles, and relationships of authority that these elites bring with them into politics are bound to reproduce themselves over time.

The ways in which Party control was institutionalized has heavily informed this legacy, as well as its varying impact across the former USSR. Robinson noted that in Africa it was "the changing bargains of collaboration or mediation" that "define[d] the actual working of imperialism at the point of impact."[31] Particularly during the post-Stalinist period, when Moscow was content to rule over the non-Russian periphery rather than transform it, one saw a strategic shift away from modes of formal control and toward more informal mediation of governance. The indigenization of Communist elites in the post-Stalinist period was part of a larger reworking of the "bargains of collaboration" that had dominated Soviet politics in the past. Indigenization raised the specter of nationalism penetrating into the Communist Party itself, particularly if indigenous elites attempted to build authority within their local populations and press local issues with the center. The alternative to this kind of populism was the proliferation of clientelism and patronage politics along ethnic lines, involving a different kind of loss of organizational control for the sake of depoliticizing ethnicity.[32]

The Brezhnev leadership clearly demonstrated that it preferred clientelism over populism, a preference that led to a blossoming of corruption throughout the USSR during its reign. These mechanisms of mediation then came under a whole new set of pressures with the initiation of glasnost. As ethnic mobilization increased, mediating elites at times found themselves pulled between irreconcilable demands emanating simultaneously from the mobilized masses and from Moscow. In cases where mobilization around nationalist issues was successful in penetrating into local leaderships, indigenous Communist elites tended to embrace populism, ultimately detaching themselves from Moscow's authority and coming to support (and even lead) the struggle for independence. In such cases, communist parties typically split internally along the lines of orientation towards independence, and in postindependence politics the independence-oriented wing usually sought to recast itself in the image of social democracy. Under conditions of market transition, it is the appeal of their economic message that has tended to fuel this faction's popularity.

By contrast, where mobilization around national issues failed to breach local institutions, patronage networks largely remained intact in spite of waning central controls. This autonomization of the Party brought about the rise of the national *nomenklatura*. Groups of indigenous local Party officials came to embrace independence only after the collapse of the USSR and largely as a means of preserving their collective power. In these states, clientelism remains at the center of postindependence politics, which itself can largely be understood as little more than an extension of local politics in the Communist period. The Soviet-era political networks remain cemented by political and bureaucratic practices embedded during Soviet rule, and the sense of continuity with the past in these states is often so palpable as to be overwhelming.

In cases in which statehood was obtained without a struggle and under the organizational guidance of former Communist elites, even the authenticity of ethnic nations remains open to question. Here, the strength of ethnic loyalties has rarely been tested. It is an open question whether Uzbeks would defend the Uzbek state, or whether regional and local ties still outweigh national allegiances. A public opinion poll conducted in Belarus in March 1994 discovered that more than 55 percent of Belarusians were in favor of the restoration of the USSR, and 63 percent favored unification of the republic with Russia.[33] Indeed, under the Lukashenka government, Soviet state symbols have been reintroduced, along with Communist-era textbooks in place of those that would instill a sense of distinct national identity, and Russian has been given official-language status.

With the exception of the Baltic states, all of the post-Soviet states are on a trajectory that will fall short of democracy, and many are headed in the opposite direction, spearheaded in particular by the growth (or in most cases, really, the persistence) of executive institutions and the institutionalization of strong presidencies. It has frequently been pointed out that the executive branch in post-Soviet states has come to play the coordinating role once played by party institutions; indeed, in many cases much of the staff of executive institutions was recruited directly from the former Party apparatus, and the new bureaucracies are often larger than those of the Party apparatus. In spite of the transitions to market economies, the weight of bureaucracy in these societies is still heavy and is likely to remain so long into the future. As one study of politics in Kazakhstan notes, "although under other names, the basic elements of the command-administrative system [in the republic] have been preserved almost in their entirety."[34]

Presidentialism, ironically, was first introduced into Soviet politics only at the end of 1989 as a way for Gorbachev to make an end run around the Party bureaucracy. In 1990 and 1991, on the eve of the Soviet collapse, presidentialism came to be duly imitated in nearly all of the Soviet republics, with the exception of the Baltic states and Belarus; of this latter group, Belarus and Lithuania eventually came to introduce presidentialism as well. The question, of course, is how to produce political, administrative, and economic coordination in societies that have traditionally relied on a party apparatus to do so and that are undergoing rapid change. In many cases, however, presidentialism has come to be the source of significant political abuse, undermining the roles of legislatures, luring mass media into executive control, and introducing or reinforcing a pervasive personalism and corruption in politics. Take, for instance, the case of the 1995 constitutional changes introduced in Kazakhstan. There, in imitation of Soviet practice in the 1920s, indirect suffrage was introduced, a process by which electoral colleges composed of representatives of local *maslikhats* (councils)— themselves appointed by the presidential administration—select members for the legislature's upper house. It is difficult to imagine a practice that comes closer to the traditional "circular flow of power" that long dominated Soviet politics.[35] As this example suggests, presidentialism has so easily grafted itself upon the body of post-Soviet politics precisely because it upholds longstanding patterns of behavior and ways of relating to state authority. Legislators throughout the states of the former Soviet Union "look at the president as a rabbit would at a boa constrictor," as one Russian lawmaker put it,[36] and the near-universal trend is to tighten the coils rather than give the rabbit room to breathe.

With minor variations, all post-Soviet states have inherited similar social structures, in which bureaucratic elites continue to figure heavily, even in the aftermath of privatization. Emergent capitalist classes remain weak and strongly tied to government—a form of state capitalism close in some senses to what Nikolai Bukharin and others wrote about in the 1920s. With the exceptions of Ukraine and Belarus, native managerial and industrial working classes tend to be small due to the structure of Soviet industry, which subordinated most significant industries directly to ministries in Moscow. This structure in turn encouraged mass migration of Russian-speaking administrators and workers into areas of development rather than the training of local cadres. What Rogers Brubaker calls the "mixing of peoples"[37] that occurs as polities seek to establish control over territories was, in the Soviet case, more than the conscious strategy of an imperial center to dominate through resettlement, though certainly this was part of the demographic legacy of Soviet rule. Instead, Russocentric institutions in Moscow that oversaw development in non-Russian regions, through the implicit cultural rules that lay at the basis of their operations, produced local managerial and working classes in their own cultural image. Native intelligentsias were created as a result of Soviet policies, but they were largely confined to the cultural sphere, as part of Soviet efforts to implement the formula of "national in form, socialist in content."

Technical expertise, however, was concentrated in Russia or Russified regions of the republics. Of course, the burden of deindustrialization that accompanies a transition from central planning to the market has disproportionately fallen on these same groups. But it is also these groups that, through *nomenklatura* privatization, have in many cases been able to sustain their control over strategic economic bases even in the aftermath of the transition from state socialism. Rural populations in most cases remain closely connected with the state through the former collective farm management structure. But even where these structures have been dissolved, emergent farmers have relied heavily on state subsidy, and toppled governments in Latvia and Estonia when such support was not forthcoming. In short, the two defining features of post-Soviet social structures remain the dominant role played by the state in the reproduction of stratification and the connection of industrial groups with groups associated with the former occupying power. Small wonder, then, that the major push for economic reintegration of post-Soviet space has come from managers and technocrats who made their careers on the basis of administration in an all-union economy.

Soviet Institutions and the Resources of Post-Soviet State Building

For all the post-Soviet states Soviet rule has had lasting institutional consequences precisely because the Soviet government did not simply seek to control geopolitical space, as it is often said that empires aim to do, but also sought to create a particular kind of state and a particular kind of society. In the process, it so transformed the social structures, technologies, demography, and social processes of these societies as to make them practically unrecognizable. In this aspect, the Soviet and Russian empires differ dramatically. By 1920, the economies of the newly independent Baltic states had suffered tremendously from the impact of World War I and the Russian Civil War, but nevertheless their societies contained large numbers of people with extensive experience in the workings of modern capitalism and international trade. The same is not true of the Baltics today.

Developmental policies and the organization of Soviet bureaucratic institutions determined to a large extent the immediate human, physical, and institutional resources that post-Soviet states inherited. The spatial decisions made in Moscow about developing particular branches of the economy have defined existing infrastructures and areas of specialization. Soviet planners invented an economy with the idea that the union would be a single, interrelated economic complex. Components of production were shipped across vast territories regardless of federal boundaries, a fact that gained painful importance when the Soviet state collapsed and efforts to assert sovereignty over these territories inhibited the free flow of goods across boundaries. Much of the immediate decline in post-Soviet economies was attributable to the deterioration of cross-boundary economic interactions. Territories were pegged into particular production roles that continue to function in the post-Soviet period and prescribe the niches on the world market into which these societies are capable of moving. As in other postcolonial societies, this specialization is especially difficult to reverse, as is shown by Uzbekistan's current efforts to wean itself of cotton production.

Jobs and foreign exchange earnings in each state remain dependent on branches of the economy that were designed to be only a part of a now nonexistent economic complex. With the exception of Estonia, which exported relatively little to the rest of the USSR in the Soviet period and has moved aggressively in the post-Soviet era to integrate itself with Scandinavian markets, the post-Soviet states all remain highly dependent economically on Russia. Among the energy-poor states of the former Soviet West, energy dependence, combined with economic collapse, has created vast debts to Russia. For Azerbaijan and Kazakhstan, the current politics of resource exploitation are defined by the physical location of Soviet-constructed oil pipelines, all of which traverse the Russian Federation. In post-Soviet Georgia, where Soviet power carved transportation routes through Abkhazia and across Mingrelia, the politics of development are similarly defined. In short, developmental decisions over the course of seventy-four years of Soviet history are seared into the bodies of post-Soviet states.

The structure of Soviet administration, and in particular the division of ministries into all-union, union-republican, and republican, determined to a great extent where institutional resources found local expression at the moment of independence. Hypercentralization created republican governments with extensive experience managing local road transportation, but little experience in the day-to-day management of important local economic sectors. Nevertheless, the very physical presence of these sectors provided post-Soviet states with the resources necessary to forge postcolonial economies. In Ukraine, where 28 percent of industrial production is concentrated in defense, the task of running a modern defense production sector essentially had to be reinvented, drawing expertise from plants located in Ukrainian territory but formerly under USSR administrative jurisdiction. In other cases, however, enterprises formerly under all-union jurisdiction suffered irreparable blows from the collapse of the all-union economy. The absence of critical expertise, spare parts, and capital to continue production, for instance, has led the government of Kazakhstan to transfer operational control of several dozen petrochemical, ore-refining, and machine-building enterprises in northern Kazakhstan to a Russian holding company[38]—an example, perhaps, of what Karen Dawisha terms *autocolonization.*[39]

The post-Soviet states all inherited well-developed police organizations—a pattern that is dictated largely by the ways in which these bureaucracies were organized in Soviet times. In some cases, such as in Latvia, the dominance of Russians within local police organizations led to the postindependence decision to rebuild them completely,[40] but in other cases Russian officials have simply been coopted into local regimes. In many of the post-Soviet states, the police forces, including the secret police, have been changed in name only, with many of the same personnel supervising operations as in the past.

Soviet organizational principles varied during the seventy-four years of Soviet power. But it was their final crystallization on the eve of Soviet collapse that profoundly influenced post-Soviet institutional life. One may well imagine how differently the postcolonial task of building national armies would have played out if the USSR had continued to create military units based on nationality, as it did in the 1920s and during World War II. However, by the late 1980s the Soviet officer corps was 95 percent Slavic and predominantly Russian, and the military establishment was unevenly distributed across the territories of the USSR; this state of affairs forced the new states to face a series of unsavory choices and significant resource disparities when the time came to provide for their own security. One option—to continue relying on Russia for basic security—made sense only where local expertise and resources were scant and when elites believed that Russia was not the only security threat. In Central Asia, for example, the threat of insurgence against local governments created an alliance between Russia and the old nomenklatura. As Uzbekistan President Islam Karimov stressed after signing a military cooperation agreement with Russia in March 1994, "The Uzbek Army has no development prospects if it does not maintain cooperation with the Russian Army."[41] In general, Central Asian armies remain weak and disorganized, with few prospects for action independent of Russia. Russian remains the language of command in the Uzbek army, and a full 70 percent of the officer corps know no Uzbek. Similarly, in Kazakhstan, 70 percent of all officers are Russian.[42] One out of every seven soldiers in the fourteen-thousand-strong Kyrgyz army deserted in 1994.[43]

A second security option—preferred in situations in which Russia itself was construed as the main threat to sovereignty—was to insist on the withdrawal of Russian armed forces, and attempt to build entirely new military organizations (as in the Baltics). However, in the absence of significant local expertise, weaponry, or defense industry, these forces are usually so small as to be of little more than symbolic value. They are incapable of providing effective security, and their primary utility is that they provide an international linkage with NATO if and when NATO membership is secured. Thus, only four out of six Latvian military helicopters were ready for action as of January 1994.[44] Only 5 percent of Estonian officers, also as of January 1994, had a higher military education, and those who did had been educated at military schools in the former Soviet Union.[45]

Other states, (such as Ukraine and Belarus, possessing considerable expertise, weaponry, and industry on their territories), opted for incorporating Soviet officers directly into the ranks of their new armed forces. Despite the required oath of loyalty, however, these officers often have only weak loyalties to the new states they serve, and it is unclear how many would actually fight in the event of a war with Russia. Some might even switch sides. By 1994, in fact, 60 percent of all Belarusian military pilots had already defected to the Russian air force.[46] Ukraine has also found it difficult to shoulder the financial burden of its four hundred-thousand-strong fighting force. In early 1995, 40 percent of Ukraine's fighter aircraft were out of action because of shortages of fuel and spare parts, and in 1994 pilots flew only a third as many practice flights as they had carried out in the Soviet era.[47] In February 1995, Ukraine joined a joint air defense system with eleven other CIS states.

Finally, some states (e.g., in the Transcaucasus) have relied on homegrown paramilitary organizations for security, with all the implications for internal instability that such a decision entails. In these different forms, in short, centralized control over the Soviet armed forces has created a severe security dilemma for most post-Soviet states, since the bulk of the Soviet military's institutional and human resources were inherited by the former occupying power. It is also worth noting here the inability of most post-Soviet states to guard their own borders. The security-poor states of Georgia, Armenia, Tajikistan, Turkmenistan, Kazakhstan, Belarus, and Kyrgyzstan utilize Russian border guards to guard their external borders with what used to be the non-Soviet world, raising questions about their effective sovereignty.

Placed within the perspective of the tsarist legacy, the post-Soviet states command significantly greater institutional resources than did the fledgling states that attempted to emerge out of the tsarist empire. Most of the non-Russian populations of the tsarist empire were almost entirely rural, and in the absence of a federal structure local institutions had to be invented anew. Military expertise—then also predominantly Russian—combined with the international system to play the decisive role in the outcomes that emerged. In comparison, the Soviet legacy is not entirely negative for the consolidation of new states. Of all the legacies created by Soviet rule, the easiest to remedy is that of limited resources. People can be trained, international alliances forged, and resources invested. But it is the cultural and political contexts in which this occurs that is likely to be decisive in determining whether these efforts prove effective or not.

The Cultural Legacies of Soviet Rule

Harold Isaacs once noted with regard to the impact of European empires on their former colonies that:

> these empires laid much more than a political imprint on the peoples they ruled. The mystiques by which they governed for so long included whole cultural systems that survived in many shapes and measures of their real or assumed superiorities, or by the sheer transforming power of what they brought with them. They left as legacies styles of life as well as of government, often of language, art, religion, and philosophy of the spirit and much of the practice of bureaucratic and legal systems.[48]

Certainly, post-Soviet societies inherited more than simply a set of calamitous political, social, economic, and ecological problems. They inherited as well whole ways of thinking and behaving which are likely to change through accretion only. Here, I am not speaking of the kind of civilizational or cultural attractiveness that Roman Szporluk sees as essential to an imperial enterprise, but rather the embedded and often unconscious ways of thinking that underlie our conceptions of politics. In spite of the oft-repeated denials that "Soviet man" ever existed, there are good reasons to believe that he is alive and well within his former homeland. Although the attempt to collapse national identities under the umbrella of Soviet identity obviously failed, the cultural impact of Soviet rule should not be underestimated.

A simple comparison of similar peoples on either side of the former Soviet border reinforces such a conclusion. Nazif Shahrani, for instance, attributes the "relatively weak, ineffectual and lethargic" opposition movements that have emerged in Central Asia to the successes of Soviet penetration into the region rather than the failure of Soviet policies. Although post–Soviet era elites are little respected by their populations, the destruction of longstanding Islamic institutions and behaviors and the institutionalization of clientelistic politics have prevented the emergence of mass oppositional movements similar to those on the other side of the Soviet border.[49] In Afghanistan, opposition movements have been strong, religious authority still plays a key role in society, and the primary loyalty of Uzbeks and Tajiks is not to the linguistic or ethnic communities propagated by post-Soviet nationalized states, but to *qawm* (the local kinship group).[50] The weak appeal of Islamicism in Soviet Azerbaijan, in spite of its long Shiite tradition, whereas Iranian Azerbaijan remains a stronghold of Islamic politics, cannot be understood outside of the varying impacts of the occupational policies of the USSR and Iran.

To inhabitants of Romanian Moldova, the idea that a Moldovan nation exists separate from a Romanian identity is an absurdity. Yet the vast majority of Moldovans living in former Soviet Moldova believe that they comprise a separate nation, voted in a referendum to remain separate from Romania, and now are officially said to speak a different language than Romanian.[51] Ironically, these are the very myths that were long propagated by the Soviet state, and against which Moldovans rebelled in 1989 and 1990. These myths are now generally held convictions, reinforced by a perception that Moldovans integrated into a greater Romania would constitute a marginalized community. Similarly, a study of Soviet Germans notes that "their speech patterns differ greatly from modern standard German, being based on traditional dialects of the various states of Germany. . . . For those who emigrate, standard German usually has to be learned as a foreign language."[52] Once returned to their ethnic homeland, they experience significant prejudice from German society and culture shock due to their "general bewilderment by the possibilities for freedom and development, and of the risks presented by democracy and a market economy."[53]

Multiple generations of life under Russian-dominated authority have left a deep cultural legacy that is likely to persist for further generations. There can be no doubt, for instance, that in spite of the transition to a market economy many aspects of Soviet economic behavior endure in the post-Soviet period. Cooked bookkeeping, an unrealistic financial sense, a seller's market mentality even under threat of bankruptcy, a reticence to dismiss employees for poor performance, and a pervasive underground economy are all features of post-Soviet capitalism inherited directly from the organizational culture of Soviet socialism. Just as German capitalism differs from American in large part because of the differing roles played by the state in economic development, post-Soviet capitalisms are likely to remain distinct from capitalist systems elsewhere because of the reproduction of attitudes and forms of behavior institutionalized under Soviet rule.

Basic attitudes toward authority persist that are inherited from the Soviet regime. In many cases, new elites imitate the lifestyles and demeanors of former occupational authority; for many, this requires simply continuing to behave in the ways to which they had become accustomed during the Soviet period. Bribery and corruption among officials at all levels are rampant—practices that were institutionalized in the Soviet period and have been exacerbated by conditions of market transition. Organized crime in the former Soviet Union also has clear origins in the Soviet period, although the breakdown of authority that accompanied the country's dissolution led to an explosion in its scope and operations. As in the past, informal, behind-the-scenes behavior remains the most important way to influence decision making and goods distribution. The spontaneous privatization of property into the hands of former state managers is universally practiced across former Soviet space, indicative of a vast, continuing confusion regarding the distinction between private and public power.

The state also remains the major vehicle for intergenerational transfer of wealth and status. During the Soviet era, Heydar Aliev, as a member of the Politburo, acquired a teaching position for his son at the prestigious Moscow State Institute of International Relations; in the post-Soviet period he has appointed him vice president of the State Oil Company of Azerbaijan, placing him in a position to appropriate huge sums for foreign oil contracts.[54] The bureaucratic red tape involved in any private sector undertaking in the post-Soviet states remains considerable. The temptation for political abuse appears almost irresistible. As in the Soviet period, election fraud remains widely practiced throughout the region. An OSCE (Organization for Security and Cooperation in Europe) analysis of the July 1995 parliamentary elections and constitutional referendum in Armenia noted "many reports by opposition candidates of intimidation and pressure to withdraw their candidacy, the Central Election Commission's arbitrary registration of candidates, and the pro-constitution position of the state-run mass media."[55]

What Margaret Levi calls the predatory theory of rule remains the fundamental paradigm through which post-Soviet populations construe the state.[56] The state continues to hang above society; it remains for the vast majority of inhabitants a distant and alien "significant other" to be deceived and feared, simultaneously an object of distrust and of booty. In the Soviet period, the distinction between subject and citizen was thoroughly blurred; everyone was simultaneously cast into both roles. In post-Soviet times, the distinction remains clouded, if only because the population has yet to discern features in prevailing authority that would allow it to recognize it as "ours."

State Building in the Shadow of the Past

As the previous discussion implies, close examination of the weakness of post-Soviet state authority reveals a situation that, in significant respects, cannot be separated from the expectations and behaviors implanted by Soviet authority. The "void" that Berliner and Motyl speak of is real only when we measure change by the world that we project as a desired materialization. But in reality, the "void" is rooted in attitudes and behaviors that still have Soviet institutions as their main point of reference. A social control that was so austere and pervasive could not help but give way to one characterized by general license and weakness. But the weaknesses themselves inhere in embedded ways of behaving and relating to authority. The fundamental problem these societies face, then, is not to fill an empty void, but rather to create new relationships and ways of interacting to replace existing ones. More than know-how or resources, this task requires deep changes in institutionalized expectations, orientations, and behaviors, a much more difficult task than filling a vacuum, and one in which a realistic assessment of prospects would push teleological outcomes out of view.

The physical and psychological legacies of Soviet rule for post-Soviet politics and societies remain profound and are likely to persist for many decades to come. Furthermore, there is good reason to believe that these legacies of empire- and state-building projects of the past represent much more serious threats to the survival of these states than was true in the case of other overseas and overland imperial projects. It is true that in Asia, Africa, Latin America, and the Middle East, former colonial powers were usually viewed as the most serious threats to state sovereignty in the immediate postcolonial period, and this threat served as a major source of national identification and national mobilization. Although the problems embedded by colonialism remained, eventually the sense of direct threat of colonial reoccupation receded, in part because of the delegitimation of colonial practice in the metropolitan center and the difficulties colonial metropoles had in projecting power over the vast distances required, and in part because other threats to effective sovereignty (ethnic conflict and separatism, border disputes, internal instability, economic collapse, or failed state building) soon emerged.

By contrast, post-Soviet states must always live in the shadow of their former occupier, a society that for the most part refuses to recognize the illegitimacy of occupation, because since occupation comprises a central element of its past state-building projects. The vitality of the Soviet state-building legacy continually casts a pall of doubt over the post-Soviet state system. The Belovezhskoe Forest agreement that abolished the Soviet state is now considered an illegal and illegitimate act by most Russian political parties and movements. The former occupying power's physical proximity and the artificiality of the Soviet federal system's boundaries only add to the uncertainty of post-Soviet borders. And the Russian diaspora, geographically concentrated in Kazakhstan and Ukraine but significant in the politics of Latvia, Estonia, and Moldova as well, injects even further confusion. Empire building and state building in post-Soviet politics remain difficult to separate, much as the Soviet Union itself represented a confused mix of the two. In the former Soviet Union perceptions of empire, a longing for empire, and a discourse of empire persist and are likely to endure well beyond most other postimperial situations.

It is in the interaction between the post-Soviet states and Russia that the constructed character of the Soviet imperial legacy is felt most palpably. With an unremitting question mark hanging over their sovereignty, nationalizing elites in post-Soviet states read imperial intent into acts that Russia construes as legitimate efforts at state building. For instance, nationalizing elites—even in states that are themselves engaged in violent struggles against separatist movements— view Russia's invasion of Chechnia as symptomatic of a broader regional threat rather than an attempt to consolidate post-Soviet state boundaries. Russia's concerns regarding the treatment of ethnic Russians abroad are viewed as interference in domestic politics, and attempted coups and outbursts of ethnic separatism are frequently portrayed as emanating from the hidden hand of Moscow. In short, these are states that are haunted by nightmares of their imperial past, a past that is omnipresent in the reality of everyday life. Indeed, even if Moscow's imperial practices were to cease entirely, given the proximity of Russia and the vitality of popular belief in its imperial strivings, elites within the post-Soviet states would probably find it in their interests to continue to construe the actions of the former metropole as threatening, if only to justify group solidarity and policies aimed at consolidating state sovereignty.

At the same time, Russia's practices in what it refers to as the "near abroad" (a term that itself emphasizes the liminal status of these states) have not allayed these fears. Within three years of the breakup of the USSR, the official frame for discourse in Moscow regarding the near abroad had moved from acceptance of the post-Soviet states' sovereignty to active attempts to influence their internal and external policies, and ultimately to agitation for full reintegration of the republics into a new political entity. It is practically impossible to perceive a clear distinction, as Moscow pretends to have found, between pursuit of Russia's "legitimate" geopolitical interests in the near abroad and the resuscitation of imperial ambitions. President Yeltsin, in a September 1995 *ukaz* (governmental order) outlining Russia's strategic course in the near abroad, noted that "the main goal of Russia's policy with regard to the Commonwealth of Independent States is the creation of an economically and politically integrated association of states," which, the decree notes, is also intended to act as "a countervailing factor to centrifugal tendencies within Russia itself." As the decree asserts, Russia seeks to strengthen its position as "the leading force" and "to intensify processes of integration" within the Commonwealth.[57] This course could be interpreted as the postimperial program of a great power. Yet, given Russia's assertive defense of its interests in the near abroad and the ambiguity that hovers over the goal of "integration," such a program could easily be construed as a program for an informal Eurasian empire. In addition, there are those in Russia and in the post-Soviet states who interpret "integration" not as the program of a great power within a system of states or even as the creation of an informal empire, but as the creation of a new polity in the territories of the former Soviet Union. Russia's current lack of internal stability does not inspire confidence that "integration" will find a consistent interpretation in the years to come.

Certainly, if empires in the late twentieth century are to be understood in part as subjective rather than merely structural phenomena, then it is clear that the primary differences between great-power ambitions, neo-imperialism, and empire building boil down to the ways in which one understands sovereignty and the degree to which diminutions of sovereignty within the post-Soviet states find legitimation within their populations. Sovereignty, of course, is divisible and has already been abridged and relativized within a world of interdependent states. States may cede control over their borders, their economies, or their foreign policies without ceding control over the selection of their leaders or their formal independence. Much of this kind of activity has already happened throughout the Commonwealth. Indeed, the problems of some post-Soviet states raise questions over whether sovereignty is any more than legal fiction. In other cases, foreign policies and economies have become mere appendages of Russia.

Moreover, failed state building and the disorder that it engenders often produce a demand for external interference, which provides numerous opportunities for the exercise of *legitimated* forms of domination.[58] Here again, the profound confusion that lies between consent and coercion in modern politics blurs the divide between empires and states. Nearly all Russian politicians—including those who openly advocate a re-created USSR—speak of integration as a "voluntary" process. The question confronting Russian politicians is not whether integration will be "voluntary," but rather what steps to take in order to create a situation in which the non-Russians of the former USSR will want such an outcome—as Russia's continual and partially successful efforts to manipulate Azerbaijani and Georgian politics show.[59] Russian foreign and domestic politics profoundly influence state-building processes in the other post-Soviet states and, in turn, the outcomes of state-building processes in these states play into Russia's strategic goals in the near abroad. In Ukraine, for instance, nonpayment of huge energy debts to Russia has been used as leverage to gain partial Russian ownership of the domestic Ukrainian gas pipeline network—an act that some within Ukraine look at with alarm. There are political forces within Russia that understand and seek to exploit the ambiguous ground that lies between state building and empire building in Eurasia. As one Russian nationalist newspaper described its preferred scenario for the re-creation of a Russian-dominated state across the territories of the former USSR:

> It is not only Belarus but also a number of other republics that have already partaken of "state independence" which can be lured by the neo-imperial possibilities inherent in a successful integration, and at the same time be dismayed at the costs of delay and "falling out of the process." Such a combination of carrot and stick, plus mounting internal problems caused by sovereignty, the grassroots aspiration toward integration, and the hidden but internally alive "Sovietness" of the overwhelming majority of the incumbent CIS leaders, could work a "unification miracle" on the expanses of Northern Eurasia.[60]

These concerns raise the larger question of how we know whether a new empire—either formal or informal—is coming into being in Eurasia. Without Vladimir Zhirinovsky and the unmasked politics of empire building, perceiving the difference between great-power politics and empire building is likely to be extremely difficult; indeed, in the eyes of millions of people (among them, the Chechens) Russia is still an empire, and many other non-Russians believe that an informal Eurasian empire has already come into existence. Perhaps the most that can be said about empires in a world of states is that contemporary empires should not be understood as an ideal type but rather as set of a constructed and illegitimate relationships that should concern us when a significant number of people come to view politics through such a prism. Empires in a world of states should be understood to involve the kind of "daily plebiscite" that Renan attributed to the nation. As the Soviet experience shows, what may be understood as state building today can easily be construed as empire building tomorrow. Imperial and nonimperial situations inhabit a continuum rather than neatly bounded boxes—a continuum that is constantly shifting and subject to negotiation.

It may be that, with time, post-Soviet sovereignties will gain real substance, national identities will coalesce around new centers of gravity, state boundaries will congeal in the face of strong international norms against their further revision, and the external pressures of the international system will preserve the post-Soviet state system in its current configuration. The international context of post-Soviet state building differs radically from that of 1918–20. The pull of the international economic system and the powerful effect of international norms place enormous obstacles in front of any attempt at fundamental revision of the boundaries of the post-Soviet state system. In today's world, established states are extraordinarily difficult to erase, and the simple juridical significance of statehood injects a degree of inertia into the post-Soviet state system. As time elapses in the aftermath of Soviet collapse, these norms will become still more powerful. But this in itself does not signal the passing of empire. The states of the Warsaw bloc also retained juridical statehood after World War II, yet were widely recognized as parts of an imperial system. The subjects at issue here are not only the formal boundaries of states, but also the substance of what lies within them and their relationships with other states. Post-Soviet state building must deal with a dual legacy inherited from the empire-building and state-building projects of the past: not only must post-Soviet states overcome the political and social consequences of the very human matter that composes them, but they must also surmount the gravitational pull of the astronomical black hole around which they orbit, a dead red star of which they were once part. Which of these forces—centrifugal or centripetal—will emerge dominant in Eurasia, what realms of motion and types of objects they will command, and how they will be understood by those who fall within their power are not subject to the conformities of physical or social law, but will ultimately be a matter of human choice, agency, and interpretation. Nevertheless, the outcome will determine whether empires in some form are to become only a part of Eurasia's history, or whether they constitute a factor of its present and future as well.

Notes

The author would like to thank the Woodrow Wilson International Center for Scholars and the Kennan Institute for Advanced Russian Studies for providing the opportunity to write this essay, as well as George Breslauer, Karen Dawisha, John Dunlop, Miles Kahler, Cynthia Kaplan, Gail Lapidus, Bruce Parrott, Avi Shlaim, and Ron Suny for their comments on an earlier draft. Pranas Ciziunas contributed skillful research assistance.

1. Robert H. Jackson and Carl G. Rosberg, "Why Africa's Weak States Persist: The Empirical and the Juridical in Statehood," *World Politics* 35, no. 1 (1982): 1–24; Robert H. Jackson, *Quasi-States: Sovereignty, International Relations, and the Third World* (Cambridge: Cambridge University Press, 1990).

2. Quoted in Anatolii Sobchak, *Tbilisskii izlom, ili Krovavoe voskresen'e 1989 goda* (Moscow: Sretenie, 1993), p. 174.

3. René Lemarchand, "The State and Society in Africa: Ethnic Stratification and Restratification in Historical and Comparative Perspective," in Donald Rothschild and Victor A. Olorunsola, eds., *State Versus Ethnic Claims: African Policy Dilemmas* (Boulder, CO: Westview, 1983), p. 45.

4. M. Crawford Young, *The African Colonial State in Comparative Perspective* (New Haven: Yale University Press, 1994), pp. 2, 9–10.

5. On the notion of the crystallization of state institutions, see Michael Mann, *The Sources of Social Power,* Vol. 2, *The Rise of Classes and Nation-States, 1760–1914* (Cambridge: Cambridge University Press, 1993), pp. 75–81.

6. John Hiden and Patrick Salmon, *The Baltic Nations and Europe: Estonia, Latvia, and Lithuania in the Twentieth Century* (London: Longman, 1991), pp. 48–49.

7. Some, such as Gavriil Popov, argued that it was possible to exorcise the imperial persona of the USSR and arrive at a legitimate state. But once the imperial persona of the Soviet state came to be widely recognized as such, even by Russians, how one might go about doing this became a nearly impossible task to conceive. See Gavriil Popov, *Snova v oppozitsii* (Moscow: Galaktika, 1994), pp. 364–65.

8. Ian S. Lustick, *Unsettled States, Disputed Lands: Britain and Ireland, France and Algeria, Israel and the West Bank–Gaza* (Ithaca: Cornell University Press, 1993), pp. 22–23.

9. Murray Edelman, *Politics as Symbolic Action: Mass Arousal and Quiescence* (Chicago: Markham, 1971), p. 7.

10. Accusations of empire building today are hardly monopolized by Russia, but can be found in many multinational states: British rule over Northern Ireland, Ethiopian rule over Eritrea, Israeli rule over the West Bank and Gaza, Chinese rule over Tibet, Indian rule over Assam, Indonesian rule over East Timor, Iranian control of southern Azerbaijan, and the United States' rule over Puerto Rico are but a few examples of current discourses of imperialism. Empire-states are a reality of modern politics, one of a number of personas or constructions that are highly embedded and by which states come to be identified or understood.

11. For an elaboration of these arguments, see Mark R. Beissinger, "The Persisting Ambiguity of Empire," *Post-Soviet Affairs* 11, no. 2 (1995): 149–84; Mark R. Beissinger, "Demise of an Empire-State: Identity, Legitimacy, and the Deconstruction of Soviet Politics," in M. Crawford Young, ed., *The Rising Tide of Cultural Pluralism* (Madison, WI: University of Wisconsin Press, 1993), pp. 93–115.

12. James N. Rosenau, "The State in an Era of Cascading Politics: Wavering Concept, Widening Competence, Withering Colossus, or Weathering Change?" in James A. Caporaso, ed., *The Elusive State: International and Comparative Perspectives* (Newbury Park, CA: Sage Publications, 1989), p. 20.

13. Ibid., p. 31.

14. Ibid., p. 19. In defining a similarly ambiguous term, *nation*, Hugh Seton-Watson noted that "[a]ll I can find to say is that a nation exists when a significant number of people in a community consider themselves to form a nation, or behave as if they formed one." Hugh Seton-Watson, *Nations and States: An Enquiry into the Origins of Nations and the Politics of Nationalism* (Boulder, CO: Westview, 1977), p. 5.

15. See, for instance, Philip G. Roeder, "Soviet Federalism and Ethnic Mobilization," *World Politics* 43 (January 1991): 196–232; Rogers Brubaker, "Nationhood and the National Question in the Soviet Union and Post-Soviet Eurasia: An Institutionalist Account," *Theory and Society* 23, no. 1 (1994): 47–78; Ronald Grigor Suny, *Revenge of the Past: Nationalism, Revolution, and the Collapse of the Soviet Union* (Stanford: Stanford University Press, 1993).

16. Suny, pp. 80–81.

17. In addition to population size, other factors used as control variables included: government repression against demonstrators, higher education, Communist Party membership, nationalist dissident activity in the pre-glasnost period, and a dummy variable for peoples of traditionally Muslim background. All of these variables, with the exception of the last, had statistically significant relationships with secessionist protest below the .10 level. Research on protest mobilization in the former Soviet Union was conducted under the auspices of grants from the National Science Foundation, the National Council for Soviet and East European Research, the International Research and Exchanges Board, and the Graduate School of the University of Wisconsin at Madison.

18. See Benedict Anderson, *Imagined Communities: Reflections on the Origin and Spread of Nationalism,* rev. ed. (London: Verso, 1991).

19. *Pravda* (Moscow), August 23, 1989, in *Foreign Broadcast Information Service Daily Report: Soviet Union,* August 30, 1989, p. 62 (hereafter cited as FBIS).

20. TASS, July 22, 1989, in *FBIS,* July 25, 1989, p. 63.

21. Moscow Televison, July 31, 1989, in *FBIS,* August 1, 1989, p. 47.

22. Victor Bârsan, *Masacrul inocenților: Războiul din Moldova, 1 martie–29 iulie 1992* (Bucharest: Intergraph, 1993), p. 20.

23. Vasile Nedelciuc, *Republica Moldova* (Chişinău: Universitas, 1992), p. 21.

24. *Ekspress khronika,* no. 47, November 20, 1990, pp. 5–6.

25. Leroy Vail, "Introduction: Ethnicity in Southern African History," in Leroy Vail, ed., *The Creation of Tribalism in Southern Africa* (Berkeley and Los Angeles: University of California Press, 1989), pp. 1–19.

26. *Russkie v novom zarubezh'e: Programma etnosotsiologicheskikh issledovanii* (Moscow: Institut etnologii i antropologii, 1994), pp. 125, 129.

27. Alexander J. Motyl, *Dilemmas of Independence: Ukraine After Totalitarianism* (New York: Council on Foreign Relations, 1993), pp. 52, 54.

28. Joseph S. Berliner, "Conclusion: Reflections on the Social Legacy of Communism," in James R. Millar and Sharon L. Wolchik, eds., *The Social Legacy of Communism* (Cambridge: Cambridge University Press, 1994), p. 382.

29. Anatol Lievan, *The Baltic Revolution: Estonia, Latvia, Lithuania and the Path to Independence* (New Haven, CT: Yale University Press, 1993), pp. xxiv-xxv.

30. Andrejs Plakans (paper presented at the annual convention of the American Association for the Advancement of Slavic Studies, Honolulu, HI, November 1994). See also Andrejs Plakans, *The Latvians: A Short History* (Stanford: Hoover Institution Press, 1995), pp. 187–88.

31. Ronald Robinson, "Non-European Foundations of European Imperialism: Sketch for a Theory of Collaboration," in William Roger Louis, ed., *Imperialism: The Robinson and Gallagher Controversy* (New York: New Viewpoints, 1976), pp. 129, 133.

32. See Mark R. Beissinger, "Elites and Ethnic Identities in Soviet and Post-Soviet Politics," in Alexander J. Motyl, ed., *The Post-Soviet Nations: Perspectives on the Demise of the USSR* (New York: Columbia University Press, 1992), pp. 141–69.

33. Radio Moscow World Service, March 21, 1994, 01:00 Coordinated Universal Time.

34. P. Svoik, E. Lan'ko, *Sud'ba Kazakhstana kak gosudarstva: Pervye shagi ot propasti* (Almaty: Evraziia, 1994), p. 17.

35. *Nezavisimaia gazeta*, October 4, 1995.

36. Viktor Sheinis, in *Nezavisimaia gazeta*, December 1, 1995.

37. Rogers Brubaker, "Aftermaths of Empire and the Unmixing of Peoples: Historical and Comparative Perspectives," *Ethnic and Racial Studies* 18 (April 1995): 189–218.

38. *Segodnia*, April 29, 1995, p. 2.

39. My problem with the term autocolonization is not the process that it describes, but the stance that it assumes. Autocolonization is practically indistinguishable from interdependence or dependency. Whether such situations are neo-imperial or not has more to do with the ways in which they are constructed by populations rather than their structure per se.

40. Lievan, p. 322.

41. ITAR-TASS, March 2, 1994 (7:35 EST).

42. See Susan Clark, "The Central Asian States: Defining Security Priorities and Developing Military Forces," in Michael Mandelbaum, ed., *Central Asia and the World* (New York: Council on Foreign Relations Press, 1994), pp. 180, 196.

43. ITAR-TASS, January 25, 1994 (4:58 EST).

44. *LETA* (Riga), January 10, 1994.

45. *Estonia News*, January 3–5, 1994.

46. ITAR-TASS, January 28, 1994 (11:18 EST).

47. Reuters, February 20, 1995.

48. Harold R. Isaacs, *Idols of the Tribe: Group Identity and Political Change* (Cambridge, MA: Harvard University Press, 1975), pp. 6–7.

49. Nazif Shahrani, "Central Asia and the Challenge of the Soviet Legacy," *Central Asian Survey* 12, no. 2 (1993): 123–35. See also Bert G. Fragner, "The Nationalization of the Uzbeks and Tajiks," in Andreas Kappeler et al., eds., *Muslim Communities Reemerge: Historical Perspectives on Nationality, Politics, and Opposition in the Former Soviet Union and Yugoslavia* (Durham, NC: Duke University Press, 1994), pp. 13–32.

50. Olivier Roy, "Ethnic Identity and Political Expression in Northern Afghanistan,"

in Jo-Ann Gross, ed., *Muslims in Central Asia: Expressions of Identity and Change* (Durham, NC: Duke University Press, 1992), pp. 75–76.

51. This latter issue actually led to strikes by five thousand students in Chişinău, chanting the slogan, "We are Romanians," and demanding that Romanian be recognized as the official language of the republic. *OMRI Daily Digest,* no. 74, pt. II, April 13, 1995.

52. Anthony Hyman, "Volga Germans," in Graham Smith, ed., *The Nationalities Question in the Post-Soviet States* (London: Longman, 1995), p. 472.

53. Klaus Bade, quoted in Hyman, "Volga Germans."

54. Turan, May 3, 1994.

55. Commission on Security and Cooperation in Europe, *Report on Armenia's Parliamentary Election and Constitutional Referendum, July 5, 1995* (Washington, DC: U.S. Government, 1995), p. 1.

56. Margaret Levi, "The Predatory Theory of Rule," *Politics and Society* 10, no. 4 (1981): 431–65.

57. "On Continuing the Strategic Course of the Russian Federation with the Participant-States of the Commonwealth of Independent States." Government Order Number 940 of the President of the Russian Federation from September 14, 1995.

58. Beissinger, "The Persisting Ambiguity of Empire," pp. 175–77.

59. Thomas Goltz, "Letter From Eurasia: The Hidden Russian Hand," *Foreign Policy* 92 (fall 1993): 92–116.

60. *Zavtra,* October 10, 1995.

7

The Habsburg and Ottoman Empires and Their Aftermaths

Dankwart A. Rustow

Europe's Exceptional Overland Empires

Five thousand years ago, human beings on this globe lived in small communities of planters or animal herders. In a few areas agricultural settlements were integrated by tribal conquerors, allowing a wider division of labor and the rise of impressive civilizations. One specific challenge was to control the flow of major rivers to fertilize otherwise arid lands and to prevent flooding of settlements along the shores. Most early civilizations—such as Mesopotamia (literally, "the land between the rivers"), the Nile valley of Egypt, or the Ganges and Indus valleys of South Asia—thus developed in valleys no larger than today's modern states.

Then came efforts at integration through regional empires, such as the Shang dynasty in China (16th c. to 11th c. B.C.), the Romans along the Mediterranean (1st c. B.C. to 4th c. A.D.), the Muslim caliphs in the Near East and North Africa (7th c. to 16th c.), the Mongols in Central Asia (13th c. to 15th c.), and the Aztecs and Incas in the Americas (14th c. to 16th c.); yet most of these empires were of short duration.

In this early history of empires, China and Europe stand out as extreme opposites. China's successive empires were based in the world's largest river valleys, which were early on interconnected by canals. A centralized religious-administrative system fostered an extensive division of labor and major technical inventions—such as paper making, printing, and gunpowder—long before these technologies were discovered in Europe, transforming China into "the largest sophisticated realm on this earth."[1] But when threatened by warriors from Asia or aggressive traders from Europe, China responded by building the Great Wall in the north and closing its coasts to all foreign trade.

China's landmass is bordered by desert and mountains in the north and west and by a semicircular seacoast to the east and south. By contrast, Europe has the world's most diversified coastline—with inland seas from the Baltic to the Mediterranean ("sea between the lands") and the Black Sea; islands such as Britain; and peninsulas from Scandinavia to Iberia, Italy, and the Balkans. Yet the diversified coastline gave each major island or peninsula its distinctive cultural (and later national) identity. In sum, Europe's coastline encouraged a pattern of unity and diversity.

The only political unity in the Mediterranean region was imposed by the Roman Empire, which was divided between Rome and Byzantium in the fourth century and soon dissolved by Teutonic invasions from the north. Under Charlemagne (768–814), unity was restored in western and central Europe, but within a few centuries the Holy Roman Empire broke up into feuding petty states. Vernacular languages replaced classical Latin in the time of Dante Alighieri's *Divina commedia* (1307–21) and Martin Luther's Bible translation (1522–34); distinct versions of Christian religion developed during the Reformation; and military nation-states, such as Sweden under the Vasa (1523–1654) and France under the Bourbon (1589–1789) dynasties, began to replace the defunct Holy Roman Empire of the Middle Ages.

This new European pattern of diversity within unity provided the major impetus for unification of the globe by competing colonial empires such as Spain, Britain, the Netherlands, Portugal, and France. By the early twentieth century, nearly all the non-European world except China, Japan, Turkey, and Thailand had become European colonies or dependencies. China saw its coastline divided into colonial enclaves; Turkey—after the Tanzimat reform decrees (1839)—and Japan—from the time of Emperor Meiji (1868–1912)—sought to avoid similar destinies by Westernizing their military, administrative, and, eventually, cultural systems.[2]

In the classical age of overseas imperialism, the Habsburg, Ottoman, and Russian tsarist realms stand out as the exceptional *overland* empires on Europe's eastern fringe; many of the fiercest wars from the sixteenth to the early twentieth centuries were fought among these. Thus, while western Europe moved toward national political identities and overseas expansion, the East became subject to frequent shifts of imperial boundaries.

The Habsburg Empire included a large variety of linguistic groups, and the Ottoman Empire contained diverse religious and linguistic groups. Such diversity gave both realms additional strength in their periods of ascendance, but proved to be a major liability in their days of decline. Thus, the structure of Ottoman Empire was based on an ethnic division of labor: Muslims provided the soldiers and administrators, and Christians and Jews dominated foreign trade and much of the domestic economy. Similarly, the ruling class of the Habsburg Empire, although exclusively Roman Catholic, was recruited from a wide variety of ethnic and regional backgrounds. The Ottoman and Habsburg (as well as the tsarist Russian) empires also encouraged a geographic intermingling of ethnicities, as evidenced by the fifteenth-century conversion of Albanians and Bosnian Bogomils to Islam.[3]

Rise and Fall of the Ottoman and Habsburg Empires

The Ottoman dynasty, descended from Prince Osman (1288–1326), emerged as rulers of the most successful of the Turkish-Seljuk warrior principalities that took over the Asian parts of the Byzantine Empire. After Byzantium (or Constantinople, or Istanbul)[4] itself was conquered in 1453, the Ottomans expanded throughout the Balkans; by the early sixteenth century the Ottomans had expanded into most of the Middle East and northern Africa, and its rulers became both sultans and caliphs (secular successors to the prophet Muhammad). Indeed, the Ottoman Empire became the largest and most durable empire west of China, extending from Algiers to the gates of Vienna and from Ukraine and the Caucasus to the Sudan and the Arabian Peninsula. And when, by 1492, the Christian conquest had destroyed the multireligious structure of the Islamic realm of southern Spain, the Ottomans benefited by welcoming into their empire Sephardic Jews, who helped make Istanbul and Salonica into major commercial centers.

In contrast to the Ottomans, the Habsburgs attained their imperial power not so much by military force, but first by election to the German emperorship (intermittently 1273–1330, and continuously 1438–1806) and then by dynastic marriages, which by the early sixteenth century made them rulers of Austria, Bohemia, Hungary, Spain, and Burgundy (including what later became the Netherlands and Belgium). Considering that the voyages of Columbus had just set the stage for the colonial conquest of the Americas, the realm of the Habsburg emperor Charles V (1519–56) turned out to be by far the largest since the fall of Rome and before the overseas expansion of Britain in the seventeenth and nineteenth centuries.

But Charles V was one of those rare rulers who put wisdom above thirst for power: he decided in 1521 to assign his central European lands to his younger brother Ferdinand, who succeeded him as German emperor; and he assigned his Western inheritance, including Burgundy, southern Italy, and the expanding overseas possessions, to his son Philip, who was to be king of Spain.

For the Ottoman Empire, the turning points from a policy of expansion to one of retreat proved to be two failed sieges (in 1529 and 1683) of the Habsburg capital of Vienna. One crucial factor in this reversal of fortune was the centralized imperial command structure whereby every major military order was given personally by the sultan in Istanbul and relayed on horseback to the front lines. Thus, the command system became less and less efficient as the imperial frontiers expanded. A second factor was the Ottoman practice of collecting food supplies for the army from the areas nearest to the front lines—an effective system while new conquests expanded the frontiers, but one that made the armies more vulnerable once they were on the defensive.

The Ottomans' defeat in 1683 thus was followed by a century of retreats. Whereas the Habsburgs were joined in victory by tsarist Russia and the Republic of Venice, the sultans lost most of the northern Black Sea region, the Caucasus, and southern Greece. Yet the Habsburgs did not press their military advances as aggressively as the Ottomans had in previous centuries. Instead, a pattern emerged in which both the Habsburg and Ottoman Empires became actively involved in the shifting patterns of European power politics; at the same time, both Vienna and Istanbul experienced a rare period of cultural flowering in the late eighteenth century.

The Ottoman military-administrative establishment was recruited from Muslims or converts from all parts of the empire; the higher its members rose in the centralized ruling class, the more they shed their ethnic affiliations to merge into the Islamic-Ottoman polyglot culture of Istanbul. There, the viziers and pashas, the beys and effendis prayed in Arabic (in mosques blending Middle Eastern and Byzantine architectural motifs) and enjoyed poetry modeled on the Persian classics. They smoked tobacco and ate maize imported from the Americas. They also eagerly adopted European fashions, such as roccoco architecture, an Italian headgear imported via Morocco and soon known as the fez, and lush varieties of tulips imported from greenhouses in the Netherlands (giving rise to an eighteenth-century Ottoman literary period known as the Tulip Era).[5] Similarly, the Habsburg capital of Vienna emerged as a major center of European musical culture: Franz Joseph Haydn (1732–1809) developed the modern symphony, his disciples Mozart and Beethoven further perfected the classical opera and symphony; and the Johann Strausses, Sr. and Jr. (1804–1849, 1825–1899), popularized the Viennese waltz throughout Europe.

Meanwhile, the ever more intensive interplay among European military powers helped both the Habsburg and Ottoman Empires survive on the political scene. In 1699 and 1718 the Habsburgs had conquered from the Ottomans all of Hungary, Croatia, northern Serbia, western Wallachia, and Transylvania. But because of involvement in major European conflicts—notably the War of the Spanish Succession (1701–14) and several wars with Prussia (1740–63), which was a rising military power—they were unable to pursue aggressively their campaigns against the Ottomans, who by 1739 reclaimed Serbia and Wallachia.

In 1761, the Ottomans concluded a friendship treaty with Prussia and by the 1780s Italian experts had been employed to restructure the Ottoman navy. By the 1840s, cadets were sent for military training to France, and eventually, most of the Ottoman armies' elite were trained by Prussian officers. When Russian armies penetrated deeply into the Balkans, the Ottomans were joined by Austria, Britain, and France in what became known as the Crimean War (1853–56). After another Russian-Ottoman war, Britain, Austria, and other European powers intervened at the Congress of Berlin (1878) to allow the Ottomans to regain some of their lost Balkan territories. In sum, it was rivalry among its Austrian and Russian imperial neighbors and diversity and conflict among the rising powers of western Europe that postponed the final Ottoman defeat for more than a century.

Imperial Collapse in the Age of Nationalism

Meanwhile, the American and French revolutions of 1776 and 1789 encouraged uprisings from Spain to Naples and the Netherlands in what one historian has called "the Age of the Democratic Revolution."[6] Although the newly proclaimed republics were soon converted into satellite kingdoms of Napoleon's empire, the ideal of popular or national governments continued to spread—major illustrations being the series of revolutions in Paris, Berlin, Vienna, and Prague in 1848, and the wave of nationalism that by 1867 had forced the Habsburgs to recognize Hungary as an equal partner within the Austro-Hungarian monarchy.

European support, notably from Britain, had helped Greece win its war of national independence (1821–29) against the Ottomans; later in the century European pressure secured first autonomy and then independence for Serbia (1817, 1878), Romania (1859, 1878), and Bulgaria (1878, 1908). After the Balkan Wars (1912–13), Albania was also declared independent and most of the Ottoman Empire's European territory was divided among those successor nation-states.

There were also important side effects of the changing political-cultural scene within the Ottoman Empire itself. An Ottoman officer, Ibrahim Sinasi, had been sent to Paris in the 1840s for artillery training, but he returned to Istanbul enamored of French romantic poetry. Soon he launched what turned out to be a major cultural revolution by introducing European-style rhymed verse into Ottoman literature, and also by founding the first private Ottoman newspaper at a time when the news bulletin from the sultan's palace had provided the only printed news. By 1876, Sinasi's disciple Namik Kemal took a leading role in the political revolution that deposed two sultans in order to establish a constitutional monarchy with representative government—an effort that was quashed at the time but revived by the New Ottoman (or Young Turk) Revolution of 1908.

World War I resulted in the collapse of four empires: not only the Hohenzollern-German, Habsburg, and Ottoman Empires on the losing side, but also tsarist Russia, which fought on the winning side but collapsed even earlier than the others in the Revolution of 1917.

The passing of these four empires seemed to make nation-states the norm; indeed, the postwar international organization was called the League of Nations. The 1919–20 peace treaties provided a more extensive redrawing of the political map than Europe had previously experienced. Finland, Estonia, Latvia, and Lithuania were created in the Baltic region of the Russian Empire, and the new Poland comprised former tsarist, Habsburg, and Hohenzollern territories. From the Habsburg realm emerged the new states of Czechoslovakia, Hungary, and Austria. Romania acquired Transylvania from the Habsburgs and Bessarabia from the tsars. Serbia was enlarged to include former Habsburg and Ottoman territories in a Kingdom of Serbs, Croats, and Slovenes (1918), renamed Yugoslavia in 1929.

In the nineteenth century the Ottoman Empire lost its African possessions: Algeria was annexed by France in 1830; Tunisia, formerly an Ottoman dependency, was occupied by France in 1881; and Libya and the Dodecanese Islands in the Aegean Sea became Italian colonies in 1912. However, the division of Ottoman territories came at a time when the Europeans clearly felt ambivalent about their colonial expansion. Thus, the British in 1882 imposed a "temporary occupation" on Egypt—although the temporary period lasted more than a half-century. Similarly, the Treaty of Sèvres, concluded in 1920 between the victorious Allies and the defeated Ottoman Empire, assigned some of Turkey's west coast to Greece, proclaimed a new Armenian Republic in the northeast, and transformed all the remaining Ottoman-Arab territories into League of Nations mandates. France assumed mandatory power over Syria (including Lebanon), and Britain over Palestine (including what later became Transjordan) and Iraq. All these territories were designated "Class A mandates," meaning that they were supposed to be in transition to full independence. These partitions imposed by the victorious World War I powers had very different effects in east-central Europe, Turkey, and the Arab countries.

New Nation-States in Eastern Europe

The national consciousness of most of eastern Europe goes back to what Karl W. Deutsch has aptly described as a process of increasing "social communication." In preindustrial times there had been a clear division between villagers and small townsmen—all speaking a variety of local dialects—and the ruling class in the capital and other major cities—who communicated in German, the imperial language of Vienna, or in Russian, the language of St. Petersburg. Yet, as industrialization drew more and more peasants and craftsmen to larger towns, a new social and linguistic consciousness formed in the emerging middle and working classes, which made the traditional empires ever more fragile.[7]

In World War I, leaders of the suppressed nationalities of the Habsburg Empire sided with the Allies. Thus, the new state of Czechoslovakia was proclaimed by political exiles in the United States and supported by a Czech Legion, which was organized after the 1917 revolution by Habsburg soldiers who had been taken prisoner by tsarist troops. But the borders drawn in the peace treaties of 1919–20 were clearly biased toward the suppressed nationalities of the dissolved empires. Poland included large populations of German, Ukrainian, Belorussian, and Lithuanian minorities; and Czechoslovakia contained a large German minority in the northwest and a Hungarian minority in the southeast. Other Hungarians wound up in Romania and Yugoslavia. Yugoslavia comprised not only Orthodox Serbs and Catholic Croats in the Serbo-Croatian language group, but also

Slovenes, Macedonians (whose language most closely resembles Bulgarian), and substantial Bosnian and Albanian Muslim minorities.

Woodrow Wilson had announced in 1917 that America was entering World War I to "make the world safe for democracy." Yet, with the exception of Czechoslovakia, none of the postimperial states of eastern Europe managed to develop into democracies. A "government of the people" requires both a *people* and a *government*. But any sense of "we the people" was undermined by the presence of large national minorities within most of the new borders; and the postimperial vacuum left most of them without any governmental tradition.[8] And in some of the successor states of the empires, such as Germany, Russia, Austria, and Hungary, the lingering resentment of defeat became a further obstacle to democracy.

For example, the World War I victors denied Austria the right to call itself *Deutsch-Österreich* (German Austria) or to merge with the newly proclaimed German Republic. And, of course, Adolf Hitler was born as the son of a customs official on the Austrian border with Germany, volunteered for the German rather than for the Austrian army in 1914, and, after seizing power in Berlin in 1933, made his first expansionist moves by annexing Austria and the German-speaking parts of Czechoslovakia in 1938. In sum, the aggressive response to the Habsburg imperial defeat was not a call for revival of the empire but for a new all-German national identity.

By one of the curious twists of history, the Habsburg imperial anthem has survived to this day within a German national setting. Composed by Haydn in honor of Francis I, the first emperor of the Habsburg-Lorraine dynasty (1745–1765), its original text was, "Gott erhalte Franz den Kaiser, unsern guten Kaiser Franz . . . " (God preserve Francis the emperor, our good Emperor Francis . . .). But by the 1840s, it was reset by a liberal German poet to the words, "Deutschland, Deutschland über alles . . . " (Germany, Germany above all . . .). By 1871, this new text became the national anthem of Germany's Second Reich (1871–1918) and then of its successor Weimar Republic and Hitler's Third Reich.[9]

Turkey: From Ambiguous Identity to National Independence

The lack of an established identity was even more evident in Turkey than in Austria. In Ottoman days, the word "Turk" was not applied to the ruling class but was used only for the lower class of the Anatolian hinterlands. Indeed, when an Anatolian poet proudly proclaimed in 1897, "I am a Turk, my race, my faith are sublime," he was not taken seriously by the Istanbul literary establishment— only one generation later he was proclaimed a national poet of the newly founded Republic of Turkey.[10] When Sultan Abdülhamid II (1876–1909) in 1878 suspended the parliamentary constitution of 1876 and reverted to strict autocracy, many political exiles fled to Europe, where they became known as *Jeunes Turcs,* although back home they were known as New Ottomans. Meanwhile, a Tatar immigrant from Russia aptly summarized the ambivalence of the late-Ottoman sense of identity in a 1904 political tract entitled "Three Types of Politics," by which he meant Ottomanism, Islamism, and Turkism.[11]

The 1908 revolution forced Abdülhamid to restore the 1876 parliamentary constitution; but the New Ottoman leaders were soon divided between liberals eager to decentralize power and right-wing militants who, in response to Ottoman defeats in the Balkan Wars (1912–13), imposed a military dictatorship. During World War I, the allegation that some Armenians secretly cooperated with the tsarist enemy was used by the government as an excuse to deport all Armenians from the northeastern region toward Syria and Iraq—1.5 million were killed en route in a mass slaughter secretly organized by military elements of the Istanbul government. By 1918, the Ottomans clearly suffered the worst of the imperial defeats of World War I. Most of their prewar territory was partitioned among the victorious Allies, and much of the remainder, including the capital of Istanbul, placed under military occupation. A Greek invasion was launched in 1919 with the intent of expanding Greece's occupied territory into central Anatolia, but the invasion was repelled within three years by armed forces organized by a top-ranking Ottoman general, Mustafa Kemal. Kemal's military strategy was supported in 1920 by an elected national assembly convened in Ankara. Significantly, however, the name of the nation that the assembly was to represent was carefully left unspecified.[12] It was only after military victory over the Greek armies in 1922 and recognition by the European powers in the 1923 Treaty of Lausanne that the new state was proclaimed as the Republic of Turkey. And, when in 1934 a law decreed that Turkish citizens adopt European-style family names, President Mustafa Kemal was conferred the family name Atatürk, meaning "Father Turk."

Thus, it was this radical turnaround—from defeat in World War I to victory in what became known as Turkey's war of independence of 1919–23—that finally resolved the collective identity problem that had made the Ottoman middle class waver between Ottomanism, Islamism, and Turkism. And, of course, the conversion to Turkish nationalism implied the final demise of Ottomanism—since none of the new Turkey's citizens even dreamt of trading their victorious nation-state for an attempt to resurrect the defeated empire. Nor was there any call for imperial restoration in other successor states. The Balkan countries, whatever their problems after independence, were glad to be liberated from Ottoman rule, and the Arab countries were immediately faced with a more acute problem—the imposition of halfhearted and divisive imperial rule by European powers.

Still, there are important elements of continuity between the Ottoman Empire and its successor state, the Republic of Turkey. Just as the close-knit military organization of the defeated Ottoman army enabled Mustafa Kemal to launch Turkey's victorious war of independence, so the 1923 merger of the Ankara government with the remnants of the Ottoman imperial bureaucracy gave the new state a solid political structure. Its borders coincided almost exactly with the Ottoman armistice lines of 1918, and the Turkish-speaking population already constituted a clear majority—even before the 1923 peace agreement with Greece, which provided for a population exchange of Muslim minorities in Greece and Greek Orthodox minorities in Turkey—except for Orthodox residents of Istanbul, which continued to be the seat of the Orthodox patriarchate.

Even so, the new Turkish republic included substantial ethnic minorities, the largest being the Kurds in the southeast, who rose up in 1925 in an Islamist rebellion that was forcibly repressed at the time but long remembered as a traumatic experience by Turkey's political and military establishment.

Arab Countries from Ottoman Rule to Western Quasi Colonialism

Today, the Arab-speaking countries from Mauritania and Morocco in the east to Oman in the west constitute one of the largest monolinguistic regions in the world, next to the Spanish-speaking American countries from Mexico to Chile and Argentina, and the former Russian Empire from St. Petersburg to Vladivostok. This Arab region was culturally unified by the military campaigns of Muhammad's successors, including the Umayyad (661–750) and Abbasid (750–1258) dynasties, who extended their empire eastward to the Indus valley; northward to Bukhara, the Caucasus, and southeast Anatolia; and westward to the Mediterranean, including most of the Iberian Peninsula and all major islands from Cyprus to Sardinia.

Like other early empires, the caliphate was based on a close combination of religion and military power—*khalifa* being the Islamic term for the successors of the prophet Muhammad in his capacity of secular ruler. Arabic, as the language of divine revelation in the Koran, became the language of the ruling class and most of their subjects. Yet, by the tenth and eleventh centuries, imperial overextension, attacks from Christian crusaders, and invasions from Central Asia began to dissolve the caliphal empire. Nonetheless, Arabic survived as the language of the populations along the southern shores of the Mediterranean, in the Nile Valley, on the Arabian Peninsula, and in the Fertile Crescent. By the sixteenth century, the Ottomans had reestablished the unity of Arab regions from Algeria to the Arabian Sea and the Persian Gulf; although the Ottoman language was based on Turkish, most of its vocabulary was adapted from Arabic, with some from Persian as well. Thus, the empire's official name, Devlet-i Aliye-i Osmaniye (High Ottoman State), consisted of three Arabic words with two Persian connectives.

By the nineteenth century, the Arab parts of the Ottoman realm were dissolving. Thus, Muhammad Ali, an Ottoman military commander of Albanian descent, established his authority in Egypt (1806–48), and, after an unsuccessful attempt to wrest control of Syria from the Ottomans, was recognized in 1839 as independent hereditary ruler of Egypt. As mentioned earlier, between 1830 and 1920 most of the Ottoman Arab areas were incorporated into the French, British, and Italian empires as colonies, protectorates, or mandates.

During World War I, the British encouraged a rebellion by the sherif of Mecca, Faisal, who, in the post-Ottoman vacuum of 1920, was proclaimed king of Syria by a national congress in Damascus. But when the French took mandatory power over Syria, they forcibly expelled him from Damascus; the British then arranged in 1921 to have him elected king in their mandate of Iraq, and in that same year they made Faisal's brother Abdullah the ruler (and in 1928, the king) of the eastern part of their Palestine mandate, henceforth known as Transjordan. The western part of Britain's Palestine mandate was opened up to Jewish immigration.[13]

The division of the Arab countries into many separate entities was one of the effects of transition from Ottoman to Western imperial rule; another was the redrawing of boundaries within the Western imperial framework.[14] Thus, whereas the Ottomans had ruled only the coastal regions and the Nile Valley in northern Africa, the Western rulers extended those borders southward, making Algeria into a country of Arabs and Berbers and adding a substantial non-Arab population to the Sudan. Also, under Ottoman rule the Christian-Arab area of Lebanon had been an independent district, but under the French mandate over Syria, Lebanon was made a separate entity and enlarged to incorporate substantial Muslim (Sunni and Shiite) and Druze minorities.

For Syria, one legacy of the interlude of French rule was a local army staffed mainly by Alawites—a religious minority that welcomed the French mandatory government as protection against discrimination by the Sunni Muslim majority, but which used its military power after the French withdrawal to establish what has become one of the most long-lasting and ruthless military dictatorships under General Hafez al-Assad (1970–).

More generally, an important legacy of the brief period of European imperial rule in the Arab Middle East was the pattern of collaboration between the imperial powers and local political leaders. Thus, the British not only established Arab monarchies in Transjordan and Iraq but also organized Transjordan's army as an Arab Legion under a British commander. Similarly, after establishing a formal protectorate in Egypt in 1914, they declared the country independent under King Fuad (an heir to Muhammad Ali) in 1922—yet the British continued their military presence throughout the country until after World War II and along the Suez Canal until 1956. Although these moves were intended to facilitate the burden of imperial rule, they tended to discredit the local rulers as tools of colonialism. An indirect effect of the European imperial interlude was the transformation of Palestine into the Jewish state of Israel, which left the Palestinians—who had emerged in the late nineteenth century as the most educated and Westernized of the Arab populations—as the Arab people without a country of their own.

Imperial Aftereffects in Southeast Europe and the Middle East

Despite these and other postimperial problems, the demise of the Habsburg and Ottoman empires in 1918 was clearly final, and restoration of either empire has not emerged as an imaginable option. Instead, as we have noted, resentment of defeat in Austria and other German-speaking post-Habsburg territories could fuel Pan-German nationalism—although the disastrous defeat of Hitler's Nazi empire and the steady buildup of European economic and political integration from the Marshall Plan to the European Union also rules out such Pan-Germanism as a plausible option. In southeastern Europe, although the Habsburg and Ottoman empires are clearly history, the lack of clear national identities—as evidenced by the recent peaceful partition of the Czech and Slovak republics (1992) and by the bitter civil war in the former Yugoslavia—may be considered part of the negative multi-imperial legacy.

On the post-Ottoman scene, the reversal from Ottoman defeat to Turkish nationalist victory definitively foreclosed the option of Ottoman imperial revival. There have been recurrent waves of political extremism in Turkey since the 1950s, but these waves have typically taken the form of Islamic fundamentalism or Pan-Turkism—that is, the idea of uniting the Republic of Turkey with the Turkic-speaking post-Soviet republics from Azerbaijan to Kyrgyzstan. In the Arab countries of the Middle East, it is clearly the legacy of the European imperial interlude, from the occupation of Egypt in the 1880s to the creation of mandates and protectorates in the 1920s, that has overshadowed the aftereffects of the Ottoman Empire.

Notes

1. Jonathan Spence, *In Search of Modern China* (New York: W.W. Norton, 1990), p. 57.

2. See Robert E. Ward and Dankwart A. Rustow, eds., *Political Modernization in Japan and Turkey* (Princeton: Princeton University Press, 1964).

3. The Bogomils were a dissident Christian sect, persecuted as heretics by both the Roman Catholic and Greek Orthodox churches; see Milan Loos, *Dualist Heresy in the Middle Ages* (Prague: Akademic, 1974). But since, under Ottoman rule, they could practice their Christian beliefs without restrictions, they welcomed the Ottoman conquest, and they soon found that, by voluntary conversion to Islam, they could enter—and rise to the very top of—the Ottoman administrative-military hierarchy.

4. Istanbul, rather than Constantinople, was the name by which its residents referred to the Byzantine capital. The most plausible source of the term is a contraction of "eis tan polin"—Greek for "in the city." And although Europeans continued to refer to the city as Constantinople, it was the colloquial Greek name Istanbul that the Ottomans retained for their newly established capital.

5. This paragraph is adapted from Dankwart A. Rustow's essay "The Military Legacy," in L. Carl Brown, ed., *Imperial Legacy: The Ottoman Imprint on the Balkans and the Middle East* (New York: Columbia University Press, 1996), p. 250. Note that of the four Ottoman titles mentioned, vizier is Arabic, pasha and bey are Turkish, and efendi is derived from the Greek word *avthentos*.

6. Robert R. Palmer, *The Age of the Democratic Revolution: A Political History of Europe and America, 1760–1800*, 2 vols. (Princeton: Princeton University Press, 1959–64).

7. Karl W. Deutsch, *Nationalism and Social Communication*, 2d ed. (New York: MIT Press, 1966).

8. On those prerequisites of democracy, see Dankwart A. Rustow, "Transitions to Democracy: Toward a Dynamic Model," *Comparative Politics* 2 (1970): 337–63.

9. The "Deutschland" poem was written in 1841 by August Heinrich Hoffmann von Fallersleben (1798–1874), who later became a liberal member of the revolutionary parliament of 1848, and whose intent, in placing Germany "above all," was that political unity in all German-speaking areas should supersede the rule of empires, kingdoms, and petty states. See Guido Knopp and Ekkehard Kuhn, *Das Lied der Deutschen: Schicksal einer Hymne* (Berlin: Ullstein, 1988). Of course, Bismarck's Second and Hitler's Third Reich interpreted those words in an aggressively imperialist way; yet the Bonn Republic in 1952, by a wise decision of Chancellor Konrad Adenauer and President Theodor Heuss, used only the words of the anthem's third stanza: "Einigkeit und Recht und Freiheit . . . " (Unity, justice, and freedom . . .), which clearly reflected Hoffmann's liberal views.

10. See Bernard Lewis, *The Emergence of Modern Turkey*, 2d ed. (Oxford: Oxford University Press, 1969), p. 343.

11. See Lewis, pp. 326f.

12. On the organization of the Turkish war of independence, see Dankwart A. Rustow, "The Army and the Founding of the Turkish Republic," *World Politics* 11 (1959): 513–52. The Latin-script reprints of the Ankara Assembly's proceedings of 1920–1923 call the assembly the Grand National Assembly of Turkey, but the Arabic-script originals call it only Grand National Assembly. For the general background of the transition from the Ottoman Empire to the Turkish nation-state, see Dankwart A. Rustow, *Turkey: America's Forgotten Ally* (New York: Council on Foreign Relations, 1987), ch. 2.

13. For a good overview of the impact of World War I and the postwar arrangements for the Arab portions of the Ottoman Empire, see George Lenczowski, *The Middle East in World Affairs*, 4th ed. (Ithaca: Cornell University Press, 1980), chs. 2–3. On the Damascus kingdom specifically, see Zeine N. Zeine, *The Struggle for Arab Independence: Western Diplomacy and the Rise and Fall of Faisal's Kingdom in Syria* (Beirut: Khayat, 1960).

14. On the Arab postimperial identity problem, see Michael Hudson, *Arab Politics: The Search for Legitimacy* (New Haven: Yale University Press, 1980).

8

Peripheral Successor States and the Legacy of Empire

Succeeding the British and French Empires in Africa

Robert I. Rotberg

The identities of the peoples of imperial anglophone and francophone Africa, and their many successor states, were germinated, nurtured, and even conditioned, by their vastly different colonial experiences, by their varying responses to nonuniform introductions to the West, and by idiosyncratic challenges and opportunities on distant frontiers. The rise of indigenous forms of nationalism, the shape of postcolonial forms of independence, and the very nature of the successor states derives from the formative quality of the colonial interaction.

For much of Africa, as for Asia and the Caribbean, the interactive experience—the responses of the conquered to the introduction of Western norms and expectations—began even before the eighteenth century, and was extended, elaborated upon, and intensified during the latter years of that century. The succeeding nineteenth century was critical to the evolution of South and Southeast Asian successor states and of the anglophone Caribbean, but only for selected parts of Africa—Senegambia, Ghana, and South Africa—was an interactive tutorial begun in that era. For nearly all of Africa, that century was characterized by conquest rather than acculturation, assimilation, and reaction—the character-forming ingredients of the personalities of the successor states.

The Administrative Age

For the peoples of black Africa, the texture of the events of the period between the two world wars—the "administrative age"—proved corrosive. This was when "things fell apart," when the British and French empires gave great bearhug embraces to their peripheral clients and possessions, smothering them with insidious attention. Societal and personal cataclysms ensued, endlessly profound, intentionally intrusive, and difficult—if not impossible—to oppose effectively. The legacy of empire in Africa originated primarily in the administrative interlude and in the triumphal period of nationalism that followed.

By the end of World War I, it was clearly evident that the "white devils" had, for all intents and purposes, come to stay. A new generation grew up that had never known any life other than that directed by Europeans. Along with some of their elders, this new generation accepted the imposed framework of acculturation and assimilation and faithfully attempted to adhere to its presumed expectations. The old ascription was replaced, at least in their minds, by forms of achievement sanctioned from above and outside—in other words, by the imperial ruling hegemon.

Africans attempted to adapt. Some did so easily. Africans in the administrative age learned the languages, customs, beliefs, and organizational methods of their overlords. They studied in schools staffed by European secular and clerical teachers; worked for white district officers, section chiefs, road foremen, traders, and missionaries; and often tended to the household needs of white families. All of these experiences naturally provided grist for mills of personal change.

Africans acknowledged the military might and technological superiority of the West. They thus tried to become "good" citizens, and relied upon the patronage of colonists to advance themselves. Generally, they sought not so much to preserve cultures and ways of life that had been crushed but to grasp whatever would develop themselves and their societies in a sustainable fashion. They were unabashedly, and sometimes consciously, syncretic.

By contrast, the colonial authorities and the colonial functionaries and their various instrumentalities were focused less on transferring skills and ideologies than they were anxious to administer—to control, to regulate, to tax, and to pay the bills. At the same time, they experimented with diverse political arrangements and rearrangements, toyed with economic development and trade stimulation, and tutored those whom they considered to be their charges or wards. The colonial approach remained for the most part static, and largely divorced from the profound social and economic changes taking place in the metropolitan heart of each empire. This divorce from chronological reality defined the context within which Africans became imperial subjects, and molded their aspirations.

Patterns of Dominance

At the onset of the administrative age (which came much earlier in Ghana and much later in the distant parts of Niger, Mali, Algeria, and Zaire), Africans appreciated that they had become objects rather than subjects; consequently, their ability to withstand the crashing tide of colonial events suffered a serious and irrevocable decline. During the administrative age there were few temporal or other limitations on the exercise of sovereignty by foreigners in nearly all of Africa. The mind-set of Africans then, and of their successors a few decades later, was influenced strongly by the almost uniform sense of objectification. Traditional elites were coopted, and the new protoelites were ignored, painfully rebuffed, or reduced to a powerless cohort of collaborators, of whom *Mister Johnson* is the caricature.[1]

Despite the putative import of the Indian paradigm of princely rule into parts of anglophone Africa, Africans themselves, in practice and in their daily lives, experienced little difference between varieties of colonial domination. This conclusion was primarily true for the new elites as well as for the masses; on the other hand, traditional elites often grew more powerful as they became administrative subcontractors (for example, in northern Nigeria, in Rwanda, and in sections of Tanzania) to the foreign hegemon.

Formally, through various rescripts, the French and the British governed differently. France itself, after all, was administered centrally, and the same pattern of rigid administrative centralization was applied to its colonies; traditional African forms of rule rarely found a place. The French consciously attempted to eradicate chiefly control, to rearrange or suborn precolonial political units, and to focus indigenous loyalties afresh. The functions of legitimate chiefs were "reduced to that of a mouthpiece for orders emanating from outside."[2] The French appointed and deposed chiefs. They recruited replacements without reference to relevant ethnic backgrounds or affiliations, and transformed the institution of chieftaincy into a branch of the overall francophone administrative bureaucracy.

The role of these new Frenchified chiefs was ostensibly different from that in British Africa; in ultimate impact, however, the distinctions were nominal. The French chiefs, like the British chiefs, kept order, collected taxes, and recruited labor on behalf of their superiors. In many areas (here the French practice was much more brutal than the British) the newly appointed chiefs were strangers to their districts (and even to Africa) and certainly no more effective than French administrators themselves in winning the short- and long-term allegiance of peoples who preferred their own methods of governance and legality to those imported from abroad and imposed *tout court*.[3]

Unlike the British, the French (and the Belgians and the Portuguese) refused to recognize the validity of indigenous custom. Whereas the British professed to respect indigenous procedures, the French and the other continental Europeans, devoid at home of common law notions and wedded to the civil law approach of the Napoleonic code, undermined, if not consciously destroyed, the bases of indigenous authority.

The rulers from the European continent were more openly repressive, too. They regulated African mobility, prevented most attempts at indigenous protest, punished those who dared to "agitate," and introduced regimes of forced labor that for several decades compromised the activities of the French in all other spheres of endeavor and greatly influenced the attitudes of their colonies' nationalist successors.

British Africa was run, Harvard-style, with every tub on its own bottom. Whereas the French centralized by instinct, the British bottom line was decreed by the government at Whitehall, but expressed idiosyncratically, possession by individual possession. This approach to the colonial endeavor, influenced heavily by the ideology of the parsimonious Treasury (which decried the colonizing impulse) rather than the French search for glory and imperial renown, should in theory have provided major benefits to British subjects in Africa (as arguably it did in India, and perhaps in the Caribbean). Hence, the differences in French and British method should—as the apologists of empire often declared—have been visible in their successor states. The nature of the postcolonial state should have been affected definitively by these and other differences in the mentalities of the colonists.

The dominant British administrative philosophy in Africa, derived from the experience of the raj in India, was indirect rule. It was flexible, it was inexpensive, and it promised evolutionary development capable of benefiting Africans. Experience in running "native authorities," or indigenous local governments, promised to prepare Africans for the eventual problems of home rule and, in the process, to preserve the "best elements" of traditional life. The British, unlike the French, were theoretically committed to home rule. Many of their possessions were in fact protectorates, in other words, territories in trust. So the notion that colonial rule was not forever was intrinsic to British (and Treasury) theory and rhetoric—but not to French and other imperial ideologies.

Indirect and Direct Rule

Almost everywhere, even in northern Nigeria, the aura of indirect rule increasingly seemed more important than the realities inherent in the model. Although nearly all the British colonies at one time or another during the administrative age attempted to shift from direct to indirect forms of governance, the preconditions for the necessary devolution of authority existed in their ideal form only in northern Nigeria, where there were large, preimperial, autocratic, indigenous states. So-called British Residents "advised" Hausa emirs, and (unwittingly) buttressed corrupt and inefficient personal rule. Indirect rule, in its fullest expression in Africa, was thus unusually static and retrogressive. It retarded the emergence of participatory rule in colonial Africa's most populous state and greatly influenced the entire history of postcolonial succession in Africa.

Outside of Nigeria, indirect rule had its best chance of full expression in the British Mandate of Tanganyika (later Tanzania), where Governor Sir Donald Cameron believed that the British "must not, in fact, destroy the African atmosphere, the African mind, the whole foundations of his race." He wanted to purge "the native system of its abuses, to graft our higher civilisation upon the soundly rooted native state . . . that [has] its foundations in the hearts and minds and thoughts of the people."[4]

Cameron's team went about its task of finding, anointing, and training native authorities with enthusiasm and energy. Nevertheless, in Tanzania as in Zambia, Malawi, and Uganda, these local authorities remained creatures of an alien British administration. Traditional procedures were honored in the breach. Financial independence, the bedrock of power in the British system, was almost always impossible for "native treasuries," particularly since British administrators, whatever the theory, feared to devolve either taxing or spending power. African native authorities were always deemed "unready," inexperienced, and so on. After 1936 (ten years after the inauguration of indirect rule in Tanzania), the government even gazetted a few white administrators as "native authorities."

In neighboring Malawi and Zambia, administrators refused to "hurry" the development of native authorities. They refused to "jeopardize the success" of indirect rule by entrusting native authorities with responsibilities that they were "not fit to exercise." Indirect rule, in practice, meant just as little to the peoples of eastern Africa as it did to those in most of western Africa. District commissioners actually carried out the services transferred on paper to chiefs and their associates. Even in the kingdom of Buganda, long established and long a favorite of the British Empire, British officials subverted smoothly functioning, potentially modern, indigenous rule in the 1920s.

Theory to the contrary, indirect rule prepared as few Africans to succeed the anglophone imperialists as did direct rule. Instead of providing a productive training ground for later leadership and a gradual, even glacial, transfer of power, as in the Caribbean and South Asia, British and French methods of domination in Africa dampened (and were largely meant to dampen) indigenous expectations and aspirations. It was otherwise in India, and to some extent in the Sudan, which trained a civil service modeled on that of India.[5]

Legislative Councils

This conclusion should have been averted in those few African colonial cases where, for one or another reason, Africans had been encouraged well before the administrative age to participate to a degree in the process of statewide government. Inhabitants of the Gold Coast (Ghana), for instance, had served on its Legislative Council since 1850. In 1916, three chiefs had joined three Africans appointed from the cities and three white businessmen on its "unofficial" (non-administrator) benches. Additional African councillors were appointed subsequently, but British officials held the majority of seats (and all real power) until after World War II. Similarly, starting in 1922, the residents of Lagos and Calabar elected four Africans to the Legislative Council of Nigeria; the governor appointed the rest of the members. Once again, the "officials" dominated until after World War II.

The pattern was the same in Sierra Leone, where white administrators predominated, but in the eastern part of British Africa the legislative councils of each territory were controlled in practice throughout this formative period by white settlers. They wielded effective power, from which Africans were systematically excluded. Even in western Africa, where Africans were included, their roles were purely advisory, often perfunctory; any questioning voices among this new elite were always outnumbered by both the officials and the accommodationists. Tutelage in the arts of self-government was almost always absent.

In French West Africa (Senegal and the contiguous states stretching to the borders of Chad), a small group of local white businessmen and African urban elites elected representatives to several *conseils d'administration.* Senegal possessed a slightly more important *conseil colonial,* which comprised forty members, half of whom were elected by the citizens of the country's four original communes. At the federal level (uniting all of French West Africa), a *conseil du gouvernement* contained delegates from these various subordinate conseils. Yet, again because of the French system (both in theory and in practice), this seemingly exemplary exercise in partial self-government was largely window-dressing. The governor general of French West Africa made all decisions, and the various conseils met infrequently and never demurred.[6]

Segregation and Land Alienation

Once they had effectively implanted themselves in Africa, the British and French empires taxed their new subjects, took their land (especially in the malaria-free upland areas of east and central Africa), demanded their labor, and welcomed white farmers, miners, and traders from the respective mother countries. These intrusions were enormously disruptive and caused bitter grievances, intermittent but sustained forms of protest, and enduring conflict. The appropriation of good grazing and growing land was inevitably destructive to African incomes and self-esteem, not least in Kenya, Tanzania, Malawi, Zambia, Zimbabwe, and South Africa. Hitherto productive indigenous farming communities were displaced and impoverished, shunted from areas of high rainfall and friable loams to regions of little rain and stiff clays or rocky soils.

The first five territories listed in the previous paragraph attracted white settlers and their families, which almost inexorably led to tense race relations, segregation, and the growth of both official and popular white antagonism toward African advancement. As a leader of the Northern Rhodesian (Zambian) Legislative Council explained: "We white people have not come to this country solely and even mainly to raise the native in the scale of civilisation. Our main objective is to survive ourselves, to improve our conditions if we can, and . . . to raise a family and perpetuate our race."[7]

In those five anglophone states—as in South Africa, Namibia, the Portuguese possessions of Angola and Mozambique, in southern Zaire, and here and there in hot, low-lying francophone and anglophone West Africa—the new indigenous elites' aspirations for assimilation and acculturation were thwarted not directly by official policies (the rhetoric was often otherwise), but by the unholy, if natural, alliance between white settlers and colonial administrators of the same pigmentation. The new elites were also derided, castigated, and denied fulfillment in northern Nigeria (because of the colonial alliance with the emirates), in neighboring Cameroon for the same reasons, and everywhere in nonsettler Africa where Africans who sought "too much" education, "real" jobs, and "undeserved" recognition were regarded as "cheeky."[8]

Much of the official ideology was paternalistic, often idealistically so, and the new African elites—the upwardly mobile, achievement-oriented, mission-educated, black proto-Frenchmen and proto-Britons—would have welcomed the genuine fulfillment of paternalistic policies. Instead, from the point of view of Africans, they were fed empty rhetoric, and thwarted in their desires to approximate the British or French paradigm. Even the few who went overseas to British, French, or American universities and returned home with respectable degrees, even Ph.D.s from Columbia or London, were regarded with suspicion. Few were embraced warmly or welcomed home to their territories with enthusiasm. For example, even after Dr. Hasting Kamuzu Banda had received undergraduate and medical degrees in the United States, and further medical training and licensing in Scotland, the colonial authorities in Malawi refused to offer him anything other than menial employment.[9] In these hostile ways the colonial successors were nurtured.

Good Works

Despite the administrative age's failure to fully prepare the future leaders of Africa for eventual transfer of authority, the powers of Europe did attempt to convey at least some of the progressive ideas and material accomplishments of their metropoles to the peoples of the colonies. They opened schools and hospitals, introduced entrepreneurial concepts, constructed roads and railways, erected impressive buildings, extracted minerals, and planted profitable crops. During the administrative age, more and more Africans became enmeshed in the Western economic web. It facilitated development and exploitation.

Missionaries were in the Western vanguard. As an integral part of their evangelical endeavor, missionaries started the first schools and hospitals in most of the colonies. In these early centers of instruction, Africans learned to count and to read and write their own and a European language. They drew, sang, mapped the physical terrain of the mother country, and memorized selected portions of the Bible. The lucky few later continued their educations in a higher primary or secondary school, where they were introduced to the history of their colonial rulers, and further drilled in mathematics, in the relevant foreign language, and in the Scriptures. Many also learned industrial or agricultural skills.

By Western standards, the educational systems of tropical Africa remained rudimentary, and Africans often complained that although white men spoke glibly of their "civilizing mission," they limited its benefits to a fortunate few and largely neglected the secondary and higher levels of instruction. The upper educational levels, the administrators believed, produced difficult, "detribalized" Africans.

Before 1939, colonial Africa could claim fewer than ten serious secondary schools in addition to a few postprimary teacher- and professional-training institutions. In West and Equatorial Africa, the French designed a pyramidal system of education that, through an orderly succession of village, district, and regional primary schools, emphasized the superiority of French culture and language. The École William Ponty, near Dakar, constituted the apex of the pyramid and, until World War II, it offered French Africa's only university entrance course. In Equatorial Africa, the sole higher primary school stayed shut between 1927 and 1935. The government of Zaire allowed most of its subjects to remain without any educational opportunities whatsoever. In anglophone central Africa, neither the missionaries nor the various colonial administrations opened any full secondary schools until after World War II.

The British put more than token funds behind projects to advance Africans educationally only in their West African colonies, in Uganda, and in the Sudan. An early governor in Ghana believed that education was "the keystone of progress"; in the 1920s he—almost alone of colonial officials—encouraged widespread expansion of and improvement in the colony's school system. He founded the Prince of Wales College at Achimota, which, after 1926, became the leading secondary school in all of British colonial Africa, and the nucleus of the eventual University of Ghana.[10] It even schooled women alongside men. Its rival in East Africa was Makerere College, also destined to become a postcolonial university.

In British Africa, the quality of these various educational systems depended on the extent to which each of the colonies paid its own way. Both Ghana and Uganda prospered during the administrative age, the first because of cocoa, the second because of coffee and cotton—all smallholder crops. In both colonies, too, their comparative wealth was enhanced when existing railways were extended from the coast into the far interior. Officials in Uganda, too, created the finest road network in all of Africa, the better to facilitate the selling of smallholder-produced coffee and cotton.

Exploitation

Much of the so-called development of Africa was more exploitative than productive. That proved to be the case wherever underground minerals could be dug by hordes of unskilled migrant laborers, as in Zambia, Zimbabwe, and Zaire. In the French Congo and in Zaire wild crops like rubber and some plantation crops were collected by *corvée* labor performing what were called communal tasks or civil requisitions.[11] Railways were constructed with conscripted labor in French

Equatorial Africa. In Zaire, Africans were conscripted into the *force publique,* or militia. Various other francophone states compelled Africans to cultivate and harvest rice, cotton (Mali), timber (Ivory Coast), fish (Mauritania), and other cash crops. And some states, like Kenya, reserved the growing of the most lucrative cash crops (coffee) to whites.

A Balance Sheet

If a form of cost-benefit analysis is at all relevant to the imperial colonial experiment in Africa, then the administrative age constituted a period (on the positive side) when literacy, health care, communications and transport infrastructures, the cash and market economies, and scientific and technological learning were all introduced in their Western forms to an Africa that was much more inexperienced and jejune than colonial subjects of the same imperial masters in Asia or the Caribbean. The negative side of the ledger looms larger, however, because of the exploitative, even brutal, methods that accompanied the introduction of Africans to the educational, economic, and other kinds of contributions of the West. Furthermore, as much as Africans desired the modernization that the West offered, and as much as they were even prepared to accept that modernization on Western terms, the imperial West enticed Africans but was largely reluctant to let the Africans advance rapidly, fully, and without barriers. Africans wanted a more rapid and a deeper embrace by the West.

Although quantitative analysis of such contentions awaits refinements of the available data, it is apparent from qualitative measures that Africans perceived a widespread imperial insincerity. Moreover, there is little objective disagreement that the French and British empires in Africa never believed in their own paternal rhetoric; neither did most whites, nor even most missionaries, practice the idealism that they and their Scriptures espoused. Throughout black Africa, the indigenous inhabitants daily contrasted Biblical teachings of equality with the actual performance of the Europeans who had chosen to settle in their midst. The successor states to the British and French empires were formed in the crucible of indigenous dismay.

Political Reactions

Protest was a natural reaction to imperialism, often taking nationalistic, anticolonial, sometimes even violent, forms. Using the political concepts and languages of their rulers, the local people claimed a democratic right to participate in the governing process. At first, they wanted no more than the right to have their collective voice heard in matters directly affecting the lives and actions of the indigenous population. To this end, those Africans to whom the white man's ways had become most familiar—primarily the lawyers, physicians, businessmen, clerks, evangelists, teachers, and journalists who had become Western in attitude and aspiration, and sometimes in achievement—established organizations in order to express their pleas for reform.

The establishment of voluntary associations, ostensibly apolitical but almost always very political, played a critical role in the eventual emergence of the full-fledged nationalistic movements of the 1940s and 1950s. From the administrative age onward, the leaders of these associations sought redress for grievances. They urged hostile or amused governments to rethink imperial policy. In the settler-impacted territories, they countered every public move made by white political groups to entrench white privilege at the expense of Africans. Elsewhere, they attempted to gain audiences for indigenous concerns through reasoned argument, petition, and upright personal behavior. These largely gentle skirmishes with authority represented an intermediate phase in the history of the rise of nationalism, during which African leaders gradually came to appreciate the essential futility of moderate, ad hoc, elitist, nonconfrontational criticism of colonial rule. Yet, at no time before World War II did the associations and their leaders genuinely seek self-government. They wanted to be accepted by the French and the British. They wanted to share power, not oust the colonists. The latter sentiment came to prevail only after World War II.

The African leaders of the anglophone administrative age were men like Joseph Ephraim Casely Hayford, Joseph Kwame Kyeretwie Boakye Danquah, and Herbert Samuel Heracles Macauley. The first two were Ghanaians, the third a Nigerian. The first two were lawyers, the third a civil engineer, journalist, and the grandson of Nigeria's first African bishop. Danquah came from a royal family, wrote a philosophical treatise for his Ph.D. from the University of London, and edited the *Gold Coast Leader,* an early voice of indigenous protonationalism.[12]

Casely Hayford set the tone for the new elites of British West Africa. Responding in part to President Woodrow Wilson's call for "self-determination" in the dependent, subjugated world, in 1920 he led other educated British West Africans to establish the National Congress of British West Africa. Its goals were the eventual union of the four colonies, self-government, creation of a university, and the appointment of African lawyers and physicians to the colonial judicial and medical services (from which they were barred). Casely Hayford and others also spoke out against segregation.

Danquah carried on Casely Hayford's efforts in Ghana. In 1929 he and others formed the Gold Coast Youth Conference. It agitated, albeit mildly and unsuccessfully, for improved employment opportunities for the indigenous intelligentsia. In Nigeria, Macaulay's National Democratic Party sought to "secure the . . . welfare of the people of Nigeria as an integral part of the British Imperial Commonwealth" and, eventually, to seek self-government within that commonwealth. As late as 1943, Danquah refused to demand self-government; critics accused Danquah and his cohorts of doing little more than "yapping"—of drifting comfortably without proposing significant change. Indeed, Danquah and his followers represented a generation that was passing: "Let them try as hard as they can," Danquah wrote, "but none can succeed to take away the sight of the White Man from the mind of the Gold Coast People. Churchill said the future of the world belongs to the educated race. In Africa the future belongs to him who fastens his sight on the White Man, the Economic individual."[13]

The first demand for complete local independence and full autonomy with the British Empire came in the late 1930s from the new Lagos Youth Movement, organized by Benjamin Nnamdi Azikiwe—returned to Nigeria from Lincoln, Howard, Columbia, and Pennsylvania universities—and his compatriot H. Oladipo Davies—returned home from the London School of Economics. But this incipient movement of nationalism and Pan-Africanism found its true spring-board in the titanic battles of World War II: the stirring enunciation of the Atlantic Charter; Franklin D. Roosevelt's and Winston Churchill's bold, calcu-lated promises of freedom to those who had been colonized; the Free French echo, with its bid to undermine Vichy's grip on potential African bases and territory; and the service together in war of white soldiers from Europe and black soldiers from Africa. Almost everywhere, Africans established new protopoliti-cal groupings to take advantage of the obvious loosening of the imperial ties. In Malawi, for example, the first president of the nascent Nyasaland African Con-gress denounced the exploitation of Africans and demanded full citizenship, equal opportunity, and representation in the national legislature for Africans. In francophone West Africa, imperial officials appealed for support to their subjects by promising to end compulsory labor and improve educational and medical facilities. In a meeting in Brazzaville, imperial leaders agreed to loosen adminis-trative controls on the various territories, but recommended against self-govern-ment. Instead, they proposed a pan-colonial assembly of mixed membership, to meet in Paris (after its liberation) to legislate for the dependencies—an idea that formed the nucleus of the eventual French Union. The spirit of this admittedly paternalistic Brazzaville declaration emboldened men like Felix Houphouët-Boigny of the Ivory Coast, Léopold Sédar Senghor and Lamine Gueye of Senegal, Yaciné Diallo of Guinée, and Léon Mba of Gabon to form political groupings within their territories and, simultaneously, to seek election under the new dispensation to the postwar French National Assembly and Council of the Republic.

These arrangements and a series of proposed reforms gave the inhabitants of the postwar colonies considerable hope for the future. But their leaders wanted the dismemberment of the empire, which France opposed. Thus, the ascendant new political elites of the francophone colonies organized themselves along national lines. In 1946, the various territorial parties came together in Bamako; more than eight hundred indigenous delegates—the new political men (and a very few women) of francophone West and Equatorial Africa—formed a pan-territorial political party. They sought full acceptance for black Africans as French persons. They wanted improved conditions of life and liberty, but still not self-government.

The End of Empire

The freeing of India and Pakistan and the struggles for independence in Indonesia and other Asian colonies greatly accelerated the pace of agitation for change in British Africa. Men who had spent the war years in Britain, where expatriate political thought was well advanced, and who had been influenced by Marxist anticolonial ideology, came home with radicalizing ideas. Men like Kwame Nkrumah and Jomo Kenyatta joined Azikiwe and others; they adopted new tactics of confrontation, thought privately and occasionally spoke publicly about full independence, and challenged the older, more complacent members of the black intelligentsia like Danquah. "Fishing in troubled waters" was the name of the game: protest marches sometimes turned into riots.[14] Wage protests were exploited. Prison became a good place to go. The shift from elite to mass politics was conscious, rapid, and successful. The Indian example was uppermost in the minds of colonized Africans.

By the early 1950s, the Sudan was self-governing, Ghana was quick to follow, and the other British African colonies were not far behind. Nor were the French ones, although in French colonies it was more exogenous factors—the failure of French arms in Vietnam, the scuttling of Gaullist imperial ambitions in Algeria, the joint French and British inability to secure the Suez Canal, and domestic political needs of all kinds—that fatally loosened the grip of empire. During the administrative age France and Britain were world powers; after World War II, they only thought that they were. The Suez Crisis and the demise of the pound sterling as a world standard currency gave proof that they were not—that the end of empire was confirmed.

Once the British and French empires in Africa were disassembled (by 1960 for the French and between 1960 and 1964 for most of the larger British possessions, but not until 1980 for Zimbabwe) the African successor states were never threatened by reassertions of metropolitan political hegemony. The empires never wanted the colonies back, no matter how contorted or embarrassing were the African postimperial experiences. At first, the French (and the Belgians) assumed that their former possessions could be kept loyal to the linguistic, cultural, and commercial empire of France (or Belgium) through the informal means of influence, sentiment, and the overseas franc. Thus, it was thought, the French Union would continue despite the loosening of formal ties. The British, on the other hand, generally assumed that the crown, the Commonwealth, common law, the Privy Council, and parliamentary example would suffice to bind their former dependencies to London.

Postcolonial Control

In fact, in the postcolonial era France exerted real, mostly informal, control over the destinies of its former colonies, whereas Britain exerted little control or influence of any kind. France quietly managed the treasuries and currencies of nearly all its weak, fragile African successor states. It also supplied the bulk of their foreign assistance funds. At the same time, France kept paratroop or Foreign Legion garrisons in several strategically located capitals; in the first two decades after the end of empire, France was rarely loath to interfere on behalf of any local francophone satrap, despotic or not. Many of the inevitable crises of presidential and regime succession in the former colonies were manipulated by France, sometimes with a public arrival of troops (as in the Comoros in 1995), sometimes through the provision of secret funds to a favored political party or politician, and sometimes by a nod or a wink, backed up with the threat of interference. Only in 1996 did France begin to reduce the backbone of its informal dominion, that is, its approximately eight thousand troops stationed in Senegal, the Ivory Coast, Chad, the Central African Republic, Gabon, and Djibuti.

The British aided their former possessions, sometimes lavishly, but only in colonial Rhodesia (later Zimbabwe) did they attempt to interfere militarily, though without success, after 1965. Indeed, more sensitive than the French to clamors against neocolonialism, the British had a diminishing influence in the political and economic affairs of the former members of their empire. This situation suited the British Treasury, which wanted as few further entanglements with the African colonies as possible. The French retained imperial longings; the British recoiled from them—except on the nostalgic, far Tory right—and never interfered (as France would have done) to prevent a dictator like Idi Amin from destroying Uganda or a succession of military coups from eliminating parliamentary democracy in Nigeria or Sierra Leone. Britain was pleased, after Suez, to wash its hands of imperial responsibilities; France never.

Postimperial France relied on the continuing influence in its fourteen former colonies of successor elites who had been sufficiently acculturated to think and behave like Gaullists, even if their democratic instincts were perfunctory. Hence, France supported the rule of cooperative individuals, so long as they accepted the cultural significance of France and were not rejectionists like Sékou Touré of Guinée. France even tolerated the rise and rule in the 1970s of Emperor Jean-Bédel Bokassa of the Central African Republic and Empire.

The Disappointments of Tutelage

Postimperial Britain assumed in Africa that the brief preindependence tutelage in participatory parliamentarianism, along with free and fair parliamentary elections and the mother country's multicentury example of beneficent government, would suffice. Britain's gift to each of the successor states was a splendidly drafted new constitution inspired by the legacy of the Magna Carta, the glorious Compromise of 1688, the nineteenth-century reform acts, the rule of law, and traditions of a sensible and impartial judiciary. At independence, few departing imperial Britons saw the need for bills of rights or judicial review, on the American model. The potential disopprobrium of the former mother country was thought to be sufficient to prevent Zaire-like disintegration of former possessions. Whereas France was cynical (and retained covert control of most purse strings and kept a mailed military fist behind its local velvet glove), Britain was idealistic, and ultimately disappointed.

One overriding assumption of the retreating imperialists regarded the durability of colonially bequeathed institutions. In a few key older anglophone and francophone outposts in Australasia and the Caribbean, this assumption has largely stood the test of the past five decades. India remains a vast, troubled, but functioning democracy at both the central and the state levels. The Caribbean island microstates also function, for the most part, in the approved parliamentary manner. Moreover, parliamentary institutions and many tenets of modern democracy undergird the governmental performances of such dissimilar Asian states as Thailand, Singapore, Taiwan, Malaysia, and Indonesia. Yet, the core of the former francophone empire in Asia—Indochina—has hardly adhered to lessons learned from or institutions derived from the French. Nor has Burma followed the usual postcolonial path, although it is as British-influenced as India. Even the postcolonial experience of today's Pakistan and Bangladesh—military dictatorships, rigged elections, subordinate judiciaries, and lackluster civil services—exhibits little more than an imperial veneer.

Arguably, at independence in India and, say, in Barbados, a democratic, parliamentary political culture was implanted and sufficiently accepted to endure the stresses of rapid population growth, economic and financial vicissitudes, natural calamities, political mismanagement, personal ambitions, and the blandishments and opportunities of the Cold War. The indomitable espirits de corps of a strong civil service reinforced the inherited political culture; a long tradition of anglophilic education among the elites was fundamental, as was wise and legitimate leadership of a kind that differentiates postpartition India from Pakistan and Burma and postindependence Barbados from Grenada, Antigua, and even from Jamaica.[15]

By these standards, the transfer to Africa of imperial institutions and ideologies must, with but a few exceptions, be judged a failure. The British attempt was the more intensive and extensive, and the more consciously and carefully designed. The original plan, in Ghana and nearly all the colonies, protectorates, and mandates that rapidly followed Ghana down the road to independence, was to empower Africans by means of new, British-modeled constitutions, and comparatively brief eras of "responsible government." During this colonial twilight, after the metropole decided to give a possession its freedom and a fresh election had been held to establish African political preferences, an African chief minister and cabinet ran their country under the supervision of a British governor and chief secretary. During this period (six years in Ghana, fewer in Britain's other possessions), the governor and chief secretary and their British subordinates "guided" the African chief minister and his colleagues, tutored them in the arts of parliamentary behavior, trained the new speaker of the House of Assembly, gave indigenous civil servants enhanced responsibilities, and attempted discretion in the exercise of their ultimate, if finite, sovereignty.

The "responsible government" phase, however long in years, was never of sufficient duration to establish a political culture where none had previously been rooted. The educational associations, the civil service traditions, and the depth of trial-and-error experience available in India, Barbados, and a handful of other anglophone possessions was absent in Africa. The situation was similar in the francophone countries, despite the experiences of four communes in Senegal.

The French and the British had started too late and educated too thinly. At independence, the sheer number of trained black senior civil servants was miniscule, and in some colonies nugatory. Politicians with participatory experience—even in Ghana, Nigeria, and Senegal—were few, and largely deemed "illegitimate" by the masses because of their collaborationist activities before the rise of nationalism. By contrast, in the Caribbean, trade unionists in a European mold were openly opposed to British and French rule starting in the 1930s; they comprised the first independent ruling cadres. Mohandas K. Gandhi and Jawaharlal Nehru gained their positions well before independence approached; they were steeped in the ruling political culture, and sought freedom by employing the Britain's parliamentary and democratic ethos against the empire.

Depth was largely lacking in Africa. The received, and obviously brittle, British and French parliamentary and democratic legacies thus shattered within the first decade, if not the very first years, of independence. No transition was as abrupt, and as fatally fateful as that of Zaire; Belgium had succeeded in educating through university level but *two* Africans by independence in 1960, and its phase of tutelage was remarkably brief, and forced. At independence, there were a hundred or so university-educated Africans in protectorates like Zambia and Malawi. The francophone educational experience produced even fewer university-trained individuals. For example, when Kenneth David Kaunda emerged from prison in the early 1960s to become Zambia's first chief minister, he had completed only the equivalent of the American tenth grade (in Britain, Form II). Apollo Milton Obote was only a high-school graduate when he became Uganda's chief minister. The exceptions were Tanzania's Julius Nyerere, a graduate of the University of Edinburgh, and Kenya's Jomo Kenyatta, with a master of science degree from the London School of Economics.

Parliamentary practices and democratic norms proved easy to push aside in favor of one-party dictatorships or authoritarian notions about what was appropriate for developing countries. Apologists justified the suborning of judiciaries and the banning of newspapers or political opponents by cloaking these actions in an indigenous African or Afro-socialist tradition—but they were rationalizing a fundamental intolerance of opposition. The first ruling elites exhibited zero-sum governmental mentalities; the presumed legacy of the metropolitan power's own political culture had been too weakly rooted, if it had taken root at all.

When the first of the many military takeovers occurred in black Africa in 1963 (in Benin) and 1964 (in Zanzibar), and when Nigeria and Ghana—the leaders of the freed continent—followed suit in 1965 and 1966, it was clear that the example of the apolitical British and French militaries had not been effectively transferred to the colonies (as it had transferred in India, though not in Pakistan and Burma). The African armies, even the small ones, wanted a share of the spoils. In some cases, too, they realized that the politicians were keeping the spoils of office to themselves, and not sharing them with the people (or with the army). Thus, some coups could be called "democratic" as well as "technocratic," but one coup often inspired another, and Africa has suffered more than fifty such forced governmental transitions between 1960 and 1996, a dozen in Benin alone.

It is true that parliamentary democracy and important rights such as free assembly and free expression are being restored one after another. Even on the least democratic fringe of the francophone zone, countries have readopted democratic forms and resurrected democratic institutions, often after agitation by emerging middle classes and pressure from Western donors. In this process, Tanzania, Zambia, Uganda, Benin, Senegal, Congo, the Central African Republic, and others rediscovered the critical parts of their colonial democratic legacies. Meanwhile, Zimbabwe, Namibia, and Botswana, among others, continued to embrace the parliamentary legacy bequeathed to them in 1980, 1989, and 1966, respectively. In 1996, eighteen African states elected governments or presidents at the polls. The imperial legacy has thus been resurrected as the dominant democratic norm. An alternative analysis would hold that, after the end of the Cold War, this paradigm is everyone's paradigm, diffused and embraced more because of the collapse of Soviet communism than because of imperial tutelage.

When they retreated from Africa and Asia, the imperial powers failed to consider the corrosive influence of the Cold War. They naturally assumed that reason, and national (not ideological or personal) self-interest would guide the successor states. But the Soviet and Chinese "devils" came with their competing blandishments; the West, led by the United States, countered. Money flowed. Guns followed. Inappropriate, if individually enriching, economic policies were adopted. Every ideological path chosen by the former colonies presumed the continued expansion of the world economic order, perpetually high raw materials prices, and a lasting ability to borrow unwisely and repay well. The leaders of the new nations, some of whom had strategic shorelines but most of whom only had United Nations votes to use as barter, ultimately assumed that they could play the newest empires—Soviet and American—against each other to their own benefit.

The Postcolonial Order

The postcolonial order demonstrated conclusively—as did the post–Cold War implosions in Somalia, Rwanda, Burundi, Algeria, and Nigeria—that the imperial legacy by itself was not conducive to survival in the international arena. What the empires had done for Africa was basic and in contrast to their legacies in much of Asia: they had provided borders and therefore states, all of which have survived (and will endure) in Africa. But the failures of the administrative age—especially the refusal genuinely to embrace African desires for full assimilation, and the brevity of the post–World War II period of rigorous acculturation—translated into a failure to create unified nations led by statesmen. Only in the unusual case of largely homogeneous Botswana, where a coalesced nationality had been present since the middle of the nineteenth century, have Western values—the rule of law, human rights, civil liberties, and press freedom—and sober political and economic management prevailed continuously since independence. Botswana's success was further ensured by the existence of a precolonial culture of village democracy and tolerance that was strengthened in the nineteenth century by the teachings of Protestant missionaries from Britain. At independence, the church was strong, especially among both the traditional and the new elites, and both the old and new nationalists harbored a cultural expectation of democracy. Botswana may have been unusually fortunate in that the old and the new were combined in its first leader, Sir Seretse Khama. In his case, as in the other positive African cases, the inspiration of gifted indigenous leadership was crucial to success, just as it was in Senghor's Senegal and Houphouët-Boigny's Ivory Coast. In these three cases, the imperial legacy may have been just as irrelevant as relevant; personal, or elite, predispositions prevailed over structural weaknesses.

The weakness of the emergent autonomous elites is among the major failures of the British and French empires in Africa, although the successor states have survived and a few have even flourished. To establish this contention depends upon a series of arguable definitions, but the palpable collapse of the civil services in almost all the former African colonies, the corrupt venality of so many of their leading cadres, the predatory quality of a few Mobutu-like regimes (in Zaire, Kenya, Somalia, and Malawi), the ascendancy of military juntas, the recurring debt crises, and fragile economies and weak developmental performances, all testify to a failure on the part of the European empires effectively to transfer to their successors the ingredients of good government and a sense of commonweal.[16]

Unlike much of Asia, Africa could not have emerged so quickly into the modern world without imperial influence and a period of foreign hegemony, however rapacious. The counterfactual cases of Liberia and Ethiopia, neither of which was ever successfully colonized by a major imperial power, make that point, as does the example of Haiti.[17] Without the West, Africa would probably have been unable to generate indigenous capital early enough (as Ethiopia and Liberia failed to do) to build roads and railways, dig mines, grow cash crops, and so on. British capital found its way to Latin America and the western United States to promote railways, but most of Africa had too few attractive investment opportunities. In the nineteenth and twentieth centuries, France and Britain provided the security that made weak infrastructural and communications investments plausible, or private sector (missionary) educational and medical investments likely. Without such sponsorship, colonial Africa would have entered the Western economic and learning spheres much more slowly than it did.

To say so is to excuse nothing. Certainly, Western powers had responsibilities to do more for Africa—at least to live up to their own promises and professions of good intention. They intended to create better successors, but never did. They intended to launch successor states on the road to modernity and provide them with the capability of survival and the characteristics of meaningful independence. But largely they did not do so, and their policies were insufficient to create forty-six viable nations out of a like number of colonies, protectorates, and mandates.

Near the end of the twentieth century, after more than a century of imperial rule in some cases and most of a full century in others, the post–World War II francophone or anglophone elites in most of black Africa demanded independence, received it with hardly a struggle (though after some appropriate agitation), and then proceeded to launch themselves onto the world stage not as newly hatched former wards but as full-fledged players in the heady game of Cold War rivalry.

From the 1960s and 1970s onward, most of Africa suffered from mismanagement, swings of boom and bust, and, since about 1975, a long period of little growth. In real terms, Africans are for the most part poorer than they were at the end of empire.[18] Ghana was more developed than Indonesia and Malaysia in 1960. Even Tanzania had prospects, and Zambia had long vied with Chile for world leadership in copper production.[19]

The Imperial Legacy

There is abundant gloom in Africa. But the imperial legacy lives, and provides hope. With the end of the Cold War and the collapse of the Soviet model, there has been a distinct swing back to the market economy, democracy, and the rule of law as paradigms for Africa. Despite military rule in nine states, including giant Nigeria, and despite the survival of dictators like Daniel arap Moi in Kenya and Mobutu Sese Soko in Zaire, the participatory, pluralistic, populist tendency is spreading—even into francophone Africa. Since 1990, fifteen states have become democratic and have reassumed the parliamentary and jural legacies of their imperial donors. France has even intervened in the Central African Republic, Cameroon, the Comoros, Djibuti, and Chad in order to assist their transitions to democracy. France's decision in 1994 to devalue the CFA franc was equally important in helping its former colonies modernize their otherwise protected economies. London and Paris also continue to educate Africans in their universities.

In ways that are appropriate to the post–Cold War, postcolonial era, the British and French imperial legacy survives intact and is probably growing. Indeed, in 1995 the British Commonwealth expanded its membership beyond South Africa, Namibia, and all of its former African possessions, to include Cameroon, a mostly French-speaking, sometime German colony that had been governed during the administrative age by separate British and French mandatory regimes (the French by far the larger and more influential). At the same time, the Commonwealth criticized Nigeria and threatened to expel it. The Association of Francophone States, of which Cameroon is also a member, meets regularly.

In these symbolic ways, the empires live. And as in the former Soviet Union, there is a growing nostalgia, not for foreign domination, but for the former rulers' stable and largely noncorrupt administration and well-managed macroeconomic policies. The legacy of the imperial era is that such qualities are now demanded of all indigenous governments, however constituted. There is little patience, especially in the wake of President Nelson Mandela's reassertion of Western political and economic values in postapartheid South Africa, for anything less.

Notes

1. Joyce Cary, *Mister Johnson* (London: V. Gollancz, 1939).
2. Lucy Mair, *Native Policies in Africa* (London: Routledge, 1936), p. 210.
3. See Stephen H. Roberts, *The History of French Colonial Policy, 1870–1925* (London: P.S. King, 1929), pp. 307–17.
4. Quoted in Raymond Leslie Buell, *The Native Problem in Africa* (New York: Macmillan, 1928), vol. I, pp. 451–52.
5. D. Anthony Low, "India and Britain: The Climactic Years, 1917–1947," in D. Anthony Low, ed., *Eclipse of Empire* (New York: Cambridge University Press, 1991), pp. 58–100.
6. Kenneth Robinson, "Political Developments in French West Africa," in Calvin Stillman, ed., *Africa in the Modern World* (Chicago: University of Chicago Press, 1955), p. 146.
7. Leopold Moore, speaking in the Legislative Council in 1933, quoted in James W. Davidson, ed., *The Northern Rhodesian Legislative Council* (London: Faber and Faber, 1948), p. 94.
8. For examples, see Joseph Thomson, "Up the Niger to the Central Sudan: Letters to a Friend," *Good Words* 27 (1886): pp. 26–28; Mary Kingsley, *Travels in West Africa* (London: Macmillan, 1897), p. 20.
9. See Robert I. Rotberg, *The Rise of Nationalism in Central Africa: The Making of Malawi and Zambia, 1873–1964* (Cambridge, MA: Harvard University Press, 1965), pp. 186–89; Rotberg, *Black Heart: Gore-Browne and the Politics of Multiracial Zambia* (Berkeley and Los Angeles: University of California Press, 1977), pp. 227–28.
10. Francis Agbodeka, "Sir Gordon Guggisberg's Contribution to the Development of the Gold Coast, 1919–1927," *Transactions of the Historical Society of Ghana* 13 (1972): pp. 51–64; Ronald E. Wraith, *Guggisberg* (Oxford: Oxford University Press, 1967).
11. See André Gide, *Voyage au Congo* (Paris: Gallimard, 1927), pp. 23, 92.

12. Dennis Austin, *Politics in Ghana, 1946–1960* (London: Oxford University Press, 1964), pp. 46–102.

13. Macaulay, quoted in Buell, p. 743; Joseph Danquah, *Self-Help and Expansion* (Accra: H.K. Akyeampong, 1943), p. 25.

14. George Padmore, *The Gold Coast Revolution: The Struggle of an African People from Slavery to Freedom* (London: D. Dobson, 1953), p. 62.

15. Bridget Brereton, "Society and Culture in the Caribbean: The British and French West Indies, 1870–1980," in Franklin W. Knight and Colin A. Palmer, eds., *The Modern Caribbean* (Chapel Hill: University of North Carolina Press, 1989), pp. 85–110.

16. See Michael Chege, "Sub-Saharan Africa: Underdevelopment's Last Stand," in Barbara Stallings, ed., *Global Change, Regional Response: The New International Context of Development* (New York: Cambridge University Press, 1995), pp. 309–24.

17. See Robert I. Rotberg, *Haiti: The Politics of Squalor* (Boston: Houghton Mifflin, 1971).

18. World Bank, *World Development Report, 1990* (New York: World Bank, 1990), pp. 2, 26.

19. See the various discussions in David Lindauer and Michael Roemer, eds., *Asia and Africa: Legacies and Opportunities in Development* (San Francisco: ICS Press, 1994).

9

The Imperial Culture of North–South Relations

The Case of Islam and the West

Ali A. Mazrui

Introduction and Overview

In much of the first half of the twentieth century, at least two-thirds of the Muslim world was lodged in the formal collective empire of the Western world. In much of the second half of the twentieth century, most of the Muslim world has existed within the informal collective empire of the West. In the years of formal imperialism, and especially after the collapse of the Ottoman Empire, Muslim countries were colonies and dependencies of such countries as Britain, France, the Netherlands, and Italy. In a special sense, Russia was also a colonizer of Muslims. In the more recent years of informal imperialism, the United States has assumed a preeminent hegemonic position, supported by two or three of the major European powers. During the years of formal empire, the Muslim world underwent substantial cultural Westernization—in values, dress code, educational systems, lifestyle, and economies. In recent years, the West has begun a process of demographic Islamization. Muslims are on their way towards outnumbering Jews in the United States, France, and potentially in all of western Europe. However, although Muslims may outnumber Jews, will they ever overshadow Jewish influence in any time span of less than a century?

If the twentieth century is the century of global war, is it also the century of global empire? The British attempted to create a global formal empire—a territorial vastness over which the sun never set—from Karachi to Kingston, from Maiduguri in Nigeria to Melbourne in Australia, and from Quebec to Kuala Lumpur. Although the British attempt to globalize formal empire was impressive, it fell far short of encompassing the world. It is the United States' informal empire that much more closely approaches real global scale. But the United States does not act alone. It is a global imperial power with subimperial lieutenants: Britain and France in global political affairs, and Germany and Japan in global economic affairs.

This chapter is concerned with the informal imperial relations between the Western hegemonic system and the Muslim world. During the Cold War the West divided the world, de facto, into *Dar el Harb* (the Abode of War—in other words, the Communist world), *Dar el Maghreb* or *Dar el Gharb* (the Abode of the West) and *Dar el Sulh* or *Dar el Ahd* (the Abode of Dependencies—Muslim countries and much of the rest of the Third World). The West used the United Nations as one of its instruments of manipulation. Informal empire had indeed gone global. In this century of global empire, it is not just the periphery that is multinational; the imperial core is also multinational. Hence, the hegemony of the multinational West over the multinational Islamic world is a special case of North–South relations.

In the second half of the twentieth century, no discussion of the aftermath of empires can be complete without a discussion of the role of the United Nations system. Applying for admission to the UN is one of the first acts of postcolonial sovereignty. And yet the UN itself is part of the machinery of Pax Occidental— the Western imperial umbrella. This chapter is partially about the United Nations' role in the reconstitution of Western imperial power.

It is also worth distinguishing between imperial reconstitution and imperial reincarnation. Imperial reconstitution involves a complete or partial resurrection of the same imperial power, recently dethroned. Imperial reincarnation, on the other hand, is a perceived transmigration of the "soul" of empire from one center to another empathetic center, usually a relative. During Harold Macmillan's premiership in Britain, Dean Acheson in the United States made the following pronouncement: "Britain has lost an empire and has not found a role." In reply, the somewhat irritated prime minister felt compelled to reassure the British people that Britain was great and would remain great.

But was Britain going to find a "role"? In fact, Britain's new role was to piggyback on the hegemonic shoulders of the United States. Britain became a lieutenant in the informal imperialism of the United States. Harold Macmillan— a classicist by education—described the situation as Britain "playing Greeks to American Romans." In other words, Britain was to play the sophisticate to America's cowboy power. Has the soul of Anglo-imperialism transmigrated from Pax Britannica to Pax Americana? In the Suez Crisis of 1956, Britain and the United States were on opposite sides politically. But the Suez Crisis occurred before Harold Macmillan became premier. Since then, Great Britain has, on the whole, largely ridden piggyback on the informal empire of the United States. Thus, we have an imperial reincarnation.

The idea of a special relationship between the two countries has been cultivated, especially by London. Although the British have not given up all diplomatic independence in their dealings with the Muslim world, a cornerstone of British policy has been to support American goals as much as possible. This policy included pro-Iraqi policies during the Iran–Iraq war; anti-Iraqi policies in the 1990s; collaboration with U.S. military and political decisions regarding Libya; and unwavering loyalty to U.S. insistence on continued UN sanctions against Iraq, long after the end of Operation Desert Storm. The two Anglo-Saxon powers have each used the United Nations to lend legitimacy to the reincarnation of Pax Britannica as Pax Americana. Even in Muslim countries previously ruled by Britain—such as Egypt, Sudan, Pakistan, and others—London is content to play second fiddle to Washington. And when the United States terminated its membership of an apparently Muslim-dominated UNESCO, Britain meekly followed.

The globalization of empire that the British attempted in the formal sense has been carried further by the Americans in an informal manner—with imperial sanctions against dissidents. The imperial soul has transmigrated. In the century of global empire, the term "world community" or "international community" is used to mean the United States and its closest allies. In Samuel Huntington's words:

> Global political and security issues are effectively settled by a directorate of the United States, Britain and France, world economic issues by a directorate of the United States, Germany and Japan, all of which maintain extraordinarily close relations with each other, to the exclusion of lesser and largely non-Western countries. Decisions made at the U.N. Security Council or in the International Monetary Fund that reflect the interests of the West are presented to the world as the desires of the world community. The very phrase "the world community" has become the euphemistic collective noun (replacing "the Free World") to give global legitimacy to actions reflecting the interests of the United States and other Western powers.[1]

Huntington goes on to show how the West has used the UN Security Council to impose sanctions against Muslim countries or to invoke the use of force. After Iraq occupied Kuwait, the West was faced with a choice between saving time and saving lives. The West chose to save time. In Huntington's words,

> Western domination of the U.N. Security Council and its decisions, tempered only by occasional abstention by China, produced U.N. legitimation of the West's use of force to drive Iraq out of Kuwait and its elimination of Iraq's sophisticated weapons. It also produced the quite unprecedented action by the United States, Britain and France in getting the Security Council to demand that Libya hand over the Pan Am 103 bombing suspects and then impose sanctions when Libya refused.[2]

This chapter agrees with Huntington that there is a clash of civilizations in the world, but disagrees about the nature and time-frame of that clash. The clash of civilizations did not begin with the end of the Cold War but much earlier. The chief cultural transgressor has been the Western world. Among the victims of Western cultural transgression has been the Muslim world. This chapter is partly concerned with the aftermath of the West's transgression.

Between Disengagement and Autocolonization

At the same time as the British have linked themselves with Pax Americana, they have even more vigorously attempted to disengage from formal Pax Britannica. They have chosen the role of second in command to the American informal empire and have decisively dismantled their own formal empire. As compared with the French, Britain over-disengaged from its formal empire and accepted comparatively little responsibility for what happened in its former colonies after independence day.

The Muslim world has been among those affected by Britain's over-disengagement. In 1964 within a matter of days after independence, a social revolution erupted in Zanzibar. Britain did almost nothing to intervene apart from giving political asylum to the deposed sultan. A civil war broke out in Sudan between Muslim north and non-Muslim south in 1955 as British rule was coming to an end. The war lasted until 1972, when the Addis Ababa Accords were signed. This was the first Sudanese civil war, and more vigorous British efforts could have ended it much sooner. A civil war broke out in Nigeria six years after independence. More robust British political involvement in the events that led to the civil war might have averted it. The Nigerian civil war cost 750,000 lives. Former British colonies in Africa that have experienced severe conflicts since independence also include Uganda, Sierra Leone, and the white settler–dominated countries of South Africa and Rhodesia (Zimbabwe). In former British Africa two to three million lives have been lost in postindependence civil conflicts. In former French Africa the casualties are in the hundreds of thousands, mainly in Chad.

Decolonization in the French Empire happened more clearly in stages. The first major stage was the granting of nominal political independence in the 1960s, without economic or monetary independence. Except for in Guinea (Conakry), the French continued to dominate the economies of their former colonies, but also helped them by backing local currencies with the French franc, and by providing budget subsidies where necessary. The French also stationed troops in Africa, and were not unduly modest about either instigating coups against rulers who were out of favor in Paris, or preventing coups against in-favor rulers.

The readiness of the French to intervene militarily did have the beneficial effect of stabilizing the former French colonies, at least relative to their anglophone counterparts. The former French colonies were not necessarily spared military coups, but they seemed less prone to outright civil wars.

In 1964, the British did respond to written requests from the governments of Uganda, Kenya, and Tanganyika by sending British troops to disarm mutinous

African solders. The British troops accomplished the job without firing a single shot. But this British intervention against mutineers (as opposed to coup plotters) at the request of three eastern African governments stands out in British policy as a glaring exception. Since that instance, the British have maintained a studied policy of almost total military and political disengagement from their former colonies. In most cases this translates into a policy of irresponsible over-disengagement from the consequences of their own colonization of these societies.

By contrast to its studied disinterest in postcolonial Africa, Britain has joined the bandwagon of Pax Americana and is trying to play second in command in the informal global dominion of the United States. Were the ties linking Britain to the United States rooted in a shared culture and civilization?

Different questions arise with regard to the French model of postcolonialism. The former French colonies maintained dependency relationships with France even after they ostensibly became politically independent. Can this be called a kind of autocolonization, as Karen Dawisha writes in chapter 14?

The concept of autocolonization has been used to refer to political relationships involving a hegemonic power in the Northern Hemisphere. The acceptance by a smaller country of the imperial hegemony of a mightier power is at the core of the concept, which is closely related to other concepts that are older and have logical connections to it.

One such older sister concept is "empire by invitation," which has been used to refer to American military protection of Western Europe after World War II and to the consequent American economic penetration of Europe. In the Arab world and from a Muslim perspective, it can also be used to refer to the role of Syria in Lebanon—a kind of Pax Syriana.

Another older sister to autocolonization is the formal concept of the protectorate, in which a weaker state seeks or is forced to accept the protective umbrella of a particular hegemonic power. Sometimes the umbrella even changes hands. In the nineteenth century, following a revolt against the Ottoman Empire, Moldavia and Walachia became protectorates of the Russians in 1829. They fell under wider international protection in 1856 and were united to constitute the sovereign state of Romania in 1878. In the first half of the twentieth century, the British used the concept of protectorate to checkmate their European rivals. For example, with the 1900 Uganda Agreement they convinced the Kabaka of Buganda to seek British protection—thus effectively keeping the French from much of eastern Africa. In the Muslim world, the British also persuaded the sultan of Zanzibar to seek British protection for the sultanate proper and for the sultan's coastal dominion in what is today Kenya. At least in theory, these were situations where weaker states sought the protection of stronger ones. The Sultanate of Oman was a more informal British protectorate.

The third sister of autocolonization is the phenomenon of "colonialism by consent." The most dramatic illustration of colonialism by consent was the 1958 referendum fostered by President Charles de Gaulle in the French Empire in

Africa. The referendum gave the colonies a choice between sovereign independence or continuing colonial association with France. All but one of the colonies in sub-Saharan Africa voted in favor of continuing relations with France. Only more radical Muslim Guinea under the leadership of Sekou Toure had the courage to vote for complete independence. Were the others voting for autocolonization? The general agreement to continue dependency had implications for France's relationship with Africa for the rest of the twentieth century, even after the former colonies became nominally independent starting in 1960.

The fourth sister to autocolonization is my own concept of self-colonization, which was introduced in 1993 and 1994.[3] Self-colonization in my sense is a South–South phenomenon in which the periphery colonizes the periphery. In Muslim Asia, examples of self-colonization could include Indonesia's annexation of East Timor. In Muslim Africa, examples include not only Morocco's attempt to annex the western Sahara but also the absorption of Zanzibar into the United Republic of Tanzania in 1964. For all intents and purposes, Zanzibar was annexed by Tanganyika to create Tanzania.

The fifth sister of autocolonization is the whole phenomenon of voluntary economic dependency. Most governments of the Third World have voluntarily submitted to economically dependent relationships with the Northern Hemisphere. Certainly most Muslim governments have acquiesced to economic imperialism. There is an overabundance of literature on economic dependency, and it must be asked: Is this economic autocolonization? Or is it a new form of participation in the wider capitalist world? It may in fact be both. Metaphorically, however, it is a Faustian compact with the Devil.

A Tripartite Political World

In the summer of 1993 Samuel Huntington unleashed a debate about the nature of conflict in the post–Cold War era. Huntington argued that the end of the Cold War meant that future conflicts would not be primarily between states or ideological blocs, but rather between civilizations and cultural coalitions.[4]

> The fault lines between civilizations will be the battle lines of the future. Conflict between civilizations will be the latest phase in the evolution of conflict in the modern world.[5]

Huntington was at his best when he discussed the West's masquerade as "the world community," and how it uses the United Nations to give universalist credentials to Western interests.

According to Huntington, the universalism of the United Nations is not what it seems. The United Nations has become the fig leaf for Western imperial actions. On becoming a member of the *ummah* (the worldwide Muslim community), a Muslim convert must recite the Shahadah, saying that "there is no God but Allah." It seems that in order to remain a member in good standing of the United Nations, all countries must acknowledge that "there is no political God but the West." Only the West has the right to determine when and how force should be used in world politics.

There is now evidence that Libya may not have been the culprit in the Pan-American Flight 103 disaster at Lockerbie, Scotland. Some other Middle Eastern country might be responsible. But the sanctions against Libya have not been lifted. Washington, London, and Paris are reluctant to eat their words even if injustice is being committed.[6] The stubbornness of power is at work again.

Following the end of World War II, a strange thing happened. Quite unconsciously, the West adopted an ancient Islamic view of the world: the tripartite division of the world by ancient Islamic jurists into *Dar el Islam* (the Abode of Islam), Dar el Harb (the Abode of War), and Dar el Sulh (the Abode of Peaceful Coexistence or Contractual Peace).[7] This last division was Islam's informal empire.

Within Dar el Islam, amity and cooperation on Islamic principles were supposed to prevail; Pax Islamica was supposed to be triumphant. Dar el Islam included Muslims as well as non-Muslims of the tolerated communities ("People of the Book" and Dhimmis), who enjoyed state protection against internal insecurity and external aggression.[8]

Dar el Harb was not necessarily an arena of direct military confrontation. It comprised the lands of non-Muslims who were often hostile to Islam, constituting the sort of situation that Thomas Hobbes would much later describe as a condition without a shared sovereign.[9] Muslim jurists developed the concept of Dar el Harb, a state of war, for cognizance of authorities in countries that did not agree on the sovereignty of God. As Majid Khadduri points out:

> Islam's cognizance of non-Islamic sovereignties merely meant that some form of authority was by nature necessary for the survival of mankind, even when men lived in territories in the state of nature, outside the pale of the Islamic public order.[10]

The countries of Dar el Sulh (the Abode of Contractual Peace or Peaceful Coexistence) were the non-Muslim countries that negotiated with the Muslim rulers for greater autonomy and peace in exchange for some kind of tribute or collective tax paid to the Muslim treasury. The relationship was neo-imperial. The Dar el Suhl was not recognized as a separate category by all Muslim jurists, some of whom felt that "if the inhabitants of the territory concluded a peace treaty and paid tribute, it became part of the dar al-Islam and its people were entitled to the protection of Islam."[11]

After World War II, the West appropriated ancient Islam's tripartite view of the world and simply substituted itself for Islam. For much of the second half of the twentieth century, during the period of the Cold War, the world comprised the following categories:

Dar el Maghreb (the Abode of the West)—instead of Dar el Islam; Dar el Harb (the Abode of War—which was essentially the Communist world); Dar el Sulh (the Abode of Peaceful Coexistence, which was the Third World). The Third World paid tribute to the West in the form of the debt burden and other forms of economic exploitation in a modern version of the tribute paid by Dar el Sulh countries to medieval Muslim rulers.

But one major proviso needs to be emphasized. Although the Western doctrine of the Abode of War was in theory the Communist world, in practice the West's actual military fighting in the second half of the twentieth century has been almost entirely in the Third World, including the world of Islam.[12]

The Korean War was in the Third World, although not the Muslim world. In the case of Korea and Vietnam it is difficult to distinguish between the Communist world and the Third World. Several million people perished in the American-led wars fought in Korea and Vietnam. In both cases, the countries of the Warsaw Pact and of NATO fought each other through intermediaries; in military terms, no member of the Warsaw Pact was directly hurt. The doctrinal Abode of War was not necessarily the literal abode of war. The United States armed itself to the teeth to fight the communist Second World—and turned on the Third World instead. In Korea the Western onslaught happened under the flag of the United Nations.[13]

Whereas in Korea and Vietnam it may have been difficult to determine where the communist Second World ended and the Third World began, the Muslim world poses no such ambivalence because the Muslim states have not been communist.[14] And yet, since 1980 at least five hundred thousand Muslims—including Libyans, Iranians, Lebanese, Palestinians, and Iraqis—have been killed by Western armaments. The West has been trigger-happy in its response to Muslim political challenges.

In the Persian Gulf War of 1991, the West used the flag of the United Nations to give its militarism a universalistic appeal and legitimacy.[15] The human toll in Iraq still rises, as a result of the deprivations caused by the Anglo-American economic sanctions, which were given universalistic legitimacy by the UN Security Council.[16] The rate of infant mortality in Iraq has doubled and tripled since the end of the war, and death rates of ordinary people from preventable diseases have escalated.[17] Yet despite the geographic and military emasculation of Iraq, Saddam Hussein's hold on the country appears to be unshakable.[18]

The ostensible reason for the sanctions is to make sure that Iraq does not rebuild weapons of mass destruction. And yet, each of the permanent members of the Security Council is possessive about its own weapons of mass destruction. Unlike France, Iraq has not yet found the necessary arrogance to test nuclear weapons thousands of miles away from its own core population, thereby endangering the population of other lands. Protests by the militarily weak Pacific nations around this issue include street demonstrations, diplomatic downgrading of relations, and boycotts of French goods like wine.[19] Nor does Iraq have a partner who is a permanent member of the Security Council, to whom to say "Scratch my nuclear back and I'll scratch yours."

The United Nations and the Cultural Counterrevolution

The UN, as a supposedly global institution, represents states and regions bu does not try to represent civilizations. Five of the past six secretaries-general o the UN have come from Christian traditions,[20] yet the Christian world contain only about one-fifth of the population of the world. There has been no Hindu Muslim, or Confucian secretary-general, despite the fact that together these pop ulations outnumber Christians by more than two to one. There has been one Buddhist secretary-general, U Thant. One Buddhist, and five Christians—al though there are probably as many Buddhists as Christians in the world.[21] The ratio raises a question: Should the UN system be more attentive to proportiona representation of cultures? [22]

A related question is whether peacekeeping in the future should be more sensitive to geocultural movements. International geocultural organizations like the Organization of the Islamic Conference (OIC) can be relevant in preventative diplomacy or peacemaking—although OIC efforts in the 1980s to stop the Iraq– Iran conflict were less than successful.[23] On the other hand, patient efforts in Liberia by the west Africa–based Economic Community of West African States' Monitoring Group (ECOMOG) appear to have been relatively more successful at least until the spring of 1996.[24]

A further question regards UN involvement in intracivilizational conflicts with extracivilizational consequences—like movements of Islamic militancy in places like Algeria and Egypt and, potentially, Saudi Arabia. Officials of NATO and some members of the League of Arab States are consulting with each othe concerning Islamic militancy. Should the UN join the discussion?

For the time being, the United Nations system is part of the cultural hege mony and informal empire of the Western world. And when Amadou-Mahta M'Bow, direction-general of UNESCO, tried to rebel against this situation, the United States and Great Britain withdrew from UNESCO—and M'Bow was ousted.[25]

The UN was formed primarily by the victors of World War II. Those victors belonged to one and one-half civilizations. Britain, the United States, France, and the European part of the USSR all belonged to Western civilization, and the Asian part of the Soviet Union provided the half. They made themselves perma nent members of the UN's powerful Security Council. They made one conces sion to another civilization—by also making pre-Communist China a permanen member. Of the five original languages of the UN, four were in origin Europear languages: English, French, Spanish, and Russian. A concession was made to another civilization by recognizing the Chinese language.

A kind of bicameral legislature began to emerge: an upper house, which was the more powerful but less representative, called the Security Council; and a lower house, which was less powerful but more representative, called the General Assembly. This bicameral concept developed by practice rather than by design and was very Western in origin. The upper house was the global House of Lords—warlords!—another concept borrowed from Western civilization.

One of the major functions of the UN is to help keep the peace according to the principles of international law. The law of nations was itself a child of European diplomatic history and statecraft. It once used to be:

The law of Christian nations, and then became,
The law of civilized nations, and then became,
The law of developed nations.[26]

That old international law was used to legitimate colonization by Western countries of other countries. The intellectual forebears of Western political thought were marked by an arrogant Eurocentrism. John Stuart Mill distinguished between "barbarians and societies worthy of the Law of Nations."[27] These were civilizational criteria, accepted by almost the whole white world. Even more appalling is the approbation of colonialism by early socialists; Karl Marx applauded Britain's colonization of India,[28] and Engels applauded France's colonization of Algeria.[29]

And then the UN began to admit not only more countries but also more cultures: Pakistan in 1947, Myanmar (Burma) and Sri Lanka (Ceylon) in 1948, and later Malaysia and Singapore. There followed some additional Arab countries (Egypt was already a member): Morocco; Tunisia; Sudan; Algeria; and newly independent black African countries, beginning with Ghana in 1957. New values were trying to express themselves through a Eurocentric infrastructure.

Later, the UN became a channel through which other countries and cultures began to insist on changes in international law. When India occupied Goa, thus liberating it from Portuguese rule, Krishna Menon enunciated the principle that "colonialism was permanent aggression"—thus delegitimating colonialism.[30]

African struggles against apartheid curtailed the principle of domestic jurisdiction as applied to South Africa's policy of apartheid. Eventually, apartheid came to be regarded as a matter of relevance to international security, and the United Nations began to take a more active role in combating apartheid.[31]

In the post–Cold War era, is the UN likely to be used by the dominant civilization (the West) against other civilizations? Is that what happened during the Persian Gulf War? Was the UN hijacked by the West to legitimate massacres in defense of its oil interests? In Bosnia, is the UN being used by the West to make sure there is no viable Muslim state in the middle of Europe?

The UN has sometimes been guilty of sins of omission, including:

1. standing by while Patrice Lumumba was taken to his death in 1961 in the Congo (now Zaire);[32]
2. standing by while thousands of people were massacred in the bombing of Iraq—euphemistically termed "collateral damage"—during the Persian Gulf War, and in the aftermath, continuing to ignore the privations of Iraqi individuals due to sanctions;
3. standing by in the 1990s while hundreds of thousands of Bosnians are maimed, murdered, mutilated, or raped.

Is this a clash of civilizations?

In an earlier work, I raised the issue of the West's, especially the United States', role as the defender of the holy places in Islam—Mecca and Medina—during the Gulf War.[33] At the time this chapter was written, the United States had reluctantly emerged as the only peacemaker tentatively acceptable to all parties—including Bosnian Muslims—in the Bosnian imbroglio. Part of the peace plan envisages reducing Serbian and Croatian armaments, while increasing Bosnian Muslim arms. The peacekeeping forces will not be directly involved in rearmament, but the United States is apparently trying to get third parties to undertake the task of arming the Bosnian forces so that they will be able to repel any future challenge.[34]

It is striking that, whereas the United Nations, the European allies, and the Clinton administration were long reluctant to lift the arms embargo and allow the Bosnian Muslims to arm themselves, conservative Republicans (like former senator Bob Dole) have long called for allowing Bosnia to arm itself.[35] Unfortunately, the world of Islam has not been come up with coherent and organized efforts to enable the poorly armed Bosnians to defend themselves.

Huntington was concerned about an alliance between the world of Islam and the countries of the Confucian legacy. In our terms, would this alliance provide a new Abode of War for the West? The UN saw omens of a potential Muslim-Confucian coalition in the 1970s. In 1971 there was euphoric reaction to the UN's recognition of the People's Republic of China.[36] Autumn 1974 saw Yassir Arafat's address to the General Assembly as a virtual head of state.[37] Third was Algeria's launching of the campaign for a New International Economic Order in 1974.[38] The fourth omen was the subsequent recognition of Arabic in 1975 as the second non-European language accepted as official idioms of the world body.

These are modest if significant achievements. On the whole the UN system, along with the Bretton Woods institutions (the World Bank and the International Monetary Fund), continue to be major disseminators of Western ideas, concepts, and values. In their conception, and in many of their operations, the institutions are rooted in the Western worldview. Future directors-general of UNESCO are unlikely to be as assertive as Amadou-Mahtar M'Bow.[39] And most developing countries have, in any case, been forced to toe the Western "party" line since the death of the Soviet Union.

At the moment the UN Security Council is primarily a "white man's club" with nonwhite visitors. Four of the five permanent members are essentially ethnically white countries rooted in a Euro-Christian legacy (the United States, France, Britain, and Russia). Has the United Nations become the inevitable future arena for a clash of civilizations? Or is the world body simply an extension of the West's informal empire?

The Bleeding Face of Islam

Both formal and informal empires carry considerable potential for conflict. The different conflicts in the Muslim world dictate an agonizing reappraisal. The majority of the victims are Muslims, but there are conflicts in which Muslims are the villains.

Has the ancient Dar el Islam now become the modern Dar el Harb? In traditional Islamic international law, Dar el Islam comprised the lands where Muslims were free and secure. But now Muslims are caught up in conflict in different countries. To what extent are these conflicts a consequence of decolonization? How much of it is due to the persistence of the West's informal empire?

Current conflicts in the Islamic world can be divided into three main categories of societies. First, there are societies in which Muslims are the victims of the violence of others. This category includes the wars in Bosnia, Chechnia, Kashmir, southern Lebanon, occupied Palestine, and Afghanistan when it was under Soviet occupation.

Secondly, there are societies in which Muslims are at war with each other. This includes Afghanistan, Algeria, the city of Karachi in Pakistan, and to some extent Egypt.

The third category comprises situations in which Muslims are more culprits than victims—where Muslims victimize others. Although the war in Sudan is not primarily a religious war, its net effect casts Muslims as the greater culprits. What about the November 1995 terrorist act in Riyadh, Saudi Arabia, against Americans? [40] Is that a case of Muslims against foreigners? Or did it signal the beginning of an inter-Muslim conflict comparable to the situations in Algeria and Egypt?

Within the ancient Abode of Islam, conflict was not supposed to be the order of the day; now, however, there is anguish and discord. The universalism of faith has yet to find a universality of peace. Both decolonization and residual imperialism carry seeds of conflict.

The United Nations is involved in some of these conflicts affecting Muslims, but not in others: there are UN resolutions about Kashmir, and many more UN resolutions about Palestine; the UN has sometimes attempted to help in the civil war in Afghanistan; the UN has kept out of the war in Chechnia. What is heartrending for the Muslim world is how much fratricide and victimization there is.

While Muslims have failed to maintain peace with each other, Westerners have managed to find it among themselves. A whole new body of literature is emerging based on the premise that "democracies do not go to war against each other." [41] The literature is not based on moralistic wishful thinking, but on the presentation of systemic and scientific analysis of the nature of the democratic process, especially in the liberal West. There is nothing about the democratic process, however, that will stop the United States from invading Panama, or stop Britain and France from joining a military coalition against Iraq in the Gulf War. But the new school of thought surrounding democratic peace asserts that these democratic countries are systemically unlikely to go to war against each other. In Huntington's words, "military conflict among Western states is unthinkable." [42] But how much of this peace is due to the presence of economic prosperity and nuclear proliferation, rather than a peacefulness inherent in democracy?

Rather than a situation in which Muslims do not war with each other (as the ancient doctrine expected), there is a situation in which Westerners do not go to war with each other (as the new political science asserts). Instead of the triumph of Dar el Islam, we have Dar el Maghreb victorious.

Furthermore, the West controls the United Nations. Islam's universalism of faith has stumbled because of the weakness of the Muslims. The United Nations' universalism of states has triumphed because of the power of the West.

Perhaps nowhere in the world was there such a stark confrontation between the universalism of faith and the universalism of states as in Bosnia. The state called Yugoslavia disintegrated, and out of the fragments emerged a country called Bosnia-Herzogovina, containing a plurality of Muslims. The idea of a Muslim-led government in the middle of Europe, however democratic, raised the specter of disturbing possibilities in some circles. Muslim Turkey is a Middle Eastern country trying to be recognized as European, and Muslim Albania is the most technologically backward country in Europe. But a relatively advanced Bosnia located in the middle of Christian Europe was a disconcerting prospect amid expert predictions of the ensuing "clash of civilizations."

Bosnia is therefore a useful case study of a number of factors, especially of the universalism of faith at war with the universalism of statehood. It is a case study of the United Nations' opposition to the aspirations of most of the Muslim world. And, in its approach toward de facto partition, it provides a case study of the clash of civilizations.

Bosnia-Herzegovina was originally invaded by both Serbian troops and Bosnian Serbs armed by Serbia. The UN imposed an arms embargo on both sides. Yet, the UN was wrong to impose the embargo on the Bosnian government for two main reasons:

1. Bosnia had the right to self-defense under Article 51 of the UN charter;
2. the Serbian side, having inherited the bulk of the armory of the former socialist republic of Yugoslavia, had undue advantage.

If the Muslims are humiliated and totally defeated in Bosnia, there may emerge new forms of Muslim guerrilla movements in the heart of Europe in the decades ahead. Humiliated Muslims have been known to haunt their tormentors for generations afterwards. The Bosnian equivalent of the Palestine Liberation Organization and the Bosnian equivalent of the Irish Republican Army might be unnecessarily created tomorrow by humiliating Bosnian Muslims today. A partition of Bosnia is unfolding. Will it be as costly as the partition of Palestine?

The irony of Bosnia is that just when the Muslim world is—in spite of the Hebron mosque massacre perpetrated by a Jewish militant—learning to accept a Jewish state in the midst of a Muslim Middle East, Europeans are reluctant to accept a Muslim state in a Christian Europe.

Bosnia could become a kind of Muslim Israel in the middle of Christian Europe. Has Europe the will to help Bosnia survive, or will Europe behave like Baruch Goldstein when he shot Muslims in prayer? Has the UN provided universalist legitimation for preventing an independent, well-armed, and advanced Muslim state in Europe?

In Afghanistan, the West provided arms for the liberation of a Muslim society in order to frustrate Moscow. In Bosnia, the West—through the UN—has temporarily disarmed a Muslim society, partly in order to not offend Moscow.

In Afghanistan, the West helped the mujahideen throw out their Soviet invaders. In Bosnia, the West and the UN were not prepared even to defend some of the UN protected zones. Fortunately, NATO protection of Sarajevo may freeze Serbian territorial gains.

In Afghanistan, the West did the right thing for the wrong reasons—it helped Muslims checkmate the Soviets. In Bosnia, the West had long done the wrong thing for the wrong reasons—appease the Serbian invaders, partially because of sectarian indifference.

Is it not time for the international community to do the right thing for the right reasons—help Bosnia survive as a united, independent country because aggression is wrong and because weak countries deserve the support of the world community? Or would the interests of the West's informal empire not be best served by such actions?

The shadow of cultural prejudice persists. Would the West and the UN have been so slow to react in Bosnia if it had been a case of Muslims slaughtering and raping Christians instead of the other way around? Would the U.S. administration and the Senate have responded so slowly if the Serbian concentration camps were for Bosnian Jews rather than for Bosnian Muslims? Would not the UN have been forced to respond more energetically if Jewish women were being raped by Muslim men as an instrument of war, instead of Muslim women being raped by Serbs?

Indeed, there is reason to believe that if it were Jews who were being subjected to such unspeakable humiliation, Israel would not have waited for either the UN Security Council or the U.S. Senate to act.[43] Israel would have staged a major, international, spectacular event to grab the world's attention—even if it meant bombing Belgrade. Fifty Muslim governments, on the other hand, content to timidly obey the demands of the Security Council, refrained from arming the Bosnian Muslims or even evacuating refugees.

The conclusion to be drawn here is that the UN ideal of universalism of states is still seriously flawed. The United Nations is still a creature of the Western world—a world that views the world through the tripartite lenses of medieval Islam. What to medieval Muslim jurists was Dar el Islam has now become Dar el Maghreb (the Abode of the West). Westerners are the preeminent pioneers. Until the 1990s, the Abode of War for Westerners meant the lands of communism. The question remains, has the Abode of War for the West now become the complex Muslim world?

To some medieval Islamists there was the Dar el Suhl—the home of contractual coexistence in exchange for tribute. The Western world has been receiving tribute from most of the Third World in the form of profits, interest on the debt burden, and returns on other forms of exploitation. And the United Nations has sometimes unwittingly provided an umbrella for this tripartite division of the world.

The UN and Islam: Allies or Adversaries?

When all is said and done, under what circumstances is the United Nations ever an ally of the Muslim world? First, the UN is an ally when it plays the humanitarian role—as in refugee crises or responses to famine, drought, and other catastrophes. In such situations, it does not matter whether the immediate beneficiaries are Muslims, as in Somalia and Bangladesh, or non-Muslims, as in Rwanda. Islam is supportive of all such efforts.

Second, the United Nations is an ally when it mediates some of the quarrels between Muslims—as in its efforts to resolve the destiny of western Sahara, or its assistance in the quest for peace between Iran and Iraq in the 1980s.[44]

Third, the United Nations is an ally to Muslims when it provides peacekeeping troops and peacekeeping auspices in conflicts between Muslims and non-Muslims. Over the years, United Nations troops have been much involved, especially prior to the Oslo peace accords, in the often thankless task of keeping the peace between the Arabs and Israelis. The UN's long-term role in Cyprus is another example of attempted mediation between Muslims and non-Muslims.

Fourth, the United Nations has occasionally allied with Muslims when the Western world has been divided—as during the Suez Crisis of 1956 when, in spite of Britain and France's Security Council veto, the world body opposed the invasion of Egypt by Britain, France, and Italy.

During periods of internal divisions with the West, the United Nations has also been able to play a major decolonizing role. The United States has historically been opposed to some of the older versions of European imperialism, a position that in the second half of the twentieth century often allied the United States and the Soviet Union against old-style European colonialism. Under these conditions it was indeed easier for the United Nations to provide one of the great arenas for the anticolonial struggle of the peoples of Asia, Africa, and the scattered islands of the seas. The anticolonial role of the United Nations was played not only by the Trusteeship Council but also by the General Assembly, especially from the late 1950s onwards. This anticolonial role was often a great service to the Muslim world.

Sixth, the United Nations can be an ally of the Muslim world when it takes seriously the idea of prosecuting war criminals and those who have committed crimes against humanity. Especially relevant for the Muslim world would be the prosecution of war criminals and of Serbs who have committed crimes against humanity in Bosnia. The United Nations has done well to appoint a tribunal, but has fallen far short of providing the necessary resources for this complicated task.

Seventh, the United Nations has been an ally when the Muslim world itself was united. At times, it has been possible to pass through the General Assembly highly contentious resolutions. The state of Israel is based on an ideology which believes that a Russian who claims to be descended from Jews, and whose family has had no connection with the Middle East for the last two thousand years, has more right to go to Israel than a Palestinian who ran away from Israel during the 1948 war. Was such discrimination racism? When the Muslims were united in 1975, they managed to persuade the General Assembly to pass a resolution affirming that Zionism was a form of racism. When the Islamic world was divided in 1991, the resolution was repealed by an overwhelming majority.[45]

When the Muslims were united, they could persuade the General Assembly not only to defy the United States but to move the assembly itself out of New York in further defiance. When in 1988 the United States refused to grant a visa to Yasir Arafat, thereby preventing him from addressing the General Assembly in New York regarding his declaration of an independent Palestinian state, the General Assembly denounced Washington's action as a violation of the host country's legal obligations under the 1947 Headquarters Agreement. The General Assembly then shifted the session to Geneva, Switzerland, to make it possible to hear Arafat. It was the first and only such move in the history of the United Nations. The unity of the Muslim members of the UN helped them persuade others to join their ranks.[46]

Finally, is the UN an ally or an adversary of Islamic values when it hosts its series of world conferences, such as the one in Beijing in 1995 on women's issues and the population conference in Cairo in 1994? Muslims themselves are divided as to whether these UN conferences lead to the erosion of Islamic values or help Islamic values find a new historic setting in the twentieth and twenty-first centuries. For example, are Muslim women being helped by new global standards of gender equity that are promoted at these conferences? These global conferences are part of the United Nations' universalism of states, which at time conflicts with Islam's universalism of faith. But this tension can be creative; the dialectic can have a human face. At the very least, Islam and the UN have one paramount interest in common—to ensure that Dar el Harb shrinks smaller and smaller into the oblivion of history, and that the planet becomes a House of Peace at long last.

Conclusion: Between Westernizing Islam and Islamizing the West

Regardless of the role of the United Nations, at some stage the focus must be switched from the broad theme of Islam and the West to a more intimate exploration of Islam *in* the West. There was a time in history when the Muslim presence in the Western world was one of intellectual and scientific influence. These were the days when Arabic words like *algebra* and *cipher* entered Western scientific lexicons.

One of the remarkable things about the twentieth century is that it has combined the cultural Westernization of the Muslim world, on the one hand, with the more recent demographic Islamization of the Western world, on the other. The foundations for the cultural Westernization of the Muslim world were laid mainly in the first half of the twentieth century. The foundations of the demographic Islamization of the Western world are being laid in the second half of the twentieth century. Let us take each of these two phases of Euro-Islamic interaction in turn.

In the first half of the twentieth century, the West had colonized more than two-thirds of the Muslim world—from Kano to Karachi, from Cairo to Kuala Lumpur, from Dakar to Jakarta. The first half of the twentieth century also witnessed the collapse of the Ottoman Empire and the more complete de-Islamization of the European state system. The aftermath included the abolition of the caliphate as the symbolic center of Islamic authority. The ummah became more fragmented than ever and became even more receptive to Western cultural penetration.

Other forces that facilitated the cultural Westernization of the Muslim world included the replacement of Islamic and Qur'anic schools with Western-style schools; the increasing use of European languages in major Muslim countries; the impact of the Western media upon the distribution of news, information, and entertainment ranging from magazines, cinema, television, and video to the new universe of computers. Finally, there has been the force of the West's omnipresent technology, which carries with it not only new skills but also new values. The net result of these forces has indeed been globalization of some aspects of culture. However, this has been a Eurocentric and Americocentric brand of globalization, meaning that an aspect of Western culture is eventually embraced by other cultures—and masquerades as universal. An informal cultural empire is born.

The globalization of two pieces of Eurocentric world culture may tell the story of things to come: the Western Christian calendar, especially the Gregorian calendar, and the worldwide dress code for men.

Many countries in Africa and Asia have adopted wholesale the Western Christian calendar as their own. They celebrate their independence day according to the Christian calendar, and write their history according to Gregorian years, using distinctions such as before or after Christ. Some Muslim countries even recognize Sunday as the day of rest instead of Friday. In some cultures, the entire Islamic historiography has been reperiodized according to the Christian calendar instead of the Hijra.

The hypothesis that globalization could mean pure Westernization is even better illustrated by another facet of ordinary life—dress code and dress culture. There was a time when Shakespeare's Polonius could persuasively argue that "the apparel proclaims the man." It used to be true that the nationality, wealth, class, taste, and education of a person could be revealed by his or her dress. This is really no longer so, because of the globalization of the West's masculine attire, especially the Western suit. By the last quarter of the twentieth century, a man from any culture on earth could wear a Western suit without looking culturally incongruous. On the other hand, no Japanese man could wear Arab dress without appearing culturally odd; nor can an African wear a Hindu dhoti without occasioning acute perplexity. Nor can a Chinese man dress like a Yoruba aristocrat without confounding all cultural expectations. In other words, although men of all cultures can and do wear Western dress, no other two cultures' fashions are so freely interchangeable.

If the story ended there, it would be bad enough but bearable. But the Western standard is now regarded to be so "normal" that a man who dresses in the custom of his own culture at an international meeting is considered to be making a political statement. It is regarded as abnormal to be non-Western. I have a nephew in Canada who is a devout Muslim, dresses in a Muslim way and keeps a neat beard. In 1995 he traveled in the Middle East for the first time. In one Muslim airport after another, his impeccable Islamic dress turned out to be much more of a liability than an asset. He was often taken aside for further interrogation by Muslim airport officials to whom he looked too Muslim! Had he been dressed in a Western suit he would have saved himself a lot of trouble at Muslim airports. The Western suit has been truly globalized and is now the norm. Islamic dress is "abnormal" and potentially "fundamentalist." An informal empire of dress, but at what cost?

The dress code for women in non-Western cultures has not been as overwhelmed by the West as has the dress code for men. Women in India are still disproportionately attired in the sari and its equivalents. And Muslim women continue to maintain strict rules of modesty in dress that far exceed contemporary Western standards.

But this informal empire of dress is not without its costs. After the terrorist bombing of the Oklahoma City Federal Building in 1995, the first suspicion was that the atrocity had been perpetrated by Muslim terrorists. This hypothesis prompted a lot of outrage against Muslims in the United States. The most often targeted Muslim group turned out to be Muslim women, not because any women were suspected in the bombing, but because Muslim women dress Islamic. Because of their dress code, they are more obviously Muslim than are most Muslim men.

This subject of anti-Muslim sentiment after the atrocity in Oklahoma City returns us to the subject of the new demographic presence of Islam within the Western world. In the second half of the twentieth century, both Muslim migration to the West and conversions to Islam within the West are consolidating a new Islamic presence. In Europe as a whole, there are now twenty million Muslims, eight million of whom are in western Europe. This figure excludes the Muslims of the Republic of Turkey, who number some fifty million. There are new mosques being built from Munich to Marseilles.

Paradoxically, the cultural Westernization of the Muslim world is one of the causes behind the demographic Islamization of the West. The cultural Westernization of Muslims contributed to the "brain drain" that lured Muslim professionals and experts from their homes in Muslim countries to jobs and educational institutions in North America and the European Union. The old formal empires of the West have unleashed demographic counterpenetration. Some of the most qualified Muslims in the world have been attracted to professional positions in Europe or North America.

But not by any means are all Muslim migrants to the West highly qualified. The legacy of Western colonialism also facilitated the migration of less-qualified Muslims from places like Bangladesh, India, Pakistan, and Algeria into Britain and France—again, postcolonial demographic counterpenetration. There have also been occasions when, in need of cheap labor, the West has deliberately encouraged immigration of less-qualified Muslims—as in the case of the importation of Turkish workers into the Federal Republic of Germany in the 1960s and 1970s.

As another manifestation of the demographic Islamization of the Western world, there are now over one thousand mosques and Qur'anic centers in the United States alone, as well as professional associations for Muslim engineers, Muslim social scientists, and Muslim educators. There are some six million American Muslims, and the number is rising impressively. Muslims will outnumber Jews in the United States by the end of the twentieth century. Islam is currently the fastest growing religion in North America.[47]

In France, Islam has the second-highest number of adherents; Catholicism has the most followers. In Britain, some Muslims are experimenting with their own Islamic parliament, and others are demanding state subsidies for Muslim schools. The Federal Republic of Germany is realizing belatedly that importing Turkish workers in the 1970s was also an invitation to the muezzin and the minaret to establish themselves in German cities. Australia has discovered that it is a neighbor to the country with the largest Muslim population in the world (Indonesia). Australia has also discovered an Islamic presence in its own body politic.

Judaism, Christianity, and Islam are the three Abrahamic creeds of world history. In the twentieth century, the Western world is often described as a Judeo-Christian civilization, thus linking the West to only two of those Abrahamic faiths. But if Muslims will soon outnumber Jews in countries like the United States, perhaps Islam is replacing Judaism as the second most important Abrahamic religion after Christianity. Numerically, Islam in time may overshadow Judaism in much of the West, regardless of future immigration policies.

The question has thus arisen about how Islam is to be treated in Western classrooms, textbooks, and media as Islam becomes a more integral part of Western society. In the Muslim world, education has been substantially Westernized. Is it now time for Western education to become partially Islamized?

The Euro-Islamic story of interpenetration continues to unfold. Is this a new threshold for globalization? Or is it just another manifestation of the postcolonial condition in world history? In fact, it may be both.

Notes

1. Samuel P. Huntington, "The Clash of Civilizations?" *Foreign Affairs* 72, no. 3 (1993): 39.

2. Ibid. Quotation on p. 40.

3. See, for example, Ali A. Mazrui, "Decaying Parts of Africa Need Benign Colonization" *International Herald Tribune* (Paris), August 4, 1994.

4. Huntington, "The Clash of Civilizations." Responses by Fouad Ajami, Kishore Mahbubani, Robert L. Bartley, Liu Binyan, and Jeane J. Kirkpartick, among others, were published in the next issue: *Foreign Affairs* 72, no. 4 (1993): 2–22.

5. Huntington, "The Clash of Civilizations." Quotation on p. 22.

6. For one account of the Lockerbie investigation that casts a net over a wider range of suspects than Libya alone, see David Leppard, *On The Trail of Terror: The Inside Story of the Lockerbie Investigation* (London: Jonathan Cape, 1991). Although Leppard emphasizes the Libyan connection, he also points to Iranian and Syrian connections in the last chapter. On the Libyan sanctions, see footnote 15 in Vera Gowlland-Debbas, "The Relationship Between the International Court of Justice and the Security Council in the Light of the Lockerbie Case," *American Journal of International Law* 88 (October 1994); and "Security Council Extends Libya Sanctions," *New York Times,* March 31, 1995), sect. A.

7. The present discussion is based on Majid Khadduri's introduction to his translation of *The Islamic Law of Nations: Shaybani's Siyar* (Baltimore: Johns Hopkins University Press, 1966), pp. 11–13, although he tends to emphasize the dual division between Dar el Islam and Dar el Harb.

8. Ibid., pp. 11–12.

9. Hobbes describes this condition in his seminal *Leviathan*; for one recent edition, see Thomas Hobbes, *Leviathan: With Selected Variants from the Latin Edition of 1668,* ed. Edwin Curley (Indianapolis: Hackett, 1994).

10. Khadduri, p. 13.

·11. Ibid., pp. 12–13. However, the distinction will prove useful in this analysis.

12. Although international relations scholars concentrated on U.S.-Soviet connections, some have pointed out that the West, particularly the United States, has had its most problematic international relations headaches in practice in the Third World. For example, see Charles W. Maynes, "America's Third World Hang-Ups," *Foreign Policy* 71 (summer 1988): 117–40; and Steven R. David, "Why the Third World Matters," *International Security* 14, no. 1 (1989): 50–85.

13. On the UN role in the Korean conflict, consult, for instance, Leon Gordenker, *The United Nations and the Peaceful Unification of Korea: The Politics of Field Operations, 1947–1950* (The Hague: M. Nijhoff, 1959). For specific examination of United States' actions in the UN regarding Korea, consult Leland M. Goodrich, *Korea: A Study of U.S. Policy in the United Nations* (New York: Council on Foreign Relations, 1956).

14. Albania is demographically an Islamic country, but the religion was ruthlessly suppressed by the Communist authorities.

15. See, for example, Burns H. Weston, "Security Council Resolution 678 and Persian Gulf Decision Making: Precarious Legitimacy," *American Journal of International Law* 85 (July 1991): 516–35.

16. For one recent analysis of the American stand on Iraqi sanctions, see Eric Rouleau, "America's Unyielding Policy Toward Iraq," *Foreign Affairs* 74 (January/February 1995): 59–72.

17. In fact, according to one study, the infant mortality rate had increased fivefold since the end of the war in 1991, killing almost 576,000 Iraqi children; see "Iraq Sanctions Kill Children, UN Reports," *New York Times,* December 1, 1995, sect. A.

18. For reports that criticize the sanctions, see the analysis by Haris Gazdar and Jean Dreze, "Hunger and Poverty in Iraq, 1991," *World Development* 20 (July 1992): 921–45; and Eric Hoskins, "Killing is Killing—Not Kindness," *New Statesman and Society* 5 (January 17, 1992): 12–13. In spite of internal unrest and prominent defections, Saddam Hussein has not been hurt by the sanctions, as pointed out, for example, by Steve Platt, "Sanctions Don't Harm Saddam," *New Statesman and Society* 7 (November 1994): 10.

19. According to one report in the *New York Times,* French Beaujolais wine has lost many markets due to a boycott of French products to protest French nuclear tests in the Pacific. Markets lost include not only the Pacific nations of Japan, Australia, and New Zealand, but also the Netherlands, Scandinavia, and Germany. See *New York Times,* November 17, 1995, sect. A.

20. The secretaries-general of the United Nations have been Trygve Lie, Dag Hammarskjold, U Thant, Kurt Waldheim, Javier Perez de Cuellar, and Boutros Boutros-Ghali.

21. For the backgrounds of the various secretaries-general, see Evan Luard, *The United Nations: How it Works and What It Does* (New York: St. Martin's, 1994), pp. 102–25.

22. Brian Urquhart, "Selecting the World's CEO," *Foreign Affairs* 74, no. 3 (1995): pp. 21–26.

23. John Bulloch and Harvey Morris, *The Gulf War: Its Origins, History and Consequences* (London: Methuen, 1989), pp. 117, 119.

24. On the Liberian peace plan and ECOMOG's role, see the following news reports: "Peace Plan is Accepted by Liberians," *New York Times,* August 20, 1995, sect. A; and "8-Nation African Force is Peacekeeping Model in War-torn Liberia," *Washington Post,* April 1, 1994, sect. A.

25. For examples of attacks on M'bow in the Western press, see "When Will He M'bow Out?" *The Economist,* October 3, 1987, p. 48, and "Flirting with Destruction," *Nature* (October 8, 1987), p. 472.

26. See, for example, Adam Watson, "European International Society and Its Expansion," in Hedley Bull and Adam Watson, *The Expansion of International Society* (Oxford: Clarendon, 1985), pp. 13–32; and Ian Brownlie, "The Expansion of International Society: The Consequences for the Law of Nations," in Bull and Watson, eds. *The Expansion of International Society,* pp. 357–69.

27. John Stuart Mill, "A Few Words on Non-Intervention," in Mill, *Dissertations and Discussions,* vol. 3 (London: Longmans Green Reader, 1867), pp. 153–58.

28. Consult, for example, Karl Marx and Frederick Engels, *On Colonialism: Articles from the New York Tribune and Other Writings, by Karl Marx and Frederick Engels* (New York: International, 1972), pp. 81–87.

29. Karl Marx and Frederick Engels, *Collected Works,* vol. 6 (New York: International, 1976), p. 471.

30. For a description of Menon's view of the Goa affair and Western reactions to the Indian action, see Michael Brecher, *India and World Politics: Krishna Menon's View of the World* (New York: Praeger, 1968), pp. 121–36.

31. Guides to the UN's role in combating apartheid may be found in "The U.N. and Apartheid: A Chronology," *U.N. Chronicle* 31 (September 1994): 9–14; Newell M. Stultz, "Evolution of the United Nations Anti-Apartheid Regime, *Human Rights Quarterly* 13 (February 1991): 1–23; and Ozdemir A. Ozgur, *Apartheid, the United Nations, and Peaceful Change in South Africa* (Dobbs Ferry, NY: Transnational, 1982).

32. See, for example, Michael G. Schatzberg, *Mobutu or Chaos? The United States and Zaire, 1960–1990* (Lanham, MD: University Presses of America and the Foreign Policy Institute, 1991).

33. Ali A. Mazrui, "The Resurgence of Islam and the Decline of Communism," *Futures: The Journal of Forecasting and Planning* 23 (April 1991): 283–85.

34. Al Gore, interview on *Nightline,* American Broadcasting Companies, December 1, 1995. Also see *New York Times,* December 5, 1995, sect. A.

35. Carroll J. Doherty, "Dole Takes a Political Risk in Crusade to Aid Bosnia," *Congressional Quarterly Weekly Report* 53 (March 11, 1995): 761–3.

36. Samuel S. Kim, *China, The United Nations, and World Order* (Princeton: Princeton University Press, 1979).

37. United Nations, *Yearbook of the United Nations, 1974* (New York: UN, 1977), pp. 189–251.

38. On the NIEO, consult, for example, Pradip K. Ghosh, ed., *New International Economic Order: A Third World Perspective* (Westport: Greenwood, 1984).

39. See Lawrence S. Finkelstein, "The Political Role of the Director-General of UNESCO," in Lawrence S. Finkelstein, ed., *Politics in the United Nations System* (Durham, NC: Duke University Press, 1988), pp. 385–423.

40. On the Riyadh bombing, see *New York Times,* November 14, 1995, sect. A.

41. A recent evaluation of the literature may be found in James Lee Ray, *Democracy and International Conflict: An Evaluation of the Democratic Peace Proposition* (Columbia, SC: University of South Carolina Press, 1995). Also, in *International Security,* 19 (spring 1995), several leading scholars on this subject, such as Bruce Russett, Christopher Layne, David Shapiro, and Michael W. Doyle, assess the state of the field.

42. Huntington, "The Clash of Civilizations," p. 39.

43. Witness the airlift of the Falasha Jews from Ethiopia, detailed by Ruth Gruber, *Rescue: The Exodus of the Ethiopian Jews* (New York: Athenuem, 1987).

44. For a probing account of the mediation, see Mohammed H. Malek and Mark F. Imber, "The Security Council and the Gulf War: A Case of Double Standard," in Mohammed H. Malek, ed., *International Mediation and the Gulf War* (Glasgow: Royston, 1991).

45. On the repeal, see "Zionism No Longer Equated With Racism," *U.N. Chronicle* 29 (March 1992): 67.

46. For a report on this incident, see "UN Votes to Move Session to Geneva," *New York Times,* December 3, 1988, sect. A, pp. 1, 4.

47. "Amid Islam's Growth in the U.S., Muslims Face a Surge of Attacks," *New York Times,* August 28, 1995.

IV

**Metropolitan Successor States and
the Question of Imperial Reconstitution**

10

The Fate of Empire in Post-Tsarist Russia and in the Post-Soviet Era

S. Frederick Starr

Introduction

How will the former territory of the Soviet Union be organized in the post-Soviet era? The answer seems simple: there already exist fifteen independent states that are recognized by the major powers and are certified by the United Nations, the World Bank, the International Monetary Fund, and other world bodies. Yet the reality is far more complex. By no means do all of the new states conform to a single ideal of sovereignty, and at the same time several different models for organizing the region as a whole compete with each other in Moscow, Kiev, Tallinn, and the other new capitals.

Many of the successor states are well constituted and stable, but others, notably Belarus, are only marginally viable; one, Tajikistan, is racked by civil war. Although, twelve have joined to form the Commonwealth of Independent States (CIS). While little more than a free-trade zone in the eyes of most members, this ambiguous body is viewed by some of its sponsors in Moscow as potentially a common-currency zone, a military alliance, and even a vehicle for achieving full political integration.

Meanwhile, Russia itself has for the first time in its history become a decentralized federation with some subject units claiming many of the same attributes of autonomy already enjoyed by the seceding states. Finally, some Russians throughout the region still cling to the hope that part or all of the former empire can still be reconstituted.

Which of these contending models for coordination or integration is likely to emerge victorious? By their nature, historical parallels and comparisons cannot provide real answers to such a question, yet they are instructive nonetheless. As a general rule, collapsing empires have not succeeded in reconstituting themselves.

True, Mogul India was partially revived in the form of the twentieth-century state of India, and China today comprises most of its former imperial territory. Also Hitler's effort to reestablish the old German Reich must be listed as an attempt at imperial reconstitution, but one that was defeated after less than a decade. Overall the twentieth century offers a panorama of failed efforts at imperial preservation or reconstruction. Because tens of millions of people have died as a result of such efforts, the burden of proof surely lies on the side of anyone claiming that a multinational territorial state can be reconstituted once it has fallen.

Significantly, the closest thing to an exception is Russia itself. After the empire's collapse in the years 1916–17, it was largely reassembled under Bolshevik rule by 1924. If the resulting socialist union initially lacked Finland, Poland, and the Baltic states (all of which had been part of the tsars' empire), it nonetheless managed to regain complete or nearly complete control over all of these lands except Finland within slightly more than a generation. The empire thus reconstituted endured for almost another half-century. Thus, Soviet Russia itself provides the most nearly successful model of territorial reconstitution of a former empire.

It is therefore important to ask what bearing, if any, this experience has on the present postimperial situation. This query can give rise to very sophisticated speculations, but in the end they all come down to the classic undergraduate examination assignment: to "compare and contrast" the two eras. Specifically, the task is to identify those conditions that fostered the reconstitution of empire in 1917–24 and to determine which of these, if any, obtain today. The same question must also be posed in the converse: What conditions permitted the five main western provinces of tsarist Russia to attain independence after 1917 and which of these, if any, can again be discerned in the present?

The Military Factor

Many factors contributed to the Bolsheviks' success in reassembling the southern and southeastern regions of the tsarist empire into a new state. None was more decisive, however, than sheer military might. It is inconceivable that success would have been achieved without the Red Army, which in many ways was an anomalous institution. Most of its best officers were recruited from the tsarist army, attracted to the new venture more by patriotic sentiment than by pro-Bolshevik sympathies. Most infantry were peasant foot soldiers with virtually no stake in the new order. The nearly three million deserters from the Red Army would together have constituted one of the largest armed forces in European history. Moreover, the Bolshevik troops were poorly equipped and miserably provisioned, and had transport that was woefully inadequate for their needs.

More than compensating for these weaknesses was Lenin's system of rigorous control over the army that he exercised through political commissars reporting directly to Trotsky, the head of the Red Army, and to himself. These commissar were backed by systematic terror that could be directed against insubordinate officers and deserters from the ranks. No less important than the several thousand executions of deserters that took place was the terrorization of local populations, which took the form of pillaging and mass executions in areas that resisted reconquest. Thus, terror or the threat of its use both firmed up the Red Army's ranks and sowed fear among its opponents.

Paradoxically, Lenin's first move after seizing power was to issue the "Declaration of the Rights of Peoples of the Russian Empire," which granted full independence to any subject nation seeking it. But when Ukraine acted on this pledge and when the three Transcaucasian states (Georgia, Azerbaijan, and Armenia) followed suit, Lenin promptly sent the Red Army to bring them back into the fold. Similar resistance by Muslim peoples in the Volga basin and in Central Asia brought the Red Army into action once more, leading, among other consequences, to the sacking and burning of the ancient center of Kokand in Uzbekistan.

The Bolshevik Revolution occurred in the midst of a relentless war against Germany and Austria-Hungary. It was inevitable that the war to the west would threaten the new Soviet regime. Lenin, recognizing the threat to Russia posed by any potential grouping of the western belligerents, signed away the Baltic provinces, Finland, and Russian-ruled Poland in the Treaty of Brest-Litovsk in order to preserve the Bolsheviks' imperiled rule.

This bloody history stands in sharp contrast to the post-Soviet situation. Again, there were mass desertions from the army of the old regime, but this time the new regime in Moscow was both unable and unwilling to organize the necessary discipline, let alone terror, that could check them. Again, arms and provisions were woefully inadequate, thanks to the failure of the Red Army to reequip itself after the war in Afghanistan and to the collapse of tax collection during the Gorbachev years. This led to an 80–90 percent reduction in arms procurement in the three years prior to the collapse of the USSR, hardly an auspicious situation for the builders of a new army in Russia.

Is there the possibility that Russia will rapidly and effectively rearm in the next few years? Such a possibility cannot be ruled out, but several factors make large-scale rearmament and the emergence of an effective fighting force extremely unlikely for now. The attempt would require wholesale diversion of capital from civilian development to the military, and at a time when Russian voters expect to be able to register their complaints at the ballot box. Moreover, such an attempt would severely weaken Russia's commercial ties abroad, further damaging economic progress at home.

Another development that vitiated the fighting capacity of the post-Soviet military was the steady de-Russification of the Red Army that had taken place gradually over the preceding generation. High birthrates among the Muslim peoples and low birthrates among the Slavs meant that each year the number of draft-age Muslims increased at the expense of the Russians. Even though the officer corps remained heavily Russian, the officers' confidence in the loyalty of their troops plummeted. The situation was made still worse by Soviet military doctrine, which had led to the stationing of over half of the old Red Army in non-Russian republics on the empire's periphery. In the short run this did much to inflame local nationalist sentiment against Moscow. Later, this meant that successor states would be able to claim these units and their vast stores of equipment as their own.

In contrast to the period 1917–24, the aspiring successor states to the USSR, especially Ukraine and Uzbekistan, immediately formed their own armies from the fragments of Red Army units left on their territories. Even if many of these forces were poorly equipped and ill-led, they nonetheless had benefited from the same training and military culture as Russia's own army. As the new armed forces coalesced in the successor states, many of their Russian officers decamped for Moscow. Not only did this help to indigenize the new armies of Uzbekistan, Estonia, Ukraine, and others, but it put thousands of former Red Army officers back in Russia, where they fomented resentment of, and grudging respect for, nationalist sentiment in the new states. Inevitably, this has caused Yeltsin's new generals to treat all talk of fighting a war with the non-Russian peoples of the former Soviet Union with caution tinged with fear.

The one military unit formed under the old regime that showed any inclination to fight to preserve the USSR was the Fourteenth Army, stationed in the Trans-Dniestria region of Moldova. Under the leadership of outspoken General Aleksandr Lebed, this force briefly appeared ready to reassert Moscow's claims in behalf of the local Russian population. Yet in the end Lebed confined himself to bluster. And no wonder, for no one knew better than such a Russian officer just how ill-prepared the troops stationed in the "near abroad" were for actual combat. When Moscow finally resolved to fight—this time to preserve the Russian state itself rather than the Soviet empire—it led to the disastrous and hugely unpopular engagement in Chechnya.

When the Kiev parliament (*Rada*) declared Ukraine's independence from Lenin's Russia, Austria-Hungary offered it nominal support, just as Germany gave verbal backing to secessionists in the Caucasus. Neither of these gestures amounted to much, but they did give the new Soviet leaders a pretext for declaring themselves the country's protectors against foreign attack.

Absent in the post-Soviet situation was even the pretext of resisting the foreign powers that were backing the successor states. Only in Tajikistan was there the slightest basis for such concern, and there the threat arose not from a foreign state as such but from Muslim guerrillas crossing the border from Afghanistan. To be sure, Moscow has successfully used this claim as a pretext for the stationing of troops along Tajikistan's southern border. But in its present form this scarcely has the look of an imperial venture, for the weakened Russian forces in Tajikistan have had to appeal to Uzbekistan for military assistance in this operation. Granted that the stationing of troops on the old border of the USSR rather than on Russia's own periphery could escalate into a more overtly neocolonial campaign, it is now mainly an effort to control the drug trade (Russia has nearly two million addicts, largely thanks to drugs from Afghanistan and Tajikistan). The new Russian military doctrine of 1994 defines the old Soviet borders as the perimeter of defense for Russia proper, yet by 1996 few leaders in Moscow were willing to commit troops or resources to a task that could well end in disaster. It is revealing that even hard-liners have decried the use of armed force in Chechnya, leaving Yeltsin with few leaders other than the widely derided fanatic Vladimir Zhirinovsky for support.

The one point on which today's Russia has successfully used the military to exert pressure on the new states has been in demanding and obtaining rights to station forces in the "near abroad." Yet even though twenty-three bases have been established outside Russia proper, only in Kazakhstan and Georgia (where there are four bases) do they constitute an immediate threat to the new sovereignties. And as in 1917–24, the Russians have had to withdraw their forces entirely from the three Baltic states.

The International Context

Further sharpening the contrast between the military situations in the post-tsarist and post-Soviet eras is the dramatically different international context in which the more recent imperial breakup has taken place. On the one hand, the fall of the Russian Empire occurred amid the general collapse of old empires, including those of Prussia, Austria-Hungary, and Ottoman Turkey. The remaining powers, notably Britain and France, were also in crisis due to the massive loss of life they had suffered during World War I and the resultant political turn inward. The United States had escaped the worst of the bloodshed, but its public was already in a deep isolationist mood even before the peace settlement was negotiated at Versailles. Thus, as Lenin was working to reassemble the empire, the major powers all favored a hands-off policy.

Soviet writers long argued that the British/American intervention at Arkhangelsk, the Japanese incursion at Vladivostok, British support for the White Army's Admiral Aleksandr Kolchak in Siberia, and the bizarre activities of the "Czech Legion" within Russia itself provide evidence that foreign powers stood poised to assist in the dismemberment of Russia's old empire and to prevent its rebirth under Bolshevik rule. Yet the number of foreign troops in all these initiatives together was pitifully small (fewer than ten thousand British and American soldiers in Arkhangelsk, for instance); they operated without any coordination or overall plan; and they viewed their mission as opposing Bolshevik rule rather than dismembering the country. Indeed, recently released documents from Soviet archives indicate that Lenin actually welcomed the Western forces into Arkhangelsk as a means of foiling Germany![1] It should be stressed, too, that all these forces had been withdrawn well before the Red Army launched the offenses that would reestablish Moscow's control in non-Russian regions. Thus, in spite of the limited interventions by several countries, and the Austrian and German support mentioned above, one will look in vain to find any serious international interest in protecting the newly sovereign regions against Russia after 1917, or in limiting Russia's activities in the Caucasus and Central Asia.

In this context, it is worth noting that all the major powers withheld diplomatic recognition from the aspiring sovereignties created on the ruins of the tsarist empire with the exception of Finland, the Baltic states, and Poland. This was due more to the jerry-built and fragile nature of these post-1917 successor states than to any coolness on the Allies' part to the principle of self-determination. Nor did there ye exist a United Nations or League of Nations to recognize and legitimize the new states politically, or any of the international financial institutions that might have engaged with and supported them in the economic sphere.

During the crucial years 1917–24, the major world powers did not take an active interest in the fledgling republics in Ukraine, Transcaucasia, and Central Asia. Even had they done so, it would have meant nothing to Moscow. The Soviets had repudiated international law and the Russian Empire's huge debt and had nationalized foreign industry in Russia. This put Russia off-limits to most foreign capital. Then Stalin adopted a policy of economic autarky. Together, these developments effectively freed the Bolsheviks from paying any further economic price for their policy of reconstituting the old empire. No loans were placed at risk; no foreign assistance or private investments were lost.

The contrast with the situation today could not be more striking. The new Russia recognizes international law, which affirms all the newly independent states as sovereign subjects. In order to gain the advantages of being treated as the legal successor to the USSR, Russia assumed Soviet debts, which further tied Russia into the international economic order. The major powers throughout the world moved quickly to extend diplomatic recognition to all of these new states at the same time enmeshing Russia in a series of loans, investments, and political agreements that are vital to making that country viable as a democratic state. Back in 1917–24, Moscow may have had to pay little or no price as it reconquered former imperial territories to the south and southeast, but there would be a very high price for similar actions today. Put bluntly, any government in Moscow using overt force against the newly independent states would find itself politically isolated and at odds with the international economic order on which it depends for its economic survival at a time of transition. A loss of credibility in either the political area or the economic sphere internationally would thus do untold damage to Russia's political stability at home.

Is Big Beautiful?

What accounts for the keen interest of the Bolsheviks in expansionism and globalism after 1917 but the relative disinterest of today's Russians in the same subject today? Ideology, as we shall see, played a big part in the change. Yet beyond ideology is the fact that in 1917–24, empire building was still very much alive throughout the world. True, Ottoman Turkey, Austria-Hungary, and Prussia had seen their empires destroyed. But the countries that destroyed these fading empires were themselves imperial or at least continental powers. Moreover, the world of the 1920s was awash with firm-willed people committed to imperial expansion, notably those Japanese who dreamed of a sphere of control in Asia, the Chinese followers of Chiang Kai-shek who wished to reclaim their country's lost territories, and those Germans who vowed after Versailles to avenge their country's humiliation by gathering German speakers everywhere into a new Reich. In short, if World War I's losers were weak or flawed empires, the winners were all proud imperialists or would-be imperialists. And the main loser, Germany, was soon to think once more in terms of territorial expansion. It is scarcely surprising that in such a world Lenin and his cohorts would think in terms of aggrandizing territory.

The Bolsheviks thought in terms of using territorial conquest to preempt a feared if insignificant military-political threat from abroad. Russians today do not rule out some future military challenge, as their anxious view of the proposed expansion of NATO suggests. Yet most Russian citizens also believe the real danger from abroad arises not from military concerns but from economic penetration of their country by foreign producers and capitalists. They know that South Korea and Singapore are territorially insignificant, yet they both intrude in Russia's economic life far more than Russia intrudes in theirs.

Stated differently, it is clear that the power that counts in today's world is less military-territorial than economic. Any Russian who reflects on the situation realizes that Japan, France, and England have thrived economically even though they shed their empires after 1945, whereas the USSR managed to hold on to its empire only at the cost of gravely retarding its economic and social development.

Social Factors

In no area is the contrast between the situation in the eras of Lenin and Yeltsin greater than in the social sphere. Although the early Soviet state may have been able to use military force and terror to attain hegemony over Ukraine, the Caucasus, and Central Asia, a series of social factors both in Russia and in the non-Russian regions facilitated this reconquest and enhanced Moscow's ability to hold on to the territories thereafter. In nearly every case these social factors are reversed today, with the result that any effort at imperial revival would meet serious public opposition both in the newly independent states and within Russia itself.

National consciousness among the non-Russian peoples of the tsarist empire was confined mainly to the few members of the educated elite in each group. To be sure, there were exceptions. A century of Russian control in western Poland had radicalized even the peasant population there; Finnish identity was strong enough to enable that small population to extract a semiconstitutional order from the tsars; and rapid social change in the three Baltic provinces had created the basis for their full independence by 1900.

Yet these were the exceptions. Ukrainian nationalism prior to World War I was limited to a few literary intellectuals in Kiev. Both Georgia and Armenia had sought the tsars' protection in the early nineteenth century, and their elites thereafter moved comfortably in St. Petersburg society, with little thought of separatism. This left the dream of autonomy in the assertive but weak hands of the radical Dashnaktsutian Party in Armenia and the more numerous Mensheviks in Georgia. Both of these parties were separatist, yet in each case their voice was drowned out by a Bolshevik fifth column with close ties to Russia—the Georgian group was headed by no less commanding a figure than Stalin.

Russia's Muslim population in 1917 lacked a strong sense of group identity and was either politically inert or so divided geographically as to be incapable of united action. Volga Tatars, for example, were prepared to settle for religious and cultural autonomy within a federalized Russia. The small Alash Orda Party in what is now Kazakhstan wanted full independence, but its call was scarcely heard by the largely illiterate population, let alone by Muslims outside the Kazakh zone.

Together, all these national elites, with the exception of those in the western provinces, were sufficiently weak and small in number that the Bolsheviks could reasonably expect to destroy them entirely. Today, by contrast, the elites in every former Soviet republic are far larger and more conscious of their nationhood. In other words, the current situation everywhere contains elements of what in 1917 existed only in the Baltic provinces, Poland, and Finland. True, when the USSR collapsed, the Central Asians were slow to declare their independence, a fact that has led more than one Western commentator to conclude that Central Asia might be a good candidate for inclusion in some kind of overtly neo-imperial or informally imperial arrangement. Such a view is wrong, however. The reason Uzbekistan was slow to declare its independence is that during the Soviet years, its leaders had already maneuvered adroitly to attain a high degree of autonomy. This, rather than any coolness toward autonomy as such, informed their actions.

In all these cases, and in the Baltic states, Moldova, and Ukraine as well, the reasoning of the local elites concerning autonomy is identical. Under Soviet rule they had acquired education and a measure of economic advancement. Yet a firm "glass ceiling" was maintained under Lenin, Stalin, and their successors, as a result of which non-Russians had virtually no hope of further advancement within the Soviet system as a whole unless they became Russified. Even then they frequently had to serve in figurehead positions while the real power remained firmly in Russian hands. Meanwhile, a series of ham-handed moves by the Soviet government, such as Moscow's insistence that all theses or dissertations for advanced degrees in the rapidly expanding Soviet university system be written only in Russian, vividly reminded non-Russians of their second-class status as colonials.

Demographic factors today also favor national independence for the former Soviet republics in a way that was not the case at the time of the Russian Revolution. It is virtually impossible to determine the precise number of Russians who lived in the tsarist empire, since pre-Revolution census measures focused on language rather than ethnicity. However, the number of Russian "colonialists" settling in the non-Russian provinces was small, with the exception of eastern Ukraine, Odessa, the Crimea, and northern Kazakhstan. And even though there existed communities of Russian traders in Latvia and Estonia, these had long grown accustomed to functioning easily under the control of the dominant German elites and gave little cause for anti-Russian hostility or violence.

By the 1980s the Muslims of Central Asia and Azerbaijan were among the fastest-growing populations on earth, whereas Russia's birthrate had plummeted, becoming one of the lowest. This meant that time was on the Central Asians' side, enabling them to look serenely at a future in which they would wield growing influence in their own region. Recognizing this, a reverse migration by Russians leaving Central Asia was discernible beginning with the 1980 census.

The opposite situation prevailed in the Baltic republics, where the indigenous populations felt that they were being overwhelmed by largely uneducated Russian immigrants implanted there by Moscow. This gave special urgency (if not desperation) to the Baltic republics' drive for independence. Here, as elsewhere, the "ethnic" public hated the Soviet system as the cause of the deaths of several hundred thousand of their conationals in the Stalin era.

In the years immediately following the Bolshevik Revolution, many people in both the European and the Asian provinces saw the USSR as offering them personal and professional opportunities. Such views were especially common among the urban lower classes. For contrasting reasons, neither Asians nor Europeans (i.e., Balts) within the Soviet Union of the 1980s saw in Russia's control of their republics anything but an impediment to their own aspirations.

Parallel to this shift was the social and psychological change that occurred within Russia itself. Among those who sided with the victorious Bolsheviks after 1917 were many nationalists whose first concern was to see their country accepted as a "great power" and who did not care whether Russia's economy suffered from the effort to achieve this. Today there are still many outspoken Russian nationalists, but they cannot ignore the likely negative impact their policies would have on people's standard of living.

In 1917 there were millions of Russians who viewed the new socialist empire as offering unlimited opportunities for their own advancement. For several generations these Russian beneficiaries of Soviet affirmative action (*vydvizhentsy*) eagerly took up political and managerial posts in the union republics, much as British and French civil servants had done in the nineteenth-century empires of those European powers. By the 1980s, however, such careers had begun to lose their attraction. Not only were Russians in the non-Russian republics regularly being challenged by upwardly mobile ethnics; they were also being eclipsed by other Russians in Russia itself who were gaining international status in science, industry, and the knowledge-based fields. Thus, when the USSR collapsed, there may have been hundreds of thousands of Communist Party officials in the non-Russian republics who tried desperately to maintain their posts, but there was virtually no backlog of disappointed aspirants to colonial careers back in Russia proper.

Together, these social factors dramatically shifted the relation between Russia and the non-Russian republics of the USSR over the period 1924–90. A social flow that had marginally favored Russian rule in 1924 had turned into a social tide opposing it by 1990.

Ideological and Cultural Factors

So strong was the early Bolsheviks' desire to spread their revolution, and hence expand the territory under Moscow's control, that they might well have been able to prevail even in the absence of ideological and cultural factors on their side. A relatively effective army, readiness to resort to terror, an international climate that was at least indifferent to their actions, and a host of domestic social and economic forces conspired to enable Lenin's Russia to prevail over many of the tsar's former colonies. But cultural and ideological factors were also present. Even though these pulled in conflicting directions, on balance they favored the aspirations of the new Communist government in 1917–24. Just as decisively, most ideological and cultural factors today favor the aspirations of the new states that gained their sovereignty by seceding from the Soviet Union.

It is tempting to dismiss Marxist-Leninist ideology as window dressing for Red Moscow's imperial aspirations after 1917. Its unique achievement may seem the very epitome of hypocrisy, for it both attacked imperialism as the last phase of dying capitalism and rationalized the Soviet Union's new globalism as the harbinger of social emancipation and economic progress. In effect, it provided Russians with a theoretical basis for condemning tsarist rule in the non-Russian regions, and then for defending Soviet rule in those same territories.

Beyond this, Marxism-Leninism provided theoretical justification for centralized rule by the Communist Party that had been wholly lacking in the tsarist state. Rejecting tsarist centralism as retrograde, it rationalized a far stricter centralization under the new Communist leaders.

Such reasoning was objectionable to the thin stratum of educated non-Russians in the old empire and particularly alien to the Muslim population as a whole. Yet within a few years it was being propounded in every school and workplace of the USSR. During the 1930s and 1940s, as grade school and then high school education expanded, and as industrialization spread, large segments of the Soviet population came to accept Marxism-Leninism, or at least to acquiesce in its claims of being a philosophy of progress for the new Soviet empire. Such acceptance was strongest among members of the urban working class and newly emancipated women, groups being willing to attribute their own progress in part to the new ideology. If it did not make them loyal Communists, it at least blunted their opposition, especially since the new ideology of expansion was backed by increasingly totalitarian controls over the populace during the Stalin era.

Rapid economic and social progress in non-Communist countries after the 1950s deeply eroded the public's faith in Marxism-Leninism. An ideology that had formerly presented itself as "progressive" now seemed to be the enemy of true modernity. As this shift occurred, all ideological defenses of Moscow's centralization came to be perceived as crude rationalizations for Russian control. Suddenly, the precepts of Lenin's attack on the old imperialism[2] could be turned against the USSR itself. It has often been noted that Asian and African opponents of western European colonialism derived their arguments from the writings of British and French opponents of their own governments' policies. In much the same way, intellectuals both in Russia and in the non-Russian republics of the USSR drew on Russian anti-imperial texts to justify their growing hostility toward Russia's imperialism. Soviet imperialism may not have been the last stage of capitalism, but it was surely the last phase of Russian hegemony and control.

Today, the neo-imperialist blowhards in Russia do not bother to justify their claims against the newly independent states with anything more than vague references to Russia's perceived interests. The closest they come to a theoretical defense of expanded Russian control over the new states is the claim that it corresponds to the process of political and economic integration going forward in western Europe. Europeans' own problems with the failed Maastricht Agreement are conveniently ignored, as is the fact that the European Union is based not on centralization but on shared sovereignty and the principal of subsidiarity.

As a practical matter, those Russians who today defend the renewal of imperial control do so more on the basis of Russia's traditional vocation as a great power than because they believe such control will foster economic and social progress. However, among younger Russians especially, the goal of economic and social betterment is seen as far more important than feeding Russia's national pride. Whereas in 1917–24 imperial revival appealed particularly to the young, now there is a lack of connection between the personal aspirations of upwardly mobile young Russians and the neo-imperial aspirations that are championed mainly by their elders. Worse, since many Russians by now are well aware that under Soviet rule they subsidized the poorer regions of the USSR, they realize that a renewal of imperial control could eventually lead to Russia's having to shoulder new burdens, even if that control is selective or partial. In the other newly independent states, varying degrees of nationalism provide the nearest thing to an ideology replacing Marxism-Leninism. Thanks to this, the Kazakhs, Georgians, and Ukrainians are willing to enter into mutually beneficial economic relations with Russia but remain cool or outright hostile toward Moscow's dream of a new political and military union.

An equally powerful transformation has taken place in the sphere of culture between 1917–24 and the present. Whereas in the earlier period many non-Russians saw Russian and Soviet culture as potentially liberating, by the 1960s their grandchildren perceived Soviet culture as a wet blanket dampening local values and aspirations. Because the more Europeanized western provinces of the tsarist empire had always enjoyed direct access to Europe via Germany or Poland and had always opposed those peddling Russian culture, they did not need to participate in this transformation. Everywhere else, if to varying degrees of intensity, Russian and Soviet culture changed from being perceived as an uplifting source of cosmopolitan values to an impediment to the attainment of personal and national goals.

The Russian language has been the focus of this shift. Throughout Turkic Central Asia and in the Caucasus, the pre-Revolution use of Arabic script had isolated local elites from European culture. The predominance of the relatively undeveloped Ukrainian language under the tsars had the same effect. Even though Soviet rule may have been imposed by force of arms, use of the Cyrillic alphabet in Turkic regions and of the Russian language throughout the USSR provided many of the country's non-Russian peoples with a window on contemporary world civilization.

Nor was this perception wrong. Ukrainian literature was expanding by the early twentieth century, but there had not yet appeared a writer who contributed centrally to the mainstream of Western letters as did Tolstoy, Turgenev, or Dostoyevsky, nor had any major scientific work been published in that language. Muslims of the Russian Empire were the bearers of a rich cultural and linguistic tradition of their own, but it had grown provincial and stale by the early twentieth century. As for the dozens of less numerous nationalities, most had no tradition of written literature in their own language before Soviet times, and had welcomed access to Russian as a ticket to the larger world.

Such considerations helped explain the degree of acceptance of Soviet centralization in the spheres of communication and transportation that existed from the Civil War down to the 1960s. To the extent that Moscow offered access to contemporary life that was otherwise lacking, subject peoples were more willing to accept the centralization that went with it.

However, the flow of this argument was easily reversible. Increasingly, the educated non-Russians of the USSR understood the relative backwardness of the Soviet bloc economies as compared with those of the West, Japan, and the Asian "tigers." They appreciated the importance of knowing English or another global lingua franca and resented the fact that whereas Russians could study these a second languages, they, as imperial subjects, could take them up only after learning Russian. A similar line of reasoning arose when economically active people in the non-Russian republics reflected on centralization in communica tions and transport. Why should a phone call between Estonia and Finland be routed through Moscow when it could be placed directly? Why should a Ukrainian businessman traveling to Vienna have to pass through Moscow when a Russian businessman in Leningrad could reach Vienna directly?

Even though ideological and cultural arguments may have made Soviet control over non-Russian territories more nearly palatable in the early period, the fact remained that such control ultimately rested on force or the threat of force. As the Kremlin's willingness and ability to exert force waned after the 1960s, all the ideological and cultural arguments against Russian control flowered. These were intensified by the growing tendency of non-Russians and Russians alike to take seriously the question of democracy that was endlessly propagandized in Soviet education and the media. The spread of education brought a growing desire to participate, or at least to have a voice, in public decisions that affected citizens' lives. When combined with growing national consciousness and the widespread conviction that Soviet rule retarded rather than fostered national development, such inchoate thoughts about democracy gained power.

Eventually they flowered in the "Popular Front" movements that began in Estonia in 1988 and then spread throughout the Soviet Union, even to Russia itself. Except in the Baltic republics, nothing like this had occurred among those opposing Soviet rule in 1917–24. Now outside the political system there arose voluntary and independent associations of Soviet citizens demanding to be treated not as subjects but as citizens. The Popular Fronts of the late 1980s represented a new development in the Soviet republics, for they based their claims not on an explicit ideology in the usual sense but on a generalized belief in the values of civil society as opposed to state centralism. The Popular Fronts reflected the extent to which transformational changes in the intellectual, cultural, and social spheres had quietly been taking place under the placid surface of Soviet rule.

Balancing Factors

This cursory overview of conditions after the fall of the tsarist empire in 1917 and the collapse of the USSR in 1990 has emphasized the differences between the two eras far more than their similarities. Such an approach gives one scant reason to believe that the renewal of empire is a real possibility for Russia today. Even if they do not prove decisive, the various factors cited above—military, international, political, social, ideological, and cultural—cannot be ignored. To be sure, many Russians in public life today—and particularly older Russians—preach the cause of imperial revival. This aspiration has steadily gained strength at the voting booth, as reflected in support for candidates like Zhirinovsky and the flowing of Russian national rhetoric among the Communists. Yet for all their passion, these neo-imperialists must eventually face the realities enumerated above. Thus, it is far easier to imagine a resurgence of nationalist bombast in

Russia's political dialogues than a revival of the practical policies that would give substance to that policy.

Acknowledging this, is it not important to ask whether there are other conditions that might strengthen Russia's hand if it tried to reassimilate the wayward republics of the former Soviet Union? Such factors indeed exist. Russian chauvinists tout them endlessly, and their critics just as tirelessly belittle or ridicule them.

First and most dubious among these factors are the twenty-five million Russians said to be "stranded" in the newly independent states. Most of these are poorly educated workers who were moved from Russia since the 1970s to work at factories in the non-Russian republics. Several million of these were on short-term assignment and expected to return to Russia when they completed their tour. As many as four million others are soldiers mustered out from bases in the non-Russian republics or eastern Europe who have no home in Russia to return to. Still others are Cossacks whose ancestors fled to Russia's borderlands hundreds of years ago, or the descendants of nineteenth-century settlers who built up Russian-speaking enclaves in such places as Odessa, eastern Ukraine, and northern Kazakhstan.

In an attempt to develop this force into a fifth column within the newly independent states, Russia's new government brazenly promoted the notion of dual citizenship. Recognizing that it would weaken or destroy their sovereignty, the new states have adamantly refused to go along with this idea, the one partial exception being Turkmenistan, where the Russian population was minute even at its peak. Meanwhile, surveys in half a dozen of the new countries reveal that the Russian-speaking population can be divided into three roughly equal groups. First, there is the less-educated and older population that desires to return to Russia. To date, this group has had little impact in the new states and surprisingly little in Russia as well. This contrasts sharply with embittered Portuguese returnees from West Africa and French *pieds noirs* from Algeria, groups that sharply affected domestic politics in Portugal and France, respectively. Second, there is the younger and better-educated population that is prepared to learn the local language and become loyal citizens of the new state while retaining their Russian ethnicity. Third, there are middle-aged and less-educated people who see no alternative to staying in what Russians euphemistically call the "near abroad" but are unable to adjust to postimperial conditions there. Several hundred thousand of these have obtained Russian citizenship on the expectation, so far totally frustrated, that the old empire will soon be reconstituted.

Viewed in this light, the mighty force of twenty-five million Russians "abroad" becomes fewer than eight million who constitute any real problem. And that number still exaggerates the situation. Even in a densely Russian area like eastern Ukraine, such people to date have voted consistently for independence from Russia. To the extent that the new states gain political and economic coherence, such assimilationist tendencies will grow. True, they could be reversed by the failure of the economy in any of the new non-Russian republics.

Yet Russians abroad have constituted more of a political irritant than the kind of powerful pro-imperial lobby their ancestors did in 1917–24.

Economic needs constitute the second factor favoring reintegration with Russia. The USSR's policy of "socialist division of labor" systematically undermined the economic autonomy of the constituent republics. As a result, Soviet-era factories that relied on materials or parts from elsewhere in the USSR are now suffering greatly. If only to postpone the death of these industrial dinosaurs, some renewal of old Soviet patterns of sourcing and trade across republic borders is called for.

Yet it must be noted that economic coordination of the type that would enable such factories to function can be achieved without political integration. Indeed, this is precisely what took place in post–World War II Europe for a generation. Moreover, throughout the region there are new enterprises based on more reliable, market-based sourcing and marketing. And of the new enterprises emerging in the Baltic states, Central Asia, and the Caucasus, nearly all treat Russia as only one possible source of parts and materials rather than as *the* source, and as only one market among many rather than as *the* market. Yet this process has its limits. The imbalance of energy sources and other raw materials among the fifteen countries carved from the former Soviet Union assures that economic links will always be important to the region and that Russia will remain a central player, if only on account of its oil and gas resources.

The needs of defense might also push the former states into each other's arms. Russia has already assured the West that the expansion of NATO could have this effect. Future threats from the Islamic world or China also could result in closer military links among the former republics of the Soviet Union. Large-scale migration to Siberia by Chinese and their purchase of urban property in Kyrgyzstan are already causing concern. Nor is the Russian army likely to remain as weak as it is today, so that within a few years one can expect the Russian forces quartered at the twenty-three bases in the "near abroad" to constitute a serious and potentially menacing military presence.

The extensive decentralization created under the Russian Constitution of 1993 could also foster reintegration at the regional level. Thanks to concessions by the Yeltsin government, ethnic "states" within Russia (Tatarstan, Bashkortistan) enjoy nearly as much independence from Moscow as do fully sovereign Kazakhstan and Moldova. The blurring of the distinction between federal units within Russia and between those units and the independent states on Russia's border opens the way to federal or semi-imperial arrangements embracing the region as a whole.

Finally, it should be noted that the global environment today is not wholly opposed to imperial or semi-imperial reintegration. True, major lenders and investors might take strong objection to Russian expansionism, and such opposition could damage Russia's economic prospects, not to mention those of its neighbors. At the same time, the crises in Nagorno-Karabakh, Georgia, and

Tajikistan have made it amply clear that neither the European powers nor the United States is prepared to commit soldiers to the cause of regional stability in the territory of the former Soviet Union, or even to allow their troops to be part of any significant international force organized under the OSCE. By their tacit consent, then, the major powers have adopted a de facto policy that recognizes a Russian sphere of interest extending through all areas of the former Soviet Union except the Baltic states and possibly Ukraine. Even in these areas it is doubtful that any other power would be prepared to respond militarily in the event the Russian army exerts pressure against its neighbors.

Concluding Observations

The value of historical analogies can easily be overstated. However attractive they may be as rhetorical devices, their usefulness is limited by the brute reality that "one cannot step into the same river twice." The bewildering welter of people and events that constitute reality is ceaselessly changing, with the result that superficial similarities between circumstances and epochs rapidly dissolve when a fuller range of elements is taken into account. Moreover, the very openness of human affairs makes predictions impossible. Chance occurrences, the sudden emergence of a strong personality, even unanticipated natural events can confound even the most confident and seemingly determined projections of future events.

Such considerations would have been of particular importance if this comparison of conditions in the territory of the former Russian Empire in 1917–24 and in the territory of the Soviet Union after 1990 had concluded that Russia is likely to promote imperial reconstruction and actually succeed at it. But this is not the case. On the contrary, nearly all the diverse factors touched upon here—international, social, intellectual, economic, and cultural—suggest that such an outcome is highly unlikely.

Lenin's globalism can now be seen as part of the "new imperialism" of the years 1920–45, a movement that touched nearly all of the great powers and would-be great powers of that era. Even though it was militantly anti-imperialist in its rhetoric, the Bolshevik variant of this current tended in practice toward the same forms of political-military hegemony practiced by the other major states. What is distinctive about the Soviet case is that the imperial realm not only survived World War II but also was confirmed by it, leading to a further half-century during which Soviet control expanded to new territories in Europe, Asia, and, in the case of Cuba, the Americas. The further distinction of the Soviet realm was that it was founded on central controls over society and the economy that were unprecedented in their scope and severity.

This may be traced to a variety of factors, all of them specific to time and place. Among these were Lenin's personality, Bolshevik readings of the experience of Hindenburg's wartime controls over the imperial German economy in

1917, the exploitation of new communications technologies to enhance centralized controls, ancient features of Russian's political culture, and the distinctive patterns of political-military integration that were the legacy of tsarism. Yet in the end, Soviet imperialism and the state-based economy that underlay it resulted in a system that was so extraordinarily brittle that it collapsed virtually overnight.

Any serious attempt at neo-imperialism in Russia today would eventually come up against the shortcomings of the old systems, whether tsarist or Soviet. Several of these realities have been touched upon in the foregoing discussion. Above all, such an attempt today would soon confront the core reality that the kind of autarkic imperialism that existed in the USSR was designed to avoid economic competition rather than to foster it. Its basic tendency was to restrain and control human nature and social energies rather than to release them. In a world dominated by "tigers" in Asia and elsewhere, such a system is doomed. For in the end the control of territory through political or military means is at best irrelevant to social and economic development, and at worst hostile to it.

This does not mean that there will be no attempt to regain such hegemony, in whole or in part. Indeed, the history of empires is replete with efforts by former colonial rulers to regain lost control. Britain's attack on Washington, D.C., in 1812, Spain's naval war against Chile in the 1860s, France's campaigns in Algeria in the 1950s, and Portugal's struggles in West Africa in the 1960s stand as evidence of the universality of this urge. Yet in the end none of these ventures succeeded, nor did any of the many examples by other former imperial powers that could be cited.

Such aspirations exist in Russian society and in the Russian government today. Political leaders have gained prominence by seeming to champion such dreams, the most recent case in point being Aleksandr Lebed, the former head of the Soviet Fourteenth Army in Moldova. Will Lebed or some future Lebed ever be elected president? If elected, will such a leader actually seek to implement the imperial program he proclaimed from the political stump? Only time will tell. But for now the prospects for success in such a venture appear very dim, for it would jeopardize the economic progress upon which the personal aspirations of ever larger parts of the Russian population depend.

This is of importance in today's democratic Russia. Lebed is only one of several public figures who entered the political stage talking like a rabid neo-imperialist but who cooled down once he was forced to lay out the implications of his policy of reintegration and its likely economic cost. Thus, even when some Russian politicians rattle the neo-imperial saber, their threats—so far—have little or no credibility beyond the narrow ranks of their own parties.

Beyond this, the deaths of several tens of millions of Russians under Lenin and Stalin and in World War II have inoculated most Russians against the use of force in politics or international affairs. The war in Chechnya has proven extremely unpopular in Russia, suggesting that even the most militant neo-imperialist would find little or no support in any use of force in the name of imperial reconstitution.

Aleksandr Solzhenitsyn, who has lent his support to political parties championing various forms of imperial reconstruction, dreams of some future Slavic union comprising Russia, Ukraine, and Belarus. As time goes by, the likelihood of Ukraine returning to the Russian fold diminishes. And Solzhenitsyn himself strongly opposes Russian expansion in the other twelve states formed from the former USSR.

It is by no means clear that many Russians dream of the state of noncivilization that is the alternative, or, if they do, that they would long persist in such dreams if they were to see the consequences for their personal lives and for the lives of their families and communities. This is the prudent lesson that the majority of Russians seem to have derived from the experience of 1917–24 and its consequences.

Notes

1. Richard Pipes, ed., *New Documents from Soviet Archives on V.I. Lenin* (New Haven: Yale University Press, 1996).
2. V.I. Lenin, *Imperialism, The Highest Stage of Capitalism* (Moscow, 1958).

11

Between the Second and Third Reichs
The Weimar Republic as "Imperial Interregnum"

Carole Fink

The German Reich is a Republic.[1]

'A curious republic that still calls itself an empire!'[2]

Between 1871 and 1945, in slightly more than two generations, Germany had not only two imperial regimes but also, between 1918 and 1933, its first republic. The Weimar Republic[3] has become this century's prime example of a major democracy whose collapse had calamitous domestic and international consequences.[4] Germany's joyful unification in 1990 paradoxically revived the Weimar demon in this manner: Can this belated successor state of the Third Reich, this smallest, richest Germany in all its history, fulfill its "second chance" to prove, once and for all, its people's aptitude for democracy?[5]

The "Weimar analogy" of a frail, doomed democracy may also be applied to the successor states of the former Soviet empire and specifically to the Russian Republic. Emerging from Cold War defeat, lacking experience in pluralist democracy, and facing huge economic, social, religious, and ethnic problems, the new Russian Republic, like Weimar, retains a similarly heavy imperial legacy and strong imperialist impulses.[6] Also like Weimar, the new Russia still possesses considerable international power and responsibility; and the sudden and unexpected reduction of its realm has made it a maimed giant, unheralded at home and still distrusted abroad.

To be sure, the collapse of the Weimar Republic has been debated since 1933. Scholars have contested the relative weight of external and internal factors, economic conditions and political decision making, as well as the impact of culture and ideas. They have also debated over structural causes: whether there was an exclusively German *Sonderweg* (exceptionalism) of authoritarianism and militarism that inevitably linked the Second and the Third Reichs, or whether Germany simply imbibed a more lethal dose of twentieth-century mass capitalism and democracy, and of Western racism, imperialism, and carnage.[7]

Weimar, as a symbol and a reality, likely will always haunt democracies in trouble.[8] The scholars' debate over Weimar has not impeded observers of contemporary Russia from attempting to draw analogies from the Weimar experience.[9] Even if we never agree over the causes of Weimar's collapse, it remains the prime cautionary text of an unsuccessful democratic transition as well as the reconstitution of an empire.

It may therefore be useful to isolate ten key issues in the history of the Weimar Republic, many still contested, in an attempt to suggest comparisons with contemporary Russia. They are as follows:

1. The imperial legacy
2. The abrupt, unexpected collapse
3. The dictated peace treaty
4. The syndrome of obsessive revisionism
5. *Minderheitenpolitik* (minorities policy)
6. Fragmented politics
7. A brilliant, brittle culture
8. The unregenerate establishment
9. Economic disaster
10. Weimar and the Third Reich

The chapter is organized around these ten issues.

The Imperial Legacy

Imperial Germany (1871–1918) was a Prussian solution to the ancient German longing for unity. Located at the very center of Europe and lacking protective borders, the divided German people were ruled for centuries by the supranational Holy Roman Empire. Further divided by the Reformation, and Europe's perennial battlefield, Germany finally achieved unification not by "speeches and majority votes" (the goal of the revolutionaries in 1848) but by "blood and iron." The Prussian Junker Otto von Bismarck succeeded in manipulating European diplomacy, the German liberals' nationalism, and Germany's military and economic power to forge a "Second Reich," which was embodied in a dictated constitution ensuring Prussian domination, an unfettered emperor and army, a powerless Parliament, and no bill of rights.[10]

The Second Reich immediately became Europe's major power. Under Bismarck it was not only the linchpin of an exclusive alliance system centered on Berlin but also an overseas power with a modest African and Pacific empire. After 1890, the regime of Wilhelm II, with greater expansionist designs, attempted to extend Germany's economic and political influence into eastern Europe, the Near East, and the Western Hemisphere. Germany's technical schools and universities fueled its world leadership in science, technology, and industry, and its institutes and seminars produced outstanding researchers in the arts, humanities, and social sciences. "Made in Germany" became an insignia of power and pride in the Reich's belated achievement of unity.[11]

The legacy of the Second Reich also includes a bleaker side as the seedbed of modern German racism and imperialism. At home, there was the persecution of the Catholics and Socialists, the virulent anti-Semitism, the expropriation of the Poles through officially sponsored colonization of the eastern provinces, and a heavily militaristic society. Abroad, especially after Bismarck's fall, the German empire was notorious for its adventurism and saber-rattling, which exacerbated every diplomatic crisis between 1900 and 1914. Historians may never agree over the "Versailles verdict" (that Germany and its allies were primarily responsible for the outbreak of World War I); and they may never agree over the "normality" of the Second Reich in its domestic and international conduct, compared with the behavior of the other imperialist powers: Britain and France, Austria-Hungary and Russia. The documents show that at the height of the third, fatal Balkan crisis in the summer of 1914, imperial Germany, the besieged land in the middle, plunged deliberately into war with the backing of an almost overwhelming national consensus.[12]

The Second Reich at war became a barracks state in which opposition was suspended by the kaiser's political truce (*Burgfriede*). By 1916, weighed down by the stalemate on the battlefield and the crippling embargo, Germany was transformed into a virtual military dictatorship under Hindenburg and Ludendorff. That year the Reich became the only combatant to impose a Jewish census to uncover "shirkers and profiteers," and the government imprisoned left-wing dissidents.[13]

Unrestrained by any opposition, imperial Germany in 1917 gambled on unrestricted submarine warfare, which brought the United States into the war; and it supported the Bolsheviks, who removed Russia from the war. But in 1918, an exhausted, strike-ridden Reich was halted in its great western offensives. Germany's *Griff nach der Weltmacht,* the attempt to dominate Europe and replace Britain as a global power, had failed.[14]

The Second Reich was undoubtedly different in character from the former Soviet Union. Despite its authoritarian tendencies, imperial Germany before World War I was neither a dictatorship nor a police state. Despite its huge land and naval forces and its economic prowess, it had no exclusive sphere in Europe and only a small overseas empire; it was no superpower, but competed with several comparable states on the world stage.

Nevertheless, the Second Reich did alter the nature of world diplomacy, and it introduced the concept and reality of "total war." In its internal affairs, it exerted almost as profound an influence on every aspect of German politics, economy, culture, and society as did the twenty-two-year-longer Soviet Union. The fates of the two empires also intersect in the circumstances of their demise. In both instances, after a prolonged period of national effort and sacrifice, the abrupt, unexpected collapse, promoted by the leaders of the old regime, prevented a thoroughgoing scrutiny of the past. In both cases, the death of an empire produced nostalgia and mythmaking over a lost order and power, even among the former victims.

Abrupt, Unexpected Collapse

When the Second Reich's leaders began negotiating armistice terms with U.S. President Woodrow Wilson in October 1918, the German public was caught unprepared. Fed the Supreme Command's exaggerated reports of Germany's might and its enemies' weakness, almost the entire German public, with the exception of a few pacifists, supported the Reich's expansionist war aims. In 1918, with German troops still on Russian, French, and Belgian soil, the German people were unaware that the Reich had exceeded its military and economic capabilities; that its leadership had panicked in August 1918; that its allies Turkey, Bulgaria, and Austria-Hungary had collapsed; that the U.S. army was growing stronger each day; and that the November armistice would save the Reich from defeat and possible invasion.[15]

The Allies also were unprepared and in disarray. One of the great "ifs" in history was what would have happened if Allied troops had invaded Germany in 1918–19 and brought home defeat to the German people. But the exhausted and divided victors made the fateful decision not to march on Berlin, which enabled the German leadership and population to live in a world of illusion, believing that victory could be snatched from defeat.[16]

Imperial Germany's strategy was extremely clever. Facing military collapse, its army leaders responded to Wilson's signals, deposed the kaiser, and promoted long-delayed political reforms, thereby hoping to split the United States off from its allies and convince Wilson to save the Reich from the draconian peace Germany had just imposed upon Russia.[17] Wilson's Fourteen Points, linking practical American interests, anti-Bolshevik politics, and humanitarian concerns, seemed to offer Berlin an easy peace of self-determination, freedom of the seas, and universal disarmament as well as an equitable economic settlement. However, the Reich's leaders overestimated Wilson's strength and underestimated the tenacity of their other wartime enemies, Britain and France.[18]

The harsh terms of the armistice, signed by two German civilians at Compiègne, baffled the German public.[19] During the interval between the armistice and the peace conference, the "stab-in-the-back" (*Dolchstoss*) legend was born. The military announced to the credulous nation that an undefeated German army had been betrayed by the civilians. This myth was facilitated by the chaotic events of November 1918. Power had suddenly fallen into the hands of moderate left-wing figures who had been loyal supporters of the Reich throughout most of the war and had proclaimed the republic on November 9 to stave off a feared Soviet uprising. The new regime believed that it desperately needed the military as a shield against the Allies and against bolshevism. Thus Friedrich Ebert, Germany's first Socialist chancellor, greeted the returning troops in Berlin with the ominous words "No enemy has vanquished you."[20]

The former elites of the Second Reich not only had orchestrated a pseudo-revolution and the transfer of power to docile patriots but also had initiated the search for traitors among the very people who were trying to build Germany's future. Army leaders insisted that the troops had been betrayed by worthless politicians. Protestant theologians blamed the Socialists for undermining the morale of the fighting troops. Pan-Germans railed against Jewish "war profiteers." The new republic thus came into the world branded as "November criminals"; and one of its first enemies, the wounded front soldier Adolf Hitler, vowed to avenge Germany's betrayal.[21]

Because the Allies had failed to manifest their victory, because Germany's new leaders were unwilling to tell the truth, and because the German public was highly vulnerable to crude formulas of exculpation and hate, the sudden, unexpected collapse of the Second Reich was reconfigured into a national shibboleth of an unvanquished Reich betrayed from within.[22]

Similarly, the sudden collapse of the Soviet empire and the Soviet Union between 1989 and 1991, to a considerable extent set in motion by the leadership's efforts to avert an economic catastrophe, shocked a largely unsuspecting Russian public that had been accustomed to official lies and massive shortages at home for the sake of a superpower presence abroad. The charges of perfidy from within or without and the presence of *Dolchstoss* theories undoubtedly, as in 1918, served those who managed and were responsible for the empire's collapse.

An Onerous Peace Treaty

The Treaty of Versailles (June 28, 1919) still raises controversy among scholars and statesmen. The climax of four bloody years of war and revolution, the treaty was undoubtedly a compromise among French, British, and American principles. Harsh as it was, dictated as were its terms, it was scarcely a "Carthaginian" peace, especially compared with the treaties Germany had dictated at Frankfurt (1871) and Brest-Litovsk (1918).[23]

The Allies, alarmed by bolshevism and by the specter of a German–Russian rapprochement, had given way on several key issues. The creation of a cordon sanitaire between Germany and Russia actually worked to Germany's advantage; at odds with each other and dependent on the West's erratic support for their economic and military survival, this group of small, nationalistic states would inevitably gravitate economically, culturally, and even politically toward Berlin.[24]

Most significant of all, the Allies had not obliterated their enemy. Germany's unity was maintained, its economy was virtually intact, and its resources and population, although reduced, were still considerable enough to make the Reich potentially the strongest power in Europe.[25]

Nevertheless, the entire German nation, from the Left to the Right, opposed the Versailles Treaty. First, there was the compulsion to sign, imposed by the continuing blockade and the threat of an invasion; then there was Article 231 (the "war-guilt clause"), widely, although incorrectly, perceived as a moral condemnation of the Reich; also, there were the considerable territorial and population cessions, especially in the east, the prohibition of *Anschluss* (union) with the German lands of Austria, Germany's exclusion from the League of Nations, the demand for the extradition of war criminals, the loss of Germany's colonies, and the one-sided commercial, financial, economic, transport, military, naval, and air regulations, which were seemingly aimed at crippling Germany for generations. There were small but irritating indignities and awkward territorial rectifications. Above all, there was the threat of huge, unspecified sums of reparations to be determined within two years. When the United States refused to acknowledge any connection between Allied war debts and German reparations, the Reich faced the full consequences of its defeat.[26]

Germany's behavior at Versailles set the tone for the new republic's diplomacy. Taking their cue from the prudent Metternich of 1809 instead of the arrogant Iron Chancellor and the mercurial kaiser, Weimar diplomats focused heavily on points of honor and on violations of self-determination. Led by a seasoned imperial diplomat, Count Ulrich von Brockdorff-Rantzau, the German delegation courted neutral delegates and Allied journalists, and spread alarm over the Bolshevik menace. Careful not to provoke the victors to invade the Reich, the Weimar Republic signed the Versailles Treaty but also intended to defy it in every possible way, including seeking future German–Soviet ties.[27]

To be sure, the international atmosphere was conducive to German defiance. Throughout the peace conference, Britain, France, and the United States bickered publicly and privately; John Maynard Keynes's brilliant polemics undermined the moral authority of the "Big Three." The refusal of the U.S. Congress to ratify the treaty bolstered Germany's attacks on Versailles.[28]

Much like the formation of the patriotic *Burgfriede* in 1914, the creation of a national opposition to the Versailles Treaty in 1919 was a key unifying factor in the history of the Weimar Republic. This powerful consensus, which included even the Communists, served to thwart a public national debate over the consequences of Germany's defeat.[29] In a longer perspective, Weimar's criticisms of Allied hypocrisy and high-handedness pale before the reality that Germany would have accepted *no* treaty based on its defeat. In his realist analysis of the structural, psychological, and moral weaknesses of the Treaty of Versailles, former Secretary of State Henry Kissinger pronounced its terms "too onerous for conciliation, but not severe enough for permanent subjugation."[30]

Nevertheless, there was enough hypocrisy and inequity in the Versailles Treaty, and enough external criticism, to sustain the myth of a "Carthaginian peace," which was disseminated by Weimar's leaders and by their Anglo-Saxon, Bolshevik, and neutral allies, a myth that had serious diplomatic and political consequences as well as an extraordinary durability throughout the twentieth century. One of Weimar's main lessons is how the defeated was able to snatch the moral and political advantage from the victors by discrediting a painstakingly negotiated treaty. Another is how the victors, through their bickering and bad conscience, allowed this to happen.[31]

Following the breakup of the Soviet empire and the end of the Cold War, the Russian Republic has not been formally treated as a defeated state. There have been no attempts to impose agreements on Russia, which retains the Soviet Union's permanent seat on the UN Security Council as well as most of its other former prerogatives. No longer the "evil empire," it also is not merely one of the fifteen successor states of the former Soviet Union but clearly the dominant power in the region.

Nonetheless, the new Russia has suffered sizable territorial and economic, as well as moral, losses since 1991, if not through the West's direct actions or decisions, then as a result of communism's collapse. The West has failed to present a concerted policy toward the new Russia. Moreover, by acknowledging Russia's reduced borders and diminished military, political, and economic stature in its former realm, the West may inadvertently have helped fuel the rise of Russian irredentism and neo-imperialism, and even the nationalist campaigns that echo Weimar's crusade against Versailles.

The Weimar Syndrome of Revisionism

Between 1919 and 1933, the diplomacy of the Weimar Republic manifested one principal aim: the revision of the Versailles Treaty. Like France after 1815 and 1871, and tsarist Russia after 1856 and 1878—but unlike the Reich between 1870 and 1914 or the two German states between 1949 and 1990—the Weimar Republic dedicated itself to subverting and overturning the status quo, directly or indirectly, immediately or over time. Weimar Germany's revisionism aimed at reducing the reparations burden, weakening the treaty's military clauses, and altering the treaty's territorial specifications. The Reich pursued these aims on many fronts: political, diplomatic, and propagandistic, mixing several factors or isolating essentials.[32]

The basis of Weimar's foreign policy was to offset the misery, disorder, and humiliation of 1919 by evoking the imperial spirit of unity and power. Heavily imbued with nationalism, the Reich government established the primacy of *Aussenpolitik* (foreign policy) as the key to the republic's success and prestige, a risky strategy that subordinated internal reform to foreign-policy victories and made the regime hostage to an expectant public and its wary opponents. To the exasperation of both, Weimar foreign policy was a balancing act between defiance and accommodation, nationalism and neo-Wilsonianism, between the West and Bolshevik Russia, between Europe and the United States. Behind the rhetoric and behavior was a consistent drive to revive its preponderant power in Europe.[33]

There were three phases of republican foreign policy. The first, between 1920 and 1924, consisted of a duel between French treaty enforcement and German defiance that was decided in Germany's favor; reparations were scaled down, and American loans flowed into Germany. In the second, between 1924 and 1929 (the "golden twenties"), Germany consolidated its gains. Finally, between 1929 and 1933, from the Young Plan to the advent of Hitler, the Reich's aggressive foreign policy eroded almost all the remnants of the Versailles Treaty.[34]

The Weimar Republic deployed several strategies in its *Revisionspolitik*. The first, defiance, was quickly discredited when France promptly responded in 1920 by sending troops into Frankfurt, Darmstadt, and Offenbach. The second was propagandistic. Berlin rapidly linked up with treaty opponents to discredit the peace settlement—for example, paying huge sums to publicists and publishing its own version of the historical record. The third was to divide its enemies, a tactic begun at Versailles. Indeed, the Franco-British bickering over treaty enforcement and colonial claims, plus the virtual withdrawal of the United States and Soviet Russia from European affairs, gave Weimar statesmen wide latitude in this area.

The fourth strategy was the continuation of Bismarck's *Ostpolitik* (eastern policy), playing East against West. This policy culminated in April 1922 at Rapallo, when the Weimar Republic initiated a rapprochement with Soviet Russia that threatened the very basis of the peace settlement. Rapallo was the culmination of earlier economic and military ties between Berlin and Moscow, which continued to expand until 1933.[35]

The fifth and most problematic tactic, borrowed from Germany's Bolshevik neighbor, was the "fulfillment policy" (*Erfüllungspolitik*), initiated by former imperial statesmen Matthias Erzberger and Walther Rathenau and executed by Gustav Stresemann. Based on outward compliance with the Allies' economic and military demands, *Erfüllungspolitik* was a cunning, complex program to strip Versailles of its moral authority and the Allies of their temporary dominance. *Erfüllungspolitik* rescued Germany from the nadir of the Ruhr occupation in 1923 and brought the liberation of the Rhineland, reduced reparations through the Dawes Plan of 1924, and brought huge U.S. loans; it isolated France, brought Germany into the League of Nations as a permanent Council member in 1926, and gained Germany's foreign minister, Gustav Stresemann, the Nobel Peace Prize. Stresemann skillfully emphasized the opposition of the German nationalists to extract huge concessions from the Allies, especially on military control. Thanks to Anglo-American pressure and French timidity, Stresemann moved Germany back to the center of European politics. He well understood that

Germany's economic and political frailty, its debts, and its geopolitical exposure gave Berlin considerable leverage in each successive stage of negotiations.[36] The damage of Weimar's *Erfüllungspolitik* lay not simply in its duplicitous nature. We now know that the other side was cognizant of Rathenau's and Stresemann's ultimate goals, if not all the details of their strategy. The publication of Stresemann's *Vermächtnis* soon after his death created only a momentary scandal, largely for political consumption.[37] Indeed, the republic's evasion of France's demands paralleled some of the economic and political goals of London and Washington.[38]

The essence of *Erfüllungspolitik* was its failure to break with the past. It was the creation of former Wilhelmine loyalists whose republican conversion was more practical than profound. Shunning the small pacifist German Left, which preached European conciliation, and the militant Right, which clamored for outright defiance, Weimar's *Erfüllungspolitik* aimed at regaining German sovereignty and power without ever acknowledging the legitimacy of Versailles or of Germany's defeat.[39]

There is no evidence that Weimar statesmen worked for more than peaceful revision. Nevertheless, Germany's *Erfüllungspolitik* placed a heavy burden on European politics, creating a domestic and international climate of high expectations and tough bargaining, and demanded payoffs in return for Germany's grudging adherence to the status quo. Britain, France, and the states of eastern Europe all had their own claims to the fruits of victory; but they were systematically forced to back down by Stresemann's patient and persistent demands. Britain, France, and the states of eastern Europe had their own obdurate patriots; but defeated Germany used its *Erfüllungspolitik* to demand a privileged status in return for its "compliance" with the peace treaties.

Stresemann's deft high-wire act ended with his death in 1929.[40] Much like Bismarck's successors, Stresemann's successors utterly failed to keep control over the German Right, which made huge gains in the autumn 1930 elections. Without Stresemann's restraint, the Locarno partnership evaporated. And even though reparations were finally canceled in 1932 and secret German rearmament accelerated, the German public disdained the "paltry results" of *Erfüllungspolitik* and sought less "devious," more forthrightly defiant leaders.[41]

One final strategy in Weimar's repertoire was the use of the economic weapon in foreign policy. Like the Second Reich, republican Germany appreciated the importance of trade and investment policy in conducting "war by other means." Although the Allies had tried to cripple Germany economically through the clauses of the Versailles Treaty (reparations, material confiscations, commercial restrictions, and one-sided most-favored-nation stipulations until 1925), the Reich still had the means to pursue its interests. It remained Europe's largest domestic market, with enormous productive and export power. All it took was leaders who were committed to thwarting the "injustices of Versailles" by wielding financial and economic weapons.[42]

The Weimar Republic used the aggressive tactics of imperial Germany to create an informal economic empire in the new Europe.[43] Stresemann offered several times to "purchase" Eupen-Malmédy from Belgium.[44] The Foreign Ministry launched a brutal tariff war against Poland between June 1925 and December 1926 to force concessions over German nationals, minorities, and even territorial revision. Poland was saved not by its allies but by the fortuitous English coal strike and the subsequent Polish economic boom.[45] Another Weimar tactic was the expansion of prewar cartel agreements with France, Czechoslovakia, and the United States, which created a dense web of private arrangements throughout Europe and overseas.[46] Germany thwarted the fledgling French-sponsored movement for European economic cooperation, which would have forced Berlin to renounce its revisionist and hegemonic goals.[47]

Weimar Germany's foreign policy was an amalgam of Wilsonian rhetoric and diplomatic finesse, weakness and strength, threats and pleas. Germany would always be a "different," dissenting, and nonconformist power because of the hated, unacknowledged clauses in the Versailles Treaty. Whatever the Allies agreed upon, the Germans would demand more. The obsessive revisionism of the Weimar Republic intensified German nationalism. Weimar's diplomats were even less prized at home than abroad, where they were feared, mistrusted, and only occasionally conciliated. Berlin's relentless revisionism stirred a climate of unfulfillable expectations at home, obscuring the important distinction between gradual, peaceful change and the nationalists' demands for huge, grand, impossible aims, such as regaining Germany's borders of 1914, or 1918.

Weimar's complex foreign policy provides an instructive case study for observers of contemporary Russia. There is some similarity in the two maimed, proud, and still-powerful former enemy states and the tactics of their representatives. Both have brought grievances into the international arena and demanded payoffs to satisfy an exigent domestic audience. Both have used their political and economic vulnerability to extract concessions and rarely have acknowledged the other side's problems.

There are obvious differences between yesterday's Weimar and today's Russia in their wealth and size, human and natural resources, ideological complexion, and military and nuclear capability, as well as in the events of the sixty years that separate them. Although voters rarely address foreign-policy issues per se, it is nevertheless important, especially in fragile democracies, to keep watch over the links between the policies of destabilization and revanchism abroad and the growth of antidemocratic forces at home.

Minderheitenpolitik

As a result of Germany's considerable territorial losses in World War I, the Weimar Republic inherited an acute minorities problem in eastern Europe. Excluding the Germans in Austria, there were almost eight million *Aus landsdeutsche,* Germans living outside the Reich. Between 1919 and 1933, the republic played the role of champion of *all* minorities in Europe. Part humanitarian, part demagogic, part revisionist, the Weimar Republic's minorities policy (*Minderheitenpolitik*) constituted both a break with, and an extension of, the imperial past.

Although the borders of 1871 had left numerous Germans outside the Reich in Austria-Hungary, Russia, and the Balkans, the realpolitiker Iron Chancellor was relatively indifferent to the status of the *Auslandsdeutsche.*[48] After 1890, the Wilhelmine empire exploded with pan-German ideologies calling for the ingathering of the German diaspora in eastern Europe. Reich law considered all ethnic Germans, even those overseas, citizens. Germany's huge conquests in eastern Europe between 1914 and 1918 achieved the *Mitteleuropa* dreamed of by the pan-Germans, and even after defeat it formed the backdrop of Weimar's foreign policy.[49]

The Paris Peace Conference produced a major innovation in the history of minority rights: the minority protection treaties that were placed under the guarantee of the League of Nations. The east European states denounced the treaties as infringements on their sovereignty and demanded a universal system of minority rights.[50] The Allies' purpose was to provide a *minimum* form of international minority protection to stabilize the new states and discourage intervention by Germany or Russia; they refused to grant cultural autonomy to minorities. Between 1920 and 1926, the League of Nations constructed a fairly restrictive system that limited the minorities' access to Geneva and generally sided with their governments.[51]

Outside the League, Weimar Germany could accomplish little to protect the *Auslandsdeutsche,* especially in Poland, where they faced the threats of persecution, expropriation, and expulsion. Berlin urged the *Auslandsdeutsche* to remain in their homes, subsidized minority schools and other organizations, publicized their grievances, and sought allies for the minorities' cause. Gustav Stresemann pledged to become Europe's champion of minority rights and hinted at using their grievances as the basis of his demands for territorial revision.[52]

After Germany joined the League, Stresemann behaved prudently while working for a reparations settlement that would remove foreign troops from German soil.[53] The German minority in Upper Silesia, which had direct access to the Council, forced Stresemann into public debate. In December 1928 he lost his temper in an undoubtedly calculated gesture to pressure Poland and France. Pounding his fist on the Council table, he challenged the League's dilatory procedures.[54] But Stresemann's crusade of 1929 reaped few results. With British and French support, the League transformed Germany's proposals into a few anodyne resolutions.[55] In 1930, after the Rhineland evacuation and the Nazis' shattering victory at the polls, Germany suddenly hoisted the minorities banner in Geneva. The Weimar Republic challenged two of Poland's key state prerogatives—the conduct of its elections and the implementation of agrarian reform—

as violations of minority rights. Neither initiative succeeded, either in alleviating the German minorities' difficult situation or in gaining outside support for their cause.[56]

Weimar's *Minderheitenpolitik* was a dangerously flawed diplomatic instrument. If its goals were to protect minorities, the best route lay through Warsaw, and through bilateral negotiations. If its goals were peaceful revision, Berlin's barrage of public accusations prevented even the smallest Polish concession. Weimar's *Minderheitenpolitik* was based on two illusions: that the Western powers accepted its goal of border revision and that Poland, considered a bloated, weak, incompetent, "transitory state," would ultimately collapse.[57] Weimar's *Minderheitenpolitik* kindled unrealistic, intemperate expectations by German nationalists and by the *Auslandsdeutsche;* many ultimately turned to the Nazis as the more ardent and effective defenders of the *Volk*.[58]

Almost sixty years later, the collapse of the former Soviet Union and the creation of numerous political borders in the region suddenly created a new minorities problem: some twenty-five million Russians are now under "foreign" control of peoples once subservient to Moscow and of governments with varying political experience and practices. The Russian Republic has exhibited impulses similar to the Weimar Republic's, both to protect and to use these minorities.

However, conditions today are far different, especially in the absence of any international form of minorities protection. Moreover, the long history of political and military aggression since 1933 in the name of "minority rights" has reinforced the world's suspicion of would-be minority defenders and has bolstered the world community's adherence to the principle of state sovereignty.

Fragmented Politics

We move from the realm of foreign affairs to the domestic side. The political conditions of the Weimar Republic have long been regarded as the twentieth century's textbook case of a lethal combination of authoritarianism and anarchy creating the basis for an incomplete transition to democracy and for an imperial restoration.

The Weimar constitution, drawn from the best foreign models and the most liberal of its time, was written under the shadow of defeat, internal uprisings, and the Versailles Treaty. A dualistic system, it contained such conflicting elements as a parliamentary system and presidential rule, extensive civil rights and emergency provisions, federalism and centralism—contradictions that impeded the formation of a robust liberal regime.[59]

The most problematic element in the Weimar constitution was proportional representation. This ultrademocratic innovation was endorsed by all the founding parties of the Weimar Republic, from the former opposition Socialists to the liberal and center–right-wing parties. Weimar's pure form of proportional representation spawned a host of splinter/interest parties and produced weak, ephemral coalition cabinets that featured a considerable number of "nonpolitical" experts. It also increased the opportunities and influence of the Communist and Nazi movements.[60]

Proportional representation still remains a controversial feature of democratic regimes. Although sixteen Weimar cabinets failed between 1919 and 1930, only two fell because of parliamentary votes of no confidence. In addition to its electoral system, historical and cultural factors contributed to the failure of Weimar's multiparty regime. The republic's political leaders, born under the second Reich, had been weaned on the belief in a state above all parties. Accustomed to their limited role in the authoritarian politics of imperial Germany, Weimar's party chiefs did not recognize their mandate, in an age of mass democracy, to function as representative, responsible parliamentarians, prepared to compete at the polls and to alternate in power and in opposition. Within Weimar's electorate, there remained deep historical fissures between Protestants and Catholics, liberals and socialists, parties of "representation" and parties of "interests."[61] Above all, there were the imperial remnants of contempt for politicians, for parliamentary government, for all the "foreign" paraphernalia of liberal democracy.

The leadership gap created by Weimar's parliamentary weakness had been filled in the constitution by a popularly elected president, a towering figure above parties, regions, and interests. Choosing the American over the French model, the founders of the Weimar Republic added a strong independent counterweight to the Parliament. The Reich president, in addition to his roles as commander in chief of the armed forces, Germany's representative in foreign affairs, and appointer of cabinets, was given extraordinarily broad emergency powers. According to Article 48 of the constitution, in cases of threats to public order and security, he could issue emergency decrees that overrode Parliament and state and local governments; and he could suspend seven of the most basic individual rights.[62] Between 1919 and the end of 1932, 233 pieces of emergency legislation were enacted. Although the Reichstag could request the suspension or abolition of presidential legislation, it could not revoke it; and the Reich president, according to Article 25, could dissolve a recalcitrant Parliament and call new elections.[63] Unfettered presidential rule undoubtedly helped destroy Weimar democracy, especially after 1930. The republic's second president, the revered octogenarian imperial relic Paul von Hindenburg, despised the republic and conspired with and abetted its gravediggers while the Parliament remained helpless to stop him.[64]

Weimar's model of pluralist democracy was amended in the postwar Federal Republic, which has a modified form of proportional representation and a president elected by Parliament. There are only superficial parallels between Weimar and post-Soviet political conditions. Contemporary Russia has both a multiparty Parliament and a powerful, directly elected president, deriving their ideologies and behavior from the Soviet past and contesting for supreme power. Current

Russian politics, however, is based on far different historic, constitutional, national, religious, and cultural traditions than Weimar Germany's.

A Brilliant, Brittle Culture

Weimar has long been known for its cosmopolitanism, experimentation, and modernism, which provoked a powerful nationalistic backlash. Its elite, born and trained under the Second Reich, failed to foresee or to fight Hitler's rise to power.[65] Under Weimar, artists and intellectuals, like the rest of German society, were unaccustomed to the crude practices of republican politics. Their spiritual ancestors, Kant and Hegel, Goethe and Schiller, had defined politics in poetic and idealistic terms.[66] The crass horse trading of democracy, defined as "who gets what," elicited not only distaste and ridicule but also flights into the aesthetization of politics, or into the "Reich of dreams."[67]

Most of the leaders of "Weimar culture" had been outsiders during the Second Reich who had attacked bourgeois values, opposed capitalism and materialism, and celebrated the sensual and the irrational; they lacked, however, a coherent viewpoint on foreign-policy, political, social, cultural, and religious issues.[68] During World War I, most had proclaimed their national loyalty in ringing patriotic tones.[69] Even after the euphoria of August 1914 had evaporated few artists and intellectuals opposed the Reich's policies.[70]

Although the establishment of the Bauhaus in March 1919 symbolized a union between Weimar's liberal politics and its modern art, Weimar's cultural elite did not align itself with their patron. The social radicalism of Kollwitz, Hauptmann, and Heinrich Mann evaporated under Weimar. The Dadaists ridiculed the parliamentarians, George Grosz savaged Weimar's big shots, and one of Germany's most eminent sociologists lamented its fall from greatness.[71] The highly individualist Weimar intellectuals shunned personal or group action to defend the regime from its critics. Few dared to puncture the myths of Wilhelmine Germany or expose the horrible realities of World War I[72] in order to contradict the militarist and imperialistic paeans of Ernst Jünger, Arthur Moeller van den Bruck, and Adolf Hitler.

Weimar's intellectuals continued to view the world as a clash of opposites, of sharp blacks and whites.[73] Enormously stimulating to artists, this polarization prevented them from valuing the small gains, distinctions, and compromises upon which liberal politics is based. In Weimar culture, the inner voice became more important than social concerns, irrationalism was held higher than intelligence, rebellion replaced the hope for universal happiness.

Technologically advanced Weimar, with its love of speed, of the new, of "Americanism," also was ambivalent over the price of its modernism, whether in flat roofs or horror films, feminist women or the prominence of Jews in German culture.[74] Weimar artists were elitists who distrusted mass society with its philistine tastes and conformity. Works like Brecht's *Three-Penny Opera* were a pseudopolitics without moral force. Peter Gay has noted that within the Weimar artist there was a "hunger for wholeness" that served to undermine the very basis of a pluralist, democratic polity.[75]

Democracy in Weimar Germany was a nebulous abstraction without a corps of engaged intellectuals like those who rallied to France's Third Republic during the Dreyfus affair or to the Fifth Republic during the Algerian crisis. For all their genius, Weimar artists retreated into a world of political innocence.[76] World-renowned figures, such as Albert Einstein, Ernst Cassirer, and Thomas Mann, who endorsed the republic, generally shunned politics.[77] The woolly thought of Weimar's finest minds was reflected in Karl Jaspers' lament in 1931 over the Germans' inability to "grasp the political," their advocacy of "authority," and their call for a "commitment to a state-bound fate."[78] The intellectual right—Spengler, Jünger, Moeller van den Bruck, and Heidegger—had a far clearer vision of the next Reich.

Like Weimar, the cultural elite of the new Russian Republic has its distinctive spiritual legacy, oppositional heritage, and apolitical tendencies along with an enormous sense of loss and change, of demotion and alienation within today's highly partisan political environment. The role of influential artists and intellectuals in politics cannot be measured. Nevertheless, Weimar presents a particularly striking example of a republican regime that was far more vulnerable than its imperial predecessor to the intelligentsia's scorn, political naïveté, and indifference.[79]

The Unregenerate Establishment

In many crucial respects, the Weimar Republic failed to detach itself from the Wilhelmine past. On the rostrum of the Reichstag, the speaker's and ministers' chairs continued to bear the imperial and royal insignia: the crown and the black eagle.[80] For several years official communications retained the letterhead of the Second Reich. The government failed to alter the old administrative establishment: law, civil administration, and education remained under the old leadership, as did the diplomatic service and, especially, the army.[81]

The judiciary constituted the most remarkable case. Under Weimar, there was an extraordinary disproportion of sentences, with right-wing assassins discharged or given light sentences, and left-wing prisoners "shot while trying to escape." Hitler received an amazingly light sentence for his attempted coup in 1923.[82]

Weimar's universities and high schools continued to be staffed by ultraconservative professors and teachers who were devoted to the imperial past, and to exclude Jews and socialists. When Rathenau, Germany's only Jewish foreign minister, was assassinated in June 1922, one Nobel Prize physicist refused to allow his students to attend the memorial service. Thus, not surprisingly, student corporations tended to be radically antirepublican, and anti-Semitic, and their members to be attracted to the youthful vigor and charisma of Adolf Hitler.[83]

The republican flag was an important issue. The black, red, and gold of 1848 and of Weimar was despised by the Old Guard; some embassies preferred to fly the flag of Germany's merchant marine, which still sported the imperial black white, and red.[84] The Second Reich had a glittering court and imperial ritual, and had been commemorated in scores of official paintings, monuments, odes, and anthems. Weimar neglected ceremonies; it had no banners, songs, medals, no parchment documents, no fetes and birthdays, and no political heroes to give it legitimacy or respect from its citizens.

Above all, the Weimar Republic made only feeble efforts to control its army. The *Reichswehr,* considered the indispensable shield against the "Red terror" of 1918–19 became a crucial link to all the clandestine military arrangements with Bolshevik Russia. It was also Germany's main hope for the eventual revision of Versailles. Military officers received generous salaries at least one degree higher than their civil service counterparts and enjoyed enormous respect from the public.

Many historians hold the *Reichswehr* heavily responsible for the downfall of Weimar democracy. Germany's military leaders, many of them imperial hold overs, were determined to maintain an autonomous position of power; they created a "state within the state" independent of the republic's control.[85] Recent scholars have referred to Weimar as a *Wehrstaat,* a militarized state that blurred the boundaries between military and civil society.[86] Throughout Weimar's history the army leadership remained openly hostile to the constitutional forms of parliamentary democracy. The political maneuvers of the Reichswehr's chiefs between 1929 and 1932 helped accelerate the republic's destruction.[87]

It is difficult to measure the continuity and influence of Soviet personnel institutions, and mentalities in today's Russian Republic. Numerous high civil servants and church leaders remain in power along with major military and political figures; Boris Yeltsin has admitted his failure to rein in the military largely as a result of the war in Chechnya. Many of the new regime's symbols rites, and language now reach back to the tsarist past, which may not reinforce democracy and may even kindle imperialist impulses.

There has never been a "ground zero" in human history, not in 1917, not in the destroyed Reich of 1945. No successor government has ever created its own structures and mentalities on a blank slate. Those successful postimperial transitions after crushing military defeats (France in the 1870s, Italy and Germany after 1945) had the advantage of rebuilding on the ruins of a totally discredited predecessor; but for Weimar, as for today's Russia, the residues of the past remained vital elements of rivalry.

Economic Disaster

The specter of economic calamity haunts the history of Weimar, the republic undermined by the hyperinflation of 1923 and ruined by the depression of 1929. At least two generations of analysts have scrutinized the economic causes of Weimar's demise in their internal and external, human and structural dimensions.

Weimar's notorious inflationary policies were inherited from the Second Reich's wartime financing tactics. After 1918, inflation became a deliberate means of evading the Versailles Treaty and reducing the Allies' reparations demands. Hyperinflation began in 1922 because of an outbreak of domestic violence and a bitter struggle with the Entente over the reparations bill; in 1923 it soared to horrific proportions when the Allies invaded the Ruhr and the Reich decided to finance passive resistance.[88]

Germany's inflation had positive domestic and foreign benefits. At home it helped stabilize the new republic by producing almost full employment, rising wages, and economic growth. Germany's elites and the Weimar government undoubtedly profited from the spiraling currency. Contrary to old myths, the whole German middle class was not destroyed by the hyperinflation. Savers, mortgage holders, and bondholders did lose their wealth, and the rentier class almost entirely disappeared between 1923 and 1924; but small tradesmen, shopkeepers, and craftsmen did well, as did some factory owners and merchants; farmers were unaffected. The main result was a sharp redistribution of wealth and status within the middle class, which prevented the bourgeoisie from forming a cohesive social and political factor in the early years of the republic.[89]

Workers, too, were diversely affected. Wages and the standard of living rose steadily after 1914 and continued to do so in the early republican period, thus inhibiting left-wing radicalism. The key economic and political result for the working class was the leveling tendency, the erosion of distinctions between skilled and unskilled, civil servants and factory workers, the old and the young, males and females, which made mass nationalistic protest movements more attractive than traditional social democracy.[90]

Abroad, inflation had a salutary effect for Germany. The Weimar Republic was spared the world economic crisis of 1920–21 in which over 20 percent of British workers were unemployed. Inflation fueled foreign opposition to reparations by discomfiting Berlin's competitors and exporting Germany's economic grievances. Inflation produced the "Weimar syndrome," a government disinclined to reduce real domestic income out of fear of encouraging the Allies' demands.[91] In 1924, Weimar's real and potential economic power convinced British and American financiers and statesmen to solve the Ruhr crisis by administering a mild form of "shock therapy" in return for the massive Dawes loans that financed German reparations and recovery during the years of prosperity until 1929.[92]

The "golden" Weimar years between inflation and depression now look less lustrous. Agriculture never recovered; savings, investment rates, and economic growth remained relatively stagnant; and class conflict intensified over mounting workers' demands and their employers' resistance.[93] Historians on the Right fault Weimar's high wages and low productivity; those on the Left cite the heavy subsidies and cartelization of German agriculture and industry, which inhibited growth and competition. Everyone seems to agree that Weimar's economy was dangerously dependent on foreign money, and that by 1929 the costs of its exports were rising too quickly to compete in world markets.[94]

Many historians now believe that the Great Depression had a more damaging impact on the Weimar Republic than on other industrialized countries because of Germany's political leadership. Chancellor Heinrich Brüning's advent to power in March 1930 and the onset of presidential government were decisive events.[95] Brüning, in order to cancel reparations once and for all, administered internal shock therapy in the form of the strictest possible deflationist policy; even if he did not deliberately aim to exacerbate Germany's financial and economic plight, his policies had the result of intensifying authoritarian trends and undermining the social state.[96]

The "Weimar syndrome," putting the revisionist *Aussenpolitik* before the nation's social, economic, and political well-being, intensified the depression just as the electoral gains of the Nazis and Communists reduced international confidence and led to massive withdrawals of foreign funds. In the winter of 1932–33, unemployment affected one out of every two German families. Buffeted and humiliated by forces that their government seemed incapable of mastering—and indeed, it turns out, was actively manipulating—many of Germany's despairing "little men" gravitated toward radical solutions.[97]

Economic parallels are difficult to draw, not only because of the vastly different imperial legacies of Weimar Germany and Soviet Russia, but also because of the huge differences in their size, resources, and wealth, their experience with capitalism, and their attitude toward democracy. This much can be hypothesized. The long-term success of major international rescue operations, whether in 1924, 1932, or today, requires a government strong, capable, and courageous enough to achieve a solid balance between international confidence, on the one hand, and political stability, social welfare, and democracy, on the other.

Weimar and the Third Reich

The transition from the Weimar Republic to the Third Reich is one of history's few examples of an "imperial reconstitution."[98] The republic not only perpetuated the ideas and practices of the Second Reich but also prepared the ground for Nazi Germany. It bequeathed to the Third Reich many of the instruments of Hitler's future diplomacy. It produced the rhetoric and cunning defiance of a discontented power as well as the practice of an unrelenting treaty revisionism that exploited the West's divisions and its bad conscience over the Versailles Treaty. It created a surreptitiously well-armed *Reichswehr,* strong links with the *Auslandsdeutsche,* firm ties with the Soviet Union, and the basis of an informal economic empire in eastern Europe.[99] Much of the Weimar Republic lived on— to be sure, in a markedly different form—in the Third Reich. Its constitution was never annulled,[100] its universities and research institutes produced racist scholarship and euthanasia programs, its courts administered Nazi justice, its diplomats represented the policies of the Third Reich, its soldiers conquered a huge empire in which they helped to slaughter millions of civilians, and its industrialists employed the slave labor of the concentration camps and provided the Zyklon-B for the gas chambers.

It is highly doubtful that the Weimar experience can ever be duplicated. For fourteen years, there was a unique concatenation in Germany of imperial nostalgia and national extremism that was grasped by Hitler and the Nazis. A generation of disappointed monarchists and disgruntled or indifferent citizens, who had been trained to revere the state over the individual,[101] supported—or at least gave insufficient resistance to—the Nazi rise to power. In Germany's last quasi-free elections, in March 1933, the National Socialists gained only 44 percent of the vote; 56 percent of the voting population still opposed Hitler. But a few weeks later, four-fifths of the Reichstag voted Hitler a blank check to establish the dictatorship, sealing their own and Germany's fate. In 1933, the Weimar Republic was destroyed not by military defeat or economic collapse, but by its cunning enemies and its unreliable defenders. Forthwith, the Third Reich established a totalitarian state and began its bid for European and world hegemony.

Whether and how today's Russian Republic may restore some form of dictatorship and empire in the near or distant future cannot be predicted. Germany's fateful imperial reconstitution more than sixty years ago will function either as a warning or as a temptation in the years ahead.

Notes

1. Article 1 of the Weimar Constitution, *Die Verfassung des Deutschen Reiches vom 11. August 1919,* 7th ed. (Leipzig: 1930).
2. Marc Bloch, *Apologie pour l'histoire,* 7th ed. (Paris: A. Colin, 1974), pp. 134–35.
3. The Republic was named after the city to which the new government had fled in February 1919, to escape the revolutionary disorders in Berlin. A shrine of German liberalism, Weimar ostensibly advanced the spirit of Goethe and Schiller over the specters of imperial Potsdam and Berlin. For histories, see Kurt Sontheimer, "The Weimar Republic—Failure and Prospects of German Democracy," in E.J. Feuchtwanger, ed., *Upheaval and Continuity: A Century of German History* (London: Wolff, 1973), pp. 101–15; Theodor Eschenburg, *Die improvisierte Demokratie* (Munich: Piper, 1964); Erich Eyck, *A History of the Weimar Republic,* 2 vols. (Oxford: Oxford University Press, 1962–64); Louis Snyder, *The Weimar Republic* (Princeton: Van Nostrand, 1966); Theodor Eschenburg et al., *The Path to Dictatorship, 1918–1933: Ten Essays by German Scholars,* trans. John Conway (Garden City, NY: Doubleday, 1966). The classic "liberal" study of Weimar is still S. William Halperin, *Germany Tried Democracy: A Political History of the Reich from 1918 to 1933* (New York: Norton, 1965).
4. Two other striking instances are Italy in 1922 and France in 1940.
5. Günter Grass, "Don't Reunify Germany," *New York Times,* January 7, 1990; see also Konrad H. Jarausch, *The Rush to German Unity* (New York and Oxford: Oxford University Press, 1994), p. 179.

6. Mark R. Beissinger, chapter 6 of this volume.

7. The main discussion of continuity is in Fritz Fischer, *From Kaiserreich to Third Reich: Elements of Continuity in German History, 1871–1945,* trans. Roger Fletcher (London: Allen and Unwin, 1986), pp. 83, 97; and of the *Sonderweg,* in Ralf Dahrendorf, *Society and Democracy in Germany* (Garden City, NY: Doubleday, 1967). Dissenting voices are in Andreas Hillgruber, *Kontinuität und Diskontinuität in der deutschen Aussenpolitik von Bismarck bis Hitler* (Düsseldorf: Droste, 1969); Thomas Nipperdey, "1933 und Kontinuität der deutscher Geschichte," *Historische Zeitschrift* 227 (1978): 86–111; Klaus Hildebrand, "Staatskunst oder Systemzwang: Die 'deutsche Frage' als Problem der Weltpolitik," *Historische Zeitschrift* 228 (1979): 624–44; and David Blackbourn and Geoff Eley, *The Peculiarities of German History* (Oxford: Oxford University Press, 1984).

8. Theodor Draper, "The Specter of Weimar," *Social Research* 39, no. 2 (1972): 322–40.

9. "Weimar and Russia: Is There an Analogy?," a forum held on April 13, 1994, by the Institute of International Studies at the University of California, Berkeley. I thank George Breslauer for calling this meeting to my attention.

10. Lothar Gall, *Bismarck: The White Revolutionary* (London: Allen and Unwin 1985).

11. Hans-Ulrich Wehler, *The German Empire,* trans. Kim Traynor (Leamington Spa: Berg, 1985); Richard J. Evans, ed., *Society and Politics in Wilhelmine Germany* (London: Croom Helm, 1978); James Sheehan, ed., *Imperial Germany* (New York: New Viewpoints, 1976).

12. Volker Berghahn, *Germany and the Approach of War* (London: Longman, 1984).

13. Jürgen Kocka, *Facing Total War,* trans. Barbara Weinberger (Leamington Spa: Berg, 1984); Werner E. Mosse, ed., *Deutsches Judentum in Krieg und Revolution, 1916–1923* (Tübingen: Mohr, 1971).

14. Fritz Fischer, *Griff nach der Weltmacht* (Düsseldorf: Droste, 1961).

15. Arno Mayer, *Politics and Diplomacy of Peacemaking: Containment and Counter Revolution at Versailles, 1918–1919* (New York: Knopf, 1967), pp. 3–116.

16. Leo Haupts, *Deutsche Friedenspolitik* (Düsseldorf: Droste, 1976), p. 416; Klaus Schwabe, "Die USA, Deutschland und der Ausgang des Ersten Weltkrieges," in Manfred Knapp, Werner Link, Hans-Jürgen Schröder, and Klaus Schwabe, eds., *Die USA und Deutschland, 1918–1975* (Munich: Beck, 1978), pp. 11–61.

17. Klaus Schwabe, *Woodrow Wilson, Revolutionary Germany, and Peacemaking, 1918–1919,* trans. Rita Kimber and Robert Kimber (Chapel Hill: University of North Carolina Press, 1985); see also John Wheeler Bennett, *Brest-Litovsk: The Forgotten Peace, March 1918* (London: Macmillan, 1966).

18. Arnold Wolfers, *Britain and France Between Two Wars* (New York: Norton, 1966), pp. 20ff.

19. Harry Rudin, *Armistice, 1918* (New Haven: Yale University Press, 1944); John Wheeler Bennett, *The Nemesis of Power: The German Army in Politics, 1918–1945* (New York: St. Martin's, 1964), pp. 3–82.

20. "An die heimkehrenden Truppen," December 10, 1918, in F. Ebert, *Schriften, Aufzeichnungen, Reden* (Dresden: Reissner, 1926), vol. 2, p. 127. On the revolution of 1918, see Eberhard Kolb, ed., *Vom Kaiserreich zur Weimarer Republik* (Cologne: Kiepenheuer & Witsch, 1972).

21. "Everything went black before my eyes as I staggered back to my ward and buried my aching head between the blankets and pillow.... The following days were terrible to bear and the nights still worse.... During these nights my hatred increased, hatred for the originators of this dastardly crime." *Mein Kampf,* trans. James Murphy (New York: Reynal & Hitchcock, 1939), pp. 176–78.

22. In 1919, Reinhold Seeberg, a leading theologian of Berlin University, began the official memorial service for students who had fallen in World War I with the words *"Invictis victi victuri."* Later, the University of Königsberg, where Kant had taught, bestowed an honorary Doctor of Medicine degree on Ludendorff with the citation "To the master of strategy whose art has saved the health and life of innumerable German warriors from hostile guns; . . . to the hero who protected the German people who were surrounded by a world of greedy enemies, with the sharp blows of his undefeated sword, until the people, trusting false words, abandoned its unbroken arms and the strong leader."

23. W.E. Wüest, *Der Vertrag von Versailles im Licht und Schatten der Kritik* (Zurich: Europa Verlag, 1962).

24. K. Hovi, *Cordon Sanitaire ou Barrière de l'Est? The Emergence of the New French Eastern European Alliance Policy, 1918–1919* (Turku, Finland: Yliopisto, 1975), pp. 11–21, 215–17.

25. Gerhard Weinberg, "The Defeat of Germany in 1918 and the European Balance of Power," *Central European History* 2 (1969): 248–60.

26. Peter Krüger, *Deutschland und die Reparationen: Die Genesis des Reparationsproblems in Deutschland zwischen Waffenstillstand und Versailler Friedensschluss* (Stuttgart: Deutsche Verlags-Anstalt, 1973); Marc Trachtenberg, *Reparations in World Politics: France and European Economic Diplomacy, 1916–1923* (New York: Columbia University Press, 1980).

27. Horst-Günter Linke, "Deutschland und die Sowjetunion von Brest-Litovsk bis Rapallo," *Aus Politik und Zeitgeschichte* 16 (1972): 27.

28. Sally Marks, *The Illusion of Peace: International Relations in Europe, 1918–1933* (New York: St. Martin's, 1976), pp. 26–42; E.H. Carr, *International Relations Between the Two World Wars, 1919–1939* (New York: St. Martin's, 1965), pp. 25–78.

29. Carole Fink, "German Revisionspolitik, 1919–1933," *Canadian Historical Papers* (June 1986): 134–45.

30. "The framers of the Versailles settlement achieved the precise opposite of what they had set out to do. They had tried to weaken Germany physically but instead strengthened it geopolitically. From a long-term point of view Germany was in a far better position to dominate Europe after Versailles than it had been before the war. As soon as Germany threw off the shackles of disarmament, which was just a matter of time, it was bound to emerge more powerful than ever." Henry Kissinger, *Diplomacy* (New York: Simon and Schuster, 1994), pp. 242, 245. The same judgment was expressed by A.J.P. Taylor in *The Origins of the Second World War* (Harmondsworth: Penguin Books, 1964), chap. 2.

31. Another is how, contrary to the evidence, scholars and statesmen continue to believe in the unwisdom, malevolence, or incompetence of the statesmen in 1919.

32. Andreas Hillgruber, " 'Revisionismus'—Kontinuität und Wandel in der Aussenpolitik der Weimarer Republik," *Historische Zeitschrift* 237 (1983): 597–621; see also Michael Salewski, "Das Weimarer Revisionismussyndrom," *Aus Politik und Zeitgeschichte: Beilage zur Wochenzeitung 'Das Parlament'* B2/80 (January 12, 1980): 14ff.

33. Peter Krüger, *Die Aussenpolitik der Republik von Weimar* (Darmstadt: Wissenschaftliche Buchgesellschaft, 1985).

34. Marshall Lee and Wolfgang Michalka, *German Foreign Policy, 1917–1933* (Leamington Spa: Berg, 1987).

35. Klaus Hildebrand, *Das deutsche Reich und die Sowjet-Union im internationalen System, 1918–1932* (Wiesbaden: Steiner, 1977); and Harvey L. Dyck, *Weimar Germany and Soviet Russia, 1926–1933: A Study in Diplomatic Instability* (New York: Columbia University Press, 1966).

36. In a December 1925 speech, Stresemann stated: "One must simply have ... so many debts that the creditor sees his own existence jeopardized if the debtor collapses. ... These economic matters create bridges of political understanding and political support." Quoted in Annelise Thimme, "Gustav Stresemann, Legende und Wirklichkeit," *Historische Zeitschrift* 181 (1956): 314.

37. Robert Grathwol, "Gustav Stresemann: Reflections on His Foreign Policy," *Journal of Modern History* 45 (1973): 52–70.

38. Stephen Schuker, *The End of French Predominance in Europe: The Financial Crisis of 1924 and the Adoption of the Dawes Plan* (Chapel Hill: University of North Carolina Press, 1976).

39. The Locarno Treaties of 1925 were Stresemann's crowning achievement. To thwart a threatened Anglo-French alliance, which would have increased Berlin's dependence on Moscow, and accelerate the end of Allied military control, Stresemann proposed the Rhineland pact, which guaranteed Germany's western, but not its eastern, borders. Germany was thereby admitted into the League of Nations without any obligation to participate in possible sanctions against Soviet Russia, thus undermining the hopes for collective security. The 1926 Berlin treaty with Soviet Russia underlined Stresemann's design of steering a deft middle course between East and West. See Jon Jacobson, *Locarno Diplomacy: Germany and the West, 1925–1929* (Princeton: Princeton University Press, 1972), pp. 4–12; and Hans W. Gatzke, "Von Rapallo nach Berlin: Stresemann und die deutsche Russlandpolitik," *Vierteljahrshefte für Zeitgeschichte* 4 (1956): 28ff.

40. Eighteen hours before his death on October 3, 1929, Stresemann, who had concluded the negotiations on the Young Plan that fixed the final sum and duration of Germany's reparations payments, terminated foreign control, and set the date (June 30, 1930) for the final evacuation of the Rhineland, five years ahead of schedule, announced: "We are again masters in our house." Cited in G. Castellan, *L'Allemagne de Weimar, 1918–1933* (Paris: Colin, 1969), p. 339.

41. Gotthard Jasper, ed., *Von Weimar zu Hitler, 1930–1933* (Cologne and Berlin: Kiepenheuer & Witsch, 1968).

42. Peter Grupp, *Deutsche Aussenpolitik im Schatten von Versailles, 1918–1920* (Paderborn: Schoningh, 1988).

43. Karl Pohl, *Weimars Wirtschaft und die Aussenpolitik der Republik, 1924–1926* (Düsseldorf: Droste, 1979).

44. Manfred Enssle, *Stresemann's Territorial Revisionism: Germany, Belgium, and the Eupen-Malmédy Question, 1919–1933* (Wiesbaden: Steiner, 1980).

45. Stresemann, *Vermächtnis* (Berlin: Ullstein, 1933), vol. 3, pp. 244, 247; Harald von Riekhoff, *German-Polish Relations, 1918–1933* (Baltimore: Johns Hopkins University Press, 1971).

46. Charles Maier, *Recasting Bourgeois Europe* (Princeton: Princeton University Press, 1975); further details in Werner Link, *Die amerikanische Stabilisierungspolitik in Deutschland, 1921–1932* (Düsseldorf: Droste, 1970); Carl-Ludwig Holtfrerich, *Die deutsche Inflation: Ursachen und Folgen in internationalen Perspektive* (Berlin: De Gruyter, 1980); and William McNeil, *American Money and the Weimar Republic: Economics and Politics in the Era of the Great Depression* (New York: Columbia University Press, 1986).

47. Hans Mommsen, Dietmar Petzina, and Bernd Weisbrod, eds. *Industrielles System und politische Entwicklung in der Weimarer Republik,* vol. 1 (Düsseldorf: Droste, 1974); Pohl, *Weimars Wirtschaft*; Hans-Jürgen Schröder, *Südosteuropa im Spannungsfeld der Grossmächte, 1919–1939* (Wiesbaden: Steiner, 1983); Manfred Berg, *Gustav Stresemann und die Vereinigten Staaten von Amerika: Weltwirtschaftliche Verflectung und Revisionspolitik, 1907–1929* (Baden-Baden: Nomos, 1990).

48. Solomon Wank, chapter 4 of this volume.

49. Fischer, *Griff nach der Weltmacht.*

50. Texts of the minority treaties in League of Nations, *Protection of Linguistic, Racial, and Religious Minorities* (Geneva: League of Nations, 1927).

51. Ibid.

52. Article 19 of the League Covenant permitted alterations in the Paris peace treaties wherever "conditions [existed] whose continuance might endanger the peace of the world." Stresemann, *Vermächtnis,* vol. 1, 581–82; vol. 2, pp. 101–104, 150–51, 172, 174–75.

53. Carole Fink, "Stresemann's Minority Policies, 1924–1929," *Journal of Contemporary History* 14 (1979): 403–22.

54. In his private papers, Stresemann kept a copy of an article by the French historian Jacques Bainville in *Liberté,* May 3, 1928, that compared his famous "restraint" with Bismarck's and stated: "On ne frappe pas du poing sur la table tant qu'on n'est pas le plus fort." Stresemann Nachlass, microfilm ed. T–120 (U.S. National Archives), 7383H/3175/H168973.

55. "Wo bleibt Minderheitenfrage?" *Germania,* September 25, 1929; "Stresemanns Minderheitenpolitik," *Nation und Staat* 3 (October 1929): 2–6.

56. Carole Fink, "Germany and the Polish Elections of November 1930: A Study of League of Nations Diplomacy," *East European Quarterly* 15, no. 2 (June 1981): 181–207.

57. Werner von Rheinbaben, "Deutschland und Polen: Zwölf Thesen zur Revisionspolitik," *Europäische Gespräche* 9 (1931): 97.

58. Norbert Krekeler, *Revisionsanspruch und geheime Ostpolitik der Weimarer Republik: Die Subventionierung der deutschen Minderheiten in Polen, 1919–1933* (Stuttgart: Deutsche Verlags-Anstalt, 1973); Helmut Pieper, *Die Minderheitenfrage und das Deutsche Reich, 1919–1933/34* (Hamburg: Metzner, 1974).

59. Eberhard Kolb, *The Weimar Republic,* trans. P.S. Falla (London: Unwin Hyman, 1988), p. 149.

60. Werner Conze, "Die deutschen Parteien in der Staatsverfassung vor 1933," in Erich Matthias and Rudolf Morsey, eds., *Das Ende der Parteien 1933* (Düsseldorf: Droste, 1979).

61. Larry E. Jones, "Sammlung oder Zersplitterung?" *Vierteljahrshefte für Zeitgeschichte* 25 (1977): 265–304.

62. Personal liberty, the inviolability of the home, privacy of one's mail, freedom of opinion, freedom of assembly, freedom of association, and the right to property.

63. H.W. Koch, *A Constitutional History of Germany in the Nineteenth and Twentieth Centuries* (New York: Longman, 1984), pp. 306–7.

64. Andreas Dorpalen, *Hindenburg and the Weimar Republic* (Princeton: Princeton University Press, 1964).

65. Henry Pachter, in *Weimar Etudes* (New York: Columbia University Press, 1982), compared the apolitical intellectual and artistic elites of Weimar Germany with those of Periclean Athens who were indifferent to the existence of slavery and imperialism. Among the voluminous literature on Weimar culture, see Kurt Sontheimer, *Antidemokratisches Denken in der Weimarer Republik* (Munich: Deutsche Taschenbuch Verlag, 1978); Fritz Stern, *The Politics of Cultural Despair* (Garden City, NY: Doubleday, 1965); Günther Rühle, *Theater für die Republik, 1917–1933* (Frankfurt am Main: S. Fischer, 1967); Peter Gay, *Weimar Culture: The Outsider as Insider* (New York: Harper & Row, 1968); Istvan Deak, *Weimar Germany's Left-Wing Intellectuals* (Berkeley and Los Angeles: University of California Press, 1969); Fritz Ringer, *The Decline of the Mandarins: The German Academic Community, 1890–1933* (Cambridge, MA: Harvard University Press, 1969); Carl Schorske, "Weimar and the Intellectuals," *New York Review*

of Books, May 1970; Otto Friedrich, *Before the Deluge* (New York: Harper & Row, 1972); Keith Bullivant, ed., *Culture and Society in the Weimar Republic* (Manchester: Manchester University Press, 1978); Walter Laqueur, *Weimar: A Cultural History* (New York: Putnam: 1978).

66. Friedrich Meinecke, *Die Idee der Staatsräson in der neueren Geschichte* (Berlin: Oldenbourg, 1925).

67. Kurt Hiller attacked the republic's "bumpkin rule" (*Pachulkokratie*) in *Die Weltbühne* 22 (1926): 412–15; and Stefan George, in *Das neue Reich* (Berlin: Bondi, 1928) mourned the demise of a nation whose gods had died.

68. Wolfgang Sauer, "Weimar Culture," *Social Research* 39, no. 2 (summer 1972): 264–65.

69. In their manifesto, "To the Civilized World," ninety-three German university professors and scientists defended Germany's violation of Belgium and declared that Germany would carry out the war "as a civilized nation, to whom the legacy of a Goethe, a Beethoven, and a Kant is just as sacred as its own hearths and homes." Quoted in Ralph H. Lutz, *Fall of the German Empire* (Stanford: Stanford University Press, 1972), vol. 1, pp. 74–78.

70. See Hermann Hesse, *If the War Goes On: Reflections on War and Politics,* trans. Ralph Manheim (New York: Farrar, Straus and Giroux, 1971); and *Wartime Letters of Rainer Maria Rilke,* trans. M.D. Herter (New York: Norton, 1940).

71. Karl Mannheim, *Ideologie und Utopie* (Bonn: Cohen, 1929).

72. Important exceptions include Arnold Zweig, *The Case of Sergeant Grischa* (1927); Erich Maria Remarque, *All Quiet on the Western Front* (1929); Carl Zuckmayer, *The Captain from Köpenick* (1931).

73. Henry Pachter, "Aggression as Cultural Rebellion: The German Example," in *Weimar Etudes,* pp. 275–84.

74. Siegfried Kracauer, *From Caligari to Hitler: A Psychology of the German Film* (Princeton: Princeton University Press, 1947).

75. Gay, *Weimar Culture.*

76. Thomas Mann: "An artist is a fellow who is no good at anything serious or useful; he only desires to be free to do his antics but will do nothing for the state or may even be subversive; incidentally he is also profoundly childish, inclined to exaggerate and even a little seedy. Society should treat him with quiet contempt.... He refuses to work for a civilizing or political purpose, to improve the world, etc. It is not fair to scold him for that. A work of art may have moral consequences, but one must not hold the artist responsible for them or ask him to have such intentions." Quoted in Henry Pachter, "Intellectuals and the State of Weimar," *Social Research* 39, no. 2 (summer 1972): 243.

77. "How do I define [the Republic]? Approximately as the opposite of what *exists* today.... The attempt to infuse something like an idea, a soul, a vital spirit into this grievous state without citizens ... no mean undertaking." Thomas Mann to Ida Boy-Ed, December 5, 1922, in *Letters of Thomas Mann, 1889–1955,* trans. Richard Winston and Clara Winston (London: Secker & Warburg, 1970), vol. 1, p. 109.

78. *Die geistige Situation unserer Zeit* (Berlin: De Gruyter, 1931), p. 90.

79. The Nazis always referred disparagingly to the Weimar period as the *Systemzeit,* an era ruled by law rather than by principle.

80. Alex de Jong, *The Weimar Chronicle: Prelude to Hitler* (New York: Paddington, 1978), p. 187.

81. On the revolution, see Sebastian Haffner, *Die verratene Revolution: Deutschland, 1918/19* (Munich: Scherz, 1969).

82. For statistics, see Koch, *Constitutional History,* pp. 282–83.

83. Matthias Schmidt, *Albert Speer,* trans. Jeachim Nevgroschen (New York: St.

Martin's, 1984), pp. 29–34, describes a young instructor's fascination with Hitler. See also Ringer, *Decline of the Mandarins.*

84. Friedrich Arnold Krummacher, *Die Weimarer Republik, ihr Geschichte in Texten, Bildern und Dokumenten, 1918–1933* (Munich: Desch, 1965), p. 223. De Jonge, *Weimar Chronicle,* pp. 188–89, relates jokes about the republican flag.

85. F.L. Carsten, *The Reichswehr and Politics, 1918–1933* (Oxford: Oxford University Press, 1966).

86. Andreas Hillgruber, *Grossmachtpolitik und Militarismus im 20: Jahrhundert* (Düsseldorf: Droste, 1974); see also Michael Geyer, *Aufrüstung oder Sicherheit: Die Reichswehr in der Krise der Machtpolitik, 1924–1936* (Wiesbaden: Steiner, 1980).

87. See, for example, Thilo Vogelsang, *Reichswehr, Staat und NSDAP, 1930–1932* (Stuttgart: Deutsche Verlags-Anstalt, 1962); J.M. Diehl, *Paramilitary Politics in Weimar Germany* (Bloomington: Indiana University Press, 1977); K.W. Bird, *Weimar, the German Naval Officer Corps, and the Rise of National Socialism* (Amsterdam: Gruner, 1977); Ernst Willi Hansen, *Reichswehr und Industrie: Rüstungwirtschaftliche Zusammenarbeit und wirtschaftliche Mobilmachungsvorbereitungen, 1923–1932* (Boppard: Boldt, 1978).

88. Carl-Ludwig Holtgruber, *The German Inflation, 1914–1923: Causes and Effects in International Perspective* (Berlin and New York: De Gruyter, 1986).

89. Gerald Feldman et al., eds., *Die deutsche Inflation* (Berlin and New York: De Gruyter, 1982).

90. Andreas Kunz, *Civil Servants and the Politics of Inflation in Germany, 1914–1924* (Berlin and New York: De Gruyter, 1986).

91. H. Aubin and W. Zorn, eds., *Handbuch der deutschen Wirtschafts- und Sozialgeschichte* (Stuttgart: Union Verlag, 1976), vol. 2, p. 700.

92. Werner Link, "Die amerikanische Einfluss auf die Weimarer Republik in der Dawesplan Phase," in Hans Mommsen, Dietmar Petzina, and Bernd Weisbrod, eds., *Industrielles System und politische Entwicklung in der Weimarer Republik,* vol. 2 (Düsseldorf: Droste, 1979), pp. 485–98.

93. See Ludwig Preller, *Sozialpolitik in der Weimarer Republik,* 2nd ed. (Düsseldorf: Droste, 1978).

94. See Gerald Feldman, *Iron and Steel in the German Inflation, 1916–1923* (Princeton: Princeton University Press, 1977); P. Wulf, *Hugo Stinnes: Wirtschaft und Politik, 1918–1924* (Stuttgart: Klett-Cotta, 1979); Bernd Weisbrod, *Die Schwerindustrie in der Weimarer Republik* (Wuppertal: Hammer, 1978); Dieter Gessner, *Agrarverbände in der Weimarer Republik* (Düsseldorf: Droste, 1976).

95. A.J.P. Taylor, *The Course of German History* (London: Hamilton, 1945), p. 205.

96. W.J. Helbich, *Die Reparationen in der Ära Brüning* (Berlin: Colloquium Verlag, 1962); Winfried Glashagen, *Die Reparationspolitik Heinrich Brünings, 1930–1931* (Bonn, 1980); Carl-L. Holtfrerich, "Alternativen zu Brünings Wirtschaftspolitik in der Weltwirtschaftskrise?" *Historische Zeitschrift* 235 (1982): 605–31.

97. "They shoved me off the pavement.... They chased me away!" Hans Fallada, *Kleiner Mann, was nun?* (Berlin: Rowohlt, 1933). Cf. Karl Dietrich Bracher, *The German Dictatorship,* trans. Jean Steinberg (New York: Praeger, 1970), pp. 156, 179.

98. See chapters by S. Frederick Starr and Miles Kahler in this volume.

99. Krekeler, *Revisionsanspruch und geheime Ostpolitik;* Valdis Lumans, *Himmler's Auxiliaries: The Volksdeutsche Mittelstelle and the German National Minorities of Europe* (Chapel Hill: University of North Carolina Press, 1993).

100. In March 1933, the Reichstag voted an enabling law establishing the Nazi dictatorship, but the Weimar constitution technically remained in force until 1945.

101. On many of Germany's World War I monuments was the motto "Germany must live, even if we die."

12

Empires, Neo-Empires, and Political Change
The British and French Experience

Miles Kahler

> . . . No immutable law decreed the obsolescence of colonial
> empires; and the circumstances which made *European* colonial
> domination unviable after 1945 did not apply universally.
> In the vast realm of the Soviet empire perhaps a hundred
> nations wait to be born.
>
> John Darwin, *Britain and Decolonisation,* p. 335

The last remaining multinational empires collapsed in the 1990s. They were very different in structure and lineage. The Ethiopian state was an ancient empire, but violent Marxist modernizers were unable to maintain its unity after overthrowing its autocratic regime. The Soviet empire included satellites (Eastern Europe, Mongolia, and an outer circle of Council for Mutual Economic Assistance, or COMECON, dependencies) and the Soviet Union itself, uncomfortable legatee of tsarism's polyglot realm. Although many contemporary multinational states oppress ethnic and linguistic minorities, none can be characterized as an empire. The demise of empires over the course of the twentieth century suggests that John Darwin's 1988 judgment could be extended: empires may not be viable in the conditions of the late twentieth and early twenty-first centuries. The rumblings of neo-imperial nostalgia in Russia make this question significant for more than historical reasons.

Empires have displayed considerable variety, however, and the end of those empires characteristic of the twentieth century may not signal the extinction of the species. In particular, decolonization of the European colonial empires was succeeded by the establishment of at least one successful neo-empire in francophone Africa. After presenting strong reasons for suspecting that formal empires have become extinct and will remain so, the course of decolonization in the two largest colonial empires—Britain and France—will be examined as supporting cases for that argument. Political changes that undermined colonialism and sustained decolonization in metropoles, colonial territories, and the international system are emphasized. Democracy—or a widening of political participation—in both metropole and colony was a principal source of imperial erosion. At the same time, decolonization produced political outcomes that enabled France to establish a neo-empire in Africa; Britain's influence over its former colonies quickly disintegrated.

The conditions for neo-imperial success are examined in the third section. Next, the recently (partially?) decolonized Soviet empire is scrutinized to assess the probability that a successful neo-empire might be established there. The most likely area for successful neo-imperial reconstruction (though not a reconstitution of Soviet-era structures) is Central Asia, which bears a striking similarity to postcolonial francophone Africa. Finally, two much more difficult questions are posed: What can outsiders do to prevent neo-empire in the former Soviet Union? Should outsiders prevent reassertion of Russian influence in this form?

The Fading of Formal Empires

Distinguishing between empires as juridical entities and the realities of imperial rule is difficult. As the British and French cases demonstrate, "empire" is best treated as a dynamic set of relations between societies rather than as a unit exhibiting certain timeless characteristics. Although definitions of empire have emphasized control or domination, variation among empires across space and time requires further differentiation.[1] Control implies a directive and simplified view of imperial rule, which always involves bargaining between colonizer and colonized. In our common understanding of empire, two dimensions distinguish imperial rule from other forms of international relations.

One is *hierarchy* versus devolution of decision making. Some empires are highly centralized. One society—the metropole or center—assumes sole (not shared) decision-making authority over internal and external policies that affect not only itself but other societies in the empire as well. In other cases, such as the most recent British empire, a substantial degree of devolution in decision making to the colonial societies is permitted. If devolution is complete, independence results; if joint decision making remains, but is based on equality of influence, empire has been transformed into confederation.

The second dimension of empire is its external face: *monopoly* of external ties versus competition for those relations. Imperial possessions are not permitted to diversify their international relations. Through political means, transactions are concentrated within the empire; constituent societies are typically permitted only limited relations with societies outside the empire. A hub-and-spokes pattern of international relations results.

In arguing that empires have become an extinct type in contemporary international relations, the case must be made that formal empire, an extreme combination of hierarchy and monopoly, is fatally disadvantaged. Changes that have undermined imperial international relations began before World War II and have accelerated since. Change has occurred in the international environment, in the politics of metropolitan societies, and in colonized societies. Perhaps the most striking international change has been a dramatic shift in norms: as signified in international law and the evolution of such institutions as the United Nations, self-determination, nonintervention, and the sovereign equality of states have with dramatic speed become governing principles of interstate relations. As Darwin notes, by the 1950s, beliefs that each ex-colony, no matter how "artificial" in ethnic or historical terms, was entitled to self-determination and that self-government was preferable to "good government" had become "dogmas so deeply entrenched in the Western world that scarcely the hardiest controversialists dared, or troubled, to challenge it."[2]

Associated with this shift in norms was an equally important and widespread acceptance of the sovereign nation-state as the principal and perhaps the only unit of international relations. Before World War II, one deterrent to colonial nationalism was recognition that the alternative to one imperial master was likely to be another and possible harsher master. After 1945 this assumption was reversed: empires became increasingly isolated and were forced, with few exceptions, to portray themselves as temporary way stations on the road to independence. Hendrik Spruyt has suggested the importance of "mutual empowerment," or the reinforcement of like units by their structurally similar peers, in ensuring the success of one institutional alternative over another.[3] The empire-dominated system of the early twentieth century swiftly tipped toward a nation-state–dominated system after World War II; in dramatic contrast to the 1920s and 1930s, empires were quickly defined as beleaguered and outdated institutional forms.

Two other systemic changes were more ambiguous in their consequences for imperial survival. The dominance of the Soviet Union and the United States that took shape soon after World War II awarded primacy in the international military order to two powers that were rhetorically anticolonial, despite their own imperial legacies. The anticolonialism of the United States will be examined below; its effects on decolonization have probably been exaggerated. The dominance of the United States economy after 1945, a temporary consequence of the world wars, brought liberalization of international trade and investment. These changes in turn reduced the advantages of empires as large-scale economic units. As barriers to international exchange declined, the need for large internal (imperial) markets declined as well.[4]

These international transformations accompanied equally significant changes that contributed to overturning the imperial bargain within metropolitan and colonial societies. In redefining metropolitan interests, territorial control in the developing world was no longer regarded as an important asset. Metropolitan interests could be satisfied by a much looser system of influence over a narrower array of domestic and foreign policies in developing areas. Postwar liberalization shifted the poles of growth in a resurgent international economy to the industrialized world; economies that concentrated trade and investment in their colonies, such as Portugal, were threatened with economic stagnation. Democracy was embedded as the dominant political system in the imperial powers after 1945, and democratic principles sat uneasily with the racially hierarchical system of values that legitimated imperial rule. Competitive political systems also undermined the control that narrow imperial interests exercised, especially when costs of imperial rule increased.

As metropolitan interests shifted, the capabilities of the periphery grew as well. Colonial uprisings and military resistance have probably been overemphasized in many accounts of decolonization; nevertheless, colonial nationalists did increase their organizational capabilities through widening political participation during and after World War II. Although they appeared sturdy at the time, colonial empires that survived World War II are now portrayed as fragile and ephemeral creations whose existence was dependent on several tenuous and short-lived conditions. As those conditions unraveled, the once-imposing imperial edifices crumbled with surprising speed.

As heirs to the era of decolonization and now to the Soviet collapse, we hold an image of empires as highly temporary and unstable structures. A new era may have opened, however, in which neo-empire, a looser and more geographically circumscribed system of influence over militarily weak and economically dependent societies, remains an alternative for certain states. Neo-empire is informal empire for a postimperial era. Unlike formal empire, in which the scope of decisions ultimately made at the center was wide, neo-empires restrict the range of policies subject to hierarchical decision making. Coercion by military means and the threat of such coercion remain in the background in neo-empires, setting limits to apparently conventional bargaining between states. Finally, neo-empires created between societies in which populations are no longer politically acquiescent must purchase political support from critical segments of the peripheral societies. Neo-empire does not serve the interests, democratically expressed, of the whole society, a feature that explains the association of lingering international hierarchy with persistent domestic hierarchy in the form of authoritarianism.

Most industrialized societies remain anti-imperialist because their connections with most developing societies are remote and because painful memories of military conflict, whether in Vietnam or in Afghanistan, persist. Nevertheless, the elites of those industrialized societies recognize interests in peripheral societies that are often in economic and political crisis. Spillover effects from neighboring societies are particularly important, whether in the form of refugee flows or drug trafficking. How to exert influence over fragile and threatened elites in those societies and how to manage their conflicts is a classic imperial dilemma. New techniques are deployed, including trade agreements (Mexico and North

Africa), foreign aid, and policies of short-term intervention (Haiti). When they are combined in a coherent strategy of tempered hierarchy and porous monopoly, neo-empire can result. What is lacking—and its absence may be a crucial break with the recent past—is concern over competition from other great powers, whether classic imperial rivalry or ideological competition during the Cold War.

Changes in at least part of the postcolonial developing world may also create the conditions for neo-empire. The colonial bargain shifted and finally unraveled because of growing political capabilities among colonial elites: their ability to mobilize populations on the basis of anticolonial nationalism and to take control of the postcolonial state. The phenomenon of failed states indicates that the postcolonial era has ended in parts of the developing world. In some countries, brittle praetorian regimes quickly succeeded postindependence democratic regimes. In the 1980s and 1990s, highly institutionalized party regimes—in Algeria, India, Mexico, and much of Africa—display signs of dissolution. Other societies seem incapable of constructing a stable political order of any kind (Afghanistan, Somalia, Tajikistan). The end of Cold War competition has cut off one steady source of external financial and military support for these regimes. Their insecurity and need for external support may make a neo-imperial solution more attractive.

Partial answers to the question of neo-imperial reconstitution in the former Soviet Union and elsewhere can be found in the experience of decolonization and neo-empire among the former colonial powers Britain and France. Although distinctions as well as analogies must be carefully defined, the two cases help to illuminate conditions for a relatively stable neo-empire (France) and the establishment of arm's-length relations with former colonies (Britain). They suggest explanations, based in part on the domestic politics of decolonization, for those outcomes and tentative predictions about the future course of Russia's relations with its "near abroad."

Decolonization and Neo-Imperial Outcomes

Decolonization was only one episode in a dynamic of bargaining and influence between the European metropolitan powers—Britain and France—and the societies of Asia and Africa. The devolution of self-rule and sovereign status to a large number of societies in a relatively short span of time was a key historical event in the twentieth century, but colonialism was preceded in many cases by lengthy periods of informal influence. Decolonization also would be succeeded by new relationships in which metropoles tried to retain their influence at lower cost.

Throughout this search for parallels with the end of the Soviet empire, certain key differences and similarities among these cases should be kept in view. First, the Soviet empire was far more important to Russia in military and economic terms than the colonial empires were to Britain and France after 1945. Second, the Soviet empire was not overseas, as the current title "near abroad" suggests. This geographical proximity may have important implications for redefinition of the metropole's national identity and disentangling the dense web of relations that bound together colonizer and colonized. The Soviet empire's economy was not a capitalist one, which meant that central political direction of economic flows was all-important; in the British and French cases, although their mercantilist colonial spheres were protected, their empires were not insulated from the international economy.

On a final dimension, the European and Soviet empires may have been more similar than is currently recognized. The dynamic view of French and British imperialism that now prevails implies numerous patterns of influence changing over time rather than a single template of imperial rule. The British empire was an extreme example of this diversity, displaying "no logic and little system in its constitutional structure; no uniformity in its political development; and no unity in its economic life."[5] French elites attempted to give their empire a more Cartesian and rationalized outline, but the status of dependent territories ranged from quasi-integration with the metropole (Algeria) to colonial territories governed directly (sub-Saharan Africa) to protectorates that were effectively ruled by France (Morocco and Tunisia). Although the Soviet republican structure imparted uniformity to Soviet governance of non-Russian peoples, the evolving pattern of relations since 1991 suggests that future historians may discover similar diversity within Soviet imperial structures.

The politics of decolonization in both Britain and France was shaped by relations binding empire and metropole that were embedded in the metropolitan societies. The political means by which the empires were anchored in metropolitan societies meant that threats to imperial relations would arouse a political— and sometimes violent—response. Colonial empires entered metropolitan politics by two principal avenues: as significant ideological assets for politicians in mobilizing party and electoral support, and as specific interests that could penetrate and attempt to influence metropolitan political outcomes.[6] Some parts of the colonial empires were of greater importance as symbols of national status and world power (empires of prestige); other parts were significant because of important economic interests and large settler communities (empires of kith and kin). One important structural distinction between France and Britain was the coincidence of these empires in French North Africa and their separation in the British case: India and the Middle East were the core of Britain's empire of prestige; East and Central Africa were home to the largest settler populations.

Decolonizing metropolitan politics meant first eliminating the ideological hold that empire had on British and French political formations. The ideological drive for maintaining empire should not be seen as a disembodied set of ideas or intellectual precepts; it was rooted in the instrumental use of imperial ideology for domestic political purposes.[7] Conservative parties found imperialism (and other nationalist ideologies) particularly useful in countering the class-based appeals of their opponents. The British Conservative Party had made attachment to the empire part of its core identity in the late nineteenth century; most French conservatives and centrists (and some to their left) became equally attached by the interwar years. In the French case, that attachment was deepened by identification of the colonial empire with the French republic and its institutions. Recent history—particularly France's defeat and occupation during World War II—made threats to imperial unity even more sensitive in French political formations.

The institutions of postwar politics made decolonizing British politics less traumatic than the loosening of empire's hold on France. Although dissent on imperial issues—from India to Suez to Rhodesia—was a persistent irritant for Conservative leaders in Britain, in France that dissent eventually destroyed one regime (the Fourth Republic) and threatened its successor, De Gaulle's Fifth Republic. Conservative parties in France were weakly institutionalized during the Fourth Republic, and they struggled to survive in a highly competitive political environment under constantly shifting electoral rules (typically a version of proportional representation). Fear of loss of party supporters to conservative competitors produced a tendency to bid for the nationalist vote and to harden positions on colonial issues within governing coalitions. Those coalitions themselves were prey to the shifting deals struck among parliamentary leaders, which rarely reflected broader political sentiment in the electorate; during the early years of the Algerian war (1954–58), government coalitions became increasingly unstable, and France became increasingly ungovernable.

Charles de Gaulle was able to decolonize French nationalism by redefining the content of nationalist ideology and changing the institutions of French democracy. His authority as an interpreter of French nationalism was unique, although political opponents eventually challenged his efforts to redefine French identity by excluding *Algérie française*. De Gaulle tapped a deeply embedded image of France as the "eternal hexagon" (metropolitan France) and substituted other international assets for the empire—nuclear weapons, European leadership, and a continuing presence in sub-Saharan Africa, the only region in which French decolonization was politically painless. He made his formidable task feasible by redesigning French political institutions. During the critical years of Algerian decolonization (1958–62), a new political formation controlled by De Gaulle, the Union pour la Nouvelle République, became the dominant conservative political formation. The Fifth Republic was designed as a presidential regime with a weak legislature that was, not surprisingly, the home of his fiercest opponents.[8] Not only did the powerful presidency give De Gaulle a means of circumventing his opponents, it also became the locus of French foreign policy and policy toward France's postcolonial sphere in Africa.

British Conservative leaders were able to overcome much less dangerous levels of dissent by engaging in an ideological redefinition that paralleled De Gaulle's: emphasizing Britain's status as a nuclear power and its place at the "top table" with the United States, sounding the increasingly empty themes of the British Commonwealth for true believers within the party. International status was disentangled from formal empire, even though British Conservatives, like their French counterparts, intended to retain influence over former colonial possessions and the informal empire of prestige in the Middle East. The political task of British Conservatives during decolonization was eased by a highly institutionalized party in which rules and governance were understood from rank-and-file to Cabinet members. The Conservative Party could also draw on widespread identification and loyalty among the electorate. The British political system, a first-past-the-post electoral system that favored the two major parties, ensured that dissidents within the Conservative ranks had no easy exit to the right (except to political oblivion).[9]

The strong anticolonial predispositions of the Labour Party, the principal opposition, served to strengthen the hand of the Conservative leadership vis-à-vis its parliamentary backbenchers. Any dissent that threatened to overturn the government would risk bringing to power a party whose views on colonial issues were even more objectionable. Throughout decolonization the British electorate evinced little interest in colonial matters, so long as British prestige remained intact. Unlike France, extreme Right reaction was absent during the years of decolonization; when extremism did appear in the 1960s, its core issue—immigration—was perversely anticolonial. Right-wing nationalism had become an isolationist "little England" nationalism, not a nationalism of imperialist nostalgia or reassertion.

Politics on the British and French Left was less crucial to decolonization but significant for future neo-imperial ties. Both British Labour and the French Socialist Party would hold power during and after decolonization, when relations with the former empires were defined and revised. For the Labour Party, whatever its hesitations during particular episodes, support for decolonization provided a useful point of unity for a party that fractured on many other foreign policy issues related to the Cold War (nuclear disarmament) and Europe. Its consistent stance in favor of a rapid transfer of power (with implications for the Conservative Party described above) and its provision of access for colonial nationalists in metropolitan politics speeded the peaceful decolonization of both metropole and colonies.

The record of the French Socialist Party during the Fourth Republic was far more ambiguous: from early support for reforms in Africa and independence for Morocco and Tunisia, it led France's war to retain Algeria during 1956–57. The peculiar ideological heritage of the party—in particular its experience of the Resistance and its association of the colonial empire with the republican ideology—had produced a less-than-resounding anticolonialism at the core of its political program. The French political system only reinforced this equivocation, since it appeared to offer political gains to the Socialists in carving out a niche as national (anticommunist) and anticlerical. The highly centralized structure of the party enabled the leadership, under Secretary-General Guy Mollet, to suppress anticolonial dissent with ease. Ironically, Mollet managed to retain his hold on a party that was shrinking in electoral appeal; it was among his opponents that the founders of the "new" Socialist Party of the Fifth Republic would be found.[10] In their attitudes toward France's neo-empire in Africa, however, there would be far less novelty.

Britain's advantages in decolonizing nationalist ideology and party politics were reinforced by the pattern of interests that joined metropole and empire. Resistance to changes in the colonial status quo by key colonial interests—economic, settler, military, and administration—was determined by perceived political exposure. Political exposure in turn was defined by two dimensions of their position in the colonial empire: dependence on state policy—whether a protected colonial market, a controlled labor market, or the expenditures of the colonial state—and probable political futures in the territory in question.[11] Certain economic interests and segments of the colonial population (such as the administration) were so dependent on the colonial political order that virtually any change in political status would mean substantial loss. If likely successor regimes were radical nationalist or socialist, and threatened nationalization or closure to the metropolitan economy, probable political futures were bleak. Active resistance by highly exposed interests was likely to increase.

British colonial economies demonstrated lower political exposure for several reasons. The British empire was more open to competitive pressures from the international economy; the colonial state also played a somewhat smaller role than in the French empire. These features lowered dependence on the colonial political regime. In addition industry, commerce, and banking played a larger role in the British colonies compared with agriculture and mining—the two most exposed sectors. This sectoral pattern favored economic interests that were less dependent on metropolitan political protection and those that were less likely to be targeted by colonial nationalists, particularly those mobilizing a primarily rural local population. In addition, the British pattern of economic development was more likely to produce moderate nationalist movements with a substantial stake in retaining the broad outlines of the colonial political economy, rather than more radical and anticapitalist movements.[12]

The same calculations can be applied to settler populations in the colonial empires, which often were core constituents of resistance to decolonization. Settlers attempted to manipulate metropolitan politics to their advantage. The level of settler resistance was dependent on the size of their population relative to the total population of the colonial territory, a proxy for their need to accommodate to colonial nationalism, and on settlers' political exposure. The latter, in turn, was dependent on the social and economic composition of the settler population, and particularly the numbers of *petits colons* (those in relatively unskilled or state-dependent occupations), who would be placed in direct competition with the local population upon independence. Under colonial rule, the politics of settler communities was dominated by notables of relatively high social and economic status, who served as emissaries to the metropole. As the end of colonial rule approached, these figures were displaced by more extreme representatives of threatened segments in the settler community. Ian Smith in Rhodesia and the OAS in Algeria represented die-hard elements in settler politics that refused to accept majority rule and resorted to attempted independence under settler domination or violent opposition to decolonization.

Although the Rhodesian case was an important exception, Britain enjoyed advantages in overcoming settler resistance to decolonization. Settler populations outside Rhodesia were small relative to African populations, and their relative affluence and social standing reduced their political exposure. Resistance was not the only determinant of settler influence on the politics of decolonization, however. Effectiveness in thwarting devolution of power to their colonial opponents also depended on the political assets that they could deploy in the metropolis and the influence awarded their rivals (the colonial nationalists) in the same political arena. Ultimately, none of the settler organizations were successful in managing the transition from the politics of notables to the mass politics of resistance while maintaining a hold on metropolitan politics. The bias in British colonial policy toward devolution to the periphery, however, meant that settlers were soon seen in London as external interlopers rather than as welcome kith and kin. British politics also offered—largely through the Labour Party and Labour-affiliated organizations—more ready access to the voices of colonial nationalism, so that settlers did not have a monopoly on the metropolitan political debate.

For French North Africa, none of these conditions held: settlers had long infiltrated French politics through metropolitan parties, and the shifting coalitions and lobbying politics of the Fourth Republic did little to curb their power. North African nationalists—in striking contrast to the leaders of sub-Saharan Africa—were excluded from the metropolis and often demonized by their settler opponents.[13]

Most important for the future of French domestic politics, however, was the resistance to decolonization by the state apparatus. The more violent course of French decolonization was due not only to the political hold of empire in France but also to bureaucratic and military attachment to an overseas role. France imposed a much heavier weight of administration on its empire than did Britain. Far from being a pliable instrument of the metropole, administrators were often captured by local colonial interests. Persistent obstruction and disobedience by the colonial civil administration, however, were not as dangerous as resistance by the French military, a development that had no parallel in the British Empire. Despite insurgencies in Kenya and Malaya, the British army after 1945 was directed primarily toward the Soviet threat and the European theater; colonial campaigns were sideshows.

The French military, after its searing defeat in World War II and the trauma of Indochina, faced a crisis when the Algerian insurrection erupted in 1954. For some members of the officer corps, Algeria became the front line of a *guerre révolutionnaire* that they intended to counter by equally revolutionary means.

Rather than disengaging from colonial responsibilities, segments of the French army redesigned colonial warfare as a counterinsurgency campaign for control of the local population. In doing so, they became deeply engaged in politics—first in Algeria and then, when the regime appeared ready to desert their effort, in France. The army in Algiers supported the settler uprising in May 1958 that brought down the Fourth Republic and returned Charles de Gaulle to power. The "generals' coup" of April 1961 shook the Fifth Republic but proved to be the final act of military resistance to decolonization. De Gaulle's decolonization of the French military was as thorough as his decolonization of French politics. He redirected French strategy toward the new *force de frappe* (nuclear weapons) and Europe, and reasserted French autonomy by withdrawing from NATO's military command structure. De Gaulle also maintained an intervention force for decolonized Africa while he firmly removed the army from direct involvement in politics.

The contrasting experiences of Britain and France during decolonization were mirrored in the nationalist movements that each confronted. French resistance to political change in the North African empire of prestige, a settler monopoly on political power, and an economy (particularly in Algeria) that was biased toward agriculture and failed to absorb the burgeoning Arab workforce encouraged more radical nationalist movements, culminating in the Front de Libération Nationale (FLN) in Algeria. In Morocco and Tunisia, the juridical structure of the protectorates eventually encouraged the French to deal with conservative nationalists such as the Moroccan sultan and the Néo-Destour. Only in sub-Saharan Africa, lacking large settler populations and peripheral to French claims of international status and security, did the French conduct decolonization successfully, *à l'anglaise:* transferring power to local elites that endorsed continued ties to France.[14] Those elites had long enjoyed access to metropolitan politics, including seats in the French National Assembly.

The British, too, confronted their greatest failures at the center of their empire of prestige: India, which dissolved in bloody partition, and the informal Middle Eastern empire, where Britain demonstrated its inability to grapple with the forces of Arab nationalism. Its informal empire dissolved as traditional political figures were overthrown (Iraq) or threatened (Jordan). Britain's move to direct intervention against the perceived source of Arab nationalism in Egypt failed at Suez in 1956. The British template of devolution to governments that would remain members of the Commonwealth eased decolonization, but it also encouraged local political mobilization in opposition to British rule at an early stage. Politicians in Britain's African colonies would prove more resistant to neocolonial bargains than their French counterparts.

Examining the collapse of the Soviet empire through the lens of the British and French experience raises one striking puzzle: Given the far greater significance of the Soviet empire to conceptions of national identity and the much denser web of interests that bound Russia and the other Soviet republics, why was the collapse so sudden and resistance to the end of the empire so weak? Given the scale of the Soviet double decolonization, one might have expected violence on the French level, and yet, apart from the lives lost in Tblisi and Vilnius and conflict in Moldova, the empire's demise was remarkably peaceful. Using the analysis presented here, several explanations can be offered. First, the outcome might have been very different if the coup of August 1991 had succeeded, and the forces seeking to maintain the Soviet Union had regained power at the center. Given their failure on that occasion and the measures taken against them after the failed coup, the center remained in the hands of those who wished to see imperial structures overturned or radically transformed. Second, important interests in the former Soviet republics—whether Russian populations or enterprises dependent on markets and goods in other republics—did not calculate a high political exposure, since likely successor regimes were not estimated to threaten them. At the time of dissolution, maintenance of the broad outlines of the Soviet political economy was a common assumption. Only in a few republics—Estonia, Latvia, Lithuania, Moldova, and Georgia—did decolonization take on an explicitly anti-Russian cast, and it was in precisely those republics that violence occurred. However painful the separation of key parts of the Soviet "empire of prestige"—the Slavic republics of Belarus and Ukraine—the perceived political exposure of Russians and key economic interests was very low, given the political coloration of the new governments.

In the politics of the metropole (Russia), widespread apathy and hostility marked attitudes toward the constructed Soviet nationality that was embodied in the empire. Russian self-assertiveness or nationalism could also assume an anti-imperial coloration, resembling certain strands of British and French nationalism. Finally, and most ominously, however, Soviet decolonization may have been swift and peaceful because it remains incomplete. In Russia and the former Soviet republics, the consequences of decolonization were not fully understood. Imperial reconstitution could remain a more attractive political alternative than it was in Britain or France. The British and French records in establishing neo-empires after decolonization shed some light on whether a Russian attempt at neo-empire could succeed.

The Sources and Stability of Neo-Empires

The turbulent and sometimes violent politics of decolonization left remarkably little trace on British and French politics. The anxious years of Algerian decolonization had produced predictions of an "Algerianization" of French politics, but France under De Gaulle did not become a latter-day Weimar. Settlers returning settlers from North Africa formed a small core of right-wing anti-Gaullism, concentrated in the south of France, but their discontents left few permanent scars on the French polity. The economic boom of the 1960s eased their integration into French society and also reduced any wider electoral concerns over loss of international status. Internal party dissent over decolonization did provide one ideological source for later right-wing and left-wing political currents: the critique of Harold Macmillan in the early 1960s fed into a broader conservative critique that ultimately brought Margaret Thatcher to power; the Socialist malcontents of the 1950s later led the transformed French Socialist Party of the 1970s and 1980s. In both cases, however, the foreign policy programs adopted hardly resembled those of the original dissidents.

A more consequential and illuminating connection to later political movements lay in the issue of immigration, one of the most significant and persistent ties between former metropole and former colonies. In both Britain and France, opposition to immigration from the former empire served as a core issue for right-wing extremists. Anti-immigrant positions became part of the Conservative Party's right wing in Britain; in France, Jean-Marie Le Pen, who began his career as a Poujadist supporter of *Algérie française,* now leads the National Front in opposition to immigration and European integration. As a political issue, immigration, one of the strongest and most visible ties remaining between the former empires and Europe, demonstrates a redefinition of nationalism away from an expansive view of a wider political community to a narrower and ethnically defined core.

Although decolonization may have left few permanent marks on British and French politics, the former imperial powers would pursue divergent paths in relations with their ex-colonies. France constructed a delimited neo-imperial sphere in sub-Saharan Africa; Britain's aspirations for future influence dissolved into the symbolism of the Commonwealth. Despite these contrasting outcomes, both Britain and France intended to retain influence in their former possessions long after decolonization. The conventional view of decolonization as a sharp rupture is at odds with metropolitan views at the time. As Louis and Robinson point out, "British officials concentrated on independence for tropical Africa after 1957—independence in the north-east, independence in the west—above all independence to prolong imperial sway and secure British economic and strategic assets. It was increasingly urgent to exchange colonial control for informal empire."[15] British governments quickly discovered, however, that their past mastery of informal empire did not translate into a network of influence after the concession of sovereignty.

France, on the other hand, designed a neo-empire in sub-Saharan Africa that exists in altered form today, although recent developments—halting democratization in Africa and the devaluation of the CFA franc in 1994—suggest that the sphere may not last into the twenty-first century. France's sphere is justifiably labeled neo-imperial when measured against the key constituents of the definition given earlier: hierarchy and monopoly. Hierarchy has persisted in the form of French military intervention, which has been undertaken to prop up and defend local governments, and in the franc zone, where final decision-making authority has rested with Paris. In contrast to formal empire, however, bargaining advantages have shifted to the ex-colonial states. The French neo-empire is sustained less by coercion than by protection and subsidies. The cost of influence for the metropole has increased since decolonization, and France's willingness to bear those increased costs is one of the puzzles underlying its African policies. Finally, neo-empire is associated with the absence of democracy in Africa. Although the francophone African states have not been the worst offenders against human rights and democracy, few are competitive democracies. The French future in Africa may depend on the mounting costs of influence and the possibility of "consensual empire," hierarchical delegation agreed upon by fully democratic governments.

The French neo-empire was not a halfway house between empire and independence. In a manner strikingly parallel to the last months of the Soviet Union, De Gaulle discovered that his plans for a French Community limiting colonial autonomy fell apart in a rush to independence. Like Mikhail Gorbachev, he found that constructing a fully devolved confederal structure directly from an imperial one is very difficult. Only after formal independence was granted could new structures of collaboration—hierarchical or collegial—emerge.[16] Federal options linking African territories, as well as the French Community designed by De Gaulle, gave way to new bilateral instruments of French influence in sub-Saharan Africa: the pillars of military cooperation (defense and military cooperation agreements), the franc zone (a currency area linked to the French franc), bilateral aid, cultural cooperation, and diplomatic coordination.

The evolving military pillar of the French sphere has been the most visible. Military collaboration originally consisted of bilateral defense agreements, which permit African governments to request French military assistance, and military cooperation agreements. The latter offer an array of technical assistance, training, and equipment from France.[17] Over time, the importance of French garrisons and bases in the region declined. Although the means of influence shifted, however, the French neo-empire was not simply a stage marking the transition from colonial status to arm's-length relations between France and its former colonies. The military sphere in particular demonstrated that the neo-empire was a new construction. Under President Giscard d'Estaing (1974–81), France demonstrated increased activism in Africa. As a gesture to African political sensitivity and to reduce costs, French governments increasingly relied on intervention forces that were stationed in France (in their most recent incarnation, the Force d'Action Rapide). Nevertheless, French military aid to Africa increased sharply in the 1970s.[18] Over time, fewer states retained formal defense agreements with France, but those that did so remained important "core" states: Senegal, Côte d'Ivoire, and Gabon.

A neo-empire must incorporate the possibility of military intervention on the part of the most powerful actor, and France has intervened repeatedly (over thirty times) in Africa since decolonization. The ambit of intervention has exceeded the web of formal agreements with African states. As Chipman points out, the absence of a defense agreement has not prevented French intervention in several cases.[19] French intervention has defended the international and domestic status quo in its neo-empire; in some cases, the interventions have been spurred by pressure from France's clients in the region.[20] Throughout, however, France has retained the freedom to intervene or decline to intervene, as it sees fit. The political acceptability of the policy of intervention in France has been maintained by keeping costs (casualties) low and avoiding high-profile military disasters.[21]

The franc zone (two groups of francophone countries and the Comoros, joined by two common central banks and a common currency) is the only currency area that links an industrialized country with developing countries. From the colonial era until the devaluation of January 1994, the common currency (the CFA franc) had been pegged to the French franc at a rate of 50:1. Members of the franc zone enjoy a number of advantages: a freely convertible currency guaranteed by France, access to pooled reserves to deal with external shocks, and low inflation rates, since monetary policy is effectively removed from national control. These conditions attracted foreign investment and, before the 1980s, contributed to a somewhat higher rate of growth among members than in other sub-Saharan African states.[22] In exchange for these benefits, African member governments gave up use of exchange rate and monetary policy as a means of economic management, since these instruments were effectively controlled by France. As David Fieldhouse suggests, these delegations of policymaking "implied a degree of dependence on a foreign state which would have been obnoxious to nationalist feeling in most other states of post-colonial Africa."[23] French authority was ensured not only by the rules of the system (and its guarantee of credit) but also by French representation on the boards of the regional central banks and the posting of French technocrats to key national economic ministries.

The franc zone remained a stable system until the mid-1980s, although a relaxation of French oversight and increased devolution to national authorities permitted abuses of credit to grow in the system. The International Monetary Fund's account of the sudden 1994 devaluation offers two explanations for this critical break in the zone's long history of stability: France's pursuit of a "strong franc" policy (for reasons of European policy), which overvalued the CFA franc and the sharp deterioration in terms of trade of all African countries over the course of the 1980s.[24] Growing costs to France, which was forced to cover the yawning deficits of the francophone states, finally brought the long-resisted decision to devalue. In the absence of devaluation, alternative policy measures—particularly fiscal austerity—would have been politically explosive. The devaluation of the CFA franc signaled that France was finding its African neo empire increasingly burdensome. Nevertheless, the franc zone remains intact and its convertibility guarantee has been maintained. The long-delayed devaluation demonstrated another important cost for the African economies: an ability to evade adjustments to international change in the interests of a political economy based on urban and elite political support.[25]

The costs to France of its trade and aid policies in Africa have been reduced over time by Europeanization. The French colonial empire had woven a web of protectionist measures that ensured prices well above those of the world market or both metropolitan suppliers and colonial producers. France's entry into the European Economic Community began an opening of export markets in its former colonies to its European partners. The ex-colonies gained preferential access to the European market through successive agreements with the European Community (most recently the Lomé Agreements). France remains the principal guardian of its former empire's interests in the all-important European Union, and it remains the largest export market for its ex-colonies in Africa (even as the its share of their small import market has declined).

France's aid has remained, in contrast to Britain's, bilateral and heavily concentrated on French Africa.[26] And to a degree unique among industrialized countries, successive French governments have dedicated large resources to the propagation of French language and culture, a key element in retaining elite loyalties to France, maintaining distance between elite and majority populations, and discouraging regional collaboration with anglophone states. These programs also help to sustain a (small) market for French cultural and media products.[27] The scale and concentration of the French aid effort reinforced the presence of French personnel in sub-Saharan Africa: as late as 1982, two hundred thousand French citizens lived in the former French colonies, although economic distress in the late 1980s brought a sharp decline in their numbers.[28]

French policy in Africa has been a sphere of presidential decision making since De Gaulle. His African adviser, Jacques Foccart, managed a complex web of military, intelligence, and economic interests through which French influence was exercised. The special status of the neo-empire was reinforced by assigning principal ministerial responsibility to the Ministry of Cooperation rather than the Ministry of Foreign Affairs.[29] The bureaucratic process was equally opaque; both democratic oversight and an accurate accounting of the costs of neo-empire were difficult. At the same time, France's relationship with Africa was surrounded with public symbolism, such as the Franco-African summits instituted by President Giscard d'Estaing. These gatherings reinforced ties between France and the leaders of francophone Africa, and expanded the French circle of influence to African states that were not former colonies.[30]

Even if the French neo-empire is transformed or disintegrates, France has retained its web of influence in Africa for three decades after formal decolonization. Britain never successfully constructed such a sphere, and the pattern of its colonialism and decolonization may have made it more difficult to do so. During the last stages of decolonization, British governments made critical decisions that eliminated any special capability to intervene east of Suez.[31] These decisions sharply reduced Britain's ability to assist either the governments of many former colonial territories (as in Malaya's confrontation with Indonesia) or dependent Arab regimes in the old empire of prestige that bordered the Indian Ocean. As the Falklands war demonstrated, Britain continues to maintain substantial force projection capabilities, but those capabilities have rarely been used for intervention in its former colonies. Apart from a handful of interventions in East Africa immediately after decolonization, British military programs and interventions in Africa were centered on Rhodesia's declaration of independence and the threat to frontline states from South Africa.[32] Britain did not attempt to replicate France's network of bilateral military agreements after the transfer of power. Its limited military engagement in the former empire and its military facilities in Africa declined rapidly after decolonization.

Britain's more open colonial economies and its belated membership in the European Community offered fewer opportunities for constructing preferential trading arrangements that might have shored up its influence. By the 1960s, imperial and Commonwealth preferences were already insignificant, and trade patterns diversified steadily after independence.[33] The sterling area also declined in importance. After independence, Britain and its former colonies decided against a hierarchically organized currency area and in favor of national autonomy in exchange rate and monetary policies. The weakness of sterling in the 1960s and 1970s made it unattractive as a reserve or transactions currency for most of the former colonies, and Britain, beleaguered by a sterling overhang in the hands of self-interested ex-colonial governments, came to see more costs than benefits from the arrangement.[34]

The pattern of British foreign aid also stood in stark contrast to French concentration on its African sphere. Under Prime Minister Thatcher, British aid was cut sharply: Britain's international decline was linked to economic decline that was in turn blamed in part on excessive public expenditure. The share of the Commonwealth within this shrinking (and increasingly multilateral) aid budget also declined from 77 percent of the total in 1980 to 68 percent in the early 1990s.[35]

Britain had hoped to use the Commonwealth as a central instrument in preserving its influence. The Commonwealth's emptiness as a diplomatic forum, however, contrasted starkly with the Franco-African summits. Despite its institutionalization (the formation of a secretariat in 1965), the Commonwealth quickly became a talking shop, one that sometimes pitted Britain against the rest of its members. In the late 1980s, acrimonious debates took place between the Thatcher government and other Commonwealth members over the issue of economic sanctions against South Africa.[36] Britain's isolation on these occasions highlighted the complete absence of hierarchy in the Commonwealth. Recent efforts to revive the Commonwealth have concentrated on its role as a principled club favoring human rights and democratization. Nigeria's suspension in November 1995 only confirmed its lack of sanctions and its image of impotence.

The symbolism of French presidents presiding over ever wider Franco-African summits while British prime ministers were assailed by their former colonies at Commonwealth meetings disguises strains that have appeared in France's neo-empire in Africa. Nevertheless, the mere existence of a French sphere in

Africa bears explanation, given Britain's unrealized expectations of a similar web of influence over its former colonies. Louis and Robinson argue that Britain's empire could be described as a neo-empire in the making, even before World War II:

> . . . imperial sway by 1939 derived mainly from profit-sharing business and power-sharing with indigenous elites overseas. At the country level, the system relied on unequal accommodations with client rulers or proto-nationalists who multiplied British power locally with their own authority for their own advantage. Contracts could not be too unequal or collaborators would lose their constituents and the system would break down. As local sub-contractors became better organized the terms for co-operation turned progressively in their favour. The final settlement would be with national successors who would secure British economic and strategic assets under informal tutelage. Local bargains could not be struck to imperial advantagē if other great powers competed in the bidding.[37]

Since Britain had long experience in the arts of informal empire, why did its efforts at "informal tutelage" fail and those of France succeed? Why was it unable to establish a new set of bargains that would satisfy its own interests and those of formally independent elites? Metropolitan, ex-colonial, and international differences explain the contrasting national experiences. The puzzle of France's persistent interest in an African neo-empire can be explained in two ways. Chipman suggests that the French elite defined their African sphere as an international power asset, a means to greater international status. Even though De Gaulle had given up the core of France's empire of prestige in North Africa, he substituted the more easily decolonized sub-Saharan colonies in order to guarantee France a non-European international role. This explanation is lent support by the consistency of French policy toward the region, from De Gaulle to the non-Gaullist conservative Giscard d'Estaing (who actually expanded France's role) to the Socialist Mitterrand, who took office promising reform and ended by embracing the old policies of his political rivals. The advantages of carefully delimiting this sphere were important for controlling the costs of neo-imperial sway. Costs were partly determined by the local elites and the bargain that they could extract, but French governments worked to reduce the political and financial burdens of their policy of influence. Those costs were also disguised by the management of African policy through the presidency and a bureaucratic maze; careful democratic scrutiny was unlikely.

A second explanation discounts the addition to France's international position that a cluster of poor, developing economies could make. Instead, persistent French attachment to neo-empire is attributed to capture by interests that persisted from the colonial era: economic interests that could still benefit from the array of subsidies and financial support that France extended to these countries. These interests maintained their political hold in Paris through intensive lobbying and political corruption, in particular the redirection of resources into illicit political funds in France.[38] Once again the opacity of policymaking contributed to the ease of capture.

Available data could support either explanation (or both). The important features of the relationship, from the metropolitan point of view, were its benefits in French domestic politics (France plays a role on the world stage that is clearly defined outside the American sphere) and its relatively low or disguised costs. Despite its numerous interventions, France never fought a costly neocolonial military conflict like Vietnam or Afghanistan. The corruption and authoritarianism of African regimes seldom registered in the French public debate.

Britain's choices as a neo-imperial metropole were more difficult. Divisions within the British empire, between the empire of prestige and the empire of kith and kin, had eased decolonization. That same divide made it more difficult to delimit a cost-effective neocolonial sphere. Retaining influence in the Middle East and the Indian Ocean was costly, because anti-British nationalists would resist, as the Wilson cabinet had discovered in Aden. Sub-Saharan Africa could not substitute for world power in the eyes of the British electorate or its political elite, nor did the region's nationalist leaders desire a neocolonial relationship. Britain's relations with African governments were complicated with its close ties to South Africa and its failure to use force against the white Rhodesian regime.

The issue of cost was crucial in moving the British elite against the instruments of neo-imperial influence, whether a military presence east of Suez or the sterling area. The Labour government in power during the 1960s was not hostile to a continuing world role for Britain; Harold Wilson, the prime minister, had proclaimed that Britain's frontier was "on the Himalayas." Nevertheless, recurrent balance-of-payments crises and a tough-minded Treasury underlined the costs of international influence for the national balance sheet. As crisis after crisis struck the pound during the postcolonial decade, domestic programs and spending squeezed Britain's capacity for intervention.[39]

Britain's elite derived political benefits from such policies of influence, particularly a Labour government that risked the accusation of being "anti-national." In contrast with France, however, Britain's leaders saw other alternatives for maintaining the nation's international position that were foreclosed to France. Most important was its close relationship with the United States, which seemed to guarantee its position at the international "top table." Membership in the European Community, sought by both Conservative and Labour governments, was often portrayed as a new avenue for maintaining global power (and one for which Britain's neo-imperial responsibilities were a liability).[40] Britain's passage through decolonization with *less* domestic political trauma than France made an independent neo-imperial sphere appear less essential. The costs of such a venture would be scrutinized very closely by civil servants dedicated to external balance and politicians seeking advantage.

These metropolitan differences were mirrored in the calculations of the postcolonial elites in Africa, Asia, and the Middle East. For the new leaders of francophone Africa, the neo-imperial exchange offered by France was an attractive one: for a modest sacrifice of autonomy (which did not impose significant domestic political costs), they could obtain security for themselves and their regimes (although the French guarantee was not unconditional), substantial financial resources, and an assurance that at least one major power would take an interest in their fate. Given the limited resources of the region, competition from other powers, which might have improved their bargaining position vis-à-vis France, was nonexistent.

The ex-colonies of Britain saw a much less attractive exchange when they considered British efforts to retain influence. Constrained financially, Britain could not offer much in the way of effective military protection, particularly against internal foes; its aid budget was in decline and distributed across a large number of countries; the sterling area reduced monetary autonomy and offered few and uncertain benefits. Given their more dynamic economies, Britain's ex-colonies had suitors other than Britain, whether driven by Cold War competition (India) or economic promise (Nigeria). Since political evolution and organization had on average proceeded earlier and more rapidly in British possessions, national autonomy was valued more highly, and local political opposition was delighted to attack close relations with the former colonial power. Britain's attachment to the American alliance reduced its role as an "alternative" and increased its liabilities for colonial nationalists. As Darwin remarks, "a small power in search of a patron was likely to choose one who promised the best returns, whether in terms of protection, diplomatic support, military or economic aid."[41] Britain's neo-imperial offer was not an attractive one, compared either with the offers of other powers or with a policy of nonalignment and national autonomy.

A final influence on French and British choices was the international system. A neo-empire requires continuing hierarchy and monopoly. Competition from other powers served to undermine a British sphere; its absence reinforced the French role. The United States was willing to have a French guardian over stretches of Africa during the Cold War; its support of a British sphere was tempered by occasional competition (particularly in the Middle East). The Cold War was not fatal for neo-empire; by heightening metropolitan interest in postcolonial influence and limiting intra-alliance competition, the Cold War may actually have sustained neo-imperial ambitions. Nevertheless, the differing positions of Britain and France, and their neo-imperial designs within a setting of superpower rivalry, may have influenced their respective failure and success.

The Politics of Soviet Decolonization and Russian Neo-Imperialism

The peculiarities of the Soviet empire and its collapse have been noted. Nevertheless, the dissolution of the European colonial empires and their divergent postcolonial histories suggest that the shock of the Soviet collapse may conceal a longer and more dynamic evolution. Rather than a rigid and uniform imperial structure that suddenly dissolved, one may, with more distance and more data, perceive more variation in the empire's history and in relations among its successor states. The tentative predictions offered here are predicated on such a differentiated view of Russia and its "near abroad."[42]

Of first importance is redefinition of metropolitan interests and the metropole's calculation of costs. Perhaps the greatest unknown is how Russian nationalism will be defined—whether as "empire saving" (now empire restoring) or "nation building."[43] Determining the domestic political incentives that derive from nationalist programs of any stripe is difficult, since protest voters may inflate the support for nationalist political formations. Since the late Gorbachev years, a majority of the Russian electorate has been reluctant to endorse the use of force for empire-maintaining ends. A neo-imperialism "lite" focused on particular regions may have domestic political payoffs, however. One part of the former Soviet empire enjoys the greatest political resonance among the electorate: the Slavic republics of Ukraine and Belarus (and possibly Kazakhstan), where the historic and long-standing empire of prestige coincides with an empire of kith and kin.[44] These countries also lie at the core of Russia's difficulties in redefining national political space and its parameters.

Economic interests embedded in the former empire also may exert influence on Russian politics and policy. Given the intensely politicized economic relations that bound together the Soviet empire and the disruption that imperial collapse caused for the former Soviet economies, an effort to reconstruct or retain the old imperial ties would not be surprising. The Russian oil and gas industry has already demonstrated its intention to construct close relations with industries in the other former republics; energy supplies also provide Russia's most significant economic lever over its neighbors. The old defense-industrial complex, hard hit by imperial collapse and military retrenchment, might be in the forefront of neo-imperial programs, together with industries, such as textiles, that were highly dependent on sources of supply that now lie in "foreign" areas. New entrepreneurs, pro-reform and more attuned to the international market, are likely to be more skeptical of neo-imperialism. Over time, unless countervailing political measures are taken to construct a neo-empire, the economic balance in Russia is likely to shift against those interests that retain lingering attachments to politicized economic exchange with other republics.

Parallel to the British and French cases, "settlers" might also be active in attempting to influence metropolitan policy toward the Russian littoral. Both the circumstances of Russian populations in the new states and the experience of Britain and France suggest that the influence of Russian populations in other republics may be weaker than expected. First, despite their large numbers, the return of Russians to their ethnic home had begun well before the imperial collapse, as early as the 1960s. This "retreat of Russians from the periphery" has been driven primarily by economic distress rather than political persecution or discrimination.[45] After French and British decolonization, settlers quickly discovered that they were shut out of metropolitan politics, as politicians lost interest in their fate. Their choices were straightforward: emigration or accommodation to the new political realities on the periphery.

Parallels with European colonial cases are complicated further by the term "settler," which does not apply to many Russians living outside Russia. Because of an attachment to the metropole, a settler occupied a permanent and privileged economic, social, and political position vis-à-vis the majority local population. Some Russians may be transformed into "expatriates" who reside outside Russia but define it as their primary home. They may also become minority populations that are ethnically dissimilar to the dominant local majority and constitute a parallel rather than a dominant part of society. Such parallel populations may still create ethnic conflict and stimulate Russian sympathies or irredentism, but their political dynamics are different from the hierarchical political order of settlers.

Perhaps the most disturbing parallel between the Soviet/Russian case and the European colonial powers lies with the intelligence apparatus and the military. Both remain bastions of imperial nostalgia and "old thinking" on the relations between Russia and the former republics. Redefinition of the military's role away from a neo-imperial strategy may be far more difficult than it was in the case of France. Nuclear weapons—which will be sharply reduced—do not provide a new military mission; the evolving security architecture in Europe does not provide either a new role or a clearly defined new threat. Instead, a principal role in "stabilizing" the borderlands of Russia has emerged as the new military mission of choice. Unfortunately, as the Afghanistan and Chechnia debacles demonstrate, the Russian army is not well suited for intervention in those conflicts that are most likely around Russia's periphery.[46] Taking on these new roles also increases the risk, evident in the French case, that Russia's army will become more politicized and intervene more readily in Russian politics.[47]

Domestic political incentives may exist for mobilizing imperial nostalgia, as the Communists have done in the recent legislative elections. Certain metropolitan interests also might support a neo-imperial role. The other key variable on the metropolitan side of a neo-imperial bargain, however, is the cost of such an undertaking. Russia's economic crisis may have contributed to the appeal of neo-imperial alternatives by hindering rapid adjustment of those interests attached to the old structures. Nevertheless, economic crisis sharply constrains the resources that any Russian government is willing or able to commit to such a neo-imperial venture. As the British and French cases demonstrate, a neo-imperial bargain implies more resources from the metropole to win acquiescence from the formally independent constituents of the new sphere. Russian elites and electorates believe that they were exploited under the old imperial arrangements (as does every other republic); convincing them to offer more resources for a looser arrangement is unlikely. The ruble zone—a key economic constituent of any neo-imperial bargain—collapsed in large measure because of Russian un-willingness to contribute resources and guarantees of the kind that have sustained the franc zone.[48]

The costs of Russian neo-imperialism are highly dependent on the other partners to the exchange: elites in the new republics. Of central importance is the trade that these elites and their electorates are prepared to make between national autonomy or self-assertion and economic well-being. Those republics that are unwilling to exchange immediate economic benefits for national autonomy are not likely candidates for neo-empire. This group includes republics with compet-itive political systems and strong (if divided) ethnic identities that have been mobilized into politics: the republics of the "not-so-near abroad" (the Baltic states, Moldova, the Transcaucasus) and the Ukraine. Belarus may be the only candidate for "consensual empire," in which an electorate freely agrees to less-than-sovereign status, transforming itself into a kind of Slavic Puerto Rico.[49] The only clear candidates for a neo-imperial bargain on the French model are the Central Asian republics. Before the breakup of the Soviet Union, these republics were generally the least enthusiastic about independence; they have remained the most vocal supporters of redesigned common arrangements for the former Soviet republics.

The Central Asian republics are ethnically divided; local and family loyalties are typically more important than national ones. Their elites cannot draw on powerful national sentiments for legitimacy; they are often politically insecure and reliant on external support to retain their power. Their economies were highly skewed to suit the interests of the metropole under the Soviet empire. Despite the damage that such distortion inflicted, they have found rapid diversifi-cation to be difficult. Retention of the old imperial economic patterns may be an attractive stopgap. Finally, they have reinforced or instituted authoritarian re-gimes (with the exception of Kyrgyzstan): only democratic competition would exert strong pressure from below on a neo-imperial bargain.[50]

Adding these features of the Central Asian republics to Russian neo-imperial constituencies may create the prerequisites of a neo-imperial sphere, but skepti-cism is merited for three reasons. First, Central Asian elites may demand re-sources beyond the capabilities or the willingness of the Russian political system. Second, the fit between Central Asia and the domestic political incen-tives for imperial restoration in Russia is poor: those Russians who seek renewed stature from reunion with their shattered empire are most intent to join the Slavic republics, not the ethnically and religiously alien Central Asian societies. Finally, a bargain between Russia and the Central Asian republics may reestablish rela-tions on the basis of hierarchy, but monopoly may be more difficult to reinstate. Other states have already demonstrated a strong interest in Central Asia, among them Iran, Turkey, and Pakistan, and they would undoubtedly attempt to resist Russian efforts to reestablish a neo-imperial monopoly. How those outside neo-imperial bargain can disrupt it, and whether they should attempt to do so, are final issues for consideration.

International Norms and the Future of Neo-Empires

The demise of empires depended in part on a dramatic change in international norms: self-determination and the sovereign equality of states were accepted as core values in the post-1945 international system (even if they were frequently violated). Self-government was uniformly preferred to good government (if good government was colonial government). The end of the Soviet empire reinforced those norms. Since President George Bush's "chicken Kiev" speech, few have argued for the desirability of any arrangement other than a purely arm's-length and autonomous relationship between Russia and the former Soviet republics.

Those outside the bargaining between Russia and its ex-Soviet partners can act to dilute the reinsertion of hierarchy and monopoly in those relations. Encouraging democratic development is likely to undermine a stable neo-imperial bargain. As the French experience in Africa demonstrates, fragile authoritarian regimes are prime candidates for neo-empire. This dimension of Western influence in the former Soviet Union, particularly Central Asia, has declined, however. Interested parties can also treat these states as international equals, dealing with each of them independently (and not through Moscow). Diversification of their diplomatic and economic relations can be encouraged. Alternatives to neo-empire can be provided both to Russia and to its prospective clients. In the Russian case, efforts to enhance its international status and to include it in great power clubs might diminish the appeal of more costly foreign policy options by shaving off some nationalist political support for neo-imperialism. Reducing the incentives for nationalist self-assertion on the part of other republics also could reduce provocations that increase the political appeal of neo-imperialism in Russia. Finally, when bargaining seems to involve the use or threat of military force that is not agreed to internationally, sanctions could be imposed.

The influence and attention of outsiders may be limited, however; interests that other great powers have in a Russian neo-imperial sphere are circumscribed. A more difficult question is whether outsiders should aim at exclusively arm's-length and nonhierarchical relations among the states of the former Soviet Union. Russophobes who believe that imperial spheres are an economic burden and a diplomatic distraction in the late twentieth century might concede Russia its "near-abroad" sandbox, so long as it excludes Ukraine and the Baltic states. Future engagements along the lines of Abkhazia or Tajikistan could keep the Russian military absorbed in costly military sideshows for some time and distract Russian foreign policy from more sensitive and important areas.

Less cynically, a neo-imperial outcome might provide benefits for both Russia and the Central Asian states that are positive for outsiders as well. The record of the French neo-empire has been mixed. One study indicates that although francophone states appear less susceptible to external aggression and debilitating civil conflict, they are more likely to experience military coups.[51] The French sphere has also been associated with widespread authoritarian rule. Despite the advantages of monetary stability and relatively high foreign investment, the franc zone served to arrest necessary economic adjustment by its members in the late 1980s and to reinforce an urban-biased political economy.

For Russia, as for France, a neo-imperial enterprise could provide a low-cost and nonthreatening way to reestablish national self-esteem and redirect diplomatic and military energies. For the Central Asian states, one must ask what their futures will be in the absence of a mildly hierarchical and monopolistic relationship with Russia. The fate of African states outside the French sphere—Guinea (which rejected the French bargain), Liberia, Sierra Leone, even Nigeria—has not been happy. Given a surplus of failed states and declining interest in their fate on the part of the international community, neo-imperialism "lite" may be the least bad alternative.

Notes

1. See, for example, Michael Doyle, *Empires* (Ithaca: Cornell University Press 1986), pp. 30–47.

2. John Darwin, *Britain and Decolonization* (New York: St. Martin's, 1988), p. 16.

3. Hendryk Spruyt, *The Sovereign State and Its Competitors* (Princeton: Princeton University Press, 1994), pp. 167–71.

4. On the relationship between open trade and scale of units, see Alberto Alesina and Enrico Spolaore, "On the Number and Size of Nations," unpublished paper, September 1994.

5. Darwin, p. 25.

6. The analysis that follows is drawn from Miles Kahler, *Decolonization in Britain and France* (Princeton: Princeton University Press, 1984).

7. John Chipman emphasizes the importance of an ideology of national power for French imperialism and neo-imperialism in *French Power in Africa* (Oxford: Basil Blackwell, 1989). The view of ideological incentives employed here resembles the instrumental view of nationalism (in contrast to the primordial).

8. Kahler, pp. 101–10.

9. Ibid., pp. 150–60. See also Philip Murphy, *Party Politics and Decolonization The Conservative Party and British Colonial Policy in Tropical Africa, 1951–1964* (Oxford: Clarendon Press, 1995).

10. Kahler, pp. 196–230.

11. Ibid., pp. 266–71.

12. Ibid., pp. 299–301.

13. Ibid., pp. 320–35.

14. For a more complete account of variation in colonial nationalist movements, see Tony Smith, *The Pattern of Imperialism* (Cambridge: Cambridge University Press, 1981).

15. William Roger Louis and Ronald Robinson, "The Imperialism of Decolonization," *Journal of Imperial and Commonwealth History* 22, no. 3: 485.

16. Raymond F. Betts, *France and Decolonisation, 1900–1960* (New York: St Martin's, 1991), pp. 123–26.

17. See the excellent account in Chipman, pp. 116–22.

18. Alain Rouvez, *Disconsolate Empires* (Lanham, MD: University Press of America, 1994), p. 53.

19. Chipman, pp. 157–58; see also Rouvez, pp. 85–113.

20. In one of the rare instances in which France intervened against a client (to overthrow Emperor Bokassa I in the Central African Republic in 1979), the intervention was engulfed in controversy, especially in Africa. See Rouvez, p. 172.

21. On the pattern of French intervention, see Rouvez, chap. 5.

22. On the franc zone, see Nicolas van de Walle, "The Decline of the Franc Zone: Monetary Politics in Francophone Africa," *African Affairs* 90 (1991): 383–405; Chipman, pp. 205–26; Jean A.P. Clément, "Rationale for the CFA Franc Realignment," *IMF Survey* (February 7, 1994): 33–36.

23. David K. Fieldhouse, *Black Africa 1945–80: Economic Decolonization and Arrested Development* (London: Allen and Unwin, 1986), p. 61.

24. On the devaluation, see *IMF Survey,* spec. supp., March 21, 1994.

25. Van de Walle, pp. 402–3.

26. Among the top twenty-five recipients of French aid in 1987–1988, only three were not francophone, and only four were not present overseas territories, overseas departments, or former French colonies or protectorates. See Anton Andereggen, *France's Relationship with Subsaharan Africa* (Westport, CT: Praeger, 1994), Table 11, p. 122.

27. Ibid., pp. 93–103.

28. Francis Terry McNamara, *France in Black Africa* (Washington, DC: National Defense University, 1989), p. 135.

29. Andereggen, p. 78.

30. Chipman, pp. 243–48.

31. On these decisions, see Darwin, pp. 290–97; and Philip Darby, *British Defense Policy East of Suez, 1947–1968* (London: Oxford University Press, 1973).

32. Rouvez, pp. 232, 255–56.

33. Fieldhouse, p. 59.

34. For a powerful assault on the role of sterling, see Susan Strange, *Sterling and British Policy* (London: Oxford University Press, 1971).

35. Anuradha Bose and Peter Burnell, *Britain's Overseas Aid Since 1979: Between Idealism and Self-Interest* (Manchester: Manchester University Press, 1991), pp. 20, 61.

36. Rouvez, pp. 215–17.

37. Louis and Robinson, p. 463.

38. Van de Walle, pp. 402–3.

39. On these crises and their effects, see Darwin, pp. 292–95.

40. Ibid., pp. 294–95.

41. Ibid., p. 300.

42. This section is based on the following sources: Douglas W. Blum, ed., *Russia's Future: Consolidation or Disintegration?* (Boulder, CO: Westview Press, 1994); Ian Bremmer and Ray Taras, *Nation and Politics in the Soviet Successor States* (Cambridge: Cambridge University Press, 1993), Stephen Sestanovich, ed., *Rethinking Russia's National Interests* (Washington, DC: CSIS, 1994); Stephen White, Graeme Gill, and Darrell Slider, *The Politics of Transition: Shaping a Post-Soviet Future* (Cambridge: Cambridge University Press, 1993); Karen Dawisha and Bruce Parrott, *Russia and the New States of Eurasia* (Cambridge: Cambridge University Press, 1994). Apologies to these expert authors for any misinterpretations of their excellent works.

43. John Dunlop, "Russia: Confronting a Loss of Empire," in Ian Bremmer and Ray Taras, eds., *Nation and Politics in the Soviet Successor States* (Cambridge: Cambridge University Press, 1993), p. 69.

44. Dawisha and Parrott, p. 65.

45. Dunlop, p. 47.

46. Sergei Rogov, "Military Interests and the Military," in Sestanovich, pp. 68–82.

47. John Lepingwell, "The Russian Military in the 1990s," in Blum, p. 121.

48. Dawisha and Parrott, pp. 172–73.

49. On the attitudes of Belarusian elites and population, see Stephen R. Burant, "Foreign Policy and National Identity: A Comparison of Ukraine and Belarus," *Europe-Asia Studies* 47, no. 7 (1995): pp. 1125–44.

50. Gregory Gleason, "Uzbekistan," and Gene Huskey, "Kyrgyzstan," in Bremmer and Taras, pp. 331–60, 398–418.

51. Robert D. Grey, "A Balance Sheet on External Assistance: France in Africa," *Journal of Modern African Studies* 28, no. 1 (1990): 101–14.

V

Changing Forms and Prospects of Empire

13

The Prospects for Neo-Imperial and Nonimperial Outcomes in the Former Soviet Space

Hendrik Spruyt

The collapse of the Soviet Union and the pattern of subsequent state relations in Eurasia poses daunting challenges to theorists and policymakers alike. Despite the high visibility of its internal problems, the end of the Soviet empire came as a surprise. Unlike other modern continental empires—such as the German, the Austrian, and Ottoman—the Soviet empire collapsed without overt defeat in war. Consequently, few scholars were able to foresee either the end of the Cold War or the disintegration of the USSR. Fewer still anticipated the tempo at which these processes unfolded.[1] But not only is the demise of the USSR befuddling: the future of this area is equally nebulous. Should one expect reconstitution of empire, given the virulent rhetoric emanating from Moscow and the power disparities in the region? Or should one expect a more benign set of international relations, premised either on cooperation or disengagement? This chapter begins an evaluation of theories that might enable informed speculation on the region's future. I start with a taxonomy of possible outcomes and policy choices. I then review what the existing theories of empire and integration would predict. Two dominant theories of international relations—neorealism and neoliberalism—profess to have considerable theoretical power in explaining whether states will form cooperative relations even to the point of political integration. What insights may be gleaned from them? The chapter then briefly reviews the developments in the Former Soviet Union (FSU) since 1991 and examines to what extent prevalent theories can explain the unfolding of these events. Finally, I review the prospects for neo-imperial and nonimperial outcomes based on the causal variables of theories explaining empire and integration.

A Taxonomy of Possible Outcomes

The current and future developments in this part of Eurasia can be captured as a set of dyadic relations between Russia and the erstwhile union republics. Russia's array of choices might range from a return to the old empire on one end of the spectrum to complete disengagement from the Newly Independent States (NIS) on the other end. It is important to emphasize that the following analysis is an attempt to model whether relations between Russia and the NIS—by which I mean the non-Russian successor states—will continue as a set of dyadic and special interactions or perhaps as nondyadic and more normalized sets of international relations.[2]

Given the vast imbalances of power between Russia and most of the NIS, the return of empire must be considered to be a possibility.[3] In certain scenarios, Russia could choose to reassert its physical control; domestic changes and renewed international competition could induce Russia to behave as it did in past decades.

On the other end of the scale, Russia could conceivably minimize its special ties with some of the former imperial holdings. For example, Russia could downgrade its connections with some of the poor states in Central Asia and instead pursue closer ties with more advanced industrial countries. In such a scenario, the international relations between Russia and the NIS would become normalized: they would assume the usual pattern of relations between fully sovereign states without implying that they had no dealings with each other at all. The point is that the NIS would not be under a hegemonic or imperial shadow.

Russia also has alternatives between the extremes of empire and normalized relations (disengagement) that are perhaps more likely. Rather than exercise imperial rule, Moscow might opt for contractual arrangements to facilitate trade and security in the region. Functional and security reasons could induce amenability to compromise and equitable bargaining. Given the asymmetry of power between Russia and the NIS, however, Moscow has disproportionate means at its disposal to manipulate such arrangements in its favor. Even though this would fall short of empire, Russia could try to use semicoercive measures to cajole states to accept less than optimal terms. Russian behavior would resemble that of hegemonic control—control, not of all aspects of their internal policy but of foreign policy elements that pertained to direct Russian interests.[4] Russia would continue to be the focal point of the new states' foreign relations, and the core actor around which new economic and security regimes might emerge. In this scenario, the relations of some of the states of the FSU would resemble the postcolonial ties that developed in the aftermath of French and English colonial withdrawal, as Miles Kahler discusses in chapter 12 of this volume.

Needless to say, this taxonomy, like all taxonomies, refers to ideal-typical classifications. The empirical manifestations of such types will tend to blend across these categories. Nevertheless, the taxonomy does serve to distinguish patterns of behavior. By disengagement I mean that Russia will no longer privilege relations with its former imperial territories over other international rela-

ions. This scenario diminishes the previous close ties between center and pe-
iphery. I use the term symmetric for a situation in which Russia opts to continue
rivileged ties with former subject territories in a manner whereby the other state
s not penalized for choosing an alternative policy. The relation is then one of
oluntary contracting, with the possibility of exit, and in the long run is based on
liffuse reciprocity.[5] Should the symmetry of benefits diminish and the contract-
ng process become less clearly voluntary, then I deem the relation to have
ecome asymmetric or even hegemonic. In other words, one state will tend to set
he terms of the bargain and retaliate against transgressions. The difference be-
ween hegemonic relations and imperial ones lies in the use of force. Hegemons,
s understood in the current political economy literature, cajole with issue link-
ge, retaliate through tariffs, or negotiate "voluntary" export restraints, but they
lo not use force. The use of physical force (i.e., the military) is the hallmark of
mperial and postimperial relations.

The NIS face a different and limited set of options. Given the vast power
mbalance between Russia and these states their choices are not symmetric. They
ave two options: maintain ties with Moscow or discontinue such ties. That is to
ay, states will either have reasons to continue some form of association with the
rstwhile imperial center—reasons can range from functional cooperation to
oleration of imperial and neo-imperial relations—or they might try to disengage
rom the previous dyadic connections. Disengagement can mean seeking alterna-
ive markets and resources or actively working against, or even fighting, Russian
versight and control. These states will not be able to unilaterally dictate the
erms of any contractual arrangements, nor will they be able to engage in imper-
al pursuits at Russia's expense. They are thus limited to the choices that lie
etween cooperation and relative disengagement, rather than between hard bar-
aining and imperial policies, vis-à-vis Russia. This menu of dyadic interactions
vould thus lead to eight possible outcomes, represented in Table 13.1.[6]

As long as Russia pursues ties with the NIS on a benign and equitable basis,
NIS behavior might be labeled cooperation. If, however, Russia uses more
eavy-handed tactics and even physical force to maintain close ties, then NIS behav-
or might be more accurately described as acquiescence in the face of overwhelming
dds. This might not be the form of cooperation that states would prefer, but they
night be too militarily and economically weak to resist.[7] Similarly, in the right-hand
olumn NIS behavior moves from disengagement to more forceful resistance, de-
ending again on the degree of coercion used by Russia.

Theories of Empire and Integration

Theories of Empire

This chapter follows Bruce Parrott's conceptualization of empire as "a dominant
ociety's control of the effective sovereignty of two or more subordinate socie-

Table 13.1

A Taxonomy of Possible Russian and NIS Relationships

		NIS Strategies	
		Cooperation/ Acquiescence	Disengagement/ Resistance
Russian Strategies	Disengagement	Spurned suitors	Parting of the ways or normalized relations
	Contractual Cooperation	Functional integration	Spurned suitor
	Hard Bargain	Hegemony	Mutual antagonism or hard bargaining
	Coercion/Domination	Empire	Cold war or war

ties that are substantially concentrated in particular regions or homelands within the empire."[8] Parrott deviates slightly from Michael Doyle's definition, but the implications are similar: empire becomes possible when great differences exist in the relative power of an imperial center and a periphery.[9] The stronger actor can utilize its superior economic and military power to pursue material gains. Empires can thus be partially explained by a rational calculus on the part of the imperial power of the costs and gains of foreign domination of a weaker power.[10]

Although imbalances of power form a necessary condition for empire they are an insufficient explanation. Not all power imbalances lead to aggressive foreign policies. Whether the opportunity for empire is acted upon depends, as Doyle points out, on the motives for empire in both metropole and periphery. Domestic political developments in the center, or metropole, are a critical intervening variable. States will rarely act on power imbalances alone, but they might choose imperialist policies if domestic elites with transnational interests manage to exert undue influence on the state's overall foreign policy. Such elites might include a military that favors imperial pursuits because they lead to larger budgets and expanded discretion, or business elites with translocal holdings and economic interests. Charles Kupchan and Jack Snyder note how, particularly in authoritarian systems and more rarely in democratic states, specific elites can capture the political agenda and subvert it to serve their own interests. Snyder writes "Wilhelmine Germany and imperial Japan ... gave rise to logrolling among narrow interest groups producing overcommitted expansionist policies. ... In contrast, the democratic systems of Britain and the United States ... strengthened diffuse interests opposed to expansion."[11]

Likewise, some elites in the periphery might benefit from empire. In point of fact, the alliance between local elites and colonial powers or advanced capitalist states is a central point for the dependency literature.[12] Karen Dawisha's discussion of autocolonization in chapter 14 notes that empires are seldom viable without some measure of local cooperation.[13] Indeed, entire ethnic groups might be co-opted even into battle to serve imperial interests. The Sikhs and Gurkhas became elite imperial troops in the British army, as did the Moluccans in the Dutch. Thus, although I suggested that overall the periphery's connections to the empire might be more accurately labeled acquiescence than cooperation, I do not deny that some elites and even entire ethnic groups actively cooperated with and even benefited from the imperial overlord.

A third causal factor resides in the level of competition between rival imperial centers. The decision to pursue foreign domination over other territories, sometimes at great distance, is not only driven by calculations of feasibility and domestic preferences, but also by the assessment of relations between the various powers that have imperial capabilities. For example, foreign control over Africa was feasible given the considerable economic and military advantages of the west European states. Imperial foreign policy became desirable and was later officially embraced due to the influence of domestic interest groups—all the while ensconced in moral self-legitimation. But imperial maneuverings in Africa reached fever pitch only when the competition between the imperial powers started to heat up on the European continent.[14]

The causes behind Russia's imperial politics also reside at the systemic and domestic levels, and in the interaction of competing centers. The modern Soviet empire thus found its roots in power imbalances between center and periphery, in the expansionist ideologies of domestic elites (endowed with a Marxist revolutionary agenda), and in the competition between Russia and rival major powers (as in the "Great Game" for Central Asia).[15] The question is whether similar causal variables operate in the current Eurasian environment.

Theories of Integration

Political association can range from relatively low-level cooperation between states to virtual surrender of sovereignty. Mario Polèse distinguishes three levels of integration.[16] At the lowest level, states agree to integrate their economies by lowering tariffs and facilitating interstate trade and transactions. This would describe the early efforts of the post–World War II Benelux countries and the European Economic Community. In the second level of cooperation, states might choose to engage in common economic policies and create common institutions. The European Court and the possible development of a Monetary Union are a step up, for example, from simply reducing tariff barriers. States at this stage are rescinding some of their autonomy. At the deepest level of integration, political units cede much of their autonomy to centralized authorities that have the capacity to carry out transfer payments among these entities. Federal systems are of this type. It is true that the USSR integrated the union republics at the deepest level, but the current question addresses the prospects for reintegration of the NIS, and asks at what level they will choose to do so.[17]

For obvious reasons, scholars of integration have focused particularly on regional cooperation in western Europe. As a cooperative venture, the European Union has proceeded further than any other organization both in terms of the level of institutionalization and the scope of joint decision making.[18] As a consequence, the academic emphasis has been on examining the underlying functional reasons for such cooperation. Karl Deutsch, echoing Emile Durkheim's arguments about the transformative effects of increases in dynamic density, suggested that increased transactions, communications, and trade would lead to pluralistic security communities.[19] Ernst Haas augmented the economic analysis of spillover effects with an account of how bureaucratic and interest groups had incentives to expand political integration.[20] Neoliberals have recently utilized insights from new institutional economics to clarify the functional reasons for regimes.[21] The bottom line of the liberal view is that states will pursue close cooperation, and even integration in the form of confederation or federation, if such ties yield economic gains.

At face value, neoliberal theories of cooperation seem to fly in the face of the realist view of the international system, in which states are defensive positionalists operating under conditions of anarchy, unlikely to cooperate to any great extent. Moreover, given that realists deny the basic relevance of international institutions, significant supranational decision making is problematic for the realist paradigm.[22]

But realists have suggested that close cooperation among states, even integration as in the European case, does not in fact challenge realist theory. States will cooperate and even integrate if they are each faced by similar threats. Thus, the realist explanation for the extent of the West European states' cooperation is that their shared concerns about the Soviet threat and the American presence mitigated European fears about Germany's revival. In this view, economic and functional cooperation is derivative of shared security objectives.

Stephen Walt, for example, bases cooperation on states' needs to balance against external threats.[23] Thus, when confronted by a threat to their territorial integrity, states will seek allies and will engage in both military and economic cooperation. Although such balancing behavior is the norm, weak states, or states that have no available allies, might bandwagon with the threatening power. That is, in the face of a preponderant threat, the weaker state might throw in the towel and hope for the best, or hope to share in the spoils of war that might ensue from conquest of a third party.

The two dominant schools of thought in international relations thus come to dramatically different conclusions regarding the motives and underlying causes for regional integration. In the liberal, functionalist view, states will tend to cooperate in pursuit of economic gains. States will be less concerned with the relative distribution of such gains and will cooperate if they believe that absolute benefits will accrue. In the realist view, regional cooperation is motivated by security calculations. States will cooperate with other states in order to balance a threat. A weak state might also cooperate, even if it fears the other state, if it believes it cannot check the intentions of the aggressor.

These different research paradigms subsequently lead to two different sets of explanations for past developments and different predictions for cooperation in the FSU. From a liberal view, the newly independent states will cooperate with Russia if they are highly dependent on Russian resources and know-how, if they depend heavily on access to the Russian market, and if they previously were dependent on Russian transfer payments. They will be less concerned with whether cooperation benefits Russia more than it benefits them or vice versa. As long as absolute gains can be achieved cooperation makes rational sense.[24]

Naturally, not all of these conditions need to occur simultaneously. Some states will be more concerned with access to the Russian market than they might be with the prospects for know-how and technology transfers. But in general, the greater the number of such considerations, the greater the incentive to pursue some measure of regional cooperation. Those states for which such conditions do not hold will be more inclined to seek alternative markets and integration with more useful trading partners. Thus, well-developed states with resources that might be attractive to the world market, or highly developed states that covet Western markets might be less concerned with maintaining close ties with Moscow.

For a realist, however, cooperation with Russia would depend on whether a state would see Russia as a useful ally against an external threat. If a state were threatened by another state and if Russia could help provide balance, then one should expect cooperation between the threatened state and Moscow. Cooperation with Russia might also result if a newly independent state feared Russia itself, but did not have any meaningful way to meet such a threat. In the absence of allies, and given the great power asymmetries facing most of the former union republics, there might be no alternative but to yield to Russian pressure. Such acquiescent behavior might include allowing Russia to station troops on NIS soil or giving Russia an effective veto over NIS foreign policies, even if Russia was perceived to be the main threat to sovereignty.

Events in the Former Soviet Space Since the Breakup

In 1990 and 1991, even as economic conditions took a dramatic downturn and as Gorbachev's political position became increasingly precarious, Moscow still pursued the idea of maintaining the territorial integrity of the USSR. It became evident, however, that Russia's economic free-fall made Moscow a less than attractive partner, particularly for the more affluent states. From its own perspective, Russia felt less and less compelled to bankroll a defunct empire. Thus, by 1990 it too defended the republics' right to self-determination.[25] After the failed coup of summer 1991, most of the union republics formally declared their independence.

Trying to resuscitate a dying patient, Gorbachev still envisioned some form of union with a common military command and a closely integrated economy.[26] But it was clear that some states (such as Ukraine, Moldova) would not tolerate a unified military command and had already embarked on the road to developing their own security forces. Once the Ukrainian parliament issued its declaration of independence, any thoughts of territorial integrity became illusory; Russia and most of the former union republics opted instead for a form of commonwealth.

The relations between Russia and the NIS since the breakup of the USSR in 1991 can be described by sorting them into several categories.[27] First, one group of states endorsed close cooperation with the former center from the very beginning. Some of these governments, such as Kazakhstan under Nursultan Nazarbaev, even favored a continuation of a union of states with an integrated military structure that would be headed by Russia along the Warsaw Pact model. This group of states also preferred a closely integrated economy.[28] These states thus endorsed the formation of a Commonwealth of Independent States (CIS) and signed most of the subsequent agreements. Uzbekistan, Kazakhstan, Tajikistan, and Kyrgyzstan fall into this category, as do Belarus and Armenia as slightly more reluctant partners. While Turkmenistan proved reluctant to join the CIS, given its desire to utilize its gas reserves at its own discretion, it has from the very beginning pursued close cooperation with Russia in security matters.

A second category of states comprises states that were far more reluctant to join the CIS—such as Ukraine, Azerbaijan, and Moldova. The latter two even withdrew from the CIS at one point.[29] At the present, however, they have been brought back into the fold, not in the least part because of Russian pressure.[30] Russia's military interference in the Trans-Dniestria region and support for Armenia impelled these states to reenter the CIS and be more accommodative. While Ukraine never formally left the CIS, it considered the organization to be a transitory mechanism. Russia has so far had less success using heavy-handed tactics with Ukraine than it has with the smaller countries, though it did set up customs barriers with Ukraine as it had done with Azerbaijan.[31] And although both Ukrainian and Russian leaders have supported the idea of cooperation, it is clear that issues such as the Black Sea fleet and the Ukranian trade deficit with Russia have strained their relations.

Finally, a third group of states refused to enter the CIS and vigorously pursued greater disengagement in the years following imperial collapse. Of this group, only Georgia has been brought back into the Russian orbit. Again, heavy-handed tactics from Moscow, most specifically its reluctance to crack down on separatist movements in South Ossetia and Abkhazia, forced Georgia to be more accommodative to Russian demands.[32] The Baltic states, however, despite some pressure, have largely succeeded in their pursuit of autonomy. In the long run their economies are the most likely to become closely integrated with the West.[33]

Table 13.2

Relations Between Russia and the Peripheral Successor States Since 1991

		NIS Strategies	
		Cooperation/ Acquiescence	Disengagement/ Resistance
Russian Strategies	Disengagement	—	—
	Contractual Cooperation	Central Asia Belarus Armenia	Baltics Ukraine 1992
	Hard Bargain	Georgia 1994 Moldova 1994 Azerbaijan 1994	Ukraine 1994? Georgia 1991 Moldova 1992 Azerbaijan 1992
	Empire	—	Chechnya?

They have even engaged in joint military exercises with Norwegian and other Baltic states' troops.[34] In September 1995 the president of Latvia restated the desire of all Baltic states to become members of the Economic Union (EU) and NATO. None of the Baltic states have engaged in open hostilities with Russia. As long as Russia abstains from overt imperial designs, such clashes are unlikely. If we were to enlarge our research design to include the possibility for continuing imperial relations within the current Russian Federation, then the war in Chechnya would constitute a case in which imperial desire clashed with a periphery's option to break away. For the sake of limiting the scope of this chapter, however, I will not deal with developments within the Russian Federation. But the Chechen case would be theoretically analogous to situations that might arise should Russia resort to renewed imperial quests.

In Table 13.2, the different policy outcomes are captured into the 4 x 2 matrix described earlier in the section "Theories of Empire."

A Theoretical Evaluation of the Post-Soviet Era

Russia has not sought to reestablish empire over those states that became sovereign with the dissolution of the USSR. This conforms with expectations of theories of empire. To reiterate, empire is largely due to the concurrence of three causes: large differences in relative power, the influence of domestic elites with transnational interests, and major-power competition. Whereas the first condition still exists in Russia, the salience of the latter two has receded. Changes within

Russia in favor of more democratic, capitalist interests have diminished the influence of groups who are more in favor of imperialist foreign policies. Moreover, the end of the Cold War and the current absence of any real challengers to Russia's regional preeminence have diminished the necessity for Moscow to hold on to these areas. Superpower competition has receded.[35]

A question less easily answered is whether the various relations between Russia and the NIS can be captured by integrationist perspectives.[36] From a realist point of view, the behavior of some of the successor states can be understood as balancing against external threat. The Central Asian states, for example, fear possible cross-border conflicts. In particular, Tajikistan has implored and received help from Uzbekistan and Russia to curtail Afghani support for some of its internal opposition. Similarly, Armenia's war with Azerbaijan explains why it would pursue close relations with Russia. In other words, the Central Asian states' and Armenia's reliance on Russian support for their security is the basis for their preference for a strong CIS and other ties to Russia.

Similarly, Russian support for movements that threatened the integrity of Georgia, Moldova, and Azerbaijan clarifies their reluctance to cooperate closely with Russia. Instead, they sought external support to balance against Russia and their internal foes. Thus, Moldova, in its early independent years, sought support from and perhaps even integration with Romania. Azerbaijan, in turn, tried to obtain support from Turkey.[37] Georgia's, Moldova's, and Azerbaijan's failure to obtain significant allies to balance against their domestic opponents, which were supported by Moscow, explains why these three states have retreated from their antagonistic stance and moved to closer association with Russia.

The Ukrainian position likewise follows realist tenets. It is the only one of the NIS that has considerable size and military strength in its own right. Indeed, its intentions to build a 450,000-member army would make its forces larger than those of Germany and would violate Conventional Forces in Europe (CFE) force limits. Ukraine's strength and the absence of an immediate threat to its territorial integrity lies at the basis of its independent course.[38] Granted, there are problems in the Crimea, but the overall integrity of the Ukrainian state is not threatened to the extent that Georgia or Moldova are by secessionist movements.

There are some states, however, such as Belarus, whose cooperation is not immediately comprehensible in realist terms. Belarus is not faced with immediate security threats. Even if it did fear renewed Russian imperialism and it bandwagoned with Russia, Belarus's bandwagoning would seem premature.

Such anomalies for state behavior might be more readily explained by liberal, functionalist arguments. For example, Belarus's cooperation and Turkmenistan's relative reluctance to sign many provisions of the CIS agreement might be due to functional and economic calculations. Belarus is highly dependent on access to the Russian market. Turkmenistan, conversely, seeks to develop its resources for the world market and is apprehensive about integration within an institutional framework in which resource prices might be artificially depressed.[39] In the FSU, Russia and other energy-producing states effectively subsidized the other states through artificially low prices. As a percentage of GDP, Turkmenistan's burden of subsidizing the other republics may even have been higher than Russia's.[40] Overall, many of the newly independent states depended heavily on economic subsidies from Moscow. Particularly, the poorer Central Asian states relied significantly on budget transfers from Russia. For Tajikistan, such transfers have supplied almost 47 percent of the overall budget.[41] The level of economic interdependence—admittedly artificially inflated due to Soviet policies that favored vertical integration of firms—was much higher in the USSR than in other federal systems or economic unions. For example, in 1992 the share of intraregional trade as a percentage of total trade was 72 percent in the USSR, but only 59 percent for the states in the EU, and only 44 percent for the Canadian provinces.[42] In short, many states continue to depend on Russia not only for external security but also for raw materials, transfer payments, and access to the Russian market. For example, Uzbekistan's attempt to turn to the world market to sell its cotton proved highly unsuccessful. Similarly, the inability of Moldova, Georgia, and Azerbaijan to go it alone is not solely due to their military weaknesses. They have relatively weak economies, and even oil-rich Azerbaijan may require Russian support to effectively bring its product to market.

Such overdetermination of causal relations makes it difficult to test the strength of a realist view against a liberal functional perspective. Whatever the theory of regionalism holds, it is clear that there are systemic reasons, both economic and security-related, for the NIS to cooperate with Moscow. Even Ukraine, larger and more powerful than the other NIS, may have to cooperate more closely in the future. The ability of the Baltics to escape out of Russia's orbit must be largely attributed to their ability to integrate more closely with Western markets around the Baltic Sea and, ultimately, with the EU. In any case, the foreign policies of the NIS can be usefully approached by using systemic theories as a first cut.

The greatest puzzle, however, is posed by Russia itself. Particularly puzzling is its preference to maintain close ties with some of the weaker states. From either a security perspective or from an economic perspective some of the newly independent states can hardly be called great assets. According to realist theory, Russia should be less adamant about retaining close ties with other states given the absence of a clear external threat (i.e., the end of the Cold War). If former Warsaw Pact allies and the current newly independent states are, from a theoretical perspective, analogous, then it makes little sense to let the former go but maintain close ties with the latter. What for example, does Tajikistan contribute to the security of Russia?

Nor can Russian behavior be easily understood to be the cost-benefit logic of a rationalist unitary state. Russian calculations, if economically rational, should be the inverse of those of the NIS. If poor states wish to integrate with Russia, the Russian motivation to integrate with them should be relatively low. Some of these states are economically underdeveloped, contribute few critical resources, and have in the past been a drain on Russian coffers.[43] It is less puzzling that Russia would prefer close contacts with the well-developed Ukrainian market or with such resource-rich areas as Turkmenistan and Kazakhstan.

In other words, Russian foreign policy is not well captured by a unitary state calculus of broad systemic cost and gains. Domestic variables must, therefore, be considered as critical elements of Moscow's foreign policy.[44] Several variables come to mind. First, Moscow might be less concerned with overall security or economic benefits than with the status of ethnic Russians abroad. This has clearly been an issue in Russia's withdrawal from the Baltics, as well as in Central Asia. In Kazakhstan, for example, a full 40 percent of the population are ethnic Russians.[45] As Carole Fink and Miles Kahler suggest in chapters 11 and 12 of this volume, concern for ethnics abroad played an important role in the postempire politics of Weimar Germany and decolonizing France. Such issues allow entrepreneurs to highlight ethnic divisions for political gain.

A second issue that is related to the first is that Moscow has a stake in mitigating virulent ethnic nationalism, given the composition of the Russian Federation. That is, should nationalist tensions spill across the borders of the fifteen former union republics into Russia, then the fragmentation of the USSR might but be the precursor to subsequent breakups and interethnic conflicts.

The Prospects for Neo-Imperial and Nonimperial Outcomes

The Probability of Empire

As stated in the previous section, Russia has so far not sought to reconstitute the empire in any formal sense. But, as Table 13.3 indicates, some of the systemic conditions for a return of empire—most notably, the asymmetry of power between Russia and the NIS—are still in place. Only Ukraine really constitutes a major power in its own right.

It is less clear whether the other conditions for empire exist. First, the political power of imperial coalitions in the center is ambiguous. Whether or not the democratic reforms in Russia will ultimately succeed is an open-ended question. In a worse-case scenario, democratic reformers might be confronted by a prolonged economic crisis and political extremists on the left and on the right who call for Russia to reassert itself. In such a situation, an alliance between Slavic imperialists and Communist hardliners might not be illusory.

Moreover, some elites in the periphery, particularly if they fear challenges to their own positions, might have incentives to favor some measures of imperial overlordship. In this sense, an alliance with Russia would provide both external balancing in Stephen Walt's sense and internal balancing in Steven David's understanding.[46] David suggests that alliances among Third World states are

Table 13.3

Former Union Republics: The Balance of Power

	GDP (billions of U.S. dollars)	GDP (millions of current rubles)	Defense Budgets (millions of U.S. dollars)		Armed Forces
	1993	1992	1993	1994	1994
Armenia	1.9	59,068	69	71	32,700
Azerbaijan	4.4	183,186	128	132	56,000
Belarus	16.0	—	520	430	92,500
Estonia	1.7	—	20	76	2,500
Georgia	2.3	134,397	87	88	—
Kazakhstan	18.2	1,119,600	707	450	40,000
Kyrgyzstan	2.9	180,500	51	57	12,000
Latvia	1.6	182,004	48	51	6,850
Lithuania	2.9	325,569	86	96	8,900
Moldova	4.1	226,700	48	51	11,100
Russia	1,160.0[a]	15,552,000	77,000	79,000	1,714,000
Tajikistan	2.5	—	110	115	2,500
Turkmenistan	3.8	—	143	153	28,000
Ukraine	54.2	4,804,590	3,900	3,100	517,000
Uzbekistan	13.8	416,892	390	375	45,000

Source: *The Military Balance 1994–1995* (London: International Institute for Strategic Studies, 1994). Source for GDP 1992 (rubles): *Statistical Handbook 1993: States of the Former USSR* (Washington, DC: The World Bank, 1993).

[a]This estimate of Russia's GDP cannot be correct. Per capita, Russia's GDP is U.S.$7,800 and Ukraine's is U.S.$4,300. Given that Russia's population is less than three times that of Ukraine (149 million versus 52 million), its GDP should be closer to five times the size of Ukraine's. This demonstrates the difficulty of assessing this data. Compare World Bank estimate.

based on balancing behavior against all threats—both external threats to the state and internal challenges to the existing government.

Finally, at the systemic level, competition between rival imperial centers for formal or informal control over some of the NIS may be conceivable, given the affinities of some of these areas with Turkic and Persian identities.[47] In the long run, the rapid growth of China may become a reason for concern. A variety of scholars have likened the combination of China's dynamic economic growth and continued authoritarianism to the problems posed by Wilhelmine Germany at the turn of the century.[48] Expansion of NATO could also be perceived as an external threat and could precipitate an imperial reaction. Expansion to include eastern European states and even some states of the FSU could be seen by Russia in traditional encirclement terms. Rather than prevent Russian imperialism, such a move could actually precipitate the very reaction that an expansion of NATO would allegedly seek to avoid.[49]

The Improbability of Empire

A wide variety of factors, however, may mitigate the probability that Russia will reassert formal domination over the NIS. The apparent decrease in rampant inflation and the support of international organizations such as the International Monetary Fund (IMF) during this transition period may improve the appeal of democratic capitalism. As Carole Fink points out in chapter 11, it was precisely the lack of international support systems for the failing Weimar Republic that facilitated the rise of extremism in Germany.

Second, a move to reestablish empire will have systemic repercussions. Any Russian pursuit of imperialistic foreign policies will spark a renewed round of military balancing not only by the United States and its current NATO allies but even by some of the eastern European states, maybe even by Ukraine, and possibly by China. A renewed and costly cold war would deny Russia the very benefits that a rational pursuer of empire would seek to achieve.[50] The harder Russia pushes some of the NIS toward reintegration, the more inclined they may be to seek external security guarantees. Thus, should Russia bargain too harshly with Ukraine, the latter would then have added incentives to seek NATO membership and would perhaps be less forthcoming on nuclear weapons disposal. Although Russia has vociferously argued against NATO's expansion and against Ukraine's acquiring its own nuclear weapons, its pursuit of empire could precipitate those very conditions.

Third, whatever the future systemic environment will be for Russia, its own security vis-à-vis other major powers must be taken as relatively good. Though limited in quantity, the nuclear deterrent continues, and is still more than sufficient to deny any major power a rational reason to seek territorial gains at Russia's expense.[51]

It is also empirically uncertain how easy it would be to reinstitutionalize the empire by military means. True, there is a considerable power imbalance. But the facility of military intervention is also partially determined by a state's ability to wield offensive force successfully. In military parlance, the latter will depend on whether the overall milieu favors offensive or defensive strategies.[52] Given the setbacks in Afghanistan and Chechnya—and against relatively underequipped forces at that—and the current status of the Russian military, offense might prove to be at a disadvantage compared to defense.[53]

Finally, the question of a renewed Russian empire must be seen in the overall obsolescence of empires in general; Miles Kahler suggests this as well in chapter 12. The modern era is a watershed. Whereas extensive empires were commonplace for much of history and for vast areas of the globe, empire today seems to have virtually disappeared as a logic of organization. The reasons for this complex phenomenon are manifold and beyond the immediate scope of this chapter. But let me suggest several possible reasons why this might be so. Foremost among these must be the gradual establishment of a comprehensive Westphalian system. States are now considered juridically equivalent, and the existence of a state system is antithetical to the universalist and translocal premises of empire.[54] Moreover, in the past, wealth and conquest seemed inextricably linked. Wealthy states were synonymous with great states. England, the Netherlands, and Spain all amassed fortunes in the process of territorial acquisition. This relationship may no longer hold. The immediate welfare of populations is driven less by the mercantilist pursuit of power and plenty than it is by the ability to tap into international investment, global capital flows, and competitive world production.[55]

Contractual Bargaining

Russia will deal with some of the newly independent states on a quid pro quo basis. And of course, if the other NIS are eager to placate Russian demands or if their preferences converge, as is usually the case with the Central Asian states, then there is no reason to pursue more aggressive policies. The question of imperial reemergence in such cases is essentially moot. However, even if interests do not converge, Russia might have to negotiate on relatively equal terms.

Moscow might lack the capacity to determine unilaterally the outcome of bargaining with some states, or the NIS might have alternative partners available, which is more likely if the other state has considerable means and resources of its own or if it has Western political allies and economic partners. Ukraine is an example of the former, the Baltics an example of the latter. Symmetric bargaining is also more likely between democracies.[56] Democracies are less likely to be captured by special interest groups or to pursue belligerent foreign policies. Democracies, especially well-established ones, tend to seek mutual compromise.[57] Democracies may also make more credible commitments. Because policies are based on broad consensus and consultation, it is unlikely that elites can easily divest themselves from established policy.[58] Thus, Russian democratic reform is one condition that will encourage contractual bargaining. Similarly, the presence of democracies in the NIS will make it less likely that such states will resort to ethnic nationalist policies that provoke Russia.

Third, as long as the region is presented with few external threats, Russia will be more amenable to bargaining and negotiation. In moments of crisis, by contrast, elites will be more likely to see the room for negotiation as limited. Particularly in a multipolar environment, they will wish to clamp down on allies and friends to make sure defection does not occur.

Fourth, the ability of the NIS to maintain autonomy will be partially determined by their ability to integrate themselves into the world market and gain access to international capital. As Hudson Meadwell has argued regarding Quebec, the ability of current and former federalist entities to break with central government will hinge on whether they can gain access to other markets.[59] Diminishing trade barriers has made this more likely than it was previously. Furthermore, IMF and World Bank transfers might make the transition to capitalism easier and diminish dependence on the former imperial center.

Hard Bargaining

Russia, however, may be inclined to unilaterally set the terms of international relations with some states. The manifest weakness of many NIS makes this an option. The relations between Russia, Azerbaijan, Georgia, and Moldova provide a clear example. When these states did not sign on to the CIS or when they withdrew from the organization, Russia retaliated by imposing tariffs (on Moldova) or by overtly and tacitly supporting secessionist movements in these three areas. All three have subsequently reentered the CIS after considerable pressure,[60] and one would be hard pressed to call their relations "consensual."

Second, even if functional reasons to cooperate exist, and I have argued in the section "A Theoretical Evaluation of the Post-Soviet Era" that for many newly independent states there are such reasons, these states still face a variety of collective action problems that raise transaction and information costs: the number of states involved, the low level of institutionalization, and the variety of economies.[61] Even in a benign scenario Russia might, therefore, be called upon to assume regional hegemonic leadership.

A third reason for Russia's pursuit of asymmetric advantages is its preference to embed agreements in a broader context. For example, if Russia does assume leadership functions, whether benign or malevolent, it will likely make such agreements contingent on issues such as the treatment of ethnic Russians, respect for existing borders, and the stationing of Russian troops. In other words, Russia has an incentive to use its asymmetric position to strike deals that go beyond the confines of immediate material costs and gains.

A final reason why Moscow could be less flexible is the desire to externalize economic hardships to other states. Just as the developed capitalist countries did in the 1930s, Russia could lean toward beggar-thy-neighbor mercantilist policies by raising tariffs, engaging in competitive devaluations, and dumping surpluses.

Conclusion

There are indubitably many factors that may influence developments in the former Soviet space. International rivalries and alliances, domestic upheavals, internally competing bureaucracies, ethnic tensions, even individual leaders' idiosyncrasies will weigh in the balance. One way of reducing the plethora of causes and possibilities to manageable proportions is to taxonomize the range of policy outcomes, and examine whether particular theoretical orientations allow one to make informed speculations on the likelihood of one outcome compared to another. Consequently, this chapter suggested an eightfold taxonomy, and analyzed the possible insights of theories of imperialism and systems-level theories of integration. All analysis of the region must start by recognizing that system imbalances are present. Excepting perhaps Ukraine, Russia has no military or economic match. From this preponderance of power springs the possibilty of cooperation, the apprehension of hegemony, and the fear of empire. Consequently, one may conjecture, as neorealists and neoliberals do, that the weaker the state, the graver the implications of the systemic condition. All analyses stressing the importance of domestic variables must keep this inverse relationship in mind.

Given the asymmetry of power and the past history of Eurasia, the first question is whether Russia will reassert itself as a formal imperial power. Should formal empire not be feasible for or desired by Russia then the question is how the non-Russian successor states will structure their relations to the former imperial center. Will they seek to dissociate themselves and pursue alternative security and economic partners, and to what extent will they be able to do so? Or will they, for military and economic reasons, continue close relations with Russia? And if so, on what terms? From a systemic perspective, in which unitary states are rational evaluators of their economic and security milieu, the likelihood of imperial reassertion must be considered remote. Renewed imperialism will be met by the combined balancing of the NIS and the West, and will gravely concern a growing China. Expansion of NATO and of counterbalancing alliances will ensue, which are exactly the outcomes Moscow seeks to prevent. Imperialist tendencies will also directly influence the availability of capital and direct investments for the continent. All this will deprive Moscow of any economic or security gains it might hope to achieve.

Short of empire, however, there are a variety of ways that the NIS will continue to interact with one another. In cases where successor states, such as the states of Central Asia, Belarus, and Armenia, largely follow Moscow's lead, Russia will have few reasons to exercise heavy-handed strategies. Relatively benign contracting will result. These NIS have security and economic reasons to prefer a relatively close alignment with Russia—demonstrated, for example, in Russian support for Armenia against Azerbaijan. One might argue that Central Asia–Russia relations might be most accurately described as neo-imperial or neocolonial. Indeed, Miles Kahler suggests with considerable plausibility that there is more than a passing resemblance between Francophone Africa and the Central Asian theater. The question is one of degree. No doubt the Central Asian states will continue to rely on Russia for military and economic support for some time to come. But whether or not these relations are neo-imperial will hinge on the latitude Central Asia has to develop relations outside of this framework and on the methods that Russia uses to maintain their dependence. For example, when Russia pursues heavy-handed negotiations, as it did with Kazakhstan regarding the location of an oil pipeline, then the relation might shade into hard-bargaining or even neo-imperial relations.

States that have alternative military allies and markets available might choose to disengage even if Russia would prefer to maintain close relations. Ukraine, given its considerable military might and relatively high level of economic development, has so far resisted being pulled too close into the Russian orbit. The same is true for the Baltic states, although their ability to separate from Moscow has largely been driven by their ability to pursue Western economic—and possibly military—partners. In other cases, Russia will pursue asymmetric advantages and will drive home tough bargains. Weak states that have sought to dissociate themselves from the Russian embrace—such as Moldova, Georgia, and Azerbaijan—but which lack military allies and viable alternative economic partners, have had to give in to Moscow. Even Russian behavior toward Ukraine may trend in that direction.

Given the systemic distribution of resources, economic power, and technological and administrative know-how, most NIS will have to accept the likelihood of asymmetric relations with Russia. Only a few states will have the ability to interact on more equal terms, either because of their own considerable material resources or because they have alternative markets and allies at their disposal. The availability of foreign capital and the ability of the NIS to export to the world market will enhance their ability to curtail the worst excesses of such asymmetric bargains.

The West can play an even more important role in mitigating Russian imperial and hegemonic tendencies. At the systemic level, ironically, it can do so by holding back. Premature enlargement of NATO to include non-Russian successor states could possibly lead to the very behavior the expansion would seek to prevent. Should Russia see such extension as the continuation of the superpower rivalry of the Cold War, then it might attempt to bring its sphere of influence under more formal control.

Finally, the advanced capitalist states can influence Russian domestic developments. By mitigating the painful costs of transition to a capitalist economy—partially through bilateral deals and partially through multilateral transfers—the West can diminish the appeal of extremist views for revenge and forcible reunification. One does well to remember that similar revanchist appeals against a bleak economic backdrop gained the upper hand in the Weimar Republic.

Notes

1. See John Lewis Gaddis, "International Relations Theory and the End of the Cold War," *International Security* 17, no. 3 (1992–1993): 5–58; Ted Hopf and John Lewis Gaddis, "Getting the End of the Cold War Wrong," *International Security* 18, no. 2 (1993): 202–210.

2. One might perhaps argue that Russia itself is a newly independent state. In this context, however, the emphasis is on postimperial ties of the non-Russian successor states to Russia—the erstwhile center of the empire. Just as Austria or Turkey, or for that matter England, would not usually be considered newly independent states after the end of their empires, as compared to their former territorial holdings and colonies, so too is Russia's status distinct from that of the non-Russian successor states. Hence, I mean to denote only the latter with the term newly independent states, not Russia itself.

3. No doubt some conservative and communist groups favor a return to the old imperial mode. For a description of some of the ongoing debates in Russia see Sherman

Garnett, "The Integrationist Temptation," *The Washington Quarterly* 18, no. 2 (1995): 35–44.

4. This difference between imperial domination and hegemonic oversight is discussed in Michael Doyle, *Empires* (Ithaca: Cornell University Press, 1986).

5. For the discussion of diffuse reciprocity see Robert Keohane, "Reciprocity in International Relations," *International Organization* 40, no. 1 (1986): 1–27. Unlike specific reciprocity, which refers to quid pro quo exchanges between specific partners, diffuse reciprocity refers to exchanges where exact equivalence is less prevalent and where partners are less specific.

6. I borrow here—with revisions—particularly from Jack Snyder, "Organizing Political Space in the Former Soviet Union" (paper presented at the Carnegie Conference on Political Order, Conflict, and Nationalism in the Former Soviet Union, New York, May 1995). Miles Kahler's comments on Snyder's paper have greatly informed my own views.

7. This does not in any way weaken Karen Dawisha's claim, in chapter 14 of this volume, that some groups in the periphery might welcome imperial overlordship. Her analysis centers on domestic coalitions that benefit from the metropole. My analysis focuses primarily on unitary rational actor estimation of the costs and benefits of cooperation.

8. See Bruce Parrott, chapter 1 of this volume.

9. Doyle, *Empires*. Jack Snyder makes a similar point in *Myths of Empire* (Ithaca: Cornell University Press, 1991).

10. For analysis of state expansion in rational, calculative terms, see Robert Gilpin, *War and Change in World Politics* (Cambridge: Cambridge University Press, 1981).

11. Snyder, *Myths of Empire*, p. 18. See also Charles Kupchan, *The Vulnerability of Empire* (Ithaca: Cornell University Press, 1994).

12. One of the seminal pieces in the dependency literature is Fernando Cardoso and Enzo Faletto, *Dependency and Development in Latin America* (Berkeley and Los Angeles: University of California Press, 1979). A good discussion of this literature is Peter Evans, *Dependent Development* (Princeton: Princeton University Press, 1979), esp. chs. 1, 2.

13. See Dawisha, chapter 14 of this volume.

14. In chapter 14 of this volume, Karen Dawisha phrases this constellation of variables as opportunity, motive, and context.

15. For the expansionist ideological agenda of the Russian and Soviet empires, see Roman Szporluk, chapter 3 of this volume. Interestingly, he suggests that the ideological combination of messianism and universalism might be characteristic of all empires.

16. Mario Polèse, "Economic Integration, National Policies, and the Rationality of Regional Separatism," in Ronald Rogowski and Edward Tiryakian, eds., *New Nationalisms of the Developed West* (London: Allen and Unwin, 1985).

17. Arguably, the USSR integrated the union republics to a far greater extent than would a "normal", i.e. nonimperial, federal system. The Communist Party effectively centralized and controlled opportunities for voice and exit, leaving only the possibility for approved demonstrations of loyalty. These terms are clarified in Albert Hirschman, *Exit, Voice, Loyalty* (Cambridge: Harvard University Press, 1970) .

18. See Joseph Grieco, "Systemic Sources of Variation in Regional Institutionalization in Western Europe, East Asia, and the Americas," in Edward Mansfield and Helen Milner, eds., *The Political Economy of Regionalism* (forthcoming).

19. Emile Durkheim believed that organic cooperation with high division of labor would occur if "dynamic density" increased. Emile Durkheim, *The Division of Labor in Society* (New York: Free Press, 1933). Karl Deutsch likewise suggested that high levels of communications and interactions would lead to pluralistic security communities. Karl Deutsch, *Political Community and the North Atlantic Area* (New York: Greenwood, 1956).

20. See, for example, Ernst Haas, "Technocracy, Pluralism, and the New Europe," in Joseph Nye, ed., *International Regionalism* (Boston: Little Brown, 1968).

21. For a functional account of regimes, see Robert Keohane, *After Hegemony* (Princeton: Princeton University Press, 1984). Game theorists might frame functional cooperation in terms of long-run iterating games; see Robert Axelrod, *The Evolution of Cooperation* (New York: Basic Books, 1984).

22. For the strongest statement of neorealism, see John Mearsheimer, "The False Promise of International Institutions," *International Security* 19, no. 3 (1994–1995): 5–49. A more nuanced view of the neorealist program is provided by Joseph Grieco, "The Renaissance of the European Community and the Crisis of Realist International Theory" (paper presented at the International Political Economy workshop, New York, October 1992).

23. Stephen Walt, *The Origins of Alliances* (Ithaca: Cornell University Press, 1987). In the preface, he predicts that European union will slow down with the waning of the Cold War. Kenneth Waltz similarly suggests that European unity hinges on security concerns. Kenneth Waltz, *Theory of International Relations* (New York: Random House, 1979), pp. 70–71.

24. For a comprehensive discussion of the absolute versus relative gains issue see the essays in David Baldwin, ed., *Neorealism and Neoliberalism* (New York: Columbia University Press, 1993).

25. For an overview of these events see, for example, Gail Lapidus, "From Democratization to Disintegration: The Impact of Perestroika on the National Question," in Gail Lapidus and Victor Zaslavsky, eds., *From Union to Commonwealth* (New York: Cambridge University Press, 1992); Ronald Hill, "The Soviet Union: From 'Federation' to 'Commonwealth,' " in John Coakley, ed., *The Territorial Management of Ethnic Conflict* (London: Frank Cass, 1993), pp. 99–122.

26. See, for example, the attempt to conclude the Alma Ata Economic Treaty in October 1991 and the draft for the Union Treaty of November 1991, as discussed in Richard Sakwa, *Russian Politics and Society* (New York: Routledge, 1993), pp. 206, 323.

27. This categorization relies particularly on Ian Bremmer and Ray Taras, eds., *Nations and Politics in the Soviet Successor States* (New York: Cambridge University Press, 1993); Karen Dawisha and Bruce Parrott, *Russia and the New States of Eurasia* (New York: Cambridge University Press, 1984); Sakwa, *Russian Politics and Society.*

28. Sakwa, *Russian Politics and Society,* p. 326; Hill, "From 'Federation' to 'Commonwealth.' "

29. For a discussion of this episode, see Bruce Porter and Carol Saivetz, "The Once and Future Empire: Russia and the 'Near Abroad,' " *The Washington Quarterly* 17, no. 3 (1994): 75–90.

30. See Suzanne Crow, "Russia Promotes the CIS as an International Organization," *RFE/RL Research Report* 3, no. 11 (1994): 33–38.

31. Ann Sheehy, "The CIS: A Shaky Edifice," *RFE/RL Research Report* 2, no. 1 (1993): 37–40.

32. Porter and Saivetz, "Once and Future Empire," p. 85.

33. Dawisha and Parrott, *Russia and the New States of Eurasia,* p. 184.

34. "Baltic Cooperation—the Key to Wider Security," *NATO Review* 44, no. 1 (1996): 7–10.

35. One might debate whether the political structure in existence in Russia today still constitutes empire. This would largely hinge on how peripheral areas are incorporated into the Russian Federation, in which case Chechnya would constitute a case of resistance to formal domination.

36. I develop a fuller test of these theories elsewhere. See Hendrik Spruyt, "Testing

Theories of Political Integration in the Former Soviet Space" (paper presented at Duke University, Durham, NC, November 1995).

37. Some Turkish military instructors were indeed dispatched but little else materialized. Sakwa, *Russian Politics and Society,* p. 358.

38. Arguably, Russia too violates the CFE provisions, although it argues that it has had to keep more troops in this zone due to the special security circumstances of the region.

39. Turkmenistan's gas reserves of eight trillion cubic meters are among the world's largest. It also has 700 million tons of oil. *Economist,* July 22, 1995, p. 36. The problem for Turkmenistan is that it might require Russian support to bring this gas to market. But note that Iran has tried to provide alternative transportation routes. "Gold at the End of the Railway," *Economist,* December 2, 1995, p. 42.

40. Marek Dąbrowski and Rafał Antczak, "Economic Transition in Russia, Ukraine, and Belarus in Comparative Perspective," Russian Littoral Project Occasional Paper #86, August 1995. Based on Lucjan Orlowski's data, Dabrowski and Antczak suggest that the net transfer of such subsidies as a percent of GDP was 10.8 percent for Turkmenistan and 3.7 percent for Russia. For a further discussion of some of the interrepublican trade relations, price distortions, and Russian subsidies, see Peter Rutland, "The Economy: The Rocky Road from Plan to Market," in Stephen White, Alex Pravda, and Zvi Gitelman, eds., *Developments in Russian and Post-Soviet Politics* (Durham, NC: Duke University Press, 1994), pp. 131–61.

41. See the figures in Barnett Rubin, "Tajikistan: From Soviet Republic to Russian-Uzbek Protectorate," in Michael Mandelbaum, ed., *Central Asia and the World* (New York: Council on Foreign Relations, 1994), pp. 207–24.

42. *Common Issues and Interrepublic Relations in the Former USSR* (Washington, DC: International Monetary Fund, 1992), p. 37.

43. For an overall view of the economic events before the breakup and the developments since then, see Anders Åslund, *How Russia Became a Market Economy* (Washington: The Brookings Institution, 1995). Sakwa suggests that Russia subsidized overall interrepublican trade by about 67 billion rubles by the late 1980s. (Sakwa, *Russian Politics and Society,* pp. 207–8).

44. For a similar argument with special application to Russia and Central Asia, see Rajan Menon, "In the Shadow of the Bear," *International Security* 20, no. 1 (1995): 149–81; Rajan Menon and Hendrik Spruyt, "State Formation, Conflict and Conflict Resolution in Central Asia" (paper prepared for the Carnegie Project on Political Order, Conflict, and Nationalism in the Former Soviet Union, New York, September 1995).

45. For a discussion of the nationalities problem, see Vladimir Shlapentokh, Munir Sendich, and Emil Payin, *The New Russian Diaspora* (New York: M.E. Sharpe, 1994). For analysis of how the Kazakh government deals with its particular problem, see Ian Bremmer, "Nazarbaev and the North: State Building and Ethnic Relations in Kazakhstan," *Ethnic and Racial Studies* 17, no. 4 (1994): 619–35.

46. Steven David, "Explaining Third World Alignment," *World Politics* 43, no. 2 (1991): 233–56. Note, however, that this deviates from the unitary state model, which is a core assumption of neorealism proper.

47. For a discussion that the influence is actually flowing in a reverse direction, see Daniel Pipes, "The Event of Our Era: Former Soviet Muslim Republics," in Mandelbaum, ed., *Central Asia,* pp. 47–93.

48. See Desmond Ball, "Arms and Affluence," *International Security* 18, no. 3 (1993–1994): 78–112; Richard Betts, "Wealth, Power and Instability," *International Security* 18, no. 3 (1993–1994): 34–77; Aaron Friedberg, "Ripe for Rivalry: Prospects for Peace in a Multipolar Asia," *International Security* 18, no. 3 (1993–1994): 5–33.

49. Moreover, as Robert Jervis has pointed out, not only would Western commitment to fighting for these states be less than credible, but even Russian conquest of some of the NIS would not significantly affect the military balance to challenge American or West European security. Robert Jervis, "Legacies of the Cold War," *Brown Journal of International Affairs* 2, no. 2 (1995): 25. Richard Betts has also suggested that exclusion of Russia would precipitate fears of encirclement and lead to counteracting behavior by Moscow. Additionally, he challenges the strategic soundness of the plan, arguing that it would lead to expanding NATO's eastward frontage just as NATO troop levels are being drawn down. (My thanks to him for sharing his private communications with Washington policymakers.)

50. See also Snyder's argument that imperial strategies lead to self-encirclement because the behavior causes counteracting behavior by the states threatened by the aggressor. Snyder, *Myths of Empire,* p. 6.

51. For the argument that nuclear weapons induce caution in major powers' foreign policies, see John Mearsheimer, "Back to the Future," *International Security* 15, no. 1 (1990): 5–56. Kenneth Waltz, "Nuclear Myths and Political Realities," *American Political Science Review* 84, no. 3 (1990): 731–45.

52. For a discussion of the importance and consequence of offensive and defensive milieus see Robert Jervis, "Cooperation Under the Security Dilemma," *World Politics* 30, no. 2 (1978): 167–214. For the causes and consequences of offensive doctrines for World War I, see Stephen van Evera, "Why Cooperation Failed in 1914," in Kenneth Oye, ed., *Cooperation Under Anarchy* (Princeton: Princeton University Press, 1986), pp. 80–117; Jack Snyder, *The Ideology of the Offensive* (Ithaca: Cornell University Press, 1984).

53. Some 70 percent of military units may be at as low as 50 percent of authorized strength. Institute for International and Strategic Studies, *The Military Balance, 1994–1995* (London: Brassey's, 1994), p. 109. See also "The Military Doctrine of the Russian Federation," *Jane's Intelligence Review* 6, no. 1 (1994).

54. This is discussed in greater detail in Hendrik Spruyt, *The Sovereign State and Its Competitors* (Princeton: Princeton University Press, 1994). See also Robert Jackson, *Quasi-States: Sovereignty, International Relations, and the Third World* (New York: Cambridge University Press, 1990). For an analysis of universalist empire see John Hall, *Powers and Liberties* (Berkeley and Los Angeles: University of California Press, 1985).

55. Richard Rosecrance has argued that a gradual historical trend has led mercantilist, war-fighting states to become "trading states." Richard Rosecrance, *The Rise of the Trading State* (New York: Basic Books, 1986). John Mueller's argument about the decreasing salience of war as a legitimate and widely accepted tool of foreign policy can be interpreted in a similar vein. John Mueller, "The Essential Irrelevance of Nuclear Weapons, *International Security* 13, no. 2 (1988): 55–79.

56. There is a burgeoning literature on the democratic peace argument. See, for example, Michael Doyle, "Liberalism and World Politics," *American Political Science Review* 80, no. 4 (1986): pp. 1151–69; Bruce Russett, *Grasping the Democratic Peace* (Princeton: Princeton University Press, 1993). See also the various discussions in *International Security* 19, no. 2 (1994).

57. See Edward Mansfield and Jack Snyder, "Democratization and the Danger of War," *International Security* 20, no. 1 (1995), pp. 5–38.

58. On the repercussions of specific domestic institutions see, for example, Peter Cowhey, "Domestic Institutions and the Credibility of International Commitments: Japan and the U.S.," *International Organization* 47, no. 2 (1993): 299–326.

59. Hudson Meadwell, "The Politics of Nationalism in Quebec," *World Politics* 45, no. 2 (1993): 203–41.

60. Elizabeth Fuller, "The Karabakh Mediation Process: Grachev versus the CSCE,"

RFE/RL Research Report 3, no. 23 (1994): 13–17; *Economist,* (August 19, 1995), p. 46.

61. For a discussion of these concepts, see Keohane, *After Hegemony;* Beth Yarborough and Robert Yarborough, "Cooperation in the Liberalization of International Trade: After Hegemony What?" *International Organization* 41, no. 1 (1987): 1–26; and Yarborough and Yarborough, "International Institutions and the New Economics of Organization," *International Organization* 44, no. 2 (1990): 235–59.

14

Constructing and Deconstructing Empire in the Post-Soviet Space

Karen Dawisha

The contemporary debate about the future of politics in the Eurasian space comes back again and again to the "Russian question": Will the Soviet Union, having collapsed, reassert itself, this time as a new Russian empire? Analysts in the West and elsewhere moved quickly from euphoria over these long-suppressed nations' new independence to concern over whether they would be able to resist or survive in the face of any renewed Russian imperial drive. Within two years of the Soviet collapse, books and articles started to fill the shelves—analyzing Russia's potential strength, assessing the foreign policy impact of its domestic political divisions, speaking of the Russian impulse to empire, and chronicling the near-total obsession that elites in neighboring countries have with managing their relationships with Moscow.[1]

Many of the authors of these new works point to the difficulties faced by elites in all the new states, including Russia, in developing a conception of national interest that would orient their foreign policies beyond the Eurasian heartland.[2] But the frailties both of the new states themselves and of the internal institutions available for formulating foreign policy limit their ability to extend the focus of their external politics beyond the Eurasian orbit. The fact that the interrelationships among these fifteen states is likely—in the foreseeable future—to occupy the first rank of their concerns means that the international system will also interact with them through the prism of these interrelationships. Consequently, the ability of the world community to effect change in these relationships will depend on having a clearer understanding of their essential nature. This fact underlines the importance of analyzing their relationships dispassionately and with a yardstick that can be applied more generally and that remains constant over time.

The task can be approached by posing a number of questions about the whole range of possible relationships between Russia, as a future potential imperial power, and the other new states.

For Russia: What are the prerequisites for the emergence of an imperial power? Could a country with low state capacity and no avowed official ideology of imperialism nevertheless be an empire? What distinctions should be made between the language of power and the rhetoric of imperialism in a country's debate about its external role? Does Russia, even if it rejects a renewed imperial role, have either rights or responsibilities toward the new states? What would Russian imperialism look like today? How could Russia's reemergence as a major regional and international power be distinguished from a reassertion of imperial power?

For the other new states: How dependent are the former republics on Moscow? Can these newly independent states break out of a cycle of dependence on Moscow—a dependence so great in some cases as to constitute what I call autocolonization? I define autocolonization as the process whereby elites or populations in a target country seek and accept a diminution in their state's sovereignty in hopes of receiving enhanced security, material benefits, or other benefits from an external power, thereby lowering the costs to that power of becoming an imperial state.

The concept of autocolonization, it should be noted, is not applicable only to Russia and the newly independent states. Nor should it be seen as a purely contemporary phenomenon. The history of imperialism in its many forms is full of examples of colonial processes in which elite or social subgroups have been willing to extend sovereign rights to external powers, trading certain kinds of authority and independence for other benefits.

For the international system: Can the international system prevent Russian imperialism from emerging? What measures can be used both to lessen the temptation of empire in Moscow and to increase the former republics' independence from Russia? Is dependence of the newly independent states on Moscow sometimes in the interest of the West and other external powers? Can one distinguish between imperial domination and voluntary economic dependency of the kind found in much of the Third World?

Imperial Prerequisites

An empire as a polity and imperialism as a system of ideas that guides policy intersect conceptually, in that the former is an outgrowth, a result, of the latter. This apparently trivial and obvious point gets to the heart of the first requirement of empires, namely that they be established on purpose. The purposeful objective, established by elites in the metropole, is to gain unfair advantage through coercion or its threat over countries or territories in the periphery, for the purpose of promoting definite state interests. Thus, the definition of imperialism provided by Joseph Schumpeter in his earliest works—"the objectless disposition on the part of a state to unlimited forcible expansion"[3]—or the old argument that the British Empire expanded "in a fit of absentmindedness" simply misses the point: states do not expand *for no reason.* As many of the contributors to this volume—including Carole Fink, Robert Rotberg, Dankwart Rustow, and Solomon Wank—underline, although there has been a wide variety of motivations for imperial expansion, and although motivations may have differed from colony to colony and period to period, intent is clearly central to the imperial temptation.

Historians are unlikely to successfully establish the defining moment in any decision to found an empire; this outcome, like so many others, is subject to what Kenneth Waltz has called the "tyranny of small decisions." [4] Thus, for example, the East India Company began establishing trading posts in India as early as 1600, whereas direct British rule of India was not imposed until after the Indian Mutiny of 1858. The intervening 250 years saw an incremental increase in British control, however, against a backdrop of sustained British interest in deriving economic benefits from the wealth of the Indian subcontinent. Jack Snyder has perceptively explored the various and often conflicting explanations for expansion.[5] As he demonstrates, imperial expansion may, in the fullness of time, prove to have been irrational or unwise, and often produces a pullback after a new generation of elites realizes that the capabilities of the state are overextended; even so, the original impulse to expand has to have been a conscious one on the part of dominant elites, designed to serve what they perceived to be state interests at the time.

It goes without saying that the original impulse may not have been the result of a unified decision on the part of the entire governing elite. Indeed, given the fact that empires more often than not have grown out of highly centralized oligarchies and dictatorships, it is unlikely that broad elite consensus, much less general support from the populace, has been sought or received in advance. Furthermore, as both Michael Fry's and Robert Rotberg's chapters make clear, those individuals with access to information required to calculate the real material costs and benefits of empires often knew from the beginning that the colonies were a drain on resources. Certainly, the historic confluence of between democratic and law-based societies on the one hand and an international system based on nation-states and devoted to self-determination on the other hand has limited the ability of elites to pursue imperial designs. Consequently, many analysts believe that the trend toward democracy and a law-based society in Russia is also a trend away from the imperial temptation, a topic that is further discussed in the final section below.

A policy of imperialism pursued by the center need not, of course, be advertised as such (although one can find countless instances in which it has been), but it is nevertheless important to include in one's conceptualization of imperialism the effort by one country to wrest formal sovereignty from another. The concept also presupposes that an entire structure of governance from the center is put in place in the colony. Imperialism is more than military expansion during wartime, and certainly more than the exercise of influence over the policies of another country. The definition developed by Alexander Motyl is useful in this regard, as is the earlier work of Johann Galtung. Motyl uses the terms *core* and *periphery* rather than *empire* and *colony* and defines core as "a multidimensional set of territorially concentrated and mutually reinforcing organizations exercising highly centralized authority in a system. The organizations must be (1) political, economic, and sociocultural (multidimensional); (2) located in a bounded geographic space (territorially concentrated); (3) supportive of one another (mutually reinforcing); and (4) endowed with significant decision-making authority (centralized)." Conversely, he defines peripheries as "the territorially bounded administrative outposts of central organizations. There must be at least two peripheries for empires to be distinguishable from bifurcated states, such as the former Czechoslovakia."[6]

As such, although it is not necessarily the case that elites in a state would openly declare in advance that they were going to create an empire, it should be more than possible to determine whether a state has the interest, the capacity, and the will necessary to pursue such a course. While there are great differences on other issues pertaining to imperialism, theorists are agreed that the drive to empire has to serve some set of overarching interests, whether economic (as with the British drive into India), geopolitical (as with the nineteenth-century competition among Russians, Turks, Germans, and Austrians for "the lands between" in eastern Europe), messianic (as with the missionary expansionism of Iberian Catholicism), or ideological (as with bolshevism in the USSR).

As concerns capacity, elites may undertake expansion to increase their state's well-being; nevertheless, to a significant degree only states with excess capacity can undertake imperial expansion. This perspective, captured by numerous writers from Lenin onward, focuses on the notion that only those states already most powerful in the international system can garner the relevant military and economic capabilities both to expand beyond state boundaries and to sustain and administer an empire in new territories. The extent of capability required to establish and sustain an empire is variable, depending as it does upon the extent of resistance met both locally and from other major powers. For example, the tendency among some Cossack and Slavic elites to identify Russia as a center of their religion and culture facilitated the early Romanov expansion into Ukraine, and freed the imperial army to deal with Poland's opposition. In Central Asia two centuries later, however, tsarist armies had to contend with opposition from both the local populations and the British, who wanted to stop Russia from expanding into the Indian subcontinent. Yet the general principle remains: the state must possess significant excess capacity in order to launch and sustain imperial expansion.

While the motivations for expansion may differ, some form of impulse must be present in order for the foreign policy of a state to be characterized as imperialistic. In this sense, Winston Churchill's statement that "the empires of the future are the empires of the mind" informs the current discussion by pointing to the central aspect of intent.[7] The elites must be motivated by what Ghita Ionescu calls a "historical mission of expansion," and they must possess a sense of "final purpose."[8]

Rhetoric and intention, however, must be distinguished from one another. For example, Ronald Reagan repeatedly renounced the Panama Canal Treaty during his 1980 campaign for the U.S. presidency, decrying the decision to return the canal to Panamanian control. Once in office, however, he did nothing to alter the treaty. Rhetoric can, in and of itself, affect the structure of the relationship between two sovereign countries, and saber rattling is destructive of amity. But unless transformed into policy and backed by a state mobilized to undertake imperial expansion, rhetoric remains both empty and quite distinct from intention.

It is also clear that there is a huge grey area in defining intent, in that a state's intention can be read differently by the various actors involved. In this respect, Mark Beissinger's work on empire is informative. He develops the notion that empire, particularly in the modern era and particularly as regards Russia, is primarily a constructed and subjective reality, built more on perceptions of the imputed meaning behind essentially ambiguous Russian behavior than on its "actual" content. As such, in chapter 6 of this book and elsewhere, Beissinger correctly points to the perceptual dimension of imperial behavior by judging whether that behavior is "accepted as 'ours' or rejected as 'theirs.' "[9] Although Beissinger contributes to our understanding of the interconnectedness between state building and empire building, it remains important to not lose sight of the essential distinctive structure of an empire.

Autocolonization

Pierre Bourdieu's observation that "social reality exists, so to speak, twice, in things and in minds"[10] points to the dual, interconnected, and equal importance of perceptions and of structure. Losing sight of structure and focusing primarily on perception would blur the distinction between neo-imperialism and great power politics, and would depend inordinately on Russia's behavior in any country being rejected as belonging to "the other" by its inhabitants. Such a focus thereby risks failing to capture a whole range of situations, including those in which empire is reasserted at the behest of local elites—in other words, autocolonization. It is certainly not being argued that the core country's interests are not being served by the reassertion of empire: what is being explored is the mutuality of interests and the range of cases in which the impulse for the establishment or continuation of an imperial-colonial relationship comes not from the center, but from the periphery.

Take, for example, relations between Great Britain and Iraq before and after Iraq gained independence in 1932. Prior to independence, when Iraq was mandated by the League of Nations to Britain, the country was indeed ruled as an administrative outpost. After independence was formally granted, however, the British remained in Iraq to continue a mutually beneficial relationship for the British and the local Iraqi elites. The pro-British ruling elites sought to maintain Britain's role in protecting their political and economic preeminence, and in return were willing to grant the British an exclusive oil concession, as well as basing rights and other privileges. This arrangement of essential Iraqi autocolonization operated in league with Britain's establishment of an informal empire. This arrangement prevented the local elite from heading the process of nation formation, and the cause of national rebirth was captured by previously disenfranchised socioeconomic, ideological, and political groups. Several nationalist uprisings took place in the 1940s and 1950s, until ultimately, in 1958, the monarchy was brought down, the entire elite was purged, and a vehemently anti-British regime was established.

Looking at this case allows one to draw the distinction between imperial disintegration and nation formation on the one hand and autocolonization and nation suppression on the other. The impulse for imperialism comes from the metropole; the impulse for autocolonization comes from the periphery. In the former the motivation to expand comes without taking into account—or against—the wishes of people in the periphery. Autocolonization takes place at the behest and with the support of either the elites or the population in the periphery. Many new states fail in the construction of viable national political and economic institutions.[11] Such failure invites renewed pressures from external powers and, as David Lake points out in chapter 2, lowers the cost of empire. Here, however, autocolonization is taken to include only a subset of new states in which the elites and/or population decline to even attempt nation construction.

Autocolonization can be distinguished from a number of other concepts purporting to explain similar phenomena. For example, as detailed by Ali Mazrui in chapter 9, "empire by invitation" has been used to refer to the American military presence in Western Europe after World War II. Another example on a more limited scale is the invitation issued to Syria in 1976 by certain sections of the Maronite Christian elite to intervene in Lebanon and establish a so-called Pax Syriana, which the Christians thought would maintain both stability and their own preeminence in Lebanese society.[12] Empire by invitation bears some similarity to the more formal concept of protectorate, denoting a weaker state that seeks or is forced to accept the "protective" umbrella of a particular regional or hegemonic power. Mazrui also identifies a phenomenon called "colonialism by consent" and uses as an example the 1958 referendum called by President Charles de Gaulle in the French empire in Africa. The colonies were given the choice between sovereign independence and continued colonial association with France. All of the colonies except Sekou Toure's Guinea (Conakry) voted in favor of continuing association with France. This vote had lasting ramifications for French-African relations well after formal independence had been granted in the early 1960s.

In theory, these were instances in which the weaker states sought the protection of stronger ones, usually as a result of a perceived threat from a neighboring state or another great power. Very often this protection is sought and established through the agency of local elites who collaborate with imperial authorities. This mechanism of collaboration for imperial control was used extensively in European imperialism and allowed indirect rule to be established in some of the more pliable colonies.[13] As discussed in the section on this subject below, autocolonization in the Eurasian space bears some resemblance to these examples.

One can cite historical examples that could broadly fit within the category of autocolonization. For example, at the end of 1917 a democratic federative republic was proclaimed in Bessarabia. The republic, under attack from the Russian Red Army, sought and received military protection from Romania. Finally relieved of Bolshevik pressure by the Brest-Litovsk Treaty, the Bessarabian parliament nonetheless voted to seek unification with Romania, not because they classified themselves as ethnic Romanians, but because, as the statement of unity proclaimed, the highest national purpose of the Moldovan people could only be attained through reunification with "Mother Romania."[14] Moldova thus became part of Romania until it was forcibly annexed by the Soviet Union during World War II, thereafter constituting the Moldavian Soviet Socialist Republic. For the first year after the collapse of the USSR, the dominant political trend in western Moldova once again favored reunion with Romania, although this time pressure from the country's Slavic populace and the more nationally minded Moldovan elites prevented it.

During the Soviet era, nondemocratically elected elites in Eastern Europe adopted a pro-Soviet stance in order to receive security assistance that would keep them in power. The argument has often and justifiably been made that the Soviet Union imposed communism as a system of power on Eastern Europe. Armed with this system, however, local Communist elites like Zhivkov, Honecker, Ulbricht, Husak, and Gottwald constructed security services and systems of rule that served Moscow's needs while maintaining their own positions of power. Their willingness to even use force to sustain their regimes, which became apparent in East Germany and Czechoslovakia in the late 1980s while glasnost and perestroika were being promoted in Moscow, is indicative of the desire of these elites to maintain their autocolonial status even as the impulse for empire was receding under Gorbachev. The same holds true of Moscow's allies in the Third World, who clung to the relationship with Moscow long after Soviet elites had begun to openly criticize them for their failure to implement domestic reforms.

One can also find Western examples of autocolonization. Frequently, these are cases in which a nation's economic well-being and independence are suppressed in the interests of the personal enrichment of the elite. Regarding the Philippines, there were those who argued that Ferdinand Marcos used American involvement to secure his corrupt regime in preference to instituting democratic measures that would have ousted him from power in short order. In francophone Africa, elites have often preferred to rule with French security assistance while plundering their own country's national wealth; and, as Miles Kahler points out in chapter 12, in the over thirty instances of French military intervention in postcolonial Africa, all except one were "spurred by pressure from its clients in the region."

In contemporary Eurasia, there are also cases of autocolonization, in which peripheral elites seek or accept a diminution primarily of the state's external authority and independence in return for assistance from the external power that may enhance domestic elite and/or state authority. This phenomenon is illustrated by Georgian President Eduard Shevardnadze's reliance on Russia for support in his fight against domestic insurgents, accompanied by cession of control of Georgia's major Black Sea bases to Moscow.

The success of autocolonization depends on the ability of local elites to convince their great-power protector that the costs of the relationship are less than the benefits. It also depends on the ability of the local elites to help shape the debate in the metropole as much as possible—by creating nostalgia for the center's rights as a great power, by promoting an imperial identity, by warning of the dire consequences of inaction, and by appealing to the duty and, if all else fails, the sheer vanity of the ruling elite.

Throughout history the Serbs have been masters at inculcating in Russian elite opinion the view that Serbia was Russia's only true ally in southern Europe. Seeing Serbia as permanently beleaguered in the Balkans, the Serbs have traditionally argued that not only was it Russia's duty to respond to their appeals, but that Russia's very ability to call itself a great power depended upon maintaining the dominance of Slavic and Orthodox brothers in Belgrade.[15]

Of course, this is a high stakes game, since the elites in the periphery risk being swept from power themselves if they invite intervention and then become subject to its rules. Thus, for example, the Georgian monarchy, concerned about Persian invasion, ceded sovereign rights to Catherine II and became a protectorate of Russia in 1783. However, seventeen years later, Paul I removed whatever rights the local elite still maintained when he annexed the entire country and abolished the monarchy.[16] Similarly, Armenians fleeing Turkey after the 1915 genocide established an independent republic under the nationalist Dashnak Party in 1918. The new Armenian authorities worried, however, that Turkey, under its own new nationalizing elite headed by Mustafa Kemal, would once again attack. Consequently, they ceded independence to the Communists and gave up their state in 1920, using incorporation into the emerging Soviet Union as a shield against future Turkish advances. Soviet rule was seen on balance to be protective of the Armenian population, language, and culture, and provides a good example of a situation in which elites sacrifice the state for the sake of the nation.[17]

As the Georgian and Armenian cases suggest, autocolonial policies pursued by elites in the periphery are often reactive, chosen out of fear or driven by th necessities of war. In such cases, the external power can be called in to impos social order and help restore stability. If successful, such policies can accru benefits for elites in the periphery while transferring the cost of imposing orde to the great powers. Clearly, however, the great power maintains significa advantage.

Although the concept of autocolonization should normally be associated wi action on the part of local elites, it should not be thought that their actions nev have a social basis. Protestants among the population of Northern Ireland, f example, have preferred union with Britain, even with direct rule, to an indepe dence that might leave them open to what they believe would be inevitab pressure for union with the Catholic south. Maronites in Lebanon welcome Syrian intervention to balance the growing power of Palestinian and Shii groups in their society. There are many other examples of the social bases f autocolonization, and it is certainly possible that there might be parallels now in the future in the relations between Russia and the rest of the new states.

Prospects for Russian Imperialism

In Russia, were imperialism to reassert itself, it would require capability, motiv and context. Russia's continuing preeminence in Eurasia as the dominant ge graphic and economic power gives it enormous natural advantage over its neigl bors. Comprising more than three-quarters of the territory of the former Sovi empire, more than one-half of its total population (a figure that rises to almo two-thirds if ethnic Russians living abroad are included), and controlling most the region's international transportation routes and energy pipelines, Russia ce tainly can be expected to continue to exert enormous pressure on the calculatio of its neighbors.

To conclude from this information alone, however, that Russia will "nat rally" exercise imperial ambitions over the other new states is both to ove determine for geography and to focus exclusively on the positive benefits Russia's size. In fact, the cost for the central government of maintaining Russ within its current boundaries has been significant, as both the war in Chechn and Moscow's failure to negotiate favorable revenue-sharing agreements wi some of the richest of its non-Russian federal republics has shown.[18]

Geography is a factor in that it enhances capability. Given the political will create an empire, the size and extent of natural resources are important inpu into any state machine bent on imperial expansion. Clearly, states build empir to become rich; but in addition, significant state resources are required to unde take and sustain colonial expansion. States seeking expansion may be motivat by the lure of wealth, but in order to launch a successful and sustained policy expansion, they themselves must possess significant capacity: full coffers, lar armies and navies, and extensive excess production capabilities large enough ipport, and profit from, wars of conquest and occupation. The level of capacity needed is of course relative and not absolute: the re-purces required are in inverse relationship to the resistance offered by the in-aded population, by other great powers, and by the international system. All the uropean imperial powers of the late nineteenth century, including Russia, were ready powerful when they entered the so-called golden age of empires: an age a which all the European powers mutually supported the scramble for low-risk, igh-yield gains in Africa and elsewhere. Indeed, the Concert of Europe's bal-ice of power was maintained at the same time, and largely as a result of, the reat Powers' abilities to vent their competitive spirit in Africa, the Middle East, id southern Asia.

When the empire costs more than it yields, institutional interests and ideas ke prestige and *mission civilisatrice* come to the forefront. However, once the opulation in the metropole begins to shoulder the burdens of expansion, a core omestic constituency for empire is lost. The collapse of internal support for mpire pulled Britain out of Aden and Portugal out of Africa. And it was this cognition of the cost of empire that informed popular Russian support for the ithdrawal from both the "external" empire in Eastern Europe after 1989 and the nternal" empire in the Soviet Union after 1991.

It is clear that Russia currently lacks the interests, capacity, and the will to unch a major military campaign to reassert imperial control over the newly dependent states of its former empire. The Russian military doctrine adopted in 993 emphasizes war prevention and maintenance of military sufficiency, and it schews the earlier doctrinal commitments to conventional superiority and war ghting in forward areas. The doctrine defines the Russian military's major role be the prevention of local wars that might arise from claims on Russian rritory (e.g., Chechnia) and deescalation of conflicts in lands adjacent to Rus-an territory that could imperil Russian interests and spill over into Russia roper (e.g., Abkhazia and Ossetia). Clearly, the doctrine that currently drives ussia's force posture does not emphasize force projection beyond national oundaries.[19]

In terms of the size of the military, in the five years following the breakup of e USSR, the Russian military shrank to less than half of its peak level in the id-1980s. Furthermore, the war in Chechnia—a war to maintain Russia's terri-rial integrity, and not definitionally an imperial war—produced widespread ilure to heed call-up notices to compulsory service. Public opinion showed that hile nostalgia for the Soviet era was widespread, revulsion for the loss of ussian life in the fight against the Chechens ran much deeper. This revulsion aped popular sentiment against imperial expansion abroad: public opinion lls repeatedly showed that only one-quarter of the population supported any rm of reestablishment of the union; and of those, usually less than 5 percent nctioned the use of military means.[20]

The reassertion of imperial capability cannot be achieved overnight, although it need not take a generation, either. As outlined by Carole Fink in chapter 11 the experience of Nazi Germany suggests that, given a few years, military capac ity can be dramatically rebuilt, particularly if the population is willing or oblige to sacrifice democracy in the process. Yet for the foreseeable future, Russia i likely to lack the military capacity for imperial reassertion. In the 1990s, th costs of empire, if it must be established by force, appear much too high fc Russia to bear.

Is it possible that the imperial idea will be reborn in Russia, even if th capacity to pursue an imperial policy is limited? A substantial number of right wing candidates and parties ran in the December 1995 parliamentary and the sum mer 1996 presidential elections on the platform of supporting the redrawing c borders to incorporate an area larger than Russia's current internationally recognize boundaries: proponents include the Liberal Democrats, the Communists, the Agrari ans, the Congress of Russian Communities, and the Derzhava party.

Certainly in all past empires, individuals and political groups have acted a agents for the germination of the imperial idea. Consider Cecil Rhodes, whos own personal vision of capitalist imperialism in South Africa came to be adopte by the British; the Pan-Turanists in Ottoman Turkey, who sought unsuccessfull in the dying days of the Ottoman Empire to revive it on the basis of the unity o all Turkish-speaking peoples; or the Russian general Mikhail Skobelev, whos conquests of Turkestan and militant Pan-Slavism helped undergird the establish ment of a brutal Russian imperial regime in the south. All these individuals an groups mobilized society and the elites to expend the resources necessary fc expansion. They worked with the intelligentsia to develop the essential myth that legitimated and sustained expansion, and they fostered an intellectual cli mate in which any challenge to these myths was seen to be subversive of th broader goals of society. In Russia, certainly, most nineteenth-century writer and intellectuals gave powerful support to the idea that Russia's identity was a imperial identity.

These right-wing groups and individuals are important in Russia today, in tha to a certain extent they have become influential and their ideas have become th ruling ideas. None of the parties has promoted or received support for an im mediate renewed military drive to retake any part of the old Soviet empire; no in the foreseeable future, would low state capacity allow such an expansion to b undertaken successfully or without enormous cost. Observers worry, howeve that if economic and internal conditions continue to deteriorate in Russia, and i particular if the public turns away from seeking Russia's entry into an interna tional economic system dominated by the West, public support for the essentiall Western institution of democracy may decline. This could become a particula problem if a genuinely charismatic leader emerges who can appeal to the sens that Russia has been humiliated and deserves redress.

The electoral success of right-wing Russian leaders and parties who served u a steady stream of anti-Western and pro-imperial rhetoric must be seen in thi light. Both the 1993 and the 1995 elections indicated that pro-imperial rhetoric has solid resonance among the population and exists as a political reserve capable of winning votes. On two occasions, in 1991 and 1993, these political forces also attempted to take power by force, and some have continued to espouse not only imperialistic but also antidemocratic slogans, making popular support for their positions both perplexing and worrying from a Western standpoint. In this scenario, one can see echoes of earlier views expressed by Hannah Arendt that imperialism may gain such popularity that the mob supporting it can rise up to displace both the bourgeoisie and the political institutions of democracy, simultaneously promoting the establishment of a regime that is both totalitarian and expansionist.[21]

This raises the question of whether Russian imperialism could be born out of the struggle of political forces within the country itself; that is, whether in their quest for power, groups would mobilize imperial sentiment for narrow political gain. This would presuppose that such forces could win an election, and that having won they would feel pressured to act according to their rhetoric. This view of motivation argues that empires are built almost willy-nilly, without what could be called a strict planning cycle, and largely as a combined result of domestic pressures and lack of constraints by the international community. Certainly there are historians, the British historian A.J.P. Taylor among them, who view the entire experience of the nineteenth-century construction of empires as largely a result of political competition and narrow diplomatic one-upmanship among the major European powers. Along these lines, Bismarck is said to have commented to a subordinate in 1884, "All this colonial business is a sham but we need it for the elections." He joined in the scramble for Africa, less because of his thirst for creating an overseas empire than because he thought that his electoral chances would be improved were he to launch what Taylor terms "a harmless colonial conflict with England."[22]

It is regrettable, though not entirely surprising, that in today's Russia—where leaders can point to so few signs of economic progress, and where the Duma has so few powers—the political life in this emerging democracy might be given over to trends that could endanger it. The success of rightist forces in both the 1993 and 1995 elections stimulated the general movement to the right of what had been the political center, and led to the adoption of numerous nonbinding resolutions in the Duma that did not carry the weight of law but nevertheless created a less-than-sound environment inside or outside Russia for a steady consideration of future policies. These resolutions included calls for military basing agreements to be signed with all states on Russia's borders; the promotion of dual-citizen agreements with Russia's neighbors and continued denunciations of stated preferences for the titular nationality in neighboring states' citizenship laws; demanding that the elimination of Belarus's central bank be a precondition for accepting Belarus's request for economic union with Russia; declaring Sevastopol in Ukraine to be a Russian city; declaring illegal the Belovezh Forest accord which brought the end of the USSR; and so forth. Moreover, elite articulation of views openly supporting Russian rights in the "near abroad" began to increase even in government and foreign ministry circles, a process that accelerated after Yevgenii Primakov became foreign minister. These events suggest that an elite consensus could emerge, supported by a minority within public opinion, favoring resurgence of strong Russian nationalism and seeking reestablishment of the union, although on a strictly voluntary basis. Such a consensus would essentially work to rebuild Russian power, might, rights, and duties in the Eurasian continent.

That the Russian populace voted in the 1993 and 1995 elections against the severe economic deprivations it has suffered is clear. What is more contested and unclear is whether the populace will continue along the path of privatization and capitalism or instead seek a return to state control and socialism. Certainly, the strength of the vote for Vladimir Zhirinovsky's Liberal Democratic Party of Russia in 1993 and 1995 and for Gennadii Zyuganov's Communist Party of the Russian Federation in 1995 and 1996 was a cry from the pensioners, the working poor, and the less highly educated, first and foremost for more economic protection.

Public opinion polls conducted in Russia have consistently shown respondents' preference for political parties they deem most capable of dealing with, in descending order, domestic economic issues, crime, the rule of law, and only then foreign policy. And even though the Congress of Russian Communities, headed by retired Lieutenant-General Aleksandr Lebed, was identified in one poll as the party most capable of resolving domestic and international military conflicts involving Russian soldiers, the lower popular perception of the party's capability to handle what was regarded as the more important issue of the economy meant that the party did not even break the 5 percent threshold required to ensure representation in the Duma.[23] It was Lebed's own personal charisma and his reputation as incorruptible and supportive of law and order, more than his views on foreign policy, that won him over one-sixth of the vote in the first round of the presidential election in 1996. This showing secured his appointment as Yeltsin's national security adviser, a position from which clearly he could shape future decisions about Russia's relations with the "near abroad."

Whatever Lebed's preferences, at the present there is insufficient state capacity to implement a sustained policy of imperial expansion, particularly if military force were required. It would appear that much of the state's capacity in the foreseeable future will be focused on preventing the boundaries of Russia from shrinking even further, particularly given the location of so many restless national minorities at the periphery, especially in Chechnia but also elsewhere in the northern Caucasus and in Siberia. Russia's involvement in Chechnia has turned into a political quagmire because of the public's rejection of military entanglements and popular sentiments against committing Russian conscripts.

Yet history has shown that the political culture of a country can change rather swiftly from the politics of humiliation to the politics of *revanche* (e.g., France after 1870, Germany in the 1930s, and Egypt after 1967). Unfortunately, the presence of an impoverished and defeated population has often in the past assisted in the reemergence of a fascistic regime devoted to the icons of social justice and heroic nationalism; this includes countries like France, Italy, and Spain that were the birthplaces of Western liberal democracy. It cannot be denied that the political culture in Russia could undergo an equally swift transformation.

Autocolonization in the Eurasian Space

When analysts consider the prospects for true reassertion of Russian imperial activities, as opposed to the mere expression of sentiment, they primarily deal with scenarios in which the new states of the near abroad, struggling to establish and maintain their independence, resist such efforts by all means available, including force of arms. To be sure, many of Moscow's actions in the period since independence have met with a stern rebuff. Indeed it could be said that a central feature in the national identity of many of the new states is the imperative of resistance to any renewed Russian drive.

This resistance to Russian control is particularly apparent in Latvia and Estonia, in western Ukraine, in western Moldova, in Azerbaijan, and unfortunately for Russia, also within Russia in the northern Caucasus. It is less a part of the central governing *raison d'etat* in Central Asia, Armenia, Georgia, eastern and southern Ukraine, eastern Moldova, Belarus, and Lithuania. Whereas in the first group, there exists a solid consensus among the elites and the population that independence means independence from Russia, the situation in the latter group is not so clear-cut. Factors that encourage continued Russian influence in the second group of states include historic memories of Russia as the savior of local populations; common Slavic and Orthodox roots; a common economic infrastructure still centered in Russia; and russophone elites and/or large numbers of Russian nationals settled in and intermarried with the local populations.

But how do conditions that favor Russian influence translate into circumstances that produce autocolonization? There would appear to be two primary motivations for autocolonization: security and the economy. In the first motivation, local leaders are so absorbed in a military conflict, whether civil or interstate, that they see a Russian presence as a means to either tip the conflict in their favor or suppress it altogether. In the second type of situation, elites perceive reunification with Russia as a preferred means to ensure economic improvement for the population.

In Georgia, both the Abkhaz separatists and the Georgian state authorities called on Russian military support to tip the balance in their favor and then to maintain peace once the threat of separation had subsided. In the process, the government acceded to Russian demands for basing rights in the country, bases that will be used both to promote Russia's interests and to support President

Shevardnadze's own embattled position if needed.

In Armenia, the state government has repeatedly tried to enlist Russian military support in its conflict with Azerbaijan over Nagorno-Karabakh, and it received critical supplies of oil for its 1994 offensive into western Azerbaijan. Both Armenia and Russia have sought to weaken Azerbaijan: Armenia so as to promote its own claims to Nagorno-Karabakh, and Russia so as to gain access to Azerbaijan's oil and to prevent Baku from reasserting its historic role as the beacon for the spread of pan-Turkic and Islamic appeals north and east from the Middle East.

Azerbaijan has been thrown onto the defensive in the face of this dual pressure. The Azerbaijani Popular Front and its leader, former president Abulfaz Elchibey, long an object of Russian concern, lost power to Gaidar Aliev, an old-time apparatchik who built his career in the old Soviet system. Aliev's strategy since coming to power has been to protect the country from Armenia by acceding to virtually all Russian demands, including ceding ever larger percentages of stock in Azerbaijan's oil industry to Russian firms. The Azerbaijani elite decided that the only way to buy security from Armenian attacks was to recognize Russian economic interests in the area.

Clearly none of the states in the Caucasus has become a colony of Russia: rather they have accepted an increase in Russia's presence in return for economic and security benefits for their own regimes. In doing so, they have increased their own dependence on Russia and made it possible for Russia to exert continuing and increased pressure on the politics of the region at a lower cost than would be required if Caucasian elites had not so easily accepted, and even invited, an increased Russian presence.

In Belarus, however, the situation is different. President Aliaksandr Lukashenka ran on a platform that promised a closer relationship, and indeed reunification, with Russia.[24] Public opinion polls conducted in Belarus four years after the breakup of the Soviet Union showed continuing support from almost half the population for significantly closer relations with Russia, including support among a small minority for complete restoration of the USSR. A popular referendum supported by the president called for union as well.[25] Belarus stands alone among the new states in actively favoring reunification with Russia. Although other states, including Kazakhstan and Kyrgyzstan, have sought improved and more unified ties with Russia, Belarus is the best and clearest example among the newly independent states of the phenomenon of autocolonization. Belarus has dismantled border posts along the frontier with Russia, restored Russian as the official language, promised to maintain its army's preparedness, agreed to continue paying pensions to the thousands of retired Soviet-era officers residing in Belarus, and granted Russia leases for two bases in Belarus. In February 1996, the two countries signed an agreement renouncing mutual debts, including the $600 million, plus millions in penalties, that Belarus owed to the Russian natural gas monopoly Gazprom. In March 1996 Lukashenka announced that the two countries would sign a treaty creating a single "unified state," although lawmakers on both sides expressed skepticism that Russia would choose to undertake the economic burden of reincorporating Belarus or that authorities in Minsk would surrender the country's sovereignty completely.[26]

In Central Asia, the elites were clearly unprepared for independence and spent much of the first year of independence trying to convince Russia to form a commonwealth.[27] In contrast to the elites in the Caucasus and the Baltics, postindependence Central Asian leaders generally had not been involved in pre-independence national struggles, had not undergone any period of imprisonment, and had not formed or led popular fronts. The exception, of course, was Tajikistan, where after a brief but very bloody civil war, pro-Moscow elites gained the ascendancy and established a regime strongly in favor of a continued Russian presence in the country.[28] In the region as a whole, elites have appeared unable or unwilling to act on their economic independence from Russia.[29] Elites trained in central planning continued to see Moscow as the center, and Russia has been able to maintain its economic advantage with relative ease. However, in none of the Central Asian countries is there a strong or increasing indigenous trend favoring surrender of political sovereignty; national elites in most countries (Tajikistan is the exception) have become more and not less committed to maintaining their countries' formal independence, though they continue to rely on Moscow for economic and military support.[30]

Needless to say, autocolonization may be transitory: given the speed and circumstances of the collapse of the USSR, the lack of preparation for independence among so many elites and populations is historically unique. It may be that with the passage of time, these elites or the next generation may come to value independence more, particularly if they are able to provide the national, security, psychological, and cultural benefits of independence. At the same time, as has been shown in other postcolonial areas, some of the new states may fail to make the transition, and their populations, especially the Slavic groups within them, may look to Moscow to generate such benefits. In addition, Russia is unlikely to recede as a geopolitical presence in the area, and the temptation to empire will have to be contained by more than the questionable will of elites in these bordering states.

Imperialism and the International Community

While empires have existed in both the modern and ancient worlds, the Age of Empires really lasted only briefly from the mid-1800s to World War I. During this time, virtually all the European powers expanded their domains, culture, and economic influence by means of the formal acquisition of territories worldwide. The very essence of the international system was itself imperialist. The wars between empires (as with the Crimean War and the endless wars in the Balkans) that broke out in this period were not about the nonacceptability of empire per se but about the fate of contested territory lying between empires.[31]

Consequently, alliances among empires could be established, agreements to not attack the flank of an empire at war could be signed, and all in all, discussions about the rights of nations and peoples to self-determination could be sacrificed to the interests of maintaining a balance of power within Europe.

But now that a century has passed, and the USSR—in some ways an empire—has collapsed, the talk of empire, specifically the possibility of the reemergence of a Russian Empire, has resurfaced. The USSR succeeded in the early 1920s, in a weak and divided international community, to establish itself and incorporate by force many of the territories of the former Russian Empire. Would the international community allow such a phenomenon to be repeated today?

Several important factors mitigate against such a repetition. First there is a greater awareness among neighboring countries' elites of the nature and potential of Russian power. For example, reabsorbing Kazakhstan today, with its cities, educated elite, developed infrastructure, and communications links to the outside world would be a far more difficult task than it was in the 1920s when the indigenous peoples were nomadic, illiterate, geographically isolated, and had no history of independent statehood. Moreover, threatened states would undoubtedly seek and receive external support from the international community for a renewed policy of containment, thereby producing the empire-defeating situation that Snyder calls "self-encirclement."[32]

Secondly, as Miles Kahler suggests in chapter 12 and as other international relations scholars have noted, the post–1945 international system has come to more fully accommodate as governing norms the principles of state sovereignty, national self-determination, and the inadmissibility of the use of force to change boundaries of legitimate, popularly elected governments.[33] In chapter 13 Hendrik Spruyt rightly makes the point that "empire today seems to have virtually disappeared as a logic of organization." The defense of the nation-state instead of the imperial state, and the promotion of decolonization, democracy, and human rights instead of the reestablishment of empire and authoritarian regimes—these are the dominant norms upheld by the international community and upon which international institutions derive their legitimacy. To the extent that force has been sanctioned by the international community through the United Nations, it has been to uphold these norms (as in Kuwait, Haiti, or Bosnia). It is virtually impossible to foresee a situation in which the use of Russian force against the wishes of a legitimately elected government would be formally sanctioned (as opposed to ignored, overlooked, etc.) by the international community and its organizations.

Unlike the Bolshevik expansion into other postimperial territories (whether Russian, Ottoman, or Habsburg), any renewed Russian imperial drive would be into new sovereign states recognized as such by the entire international community. It is inconceivable that the international community would support a wholesale Russian policy either of using force to absorb states or parts of states that are recognized as sovereign and independent or of systematically undermining by the use or threat of force democratically elected governments within those states. Not only would such a policy bring international censure, but many of the Western-oriented international institutions to which Russia has turned in an effort to restructure its economy would undoubtedly conclude that the upturn in military spending that such a policy shift would necessitate would so weaken Russian economic recovery as to negate the very basis on which the original loans and investments were made. In this way, the international community could both isolate and punish Russia economically for any policy of expansion.

The success of an international policy aimed at preventing any renewed imperial drive from succeeding is obviously highly conditional. It would depend first of all on the extent to which such a policy had domestic support within Russia that could be sustained even with hardships. This in turn obviously depends on the context: if Russian nationals are being subjected to fierce repression abroad, then Russian sentiment might indeed support military action irrespective of the consequences. In similar situations, the international community has in the past helped defuse some of these situations by siding with Russia and working through the Organization for Security and Cooperation in Europe to provide monitors.

Secondly, international policy will only succeed if the Russian economy first becomes integrated within the international economic system. Russia has moved significantly to introduce capitalism and integrate itself into the international political and economic system, to the point that some economists think the economy could not be returned to an autarchic and state-planned model without catastrophic disruption.[34] Yet clearly the success of the Communists, the Liberal Democrats, and their allies in the 1995 elections indicate that there will be a continuing pressure from the Duma, supported by a solid domestic base, in favor of a return to an economy based on social and economic equity, irrespective of the consequences. Indeed, some favor a decisive break from the trend toward integration with the international economic system, not least because of the common view within this group that the West plans to integrate Russia into this system not to make it strong and capitalist but to keep it weak and dependent.[35] Yet unlike in the past, when Russia could break with the West and seek alternative trading partners with a bloc of communist and left-leaning developing states, the Eastern bloc cannot be reconstructed and, as S. Frederick Starr argues in chapter 10, a turn toward communism, ultranationalism, and empire in Russia would leave the country isolated as never before.

Russia's National Security Zone

Russia has moved from pursuing an inchoate policy toward the countries on its border to one that has clearly marked the area out as an area of vital interest, akin to Michael MccGwire's concept of a "national security zone."[36] Even though

Russia may not move to reestablish empire, the area surrounding its state borders will remain critical to its well-being and security. All states have national security zones, and only the strongest have the capability to define zones beyond their borders in which to promote their interests. The conceptual distinction between an empire and a national security zone is more than a difference of degree: the former has no basis in current international norms or laws, the latter allows one to focus on the natural interplay of relations between great powers and smaller states, an interplay in which great powers are infinitely more constrained than imperial powers and in which small states have significantly more leeway than colonies. In policy terms, it is highly unlikely that the international community would support reassertion of Russian imperialism, but it is by no means certain that all Russian activities in its national security zone would be condemned.

The distinction between empire and a national security zone is blurred somewhat, however, in some cases or types of autocolonization. If, for example, Belarus chooses to reunify with Russia and the international community recognizes the reunification, then an autocolonized imperial expansion would have a basis in international law and at least some legitimacy within the international community. Neither has the international community begrudged Russia's manipulation and domination of its neighbors when they were experiencing acute civil conflict, as in the case of Georgia. In cases where weaker neighboring states descend into chaos and civil war, renewed imperial or neo-imperial control by a more powerful state may look more like foreign policy within a security zone or even peacekeeping than reassertion of empire. Likewise, Western powers have encouraged Russian involvement in Tajikistan. In such cases, the costs to the strong state of not intervening escalate (or appear to rise), thereby shifting the cost-benefit calculations in favor of intervention. From the international perspective, great-power intervention under such circumstances can be supported so that overtaxed organizations such as the UN are relieved of the burdens of additional actions, and so that the international community is spared the prospect of dealing with another Islamic-dominated (or so Russia would have had us believe) government in Central Asia.

As the largest and strongest country of the former USSR, and as the one that benefited the most from the institutional inheritance of the Soviet state, Russia is in a position of enormous comparative advantage. Russian leaders have often but not always exercised this advantage to the detriment of the other new states. Thus, Russia has used its position as the least-dependent economy in the former Soviet space to exert economic pressure, particularly through the supply or withholding of energy or access to Russian-controlled pipelines. Russian leaders encouraged all the new states to join the Commonwealth of Independent States (CIS), which originally included a joint military command dominated by Russia. And the Russian military, via a network of formal basing agreements, contingents "temporarily" stationed abroad, loan-service personnel, and peacekeeping missions sanctioned by regional treaties, is the only force in the Eurasian space capable of sustained independent action beyond its borders. Because of the fragility and comparative weakness of most of the new states, Russia is able to exert enormous leverage with relatively little effort. The way in which Russia has been able to shift support between the Armenians and the Azerbaijanis, by supplying energy to one side and then to another, or by withdrawing relatively small numbers of forces here and then deploying them there, demonstrates its ability to both punish and to reward without suffering significant or proportionate loss itself.[37]

Russia's military presence in Tajikistan, its legal claims to the Crimea, and the protection accorded by Russia's military doctrine to ethnic Russians living abroad are issues that spring from differing situations and political motivations. But they nevertheless reflect an overall consensus in Russia that at a minimum the former Soviet area constitutes a "natural" russophone zone over which Moscow has "always" been able to exercise influence. Even Boris Yeltsin, who initially aligned with a foreign policy view that emphasized international and Western links, has long come to embrace the notion that "the sphere of Russia's economic, political, and humanitarian interests extends to the entire post-Soviet space."[38]

The central point is that the other new states may be hostile to Russia, but they are also weaker and more fragile, and nevertheless need Russia. The fact that Russia has been willing to provide substantial and continued energy and trade subsidization (to the tune, according to International Monetary Fund estimates, of $17 billion in 1993 alone—making Russia the single largest aid donor to the other newly independent states) shows the extent to which Russia is both aware of these needs and concerned for the stabilization of these countries. Certainly, not all the new states regard Russia as inherently untrustworthy as a partner. Nor do they necessarily buy into the argument that Russia, for its own economic well-being, should avoid the temptation of empire. As Roman Szporluk rightly notes in chapter 3, neither the Russian decision to expand nor the decision of any of the neighboring presidents to invite Russian expansion would be made using rational cost-benefit calculations.

Belarus, with an economy that is even more inflation ridden than Russia's, has been at the forefront of efforts to forge a stronger union with Moscow, and was initially kept at arm's length by Russians concerned about the impact on Russia's economy and democracy should the Belovezhskaia accords be canceled. Belarus has been the most extreme example, but all the states have continued to rely on Moscow to varying degrees for continued trade, expertise, security assistance, and as the center of Eurasia's communications network. Certainly, in the modern era it has never before occurred that the imperial center has collapsed with some of the "colonies" so psychologically unprepared for independence. This reliance on Russia comes about not necessarily because of any nefarious design by the current Russian government, but because these countries (with the partial exception of Estonia) have yet to be incorporated into any regional or global network that bypasses Moscow. One is reminded in this context of the words of British Conservative politician, and later prime minister, Benjamin Disraeli, who said in a speech before Parliament in 1863, "Colonies do not cease to be colonies just because they are independent."

In this context, therefore, it is necessary to distinguish between the fact of Russia's self-perception as the dominant power in the region and the other countries' objective dependence. The legacy of the Soviet empire has left them dependent, but the primary responsibility for overcoming the consequences of that dependence resides with these new states themselves. A similar phenomenon to that witnessed following the emergence of postcolonial Africa and the Middle East can be expected in Eurasia. Many leaders in the newly independent states, faced with almost intractable problems, have chosen either to seek salvation in a renewed Russian embrace or to blame Moscow for their own inability to implement a credible development strategy.

Looking at the patterns that have emerged in the decades since decolonization began in the developing world, one can find many reasons to conclude that the process in Eurasia will be equally difficult but substantively different. The proximity of the former colonial power, in particular, and the harsh economic straits that Russia finds itself in, predispose one to conclude that the interrelationship between Russia and its neighbors is likely to be more intense than between most former colonial powers and their newly independent states. Russia will not have the "luxury" of having a debate about casting off "the white man's burden," as the British did when discussing the benefits of withdrawal from India, because twenty-five million Russians found themselves in the successor states after the breakup of the USSR, and because Russia's weak economy makes these states a more natural partner for Russia than India was for Britain. And as for the other new states in Eurasia, they cannot easily form regional security systems to bolster their independence from their former colonial masters (as the newly independent African and Middle Eastern states did through the Organization of African Unity and the Arab League) because, whereas Britain, France, and Portugal withdrew over their horizon when these empires collapsed, Russia continues to reside in their midst.

Russia, too, lacks a regional alternative to cooperation with the other new states. Although it is abundantly richer in natural resources than its neighbors, the psychological and organizational detritus of the Soviet era has created many barriers to cooperation with alternative partners in Europe or elsewhere. Whereas Britain and France could simultaneously pursue decolonization in Africa and Asia and integration with Europe, Russia has little alternative but to pursue decolonization in Eurasia as it simultaneously seeks regional reintegration with these same countries. Naturally, such a policy is fraught with potential for misunderstanding. It is indeed difficult to read the official Strategic Course of the Russian Federation, signed by Yeltsin in September 1995, without wondering whether the successful pursuit of this course of action regarding the countries of the commonwealth would not under certain circumstances pave the way for a de facto imperial reassertion. At a minimum, the edict clearly asserts Russia's great-power status over the other states. The policy states Russia's main objectives toward the Commonwealth of Independent States to be (1) creating "an economically and politically integrated association of states capable of claiming its proper place in the world community"; (2) establishing Russia as "the leading force in the formation of a new system of interstate political and economic relations"; and (3) securing the agreement of the UN and the Organization for Security and Cooperation in Europe that, as regards peacekeeping in the CIS, "this region is primarily a zone of Russian interests."[39]

By far the most realistic course, therefore, to avoid both renewed Russian imperialism and autocolonization among the new states would be to promote interdependence and democracy. Such a course would be difficult for the reasons elaborated here: the legacy of *diktat* and distrust; a domestic political climate in which democratic institutions are skirted or assailed by former Communist elites; and an international climate that alternately promotes Russia as a great power in its national security zone and punishes it for exercising the prerogatives of such a power. Contributing to the problem is an absence of consensus and inherent definitional confusion about the distinction between illegitimate imperial behavior on the one hand and Russia's available range of legitimate actions to promote self-interest within its national security zone on the other hand. Moreover, states that are neither truly independent nor moving toward democracy cannot easily participate in an interdependent world; and until more of the states bordering Russia make further strides, their full participation will remain only a distant objective.

Notes

1. Fiona Hill and Pamela Jewett, " 'Back in the USSR': Russia's Intervention in the Internal Affairs of the Former Soviet Republics and the Implications for United States Policy Toward Russia," Ethnic Conflict Project, John F. Kennedy School of Government (Cambridge, MA: Harvard University, January 1994), pp. 1–90; Richard Pipes, "Imperial Russian Foreign Policy," *Times Literary Supplement,* May 20, 1994, pp. 3–5; Peter Reddaway, "The Role of Popular Discontent," *The National Interest* 31 (spring 1993): 57–63; Reddaway, "Russia on the Brink," *New York Review of Books,* January 28, 1993, pp. 30–36; and Reddaway, "Yeltsin and Russia: Two Views," *New York Review of Books,* April 22, 1993, pp. 16–19. From a completely different perspective, some Russian intellectuals joined in the debate, arguing that Russia's "natural" cultural superiority would produce a reuniting tendency. See, for example, Tatiana Tolstaya, "Intellectuals and Social Change in Central and Eastern Europe," *Partisan Review* 59, no. 4 (1992): 568–73; and Tatiana Tolstaya, "The Struggle for Russia," *New York Review of Books,* June 23, 1994, pp. 3–7.
2. Elena Bonner, "Yeltsin and Russia: Two Views," *New York Review of Books,* April 22, 1993, pp. 16–19; Suzanne Crow, "Why Has Russian Foreign Policy Changed?"

RFE\RL Research Reports 3, no. 18 (May 6, 1993); Karen Dawisha and Bruce Parrott, *Russia and the New States of Eurasia: The Politics of Upheaval* (Cambridge: Cambridge University Press, 1994), ch. 6; Adeed Dawisha and Karen Dawisha, eds., *The Making of Foreign Policy in Russia and the New States of Eurasia* (Armonk, NY: M.E. Sharpe, 1995); and John Lough, "The Place of the 'Near Abroad' in Russian Foreign Policy," *RFE\RL Research Reports* 2, no. 11 (March 12, 1993).

3. Joseph A. Schumpeter, *Imperialism and Social Classes,* rev. ed. (New York: Kelley, 1951), p. 7.

4. Kenneth Waltz, *Theories of International Politics* (Reading, MA: Addison-Wesley, 1979), p. 111.

5. Jack Snyder, *Myths of Empire: Domestic Politics and International Ambition* (Ithaca: Cornell University Press, 1991).

6. Alexander J. Motyl, "Thinking about Empire: A Conceptual Inquiry with Some Implications for Theory," in Karen Barkey and Mark von Hagen, eds., *Imperial Collapse: Causes and Consequences* (Boulder, CO: Westview, forthcoming).

7. Winston Churchill, speech at Harvard University, September 6, 1943, printed in *Onwards to Victory* (Boston: Little Brown, 1944), p. 238.

8. Ghita Ionescu, *The Break-Up of the Soviet Empire in Eastern Europe* (Baltimore: Penguin, 1965), p. 7.

9. Mark R. Beissinger, "The Persisting Ambiguity of Empire," *Post-Soviet Affairs* 11, no. 2 (1995): 155.

10. Pierre Bourdieu, *The Logic of Practice* (Stanford: Stanford University Press, 1990); cf. Beissinger, "The Persisting Ambiguity of Empire," p. 154.

11. The concept of "collapsed states" is developed theoretically and explored particularly as it pertains to certain postcolonial African cases by I. William Zartman, *Collapsed States: The Disintegration and Restoration of Legitimate Authority* (Boulder, CO: Lynne Rienner, 1995).

12. See Adeed I. Dawisha, *Syria and the Lebanese Crisis* (London: Macmillan, 1980), pp. 107–9, 130; and John Bulloch, *Death of a Country: The Civil War in Lebanon* (London: Weidenfeld and Nicolson, 1977), pp. 126, 142, 145.

13. This notion of a collaborative mechanism is developed by Ronald Robinson, "Non-European Foundations of European Imperialism: Sketch for a Theory of Collaboration," in Roger Owen and Bob Sutcliffe, eds., *Studies in the Theory of Imperialism* (London: Longman, 1972), pp. 117–43.

14. Ion Nistor, *Istoria Basarabiei* (Bucharest: Humanitas, 1991), pp. 277–95. The author wishes to thank Professor Vladimir Tismaneanu for bringing this citation to her attention.

15. This relationship is the subject of an interesting article by Sergei A. Romanenko, "The Yugoslav Question in the Foreign Policy of Russia at the Beginning of the Twentieth Century," in S. Frederick Starr, ed., *The Legacy of History in Russia and the New States of Eurasia* (Armonk, NY: M.E. Sharpe, 1994), pp. 41–61.

16. Ronald Grigor Suny, *The Making of the Georgian Nation,* 2d ed. (Bloomington: Indiana University Press, 1994), pp. 58–59.

17. Ronald Grigor Suny, *Looking toward Ararat: Armenia in Modern History* (Bloomington: Indiana University Press, 1993), p. 130.

18. Christine Wallich, "Reforming Intergovernmental Relations: Russia and the Challenge of Fiscal Federalism," in Bartlomiej Kaminski, ed., *Economic Transition in Russia and the New States of Eurasia* (Armonk, NY: M.E. Sharpe, 1996).

19. For a fuller discussion of the doctrine, see Raymond L. Garthoff, "Russian Military Doctrine and Deployments," in Bruce Parrott, ed., *State Building and Military Power in Russia and the New States of Eurasia* (Armonk, NY: M.E. Sharpe, 1995), pp. 44–64.

20. U.S. Information Agency, *Briefing Paper*, Washington, D.C., September 13, 1994.

21. Hannah Arendt, *The Origins of Totalitarianism*, rev. ed. (New York: Harcourt, Brace, Jovanovich, 1973), pp. 124–57.

22. A.J.P. Taylor, *The Struggle for Mastery in Europe, 1848–1918* (Oxford: Clarndon, 1954), p. 293.

23. See Sarah Oates, "Vying for Votes on a Crowded Campaign Trail," *Transition* 2, no. 4 (1996): 26–30.

24. Kathleen Mihalisko, "Democratization in Belarus" (paper presented at University of Maryland/School of Advanced International Studies Conference on Democratization in Post-Communist Countries, College Park, November 1995).

25. See Foreign Broadcast Information Service (hereafter, FBIS), *Central Eurasia Daily Report*, March 20, 1996, p. 65, for details of an opinion poll showing that 47 percent of the Belarussian respondents supported a call for the unification (integration) of the two countries; and of those, 33 percent spoke in favor of "complete fusion," as in Soviet times.

26. Details are from FBIS, *Central Eurasia Daily Report*, March 5, 1996, pp. 55–56; FBIS, *Central Eurasia Daily Report*, March 6, 1996, p. 50; and *Washington Post*, March 24, 996.

27. Martha B. Olcott, "Central Asia's Catapult to Independence," *Foreign Affairs* 71, no. 3 (1992): 108–31.

28. Muriel Atkin, "Democratization in Tajikistan" in Karen Dawisha and Bruce Parrott, eds., *State Formation and Political Participation in Central Asia and the Caucasus* (Cambridge, UK: Cambridge University Press, 1997 forthcoming).

29. Bartlomiej Kaminski, "Factors Affecting Trade Reorientation of the New Independent States," in Bartlomiej Kaminski, ed., *Economic Transition in Russia and the New States of Eurasia* (Armonk, NY: M.E. Sharpe, 1996).

30. The extent of the economic, military, political, and cultural ties between Central Asian states on the one hand and both Russia and the Middle East on the other is the subject of a Ph.D. dissertation by Ibrahim Arafat (University of Maryland, College Park, 996). Arafat shows the trend toward increased ties with Russia after a brief period of decreased ties, beginning in 1993 for all Central Asian states with the exception of Turkmenistan, whose ties with the Middle East became more significant.

31. See Marcus Cunliffe, *The Age of Expansion, 1848–1917* (Springfield, MA: G. & C. Merriam, 1994).

32. Snyder, *Myths of Empire*, pp. 6–7, 213–14.

33. Peter J. Katzenstein, "Coping with Terrorism: Norms and Internal Security in Germany and Japan," in Judith Goldstein and Robert Keohane, eds., *Ideas and Foreign Policy: Beliefs, Institutions, and Political Change* (Ithaca: Cornell University Press, 1993).

34. Anders Åslund, *Economic Transformation in Russia* (New York: St. Martin's, 994); and Åslund, "Russia's Success Story," *Foreign Affairs* 73, no. 5 (1994): 58–71.

35. Ilya Prizel, *Russia, Poland and Ukraine: National Identity and Foreign Policy Formation* (Cambridge, UK: Cambridge University Press, forthcoming). Veljko Vujacic, "Gennadiy Zyuganov and the 'Third Road,' " *Post-Soviet Affairs* 12, no. 2 (1996): 118–55.

36. Michael MccGwire, *Perestroika and Soviet National Security* (Washington, DC: Brookings Institution, 1991).

37. A partial catalogue of Russian activities abroad and a full justification of all such activities was presented in a report by the then-director of the Russian Foreign Intelligence Service, Yevgenii Primakov, and published in full in *Rossiiskaia gazeta*, Moscow, September 22, 1994.

38. *Segodnya*, Moscow, September 30, 1994.

39. *Rossiiskaia gazeta*, Moscow, September 23, 1995.

Appendix: Project Participants

Mark Beissinger, University of Wisconsin
George Breslauer, University of California at Berkeley
Barbara Butterton, Institute on Global Conflict and Cooperation
Adeed Dawisha, George Mason University
Karen Dawisha, University of Maryland
Janine Draschner, Russian Littoral Project
Mary Ann Drinan, Palomar College
Patrick Drinan, University of San Diego
John Dunlop, Hoover Institution
Robert Edelman, University of California at San Diego
Arun Elhance, Social Science Research Council
Carole Fink, Ohio State University
Kathleen Hancock, University of California at San Diego
Jon Jacobson, University of California at Irvine
Miles Kahler, University of California at San Diego
Cynthia Kaplan, University of California at Santa Barbara
David Lake, University of California at San Diego
Gail Lapidus, Stanford University
Wayne Limberg, Department of State
George Liska, School of Advanced International Studies
Ali Mazrui, SUNY at Binghamton
Kendall Myers, Foreign Service Institute
Vali Nasr, University of San Diego
Bruce Parrott, School of Advanced International Studies
Philip Roeder, University of California at San Diego
Richard Rosecrance, University of California at Los Angeles
Robert Rotberg, Harvard University
Alvin Z. Rubinstein, University of Pennsylvania

Nikolai Rudensky, Institute for Economy in Transition, Moscow
Richard Rudolph, University of Minnesota
Dankwart Rustow, City University of New York
Avi Shlaim, Oxford University
Hendrik Spruyt, Columbia University
S. Frederick Starr, The Aspen Institute
Ronald Suny, University of Chicago
Roman Szporluk, Harvard University
Stacy VanDeveer, University of Maryland
Solomon Wank, Franklin and Marshall College
Fred Wehling, University of California at San Diego
David Wilkinson, University of California at Los Angeles
Marc Zlotnik, Central Intelligence Agency

Index

Mill, John Stuart, 227
Millet system (Ottoman), 99, 105–6
Milosevic, Slobodan, 19
Minderheitenpolitik, 270–72
Mitteleuropa plans, 97–98
Mitterrand, François, 303
Mobutu Sese Soko, 215
Modern empire, 7
Moeller van den Bruck, Arthur, 274
Moi, Daniel arap, 215
Moiseyev, N.N., 85–86, 92*n.55*
Moldova, 55, 322, 323, 324, 325,
    327
Moldovans (ethnic), 176, 344
Mollet, Guy, 293–94
Molotov, Vyacheslav, 124–25, 131
Moluccans, 319
Mongol empire, 67
Monopoly state, 44–53, 56, 287
Morgenthau, Hans, 32
Motyl, Alexander, 341
Mozart, Wolfgang Amadeus, 189
Muhammad Ali, ruler of Egypt,
    194–95
Multinational state, 12
Muscovites, 67–68, 70–71, 74
Muslims. *See* Islamic people

Napoleon Bonaparte, 32
Nationalism, 16–18, 68, 69–71, 72,
    127
  French and American revolutions
      influencing, 106, 190
  post-World War I, 190–91
  Young Turk ideology and, 108
Nationalities
  language-based, 163–64
  See also Ethnic groups
National security zone, 355–59
Nation-state, 9–10, 26*n.21*
NATO. *See* North Atlantic Treaty
    Organization
Nazarbaev, Nursultan, 322
Nazi Germany, 9, 17, 192, 278–79
Nehru, Jawaharlal, 212
Newly Independent States (NIS), 316,
    320, 322–27; *See also specific
    countries*

Nicholas II, emperor of Russia, 72, 77
Nigerian civil war, 221
NIS. *See* Newly independent states
Nkrumah, Kwame, 209
Nomenklatura, 170
North Atlantic Treaty Organization,
    34, 174, 225, 226, 231, 323, 327,
    328, 331, 332, 336*n.49*
Nyerere, Julius, 212

Obote, Apollo, 212
Obsolescing bargain, 60*n.40*, 42
OIC. *See* Organization of the Islamic
    Conference
Oil prices, 44
Opportunism, costs of, 39–41
Organization of the Islamic
    Conference, 226
Orthodox Christianity, 68, 69–70,
    88*n.10*, 99, 191
Osman, Prince, 188
Osmanli dynasty, 98, 107, 188
Osmanlilik. *See* Ottomanism
Ossetians, 164
Ostpolitik, 268
Ottoman Empire, 13, 15, 16, 84
  disintegration and aftermath,
      94–115, 122, 186–96
  history, 102, 188–90
  as "sick man of Europe," 95–98
  See also Turkey
Ottomanism, 105, 106, 107

Pacific Ocean territories, 148, 149
Palestine, 134, 191; *See also* Israel
Palestinians, 233
Pan Am 103 bombing, 220, 224,
    237*n.6*
Panama Canal Treaty, 342
Paris Peace Conference, 271; *See also*
    Versailles, Treaty of
Paul I, emperor of Russia, 345
Pax Americana, 221, 222
Pax Britannica, 221
Peasantry, 74, 75
Pericentric theories, 32
Periphery, 341
Persian Gulf War (1991), 225